Russian Corporate Capitalism from Peter the Great to Perestroika

Russian Corporate Capitalism from Peter the Great to Perestroika

THOMAS C. OWEN

New York   Oxford
OXFORD UNIVERSITY PRESS
1995

Oxford University Press

Oxford New York
Athens Auckland Bangkok Bombay
Calcutta Cape Town Dar es Salaam Delhi
Florence Hong Kong Istanbul Karachi
Kuala Lumpur Madras Madrid Melbourne
Mexico City Nairobi Paris Singapore
Taipei Tokyo Toronto

and associated companies in
Berlin Ibadan

Copyright © 1995 by Oxford University Press, Inc.

Portions of Chapter 2 originally appeared in "The Population Ecology of Corporations in the Russian Empire, 1700–1914," *Slavic Review* 50, no. 4 (Winter 1991), 807–26. Copyright © 1991 by the American Association for the Advancement of Slavic Studies, Inc. Used by permission.

Portions of Chapters 2 and 3 originally appeared in "La Démographie des sociétés anonymes dans l'Empire russe (1821–1914)," in *Naissance et mort des entreprises en Europe aux 19ème–20ème siècles,* ed. Philippe Jobert and Michael Moss (Dijon: Éditions de l'Université de Dijon, 1995). Used by permission.

Published by Oxford University Press, Inc.
198 Madison Avenue, New York, New York, 10016

Oxford is a registered trademark of Oxford University Press

All rights reserved. No part of this publication may be reproduced, stored in a retrieval system, or transmitted, in any form or by any means, electronic, mechanical, photocopying, recording, or otherwise, without the prior permission of Oxford University Press.

Library of Congress Cataloging-in-Publication Data
Owen, Thomas C.
Russian corporate capitalism from Peter the Great
to perestroika / Thomas C. Owen.
p. cm. Includes bibliographical references and index.
ISBN 0-19-509677-0
1. Capitalism—Russia. 2. Capitalism—Soviet Union.
3. Corporations—Russia. 4. Corporations—Soviet Union. 5. Russia—
Economic conditions. 6. Soviet Union—Economic
conditions—1985–1991. I. Title.
HC335.O83 1995
338.7'0947—dc20   94-49317

1 3 5 7 9 8 6 4 2

Printed in the United States of America
on acid-free paper

To Sue Ann

Preface

Historians justify their work with the general argument that an understanding of the past prepares us to meet the challenges of the future. The study of ancient and faraway civilizations reveals the great variety of human experience and teaches an appreciation of cultural norms different from our own. Recent history sharpens our awareness of current realities and future possibilities by showing the momentous consequences of social and cultural institutions inherited from the past.

In this case, it is incumbent upon an American historian of Russian capitalism to draw lessons that might prove useful to those who seek to understand and engage the new capitalist institutions in the former Soviet Union. What began as a historical investigation of an apparently extinct economic system became a commentary on one of the great social and economic dramas of our century: the transformation of the economy and society of the largest country in the world after centuries of autocratic rule, both tsarist and Soviet. The study of corporations under the tsarist regime has some relevance for an understanding of post-Soviet capitalism because it makes clear the strength of anticapitalist attitudes in Russian culture, not only under Soviet Marxism, but under the tsarist regime as well.

This new context imposes on the book a rather unusual chronological structure, one that embraces both the tsarist and Gorbachev periods. The introduction discusses the main historiographical issues and sources used for the pre-1914 study, including the database of corporations in the Russian Empire. Chapter 2 analyzes patterns of corporate formation and survival primarily from the perspective of population ecology, a branch of the sociology of organizations. Chapter 3 portrays the evolution of the Russian corporate elite, with attention to previously unknown patterns of ethnicity and social status in the major economic regions of the empire. Chapter 4 leaps forward to the era of perestroika in an effort to examine the institutional obstacles to incipient capitalism laid down during seven decades of Soviet economic policy. (No database is yet available for the study of Soviet corporations in the period from 1921 to 1928, although the material for such a study exists in periodicals of the period. Such a statistical analysis would illuminate the institutional background of Stalin's abrupt bureaucratization of the Soviet economy.) Chapter 5 offers historical parallels between the imperial and late Soviet economies and places the radical and reactionary critiques of capitalism within the long tradition of Russian xenophobia. The conclusion draws attention to several possible directions of economic evolution in the decades to come. It is for the reader to judge whether this attempt by a historian to compare economic institutions across the great abyss of the Soviet period succeeds or not.

Many institutions and individuals contributed generously to the realization of this project. Several research grants provided access to rare materials in major libraries and archives. Two visiting grants from the Kennan Institute for Advanced Russian Studies in 1979 and 1981 enabled me to use the incomparable resources of the Library of Congress. For this support I am grateful to the directors of the institute at those times: S. Frederick Starr and Abbott T. Gleason. I also received support from the International Research and Exchanges Board (IREX), with funds provided by the Andrew W. Mellon Foundation, the National Endowment for the Humanities, and the U.S. Department of State. This grant funded my stay in Moscow, Leningrad, and Helsinki from January to May 1980 for research on Russian corporations, exchanges, and trade associations. During that visit, I received encouragement and guidance from Valerii I. Bovykin and the late Vladimir Ia. Laverychev in Moscow and from Boris V. Anan'ich, Leonid E. Shepelev, and Galina A. Ippolitova (Shepelev's wife, an archivist at the Central State Historical Archive) in Leningrad. In 1981, I spent a productive semester in New York thanks to a Senior Research Fellowship at the Russian Institute (now the W. Averell Harriman Institute) at Columbia University. Particularly generous with their expertise were Jonathan Sanders, Wesley Fisher, Harold B. Segel, Seweryn Bialer, John L. P. Thompson, Andrew A. Beveridge, and the staffs of the Columbia Law School Library and the New York Public Library.

A grant to Louisiana State University from the National Science Foundation (SES-8419943, in economics) provided funds for computer equipment, software, graduate student wages, and other items essential to the completion of the RUSCORP database in 1985–8. A grant-in-aid from the Economic History Association in 1983 facilitated the coding of data; and short-term grants from the Hoover Institution at Stanford University (under the Soviet–East European Research and Training Act of

1983, Public Law 98-164, Title VIII, 97 Stat. 1047-50) and the American Philosophical Society supported preliminary statistical work in 1988. The University of Illinois Library generously loaned many microfiches and microfilms, including the entire set of the *Sobranie uzakonenii i rasporiazhenii* (Collection of Statutes and Decrees, 1863–1917) and many rare publications obtained from Soviet libraries. Access to the rich holdings of Widener Library and the Harvard Law Library was kindly provided by the Russian Research Center of Harvard University in 1988. A Manship Summer Fellowship in the Humanities from Louisiana State University supported the initial composition of the manuscript in 1990, and a second grant from the National Science Foundation (SES-9022486, in sociology) funded the final statistical analysis of the data in 1991–3.

Many scholars provided essential advice on the creation of the database, particularly in the history of ethnic minorities in the Russian Empire. All are named in the RUSCORP manual. A special word of thanks is due to Erik Amburger, of Heuchelheim, Germany, who, shortly before his eightieth birthday, in 1987, kindly shared materials from the history of his family's enterprises in prerevolutionary St. Petersburg. He also put at my disposal his unique card file of foreigners in Russia, containing biographical data on over a quarter-million individuals. Others who gave expert advice in the compilation of the database include Boris V. Anan'ich, J. Arch Getty, Paul R. Gregory, Patricia Herlihy, and John P. McKay.

At Louisiana State University, several undergraduate and graduate students helped to extract and encode data: Beata Kochut, Michael Rechelman, Thomas R. Trice, Stephen S. Triche, and Christopher White. Useful advice on the ethnic identification of corporate founders in Odessa and Poland was provided by Rechelman, a native of Odessa; Kochut, a former history teacher in Warsaw; and Trice, an exchange student in Lublin, Poland in 1983–4. The feasibility of a quantitative study of corporations based on data from the corporate charters was first demonstrated by a graduate student at LSU, Whitney A. Coulon III, in 1979. Elizabeth T. Cahoon and Charles Mann helped prepare grant applications to the National Science Foundation and the American Philosophical Society.

During an extended stay in Madison, Wisconsin, my colleague at Southern University in Baton Rouge, Michael J. Fontenot, kindly obtained copies of the Soviet corporate laws of 1990 from the University of Wisconsin library. From Moscow, Inna A. Simonova supplied copies of current newspapers.

My efforts to apply quantitative methods to Russian social and economic history received encouragement and assistance from many specialists in the social sciences: Paul F. Paskoff, Lawrence P. Falkowski, Wayne Villemez, John J. Beggs, Michael Irwin, Dawn Robinson, and Leonard Hochberg of Louisiana State University; Andrew W. Creighton, Elaine Backman, W. Richard Scott, Alex Inkeles, and Terence Emmons of Stanford University; David W. Griffiths of the University of North Carolina,

Chapel Hill; Kenneth Sokoloff and Jean-Laurent Rosenthal of the University of California, Los Angeles; Robert W. Gallman of the National Bureau for Economic Research in Cambridge, Massachusetts; and Herman Daems at the Graduate School of Business Administration at Harvard University. Several colleagues offered useful comments on my paper "Radical and Reactionary Critics of Russian Capitalism, 1890–1917: The Role of Xenophobia in the Russian Revolution," presented at a panel devoted to Russian capitalism at the convention of the American Association for the Advancement of Slavic Studies in November 1992. One member of that panel, Samuel C. Ramer of Tulane University, also provided an incisive critique of Chapters 5 and 6.

The opinions, findings, conclusions, and recommendations expressed in this book are those of the author and do not necessarily reflect the views of the National Science Foundation or other agencies. Any errors, of course, are those of the author.

To my wife, Sue Ann, I owe special thanks for her steadfast support during the many years that these projects required.

Baton Rouge T. C. O.
January 1995

Contents

1 Introduction: The Challenges of Russian Business History, 3

2 Corporations in the Russian Empire, 1700–1914, 16
   The Population Ecology of Russian Corporations, 16
   Railroads and Banks, 30
   The Formation and Survival of Corporations
      in Ten Large Cities, 37

3 Corporate Entrepreneurs and Managers, 1821–1914, 50
   Patterns of Entrepreneurship, 51
   Corporate Managers in 1905 and 1914, 65
   Russian Entrepreneurship in Comparative Perspective, 78

4 Perestroika and the Failure of Soviet Capitalism, 1985–1990, 84
   Cooperatives and the Culture of Communal Envy, 85
   Corporations and Exchanges, 100

5 Capitalism and Xenophobia in Russia, 115
   Radical and Reactionary Critiques of Capitalism
      under the Tsarist Regime, 116
   Slavophile Capitalism, 126
   War and Revolution: The Origins of Economic Xenophobia in
      Soviet Ideology, 138

6 Conclusion: Varieties of Russian Capitalism, 151

Appendix A: The RUSCORP Database, 173
Appendix B: Basic Capital as an Indicator of Corporate Size, 175
Appendix C: Tables, 180
Appendix D: Figures, 190
Notes, 201
Works Cited, 231
Index, 251

Russian Corporate Capitalism
from Peter the Great
to Perestroika

The main industrial areas in European Russia up to 1917. From Hugh Seton-Watson, *The Russian Empire, 1801–1914,* 1967, by permission of Oxford University Press.

1

Introduction: The Challenges of Russian Business History

The most beautiful order of the world is still a random gathering of things insignificant in themselves.

Heraclitus[1]

The evolution of the new institutions of Russian capitalism since the breakup of the Soviet Union in December 1991—corporations, commodity and stock exchanges, and trade associations—has proceeded too rapidly to be analyzed in a historical survey. However, the outlines of the new economic system had become clear by 1990. Mikhail S. Gorbachev's experiment in political and economic restructuring (perestroika), although introduced simultaneously with the exhilarating expansion of freedom in the media and political arena (glasnost), failed to halt the disintegration of Soviet industry, trade, and finance. The political crisis of August 1991 opened the way to the victory of Gorbachev's rival, Boris N. Yeltsin, in the Russian Federation and the dissolution of the Soviet Union at the end of that year.

But why did Gorbachev's economic reforms of 1987—the legalization of profit-oriented cooperatives, the imposition of rational cost accounting in the finances of state enterprises, and the encouragement of joint ventures with foreign capitalists—fail to lay the foundations of a market-oriented economy? To what extent can the slow pace of economic reform be attributed to ideology, particularly anticapitalist attitudes prevalent not only in the leadership of the Communist Party but among the Russian public as well?

Cooperatives and corporations sprang up in response to the dismantling of the instruments of central control. By the end of 1991, Gorbachev's economic reforms, including the legalization of capitalist enterprises, had been in place for many months, but his policies had failed to invigorate industry and trade, stabilize the currency, or maintain (much less improve) the modest Soviet standard of living. The dilemmas of social and economic change that became visible in the Gorbachev era promised to exert their influence well into the twenty-first century.

Numerous conceptual problems arise in drawing analogies between the new Soviet capitalism and capitalist institutions in other times and places. The first is what one student of the USSR called "the indiscriminate use of the terms capitalism, socialism, and class," which have "never been defined in any sort of precise, meaningful, and generally acceptable way."[2] The present study adopts the classic six-part definition of the elements of "modern capitalism" offered by Max Weber: rational accounting for business, separately from the finances of individuals and families; a free market open to persons of any social status; the use of advanced technologies, especially those requiring large investments of capital; a system of law free of arbitrary exceptions and unpredictable changes; a labor force recruited and organized by financial incentives and unrestricted by such impediments as serfdom or slavery; and corporate enterprises based on the public sale of shares.[3] That such a system has never existed in its pure form does not invalidate the use of the definition by social scientists. Its benefit consists in its clarification of the extent to which specific aspects of the Weberian "ideal type" arose in a given historical situation. In any case, the corporations that operated in Russia and the USSR deserved the label "capitalist institutions" because they fit the sixth part of Weber's definition and, in fact, flourished or stagnated to the extent that the other five aspects prevailed or not. Indeed, the stultification of capitalism under the tsarist and Soviet autocracies and during the era of perestroika demonstrated the validity of Weber's logical connection between law and economic activity.

In an effort to explain the failures of the Gorbachev era, this study places in historical perspective the peculiarities of Russian capitalism in the 1990s. Capitalist institutions were abolished soon after the Bolshevik Revolution in 1917, but Stalin's dictatorship, however "totalitarian" in its pretensions to absolute control from 1928 to 1953, failed to extinguish habits of private gain. Numerous studies of what economists call "opportunistic behavior" by managers and workers testified to the imperfect administrative control of the State Planning Committee (Gosplan) and the ministries.[4] The relaxation of centralized controls from 1985 onward did not, however, call forth a new stratum of capitalist entrepreneurs equal to the task of creating a modern market economy on the ruins of the old Stalinist edifice.

The new forms of economic activity that emerged in the late 1980s bore a curiously ambivalent character. The decrees that legalized private economic activity contained logical inconsistencies that echoed those of the tsarist regime a century before. Reforms promulgated in Moscow met resistance from local officials, who implemented them in arbitrary ways, so that the line between legal and illegal activity often remained unclear. The rapid expansion of the illegal and semilegal markets in the so-called second economy, itself an important phenomenon since the Khrushchev era, and the proliferation of thievery, bribery, extortion, and organized crime made it impossible to measure the size and scope of private economic activity.[5] More important than the Soviet autocratic tradition for an understanding of the failure of Gorbachev's reforms, from the historian's point of view, was the legacy of the weak development of capitalism in the centuries prior to the Bolshevik Revolution of 1917.

To grasp the interplay of economics and ideology in Russia today requires an understanding not only of the familiar anticapitalist rhetoric of Soviet Marxism but also of the debate over capitalism that resounded in the last decades of the imperial period. Diligent empirical spadework in Russian intellectual history has revealed the origins of several varieties of socialist ideology, from anarchism to Bolshevism, and occasional defenders of capitalist institutions, notably the scientist Dmitrii I. Mendeleev and the economist Petr B. Struve.[6] Someday, perhaps, the leading personalities of Russian capitalism will receive the attention that they deserve. To date, the institutions of capitalism in the Russian Empire have remained at the periphery of historical writing, to be mentioned in passing in a study of the tsarist economic policy or in terms of the social history of merchants or workers. There exist only a handful of case studies of prominent entrepreneurs, their companies, and industrial regions.[7]

In their analyses of economic development in the Russian Empire, Soviet historians generally maintained that Russian industry and trade developed according to a universal "capitalist" pattern. Evidence of an indigenous Russian capitalism was found in the textile industry, which utilized hired serf labor decades before the abolition of serfdom in 1861. "Monopolies" in the last quarter-century of the imperial period received special attention because they appeared to coordinate production and sales of key products—coal, iron and steel products, locomotives and rolling stock, copper products, and metal roofing—on the model of imperial Germany. The Soviet treatment of the role of the largest banks in financing industry also employed a quintessentially Marxist term, "finance capital," which likewise implied a high level of organizational sophistication on the eve of World War I. Soviet historians emphasized the activities of the tsarist state in sponsoring these giant enterprises and stressed the financial benefits derived by the great magnates in railroads, banks, and industry.[8]

These essentially polemical interpretations neglected, however, the vast majority of economic units in favor of the several dozen largest firms. Part of this neglect can be attributed to the lack of statistical tools to analyze the several thousand corporations that came into existence under the tsarist regime, although the inexcusable refusal to acknowledge the work of an early pioneer of statistical analysis of Russian economic trends[9] suggested that ideological as well as purely technological considerations were at work.

The most prolific Soviet researcher on the history of prerevolutionary corporations, the archivist and historian Leonid E. Shepelev, analyzed a vast number of sources in the imperial archives to sketch the interplay of policy and corporate development in the Russian Empire.[10] His articles and monographs inspired admiration for their meticulous empiricism, rare in Soviet scholarship before the Gorbachev era. Shepelev's pioneering study of corporations presented some aggregate statistics of formation and survival, but its major contribution was to trace the evolution of tsarist policy toward corporate enterprise. He concluded that the tsarist state was far less accommodating toward the so-called Russian bourgeoisie than most other Soviet accounts claimed.[11]

Shepelev's work maintained a high degree of factual accuracy, but he erred in asserting that all corporate charters confirmed by the imperial government were printed in the *Polnoe sobranie zakonov* (Complete Collection of Laws) until 1912.[12] In fact, the charters of only the largest companies, primarily railroads, appeared in full in the third series of the *PSZ*, containing laws confirmed from March 1881 to the end of December 1913. The charters of all new corporations, with the exception of those omitted because of slipshod bureaucratic procedures, were published in the *Polnoe sobranie zakonov* from the early eighteenth century to the end of February 1881 and in the *Sobranie uzakonenii i rasporiazhenii*, published from 1863 to the end of 1917.

Previous studies of corporations in Russia accepted uncritically tsarist statistics, often of dubious quality, so that some false notions appeared from time to time in the secondary literature. The most common was the identification of the Russian-American Company as the first corporation founded in the empire, in 1799,[13] when in fact twenty-seven enterprises that qualified for definition as companies had received charters between 1704 and 1782. One scholar who relied on official reports found only eight incorporations in the empire before 1836. Another asserted that "from 1799 to 1836, only ten companies were established." In fact, forty corporate charters received the imperial signature from 1800 to the end of 1835.[14] Researchers in Russian business history also had to contend with the unfortunate deterioration and loss of many prerevolutionary corporate records at the hands of negligent Soviet archivists in the 1920s and 1930s.[15]

By the end of the 1970s, Soviet researchers had seen the need for detailed statistical study of Russian corporations and had identified the requisite published sources,[16] but little empirical research appeared. The genre of biographies of leading industrialists and financiers did not exist. Post-Soviet works by Russian historians often adopted a journalistic tone typical of preliminary studies. These articles sometimes had a clear polemical purpose as well, as they contrasted some newly rediscovered heroes of Russian economic development in the nineteenth century to the speculators of the Yeltsin era.[17]

At this early stage of Russian business history, it seems essential to analyze the evolution of capitalist institutions in the aggregate, both for an understanding of the stages of historical evolution and for an appreciation of the polemics that raged around them. Besides corporations, these included several dozen exchange committees (*birzhevye komitety*), which oversaw trading in commodities, government bonds, and corporate securities in large cities. Equally important were the many business organizations, called "trade associations" in current American parlance, that defended the economic interests of manufacturers and traders in specific sectors and regions and, after 1906, on the national level. As Alfred J. Rieber has recently noted, "social historians ought not restrict themselves to examining the activity of those groups solely within the socioeconomic sphere. The dynamics of social groups penetrate political institutions, for example, filling them with social content, profoundly affecting their formal, legal-administrative structures, and often transforming them beyond the intentions of their original architects."[18] Exchange committees and business organizations tried in vain to convince the tsarist bureaucracy and the public that policies conducive to industry would benefit the entire society. Their failure in this regard requires explanation. A serious logistical problem arises, however, because the creation of an adequately detailed history of just one business organization could easily demand a researcher's undivided attention for many years, as several case studies have demonstrated.[19]

Moreover, historians of Russian capitalism have found it difficult to apply to their subject the kind of comparative methods used by their colleagues in Europe, North America, and Japan. The study of comparative corporate finance presupposes the availability of preliminary research findings on such basic factors as stock exchanges, interest rates, and enterprise debts and profits in various European countries. Although some Russian corporate directories presented data on stock and bond issues and profits, the nonexistence of standard accounting practices prior to 1914 made any statistical study of these figures extremely dubious. Shortly before its liquidation by the Bolshevik government in early 1918, the Russian Banking Association complained that Russian banks still used a variety of incompatible techniques for computing balances (*balansy*) and accounts (*otchety*). The association favored a uniform system based on a model proposed in 1915 by the Ministry of Finance, consisting of thirty-six categories of assets and nineteen categories of liabilities, but the chaos of war prevented the adoption of this system.[20]

For these reasons, this research project focused not on business organizations or statistics of corporate profits but on the corporation as an institution in the Russian Empire and the Soviet Union: a legally distinct entity with unambiguous characteristics that could be described and analyzed in quantitative terms, such as the size of basic capital, the price of shares, and the number of years from founding to liquidation, when the latter date was known. Qualitative aspects, such as function, location of headquarters and operations, and ethnicity and social status of founders and managers, also lent themselves to a variety of statistical tests. Unlike business organizations, corporations and stock markets could be studied in the aggregate in the course of centuries, and basic patterns of corporate entrepreneurship could be discerned.

The obstacles of insufficient biographical data and the lack of institutional case studies were overcome to a large degree by analyzing the evolution of the entire population of corporations in the Russian Empire over the long term, from their first appearance, in the reign of Peter the Great (1689–1725), to the period of their highest development under Nicholas II (1894–1917), on the eve of World War I. An unprecedented level of accuracy was possible because the database of corporations includes information from every charter published by the tsarist state in the *Polnoe sobranie zakonov* (covering 1649–1913) and its supplement, the *Sobranie uzakonenii i rasporiazhenii* (Collection of Statutes and Decrees, covering 1863–1917), and from six corporate directories published between 1847 and 1914.

What, then, were the main elements of continuity in the history of Russian capitalism? The first was the fact that, in the tsarist period, *capitalism in Russia was weakly developed in comparison to capitalism in Europe and North America*. The number of corporations lagged significantly behind that of European countries and the United States. These data indicated more than "economic backwardness." This phrase, the cornerstone of the influential analysis advanced by the great economic historian Alexander Gerschenkron, implied that the gap would eventually disappear once Russia managed to "catch up" with the early starters in the process of industrialization. Another of Gerschenkron's famous concepts, that the Russian state substituted for the function of markets and investment banks in European countries until about 1905, after which the largest Russian banks took the initiative in directing investment capital into industry, also carried the same implication.[21]

However, some of the most enduring elements of Russian culture prevented a rapid closure of the gap. These included the overwhelmingly agrarian nature of the society well into the late twentieth century; the relatively low levels of urbanization, literacy, and political participation in the imperial period; the small size of the Russian commercial-industrial elite, which did not deserve the European label "bourgeoisie" until the Revolution of 1905 and even then remained fractured along lines of social status, ethnicity, and geography; and the refusal of the tsarist bureaucracy to relinquish power to constitutionally elected government.

(To my knowledge, the first published admission to this effect by a member of the Soviet historical profession occurred only after the collapse of the USSR, when P. V. Volobuev noted in passing that "after all, Russia suffered not so much from the development of capitalism as from its insufficient development." The precise dimensions of this institutional weakness remained unclear because, in scholarship on Russian social classes before 1917, "the main inadequacy of Soviet research involved, as we would say, the 'other side of the barricade': until 1985 its tendentiousness and one-sidedness could not be surmounted." In other words, no objective account of the so-called Russian bourgeoisie was possible for seven decades in Soviet universities and research institutes.)[22]

Second, *capitalism in Russia was geographically concentrated*. The Russian Empire, the largest country in the world, stretched from the Baltic Sea to the Pacific Ocean, but two cities accounted for more than half the total corporate headquarters: St. Petersburg, with almost a third, and Moscow, with one-fifth. Another eight cities—Warsaw, Kiev, Odessa, Riga, Kharkov, Lodz, Baku, and Rostov-on-Don, in that order—together brought the cumulative proportion to almost three-quarters. The vast majority of citizens in the empire associated the corporation with the wealthy urban elite. Some corporations exploited the rich natural resources of isolated areas, such as gold in Siberia and coal in the Donets Basin, where unincorporated firms could not amass the requisite capital and technical expertise, but many of these companies maintained their headquarters in St. Petersburg, and the process of geographical diffusion remained slow throughout the tsarist period.

Third, *capitalism in Russia remained essentially foreign*. The corporation, elaborated and modified by European merchants and statesmen over the past several centuries, came to Russia as a fully mature economic institution. Efforts by Russian merchants to emulate the creators of the great trading companies of the Dutch, English, and French empires came to naught in the reigns of Peter the Great and Catherine the Great (1762–96). Insurance companies, banks, and stock exchanges succeeded best in Russia when they combined the organizational structure of their European counterparts with intelligent accommodations to Russian economic realities. Because no native entrepreneurial class capable of adapting the corporation to Russian life emerged until late in the nineteenth century, however, foreigners (primarily German, French, English, and Swedish expatriates) and members of minority nationalities in the western borderlands of the empire (especially Poles, Jews, Germans, and Armenians) filled the crucial mediating role during most of the imperial period.

To demonstrate that the Russian political system hindered the emergence of a native version of the corporation, it suffices to mention just one factor: the legal essence of the European corporation, which found no counterpart in the Russian political system. The roots of this contrast between Russian and European commercial law can be traced to the late medieval period. The disparity persisted to 1917 because the tsarist regime consistently refused, despite many initiatives for reform, to introduce a system of corporate law modeled on European legal norms.[23]

Although the Soviet regime allowed some petty trade and manufacturing, out of economic necessity, in the 1920s[24] and authorized the creation of corporations that issued stock to various ministries and agencies, it obliterated virtually all vestiges of private enterprise during the five-year plans in Stalin's time (1928–53) except the peasants' private plots under the system of central planning. Buying goods at one price and selling them at another constituted "speculation," a serious crime under Soviet law until 1986. The Gorbachev regime did not legalize the corporation in its prerevolutionary form until 1990, just one year before the collapse of the USSR. The Russian corporation, therefore, once again bears an alien physiognomy in the 1990s.

Finally, and most importantly for the future, *capitalism in Russia was resented*. By its nature, the corporation brought together a relatively small number of individuals who had sufficient wealth to invest in an enterprise and expected to reap significant financial gain. Sources of the Soviet antipathy against the corporate elite included not only the well-known Leninist and Stalinist condemnations of monopolies and banks, whether foreign or domestic, but also strong traditions of anticapitalism among the Russian peasantry, working class, intelligentsia, landed gentry, and bureaucracy before the Bolshevik Revolution of 1917. Although the Soviet regime directed innumerable propaganda campaigns against the evils of capitalism, it did not invent the stereotypes of the kulak (greedy peasant), the coarse merchant millionaire, or the grasping Nepman (trader during the New Economic Policy, 1921–8). What Hedrick Smith called "the culture of envy" during the period of perestroika[25] had deep roots in Russian culture. Most importantly, elements of Soviet Marxism explicitly reiterated xenophobic attitudes drawn from the reactionary and anti-Semitic tradition of tsarist Russia. Xenophobia—the fear and hatred of foreigners—had an economic component: anticapitalism. Then and now, corporate capitalism was hated in Russia because it was foreign.

The four characteristics of Russian capitalism developed according to a certain symmetry. Two (weak development and geographical concentration) may be considered objectively defined, the first in comparison to Europe; the second, by a statistical study of geographical patterns within Russia. The other two features (foreignness and resentment) appeared to be essentially subjective; again, one was defined with reference to Europe, and the other described a powerful current in Russian culture.

The main conclusion of this study is that the antipathy toward capitalism among most social groups in prerevolutionary Russia emerged once again with undiminished force, to judge by the distrust of the free market shown by Soviet bureaucrats, workers, and peasants in the era of perestroika. To account for this persistence requires more than proof that these attitudes existed before 1914 and after 1985. Ideas do not live by a momentum all their own. As Barrington Moore, Jr., observed with characteristic brilliance more than a quarter-century ago, historians should view with skepticism

> the conception of social inertia, taken over probably from physics. There is a widespread assumption in modern social science that social continuity requires no explanation. Supposedly it is not problematical. Change is what requires explanation. . . . The assumption of inertia, that cultural and social continuity do not require explanation, obliterates the fact that both have to be recreated anew in each generation, often with great pain and suffering. To

maintain and transmit a value system, human beings are punched, bullied, sent to jail, thrown into concentration camps, cajoled, bribed, made into heroes, encouraged to read newspapers, stood up against a wall and shot, and sometimes even taught sociology.[26]

The critique of capitalism under perestroika did not simply reflect the official Marxist slogans and other, more brutal, measures of persuasion employed by the Soviet regime in the course of more than seven decades of its autocratic rule. In fact, some anticapitalist attitudes of the prerevolutionary period, particularly Russian nationalist prejudices, which were officially discouraged in Soviet Marxist ideology, survived two of the greatest political and economic upheavals of the twentieth century: the Russian Revolution of 1917 and Stalin's rule in the 1930s, which included the collectivization of agriculture, forced industrialization, mass purges, and the imposition of state censorship that far surpassed in its severity the relatively stringent system of the tsars.

Somehow, then, cultural attitudes toward capitalism passed from one generation to another, not only via the Marxist-Leninist propaganda of the Soviet state but also by other, more informal means. These apparently included families and churches; indeed, the xenophobic rhetoric of the Russian Orthodox Church in the early 1990s had a particularly strong anticapitalist component that recalled prerevolutionary religious attitudes. For the moment, it suffices to mention the influence of economic and cultural geography, in the sense that the challenges that Russians perceived in their dealings with the outside world remained more or less constant over the generations, from the invasions of Charles XII, Napoleon, and Hitler to the economic threats posed by Germany and other industrially advanced neighbors in our own time.

The case for historical continuity draws support from recent theoretical work in economic history, which stresses the contribution of the institutional environment, especially legal systems and norms of behavior in business, to the efficient functioning of enterprises. As Douglass C. North observed:

> In developed countries, effective judicial systems include well-specified bodies of law and agents such as lawyers, arbitrators, and mediators, and one has some confidence that the merits of a case rather than private payoffs will influence outcomes. In contrast, enforcement in Third World economies is uncertain not only because of ambiguity of legal doctrine (a measurement cost), but because of uncertainty with respect to behavior of the agent.... Third-party enforcement means the development of the state as a coercive force able to monitor property rights and enforce contracts effectively, but no one at this stage in our knowledge knows how to create such an entity.[27]

To insist on resemblances between imperial Russia and the post-Soviet states on the one hand and Third World countries on the other may seem bizarre, but the continuity of autocratic government and cultural hostility to the West appear to have combined to hinder the emergence of institutions of capitalism and of attitudes conducive to corporate enterprise, then and now.

The concept of historical causation employed here rejects both randomness and rigid determinism. Rather, it adopts what North and other theorists of economic history call "path dependence," borrowed from the history of technology. This approach examines the ways that any choice made by historical actors in pursuit of a given policy will limit the range of future choices by the incremental creation of institutions resistant to rapid change. Particularly relevant for the Russian case is the phenomenon of economic stagnation within states ruled by powerful bureaucracies. In specific historical circumstances, "unproductive paths" may lead to "disincentives to productive activity," which limit economic productivity for centuries. "Incentives that may encourage military domination of the polity and economy, religious fanaticism, or plain, simple redistributive organizations" tend to limit "the stock and dissemination of economically useful knowledge." The repressive ideology often associated with such a regime "not only rationalizes the society's structure but accounts for its poor performance," so that new policies "reinforce the existing incentives and organizations."

North placed particular stress on the shortcomings of neoclassical theory in explaining economic development. "Our preoccupation with rational choice and efficient market hypotheses has blinded us to the implications of incomplete information and the complexity of environments and subjective perceptions. . . . Ideas and ideologies shape the subjective mental constructs that individuals use to interpret the world around them and make choices." Indeed, he called for "much more integration of politics and economics than has been accomplished so far."[28]

To understand the shape of Russian capitalism under tsarism and perestroika, therefore, it is necessary to grasp the structural and cultural impediments to its development bequeathed by the perennial realities of geography, autocratic politics, and xenophobic cultural attitudes. Perhaps the exaggeration of cultural continuities across time constitutes one of the historian's occupational hazards. Nevertheless, the anticapitalist attitudes expressed during the late tsarist period and those that emerged in the era of perestroika bear a striking resemblance to one another because they grew out of the same cultural tradition.

There is an important political dimension to this investigation as well. The fate of Russian capitalism mirrored the weakness of the liberal tradition in Russian culture, in contrast to the enormous power of both the radical and reactionary political traditions on the eastern periphery of European civilization. The effort to explain statistical patterns of corporate development in Russia and the Soviet Union therefore constitutes part of an attempt to understand institutional impediments to political freedom in the largest country in the world. Moore expressed this point of view in terms that appear to me to strike just the right balance between moral commitment and scholarly detachment: "Whether the ancient Western dream of a free and rational society will always remain a chimera, no one can know for sure. But if the men of the future are ever to break the chains of the present, they will have to understand the forces that forged them."²⁹

The pace of market reforms in the Soviet and post-Soviet economies has aroused heated debates. Would a rapid shock, painful in the short term, clear the ground for steady progress later on, or could gradual reforms maintain the bond of political trust between the rulers and the ruled? Some American advisers to the Yeltsin government prior to 1994 cited the necessity of applying economic reforms, such as stabilization of the currency and balanced budgets, that contributed to the creation of conditions favorable to capitalism elsewhere in the world. International communications have reached such a level of speed and sophistication that experts like Jeffrey D. Sachs, a professor of economics at Harvard University, could prescribe a massive reform program for the Polish economy in 1990 and, less than two years later, lay out an even more ambitious blueprint for Russia.³⁰

Whether or not the economic policies of Yeltsin and Gaidar qualified as genuine "shock therapy" remained a topic of lively discussion among economists. Meanwhile, a veteran observer of Soviet politics issued a cogent warning of the dangers of excessive American ethnocentricity in our handling of the Russian crisis.

> The anti-American backlash is also gathering force among the general population, despite a large reservoir of pro-American sentiment. The Yeltsin-Gaidar free-market shock therapy has inflicted enormous social pain. To millions of Russian citizens the loss of their life savings, their growing misery, their inability to care properly for young and old family members, and their anger over rampant "corruptalism"—all seem to be "made in the U.S.A." That is not true. But given U.S. rhetoric and effusive support for the Yeltsin-Gaidar measures, given the hordes of American "advisers" swarming over Russia, given the absence of effective U.S. relief but abundance of American trash movies dumped on the Russian market—why would they think otherwise?³¹

The debate over economic welfare during the transition from the Soviet system raised complex questions regarding the relationship between the corporation and democracy. To explain the uneasy accommodation of the corporate elite to the tsarist autocracy, a fascinating feature of late imperial Russian history, Timothy McDaniel coined the felicitous term "autocratic capitalism."³² It will also be recalled that Max Weber, as he pondered the fate of Russian democracy in the wake of the Revolution of 1905, detected in the modern corporation a tendency toward bureaucratization inimical to the constitutional freedoms that had developed in Europe in the preceding centuries. The very nature of the corporation, he warned, made a "new servitude" likely. Without constantly increasing technological progress, the division of labor and expansion of the population would create "ever-new work for clerks, and ever-new specialization of functions," all of which would lead to the creation of "caste." "It is utterly ridiculous to see any connection between the high capitalism of today—as it is now being imported into Russia and as it exists in America—with democracy or with freedom in any sense of these words. . . . We are 'individualists' and partisans of 'democratic' institutions 'against the stream' of material constellations." In his opinion, "freedom and democracy are only possible where the resolute will of a nation not to allow itself to be ruled like sheep is permanently alive."[33] A recent analysis of the corporation concluded that "in the vast majority of cases, corporate elections are like old Soviet elections, . . . not like those that we would normally recognize as democratic."[34] These observations constitute a useful antidote to the simplex equation of corporate capitalism with liberal democracy.

All the signs of both creative entrepreneurship and enormous abuse evident in the early 1990s suggested that Russian capitalism would eventually reflect both tsarist and Soviet historical experience. For this reason, capitalist institutions appeared likely to evolve relatively slowly in the face of attitudes deeply rooted in Russian culture, just as the capitalist systems now prevalent in Japan, India, and Nigeria, for example, owe much to the specific cultural and legal environments of those countries, far from the European birthplace of capitalism. The corporation has shown a remarkable ability to adapt to a wide variety of cultural and political environments in its rise to predominance in the world economy during the past several centuries. As Boris Yeltsin recently announced with characteristic bravado, Russia "is a unique country. It will not be socialist or capitalist."[35]

Notwithstanding the failure of Gorbachev's reforms, it seems excessively fatalistic to maintain that the weight of centuries of autocratic rule and hostility to individualism will prevent the gradual emergence of some sort of decentralized market economy in Russia.[36] Equally untenable is the opposite presumption of the inevitability of corporate capitalism in Russia on the European or American model: the evaporation of the Russian xenophobic tradition and the triumph of the West. Some might dream of remaking Russia and its neighbors in the image of the United States, but the notion is absurd. One prediction of a rosy future for Russian capitalism drew an analogy between Russia in the 1990s and the United States in the era of Alexander Hamilton,[37] a comparison that, in my opinion, ignored every relevant fact of Russian economic, social, and cultural history.

At this point in the historic drama, both extreme positions in this argument—the notions that Russia is fated to remain mired in its autocratic tradition and that the West should endeavor to make Russia a junior partner in an American-German-Japanese capitalist condominium—appear flawed on both logical and factual grounds. On the one hand, although it seems inevitable that Russia will rejoin the international economy, the terms of the eventual accommodation remain unclear. On the other hand, even the most vigorous enthusiast of technological determinism must recognize that the wholesale importation of capitalist institutions will take decades to influence everyday economic behavior in the largest country in the world. Thus, between the untenable extremes lies a vast area for fruitful disputation.

The main purpose of this book, then, is to explore the political and cultural currents that have shaped the institutions of corporate capitalism in the Russian Empire before 1914 and in the era of glasnost. If this account helps to explain the uniqueness of Russian capitalism in the near future, then it will have achieved its purpose.

2

Corporations in the Russian Empire, 1700–1914

> *By assiduously entering into detail, . . . each researcher into local history . . . lets us see a city, a village, a guild, a monastery, a family—alive in its past. And if we carry this over to the larger complexes—an area, a people, a state, a continent—where is the borderline between the unimportant and the merely interesting? There is none. Every historical fact opens immediately into eternity.*
>
> Johan Huizinga[1]

Although the notion of the imperial Russian state as the leading sponsor of corporate capitalism has lost much of its explanatory power in recent years, the sheer size of the tsarist bureaucracy and the lack of legislative and judicial restrictions on its arbitrary exercise of power make plausible what might be called the negative variant of the model advanced by Gerschenkron and Von Laue. The tsarist state exerted direct and significant influence on the pace and direction of corporate capitalism but erected impediments to corporate entrepreneurship instead of promoting it. Indeed, a close reading of criticisms leveled at the tsarist policymakers during the Russian Revolution, but since neglected by historians, lends support to this hypothesis.

The Population Ecology of Russian Corporations

The eminent economic historian Paul R. Gregory recently offered a cautiously sanguine assessment of Russian economic performance in the late tsarist period, especially in contrast to the five-year-plans. "The amount of structural change, as measured by the changes in Russia's agriculture and industry shares between 1885 and 1913, was average or slightly below average" compared to that of the major European countries, the United States, Canada, and Japan before World War I. Although he rejected many of Gerschenkron's findings with regard to stagnation in peasant agriculture, Gregory agreed that "the statistical profile of the Russian economy was that of a market economy taking the first decisive steps toward modern economic growth."[2]

The difference between this positive view and the more somber evaluation offered in the present study is to be explained largely by the dissimilar perspectives of analysis. Gregory surveyed the entire range of statistics for national income, which embraced government spending, peasant agriculture, and all forms of enterprise, whereas the new statistics in the RUSCORP database portrayed the immaturity and institutional weakness of corporate capitalism. To the extent that corporations represented the most technically advanced forms of economic activity, this negative finding constitutes a small, but important, qualification to Gregory's comprehensive analysis.

A relatively new theory from organizational sociology—the population ecology of organizations—helps to place the Russian corporate data into a coherent explanatory framework. This theory has particular relevance to the study of Russian corporations because it focuses on such environmental influences as geography, culture, and legislation. Drawing on "the natural selection model of biological ecology," researchers in this field of sociology examine "the nature and distribution of resources in organizations' environments" and "variation, selection, and retention" of organizational forms to explain "how organizational forms are created, survive or fail, and are diffused throughout a population."[3]

Published sources on Russia do not provide adequate information for many of the complex statistical tests used to analyze extensive populations of companies, such as those that are available on the largest one hundred or two hundred companies in Europe and the United States in a given year.[4] However, the RUSCORP database provides statistical data amenable to analysis by the theory of organizational ecology. (See Appendix A.)

Population ecology identifies at least six dimensions of the environment: capacity, homogeneity, stability, concentration, defense, and turbulence. These dimensions affect the emergence and survival of organizations. A thorough exploration of the theory's implications for Russian economic history and, conversely, of the strengths and weaknesses of the theory in light of that history would lead far beyond the analyses offered here. It is sufficient to note that, although the theory provides stimulating approaches to the history of Russian corporations, it appears unduly specific, in respect to its implied political and legal theory, to the history of western Europe and the United States.

Capacity indicates the maximum number of organizations that a given environment can support. The capacity can be placed on a spectrum that ranges from "lean" (small) to "rich" (large). Despite the more than thirtyfold increase between 1847 and 1914, the number of Russian corporations, and therefore capacity, remained relatively low. Even at the end of this period, corporations in the major European countries far outnumbered those in Russia, in both absolute and per capita terms. (See Table 2.1.)

Of the 4,542 corporations chartered between 1700 and December 31, 1913, only 33—too few to inscribe a curve on a graph—came into existence in the first 120 years. The first published list of companies in existence appeared in 1847, so it is impossible to know how many corporations survived to a given date before then, but the numbers appear to be tiny.

Companies founded in the first half of the eighteenth century managed mostly commercial or hunting and fishing enterprises modeled on those in Britain, France, and the Netherlands, but without the slightest financial success.[5] Between the publication of the first corporate charter, in 1704, and 1750, only eighteen companies came into existence, of which seven were devoted to whaling, fishing, and trapping, six to textile production, and two to other forms of manufacturing: needles and gunpowder. Of the nine companies founded in the reign of Peter the Great, one, the Spanish Trade Company, chartered in 1724, sought to implement the emperor's plan to make Russia a major maritime power, but it apparently failed soon after receiving its charter. The appeal of Empress Anna Ivanovna in 1739 for merchants to create a China Caravan Company had no more effect than Peter's admonition to Russian merchants, forty years before, to create trading companies in Archangel, Astrakhan, and Novgorod.[6]

The second half of the century witnessed the chartering of only eleven new companies, even fewer than in 1704–50. Catherine the Great, despite her professed devotion to European principles of statecraft, signed only four charters. All seven of the companies launched between 1751 and 1800 for the purpose of foreign trade—whether to foster commerce with Astrakhan (1752), Constantinople (1757), Persia (1758), the Caspian seacoast (1760), and the Mediterranean (1763) or to increase the export of grain from Nizhnii Novgorod (1767) or Voronezh (1772)—soon expired. Indeed, in 1762 Catherine abolished the Constantinople, Persia, and Caspian companies on the grounds that they enjoyed state monopolies, which she opposed in principle.[7] Although these monopolies might have had deleterious consequences, no companies arose to take their place after 1762.

The Russian-American Company received its original charter in 1797 as the American Company, capitalized with the considerable sum of 509,000 silver rubles, the first specific capital amount to appear in any charter. In 1799, it merged with another new company and assumed the famous name. The rich fish and animal resources of Alaska sustained this enterprise until its abolition in 1868, shortly after the transfer of Alaska to the United States. However, because the company did not provide limited liability to its investors until 1821 and functioned under strict governmental control for most of its existence, it hardly served as a model for corporate enterprise in the Russian Empire. A comparative study of this enterprise and the Hudson's Bay Company, which operated in a similar geographic environment in Canada but enjoyed far more economic success and survives to the present day, would probably illuminate crucial institutional differences between British and Russian corporations. Certainly, the British government's liberal policies, the managerial skills of the corporate directors, and the flexibility of the local traders contrasted sharply with the Russian bureaucrats' tutelage, the inexperience of the Russian-American Company's managers in St. Petersburg, and the tendency of local agents to deplete as rapidly as possible the stock of fur-bearing animals on the northern Pacific coast.[8]

Corporate growth in the Russian Empire remained unimpressive until the Crimean War (1853–6). Several trading and insurance companies founded in Odessa in the early nineteenth century failed within a few years of chartering. The fifteen corporate charters approved by the tsarist bureaucracy in the decade 1821–30 represented a significant increase in comparison to the thirty-three granted in the previous 120 years, but of the five largest companies chartered in the 1820s, including two steamship lines, only one, the First Russian Insurance Company, survived until 1914. Founded in 1827, it was called the First Russian Fire Insurance Company until 1896, when it began issuing transport and accident insurance.[9]

(Foreign companies, of which 262 were recorded in existence in Russia in 1914, do not figure prominently in this study because published documents did not provide statistics of their creation and growth. Moreover, they are peripheral to the issue of corporate entrepreneurship within Russia. The role of foreigners in the Russian corporate economy is discussed in Chapter 3.)[10]

Indications of the limited capacity of the Russian corporate environment in the reign of Nicholas I (1825–55) included the small number of new companies founded in this period—136, or less than 5 per year on the average—and the tiny number of those with large capitalizations. (On the use of the basic capital figure as an indicator of corporate size, see Appendix B.) Only 18 of the 136 charters contained capital amounts in excess of one million rubles. (See Table 2.2.)

Although the precise number of corporations in existence in a given year before the mid-nineteenth century is not known, it probably did not exceed a dozen well into the 1830s, so few were the charters issued before then and so high was the rate of failure. Two persistent patterns of Russian corporate development emerged at the outset: the geographical concentration of corporations in St. Petersburg and the relative success of insurance companies and textile manufacturing companies, in contrast to the short lifespans of large enterprises in metallurgy and transportation. The era of corporate railroad management, manufacturing, and banking lay in the future. Particularly ominous was the failure, within two decades of its founding, of the Russian Livestock Insurance Company, the only large corporation specifically devoted to the improvement of agriculture in this predominantly agrarian society.

The irregular expansion of the capacity of the corporate environment remained the dominant pattern. The theory of population ecology holds that, if capacity remains stable, the population growth of organizations generally inscribes an S-curve. The growth rate increases rapidly at first but then declines as the number of organizations approaches the maximum carrying capacity of the environment. As the carrying capacity increased, the resultant pattern of annual totals would have inscribed a series of S-curves, each ending at a plateau higher than the previous one.

World War I and the Bolshevik Revolution prevent our knowing the ultimate carrying capacity of the Russian economy in the early twentieth century. However, substantial growth occurred only in the six decades between the Crimean War and World War I. In seven cycles of incorporation, of which the first two were extremely weak, booms alternated with equally important periods of stagnation.[11] (See Figure 2.1. Cycles are measured in this analysis from the first rise at the end of one trough to the low point of the next trough.) Only in the early twentieth century did the statistics of existing companies and corporate capital reach impressive heights. (See Figure 2.2.)

Cycles of incorporation and the pattern of gradual increase must be considered in their social context, especially the expanding population of the empire. That is, these data do not demonstrate rapid and relentless progress toward a modern corporate economy. (See Figure 2.3.) Per capita capitalization rose dramatically in the two decades after the Crimean War, but then sluggishness persisted from the mid-1870s to the mid-1890s. The high point of the cycle that peaked in 1881 was only one-quarter as great as in the previous cycle. Even during the corporate boom of 1906–13, the highest per capita capital amount fell short of that of 1871, four decades before. (All annual capitalization figures refer only to the authorized value of shares of newly chartered corporations. These figures do not include new issues of shares by existing companies, for which no comprehensive published data are available. The financial literature in the decade before World War I suggests that this phenomenon added substantial amounts of capital to the market. The effects of such subsequent share issues appeared in the RUSCORP database only in the profiles of corporations that survived to 1847, 1869, 1874, 1892, 1905, and 1914.)

Although the number of existing corporations increased by a factor of almost thirty-two in the course of seven decades, from 68 in 1847 to 2,167 in 1914, it rose less than five and one-half times in per capita terms. Capitalization rose at a more impressive rate, from 0.51 ruble per person in 1847 to 33.3 rubles in 1914, but scarcely any increase occurred in the three decades before 1905.

What accounted for these and other patterns of corporate creation and development, both in the empire as a whole and in key sectors and regions? Variations in the availability of capital (as measured by the interest rate), incentives to specialization offered by the increasing diversity of the economic environment, and governmental encouragements and prohibitions all affected these incorporation patterns. (The entrepreneurial behaviors of various social and ethnic groups are examined in Chapter 3.)

Until 1917, the concessionary system of incorporation obstructed the free establishment of corporations by delaying the granting of charters, often for many months, and imposing restrictions on charters granted to foreigners and non-Russian citizens of the empire.[12] Business leaders failed to convince the imperial government to permit incorporation by registration, the system adopted in most advanced countries, including Japan, by the late nineteenth century. The tsarist bureaucracy thereby demonstrated its peculiar suspicion toward unfettered commercial and industrial activity. Rejections of petitions for corporate charters between 1799 and 1836 included four in insurance, three in transport, two in municipal services, one in agriculture or animal products, and five in other commercial or industrial fields.[13] (The Soviet regime evinced a much stronger antipathy in later decades.) Because dozens of charters received approval in large batches every few months, especially toward the end of the tsarist period, neither the emperor nor his ministers could have perused every application. The importance of the concessionary policy lay less in the weeding out of particular enterprises than in the maintenance of a high threshold to corporate entrepreneurship.

The seven cycles of incorporation reflected a variety of causal influences, but the major factor appeared to be the finance ministry's manipulation of interest rates. The abrupt lowering of interest rates paid to depositors in the state's savings banks served as catalysts for the flurries of incorporation in the 1830s, 1850s, and 1890s. During each of these episodes, savers who sought the highest possible rate of return transferred their cash out of savings accounts and into corporate securities. Only after the state raised its lending rates once again, thereby reducing the attractiveness of the stock market, did the corporate boom subside.[14]

To be sure, the staying power of particular corporations in their "niches" was evident from the 1830s onward across the spectrum, from tiny mineral water companies in Petersburg, Odessa, and Riga to the venerable First Russian Insurance Company, the oldest company in the empire between 1869 and 1914. Corporations founded in boom periods—the quinquenniums 1836–40, 1856–60, 1871–5, and 1896–1900—had low survival rates to 1914. Survival rates of companies founded in the peak years—1838 (zero), 1873 (28.1 percent), 1881 (40 percent), and 1899 (33.8 percent)—likewise fell below those of companies chartered in immediately preceding and following years. The sharp alternation between these occasional outbursts of "speculative mania" (*griunderstvo*, from the German *Gründertum*, current in the early 1870s) and deep troughs indicated the immaturity of the Russian corporate economy.

Another symptom of this immaturity appeared in the age structure of corporations, which showed the effects of cycles of incorporation in later years. (See Figure 2.4.) The small number of Russian corporations in 1847, 1869, 1874, 1892, and 1905 meant that the cyclical peaks of incorporation reached, for example, in 1873 and 1898 distorted the age structure for years thereafter. Only in 1914, after eight years of unprecedented growth in the number of new companies, did the age structure begin to reflect a clear pattern composed of large numbers of recently founded corporations and a gradually declining percentage of the total number of corporations in successive age groups, the result of a steady attrition rate of new enterprises over time.[15] Even in 1914, however, the tapering remained imperfect, as the influence of boom years continued to be felt after forty and fifteen years, respectively.

The second characteristic of the environment is *homogeneity*. The degree of homogeneity of a population can be seen in two important dimensions: function and size. A high degree of homogeneity was to be expected in the early stage of economic development. Indeed, the concentration of corporate headquarters in St. Petersburg; the predominance of companies in two leading sectors, insurance and light industry; and the importance of large companies in the reign of Nicholas I (shown in Table 2.2) demonstrated a pattern of homogeneity typical of immature populations. In contrast, a mature corporate population would be characterized by decreased homogeneity (increased heterogeneity), as expressed in lower ratios between the number of corporate headquarters in the largest and, for example, the tenth largest city; between the number in the largest and smallest functional categories; and between selected high and low percentiles of capitalization. Did the Russian corporate economy develop in this direction prior to World War I?

The phenomenon of geographical dispersion is examined in the third section of this chapter. As for function and size, the Russian corporate population evolved toward heterogeneity between the 1870s and 1905, but the industrial boom of the last prewar decade increased the degree of homogeneity once again. Thus, although the corporate economy grew increasingly diverse, as new enterprises sprang up in a variety of economic sectors, heterogeneity of function increased only slightly. (See Figure 2.5.) Financial primacy, as measured by totals of authorized corporate capital, passed from one sector to another: finance (mainly insurance) in the first two cycles; transportation (especially steamship lines) in the third; transportation again (led by railroads) to an even greater extent, in the fourth; light manufacturing (especially textiles) in the fifth; heavy manufacturing (mainly ferrous metallurgy and mechanical engineering) in the sixth; and transportation (railroads again) in the seventh. Heterogeneity increased as the leading sector's share diminished from the late 1870s onward, but the degree of homogeneity in terms of capitalization declined more slowly than in the case of corporate units, primarily because of the enormous size of railroad companies.

Similarly uneven progress toward heterogeneity occurred among surviving companies. (See Figure 2.6.) The persistence of the large proportion of corporations in light industry over the decades consistently limited the functional heterogeneity of the corporate population. Likewise, in

1914 the most heavily capitalized sector, transportation, accounted for almost two-fifths of the total capitalization.

A third indication of the slow evolution of capitalism in Russia toward heterogeneity emerges from an analysis of the size of existing corporations over the decades. (See Figure 2.7.) Although the narrowing of the distance between high and low percentiles after 1874 suggests a trend toward greater heterogeneity according to size by 1905, this aspect of economic maturity came at the expense of the expansion of the economy as a whole, in contrast to the marked expansion expressed in the uniform increase of all percentile values from 1847 to 1874. The median (by definition, the 50th percentile) declined after 1892, and the high points for the 95th, 90th, and 75th came in 1874, shortly after the remarkable flurry of incorporation during the era of the "Great Reforms." This peak in the three highest percentiles remained unsurpassed in 1892, 1905, and 1914. On the eve of the war, the two selected percentiles below the median—the 25th and 10th—stood far above their levels of 1847, but, like the median, they had reached their high point in 1892, on the eve of the famous industrial drive masterminded by Finance Minister Witte.

A positive interpretation of these data might be that the steady increase in the number of existing companies, shown in Figure 2.2, reduced the ruble amounts of the percentile levels, as small companies outnumbered the giants by wider and wider margins as time went on. However, the dismal performance of the very largest companies—corporate railroads, discussed later—dragged down the three highest percentiles after 1874. The 99th percentile (not shown) reached its peak of 81.4 million rubles in 1892, just before the state's purchase of the Russian Railroad Company, the largest corporation ever founded in the empire.

Owing apparently to the failure of many large corporations in the industrial crisis at the turn of the century, the distances between percentiles reached their lowest point in 1905. For example, the ratio between the 95th and 10th percentiles fell from 147.1:1 in 1874 to 24.0:1 in 1905. (The ratio may have increased during the industrial boom of the 1890s, but the database contains no statistics for corporations in existence in 1900.) This trend reversed itself in 1905, as the ratio between the two percentiles increased to 40.0:1 in 1914, reflecting the creation of a handful of huge new railroad companies in 1908–13. If a mature economy is defined as having a fairly even distribution of units of all sizes, so that large, medium, and small enterprises coexist and supplement one another, then the renewed increase in homogeneity from 1905 to 1914 demonstrated once again the immaturity of the Russian corporate economy.

The third element of population ecology is *stability*. Although the geographical and social contexts evolved slowly, from time to time corporations faced abrupt changes in their financial environment, particularly as a result of shifts in governmental policies. These changes called forth new corporations but also threatened the survival of existing ones. The "liability of newness" posited by Michael T. Hannan and John Freeman is clearly shown in the rapidly falling survival rates during the initial years of each cohort's existence. (See Figure 2.8, which sets the 100 percent mark at the midpoint of each cycle.) Entrepreneurs in Cycle 5, the least impressive because of its failure to rise above the trend line, won the benefits of caution in the form of a higher survival rate in 1914 than those in Cycle 6, which included the speculative boom of the 1890s.

Particularly significant in the Russian case was the fourth element of population ecology: *concentration* of resources. The Russian Empire, the largest country in the world, contained a dozen regional economies, each with distinctive resource endowments and cultural traditions. This diversity created an extremely uneven environment, despite the uniformity of the legal structure. Ores, fuels, and appropriate soils and climates for specific crops, such as grain and sugar beets, were distributed unevenly in the empire. Other resources, notably governmental assistance, investment capital at relatively low interest rates, and managerial expertise, remained concentrated in the few large cities. These environmental factors help to account for the extremely uneven geographical distribution of corporate headquarters. The rate of diffusion of corporate headquarters and operations into new areas increased toward the end of the imperial period, but slowly.

Ten centers of corporate headquarters accounted for the vast majority of new corporations. After minimal activity before 1851, too slight to be shown on a graph, the strikingly uneven pattern of geographical distribution took shape. (See Figure 2.9.) The essential similarity of cyclical patterns of incorporation is shown by Spearman correlation coefficients of rank orders of corporate headquarters in consecutive quinquenniums: 1821–5/1826–30 to 1906–10/1911–3. Coefficients for the eighteen pairs of consecutive quinquenniums ranged from lows of +.6240 in 1831–5/1836–40 and +.6494 in 1901–5/1906–10 to highs of +.9259 in 1856–60/1861–5 and +.8951 in 1876–80/1881–5.[16] (Here and elsewhere, the three-year period from January 1, 1911 to December 31, 1913 is called a quinquennium for the sake of convenience.) The lowest coefficients draw attention to changes in the regional dispersion of corporations. During the petroleum boom in 1901–5, for example, Baku surpassed Odessa and Riga in the creation of new companies, but after 1905, when ethnic violence between Armenians and Azeris severely damaged its oilfields, Baku fell to tenth place in the last two quinquenniums, while Rostov-on-Don moved from a tie for tenth place in 1901–5 to sixth place in 1911–3.

Geographical concentration persisted despite the rise of provincial centers of corporate activity. St. Petersburg remained the favored home of large corporations, especially railroad, shipping, and mining companies, because their managers depended on access to its relatively well-developed capital market and to the governmental ministries that subsidized strategically important economic activities.

An organization's *defense* of its domain against competitors and the state constitutes the fifth element of organizational ecology.[17] At least three aspects of defense are evident in the case of Russian corporations. First, the perennial shortage of investment funds meant that any corporation capable of amassing large amounts of capital enjoyed a distinct advantage in the Russian economy. No less important a factor was entrepreneurial ability. The cases of two American corporations, International Harvester and Singer, illustrated how capital and entrepreneurial ability constituted keys to success.

In 1914, International Harvester's huge basic capital—77.7 million rubles, or approximately $40 million—made it the largest of the 262 foreign corporations authorized to operate in Russia, an unusual accomplishment in view of the fact that its agricultural machinery factory at Liubertsy, near Moscow, had begun production only three years before. Singer's 50 million rubles of basic capital earned it fourteenth place among the 2,167 corporations founded under Russian law and first place among all manufacturing corporations that survived to 1914. As Fred V. Carstensen observed,

> In Russia, the very expanse of the country, its comparative poverty, its poorly developed transportation infrastructure, and its inadequate credit services all compounded the usual costs of doing business. International Harvester, with a selling investment of Rs. 53 million, found doing business in Russia two to three times more expensive than in the United States. Singer, with operating capital of Rs. 85 million, had one and a half to two times as much capital tied up in Russia as was necessary relative to its business in France. In making such large investments, both firms evidently broke a bottleneck for Russian purchases.

That is, these integrated American companies prevented Russian competitors from finding profitable niches and thereby defended their domain. Singer created its own sales network, which "probably reached deeper into the stretches of the Russian Empire than any other organization save, perhaps, the government"; and International Harvester used marketing techniques perfectly suited to Russia, such as the provision of more than two years' credit to purchasers of its reapers and binders. Even International Harvester's difficulties illustrated the importance of managerial expertise. Because its managers failed to maintain high quality standards and chose an imperfect product mix, the company did not turn a profit on its Russian manufacturing operations in 1909–13 and barely "broke even" in 1910–14.[18]

Third, the concept of defense in the theory of organizational ecology reiterates in a new way the enormous importance of the state in the Russian economy. For example, to the extent that various cartels or syndicates succeeded in receiving governmental approval despite the formal illegality of their activities, these organizations may be considered to have defended their domain. Of crucial importance for sugar enterprises, for example, was the market control exercised by the Society of Russian Sugar

Producers, founded in 1897 as the successor to a sugar producers' bureau created ten years before. The society strove to limit the supply of marketed sugar as the number of companies expanded and productivity rose as a result of improvements in technology. The state cooperated with the cartel by regulating the amount of annual sugar production after 1895 and by coordinating the dumping of the surplus, at mandatorily low prices, in the Ottoman Empire and Persia to maintain stable profit margins in Russia. In return, the bureaucracy derived a financial benefit because it collected no less than 21 percent of its excise revenues from sugar.[19]

However, when the interests of the state clashed with those of cartels or syndicates (as cartel sales offices were called), they found it difficult to defend their domain. The coal syndicate, Produgol', incorporated on May 11, 1904, complained that the state exerted downward pressures on prices for the benefit of the navy and government-owned railroads, which consumed vast amounts of coal.[20]

The last major element in an organization's environment is *turbulence*, defined as "externally induced changes in the nature of environmental selection criteria, produced by forces that are obscure to administrators [of organizations] and therefore difficult to predict or plan for."[21] Into this category fell economic forces that swept through the international economy according to their own logic. From the 1850s to the early twentieth century, the Russian corporate economy became integrated with that of western Europe. The effect of the Panic of 1873 was especially evident, as only 46 charters were issued in 1874, compared to 114 in 1873, a 59.6 percent decline. (See Figure 2.1.) St. Petersburg proved particularly responsive to foreign trends, the more so because of its relatively large colonies of European businessmen, as discussed in Chapter 3. As Gregory noted,

> Russian prices, investment spending, and national income appeared to move strongly with business cycles in other countries. This is readily apparent from the price data. The relationship between Russian investment and output cycles and those of the major industrialized countries is more complex and is deserving of further analysis. One point is fairly clear: The political events of 1905 and 1906 caused Russia to diverge from the world investment and output cycle.[22]

More significant than the strikes, peasant rebellions, and other economic dislocations caused by the Revolution of 1905, however, were structural changes that gradually reduced the effect of foreign influences on the Russian economy. The Soviet economist Pervushin found that the Russian business cycle, as measured by a variety of quantitative indicators, began to diverge from that of Europe after 1905, when it reflected, for better or worse, trends in Russian agriculture. Russian grain prices, in turn, felt the influence of the world market from the 1880s onward, as the extension of the domestic railroad system lowered costs of transportation to Europe.[23]

The concept of turbulence highlights the crucial role of the tsarist state in the corporate environment, but it also reveals a weakness in the theory itself. Theorists of economic organization often stress the positive contributions of the state. In the words of one sociologist: "Political stability and ideological legitimacy reduce environmental uncertainty and thus encourage future-oriented behavior, giving organizational entrepreneurs the confidence to found new organizations. Nation-states facilitate and protect organizations both directly and indirectly. . . ."[24] This characterization might apply to states based on a firm legal foundation, particularly those that have provided institutional protection for private property, but it hardly describes the notoriously arbitrary tsarist state. Whether the immense influence of the state as a factor in the organizational environment promoted or hindered organizational development must remain a matter of empirical determination.

As early as 1949, W. T. Easterbrook criticized the tendency of neoclassical economic theory to prescribe a role for the state that consisted in providing legal safeguards for private property and the implementation of "corrective" methods to ensure competition. "State action may be repressive as well as 'constructive.' There is a tendency to overemphasize the importance of the state as a positive agent. . . . It is impossible to separate state from law, . . . and the legal system as a stabilizing force, a sanction element, protector of property rights, and so on, is to be regarded as one of the elements most crucial to the power and freedom of the entrepreneur." He stressed the negative effects on entrepreneurial activity of the repressive policies of the governments of Spain and Russia over the centuries.[25]

Thus, the tsarist autocracy, which refused to implement a rational system of corporate law, provided an excellent example of a negative environmental influence. To accept the widespread concept of the state "as an agent of society" that generally acts "to mobilize, control, and redistribute societal resources on a stable basis"[26] is therefore to ground the analysis in the modern democratic tradition, a recent and rare phenomenon in human history and geographically specific to Western Europe and areas of the world under its cultural influence.

The inability of the tsarist government to implement a rational policy of industrial development also requires emphasis. Historians have accepted uncritically the Russian autocrats' declarations in favor of economic development. Peter the Great is generally viewed as a brutal but effective champion of "forcible industrialization" against the resistance of boyars and peasants, but the damage inflicted on hapless merchants by his impetuous rule has not been adequately appreciated. The minuscule numbers of corporations founded under the impetuous Peter (nine) and the allegedly enlightened Catherine II (four) show that they did not provide a favorable legal environment for corporate entrepreneurship in the eighteenth century. Thus, much of what Aldrich called "environmental uncertainty"[27] emanated, in Russia, from the autocratic state itself.

In vain did the Swiss philosopher Frédéric-César de La Harpe admonish his pupil, Emperor Alexander I, to provide a firm structure of property law in the early nineteenth century:

> I believe that numerous capitalists will arise, and in order to prosper their enterprises need only the simple protection due all from the government, which always does well not to meddle too often in private affairs. . . . When good laws known to all protect persons and property against arbitrariness, and the course of justice is regulated by men dedicated to the study of law, virtuous, executing the latter for all, human ingenuity cannot fail to make the steppes fertile.28

However vigorous the economic policies of the tsarist government, they did not lay a firm foundation of legality.

By the early twentieth century, manufacturers felt emboldened to criticize not only specific measures—the degree of tariff protection and the amounts of subsidies to favored industries—but the entire program of state tutelage. As the mining and metallurgical industrialists of the Ural region complained in 1905:

> Economic life can develop successfully only under a firmly established system of law [*pravovoi poriadok*]. The spirit of initiative and entrepreneurship [*predpriimchivost'*] can live only when every individual is confident of strict observance of sensible [*razumnyi*] and just laws, of the independence of the courts, and of a lack of administrative arbitrariness.

Unfortunately, the tsarist bureaucracy was "so cut off from life and so biased and suspicious in dealing with [industry's] needs" that it tended to "hinder the development of the state's productive forces. . . . An entrepreneur is ready to take into account all kinds of risks, one American has said, except the risk of arbitrariness." Whether or not the Ural manufacturers had read La Harpe's works, they accurately sensed the failure of the tsarist government to provide such a system of guarantees. Beet-sugar producers also demanded liberal reforms during the Revolution of 1905, including the abolition of ethnic restrictions on entrepreneurs in the sugar industry.29

However, Nicholas II and his ministers refused to reform the Russian legal system in the decade prior to World War I. The Association of Industry and Trade, the national business organization created in 1906, repeatedly complained of the state's interference in industry, its refusal to relinquish control over key sectors of the economy, such as railroads, and its competition with private industry.30

The effects of state sponsorship of industry were often ambiguous. Rising import tariffs provided increased protection from foreign competition, but manufacturers complained of the arbitrary and unpredictable manner in which tariffs, subsidies, interest rates, and other measures were imposed by the bureaucracy. (Gregory correctly noted the important fiscal purpose of import tariffs imposed by the tsarist government,[31] but he understated their economic impact in protecting traditional industries, such as textiles, and in calling forth whole new sectors, such as coal mining and mechanical engineering in the 1880s. The many polemical battles over tariff protection indicated their importance in the last century of the tsarist period.) In addition to fostering commercial banks between 1864 and 1874, Finance Minister Mikhail Kh. Reutern maintained strict tutelage over them. He intervened to rescue favored banks from collapse in moments of crisis but refused to help those whose bankruptcy appeared to result from careless management.[32]

Without adequate statistical data on corporate finances and on the effects of various policy changes in the imperial capital, it is difficult to measure precisely the costs to the Russian economy of inflexible bureaucratic guardianship of capitalist institutions.[33] Someday, historians of the Russian economy may attempt to emulate the methods employed in U.S. economic history, where researchers have sought "to determine the size and/or growth of the firm over time in association with major strategic variables such as advertising, diversification rates, price policy and especially stock market value."[34]

The inadequacy of economic data is only one aspect of the problem, however. The key challenge for the economic historian of Russia lies not in fitting corporate data into economic theory but in the attempt to lay bare causal relationships among political, social, and economic trends. Even if adequate data on profits, dividends, and stock-market prices were available, economic theory by itself would illuminate only part of the great drama of economic development. As Peter D. McClelland has observed,

> although the core of economics is fairly well defined, the margin remains obscure. The historian concerned with the causes and consequences of institutional change, with the interaction of the economy with political, social, and cultural factors, is drawn irresistibly toward that margin and away from the main body of economic theory. Put another way, the usefulness of economic theory is crucially dependent upon the questions asked, and many of the questions asked by the historian with a broad focus cannot be readily answered by using the type of causal generalizations that are the core of contemporary economic theory.[35]

Finally, organizational ecology not only assumes beneficial legal norms established by the rational state, a notion that is geographically and culturally unique, but also, in its simplest form, takes for granted the identity of units in the population to be examined. As Herman Daems once quipped, the theory of population ecology applies to sharks because we know what a shark is, but corporations are not necessarily separate entities. In addition to multinational companies, which operate through a complex system of subsidiaries organized on functional and geographical lines, Daems had in mind the Belgian "mixed banks" and, especially from the 1930s onward, holding companies and their allied firms, which functioned together as a single economic unit but retained separate institutional identities in the eyes of the law.[36]

Researchers in organizational ecology have identified this phenomenon.[37] It embraces as well the unincorporated trading firms that some of the leading corporate entrepreneurs in imperial Russia used to coordinate the investment of rare capital. The most prominent of these, the Wogau firm, represented the application of German managerial ability to a great variety of industrial undertakings. The huge financial resources of this firm, 50 million rubles on the eve of World War I, surpassed those of all but the largest industrial corporations in Russia at that time. It might be objected that real patterns of entrepreneurship in Russia will remain obscure until the activities of these invisible actors is illuminated. However, the few sketches of trading firms already available make clear that their fortunes rose and fell in response to general economic trends, as did those of corporations.[38] Although much empirical spadework is still required to reveal the hidden structures of Russian capitalism, especially the coordinating activities of trading firms and banks, the RUSCORP database adequately reveals the most basic patterns of cyclical development, geographical concentration, and functional specialization. Because of their enormous size and crucial functions, railroads and banks exerted a decisive influence on the entire population of Russian corporations.

Railroads and Banks

Railroads occupied a key position among corporations in all major industrial countries in the modern world. They spearheaded economic development not only by reducing transportation costs and increasing the demand for rails, locomotives, rolling stock, and coal, but also by creating efficient forms of large-scale economic organization. Alfred D. Chandler called railroads "the first private enterprises in the United States with modern administrative structures" because their far-flung operations required "a concentration of effort on coordinating, appraising, and planning the work of the specialized units." The Pennsylvania Railroad's centralized administrative structure in the 1880s provided the first example of the "line-and-staff concept of departmental organization." This model was utilized by the great manufacturing corporations that appeared at the turn of the century—the National Biscuit Company, International Harvester, International Paper, and the United States Steel Corporation—before the emergence of the decentralized "multidivisional" giants in the 1920s, some of which have remained dominant in their sectors since then: du Pont, General Motors, Standard Oil of New Jersey (now Exxon), and Sears, Roebuck and Company.[39]

Seen in this international context, Russian railroad companies performed poorly. Three bursts of entrepreneurship—in the aftermath of the Crimean War, from the mid-1860s to the mid-1870s, and in 1908–13—

were separated by decades of stagnation. Despite their enormous size, railroads failed to provide an administrative model for successful corporations of the late imperial period, such as the Nobel Brothers Petroleum Company, the largest industrial corporation in 1905 and the second largest, after Singer, in 1914. Indeed, owing largely to generous financial subsidies from the state in the 1860s and 1870s, Russian railroads left a record of enormous extravagance, waste, and inefficiency. Railroad companies founded in the era of the so-called Great Reforms absorbed huge amounts of investment capital but failed to create a national rail network equal to the task of providing efficient overland transportation. After spending millions of rubles in guaranteed dividend and interest payments on railroad stocks and bonds, the state saw few positive results. In 1886, for example, the debts of railroad companies totaled 850 million credit rubles, far more than the 618 million rubles represented by their combined basic capital.[40]

The tsarist state gradually lost patience. Years of investigation by the Baranov Commission led to the promulgation in 1885 of a comprehensive law of railroad management and to the state's purchase of many unprofitable companies in the 1880s and 1890s,[41] a process that dramatically reduced their number. (See Figure 2.10.) Only in 1908 did the bureaucracy once again begin to confirm charters of corporations that were intended to build ambitious long-haul railroads, mostly on the periphery of the empire, in the Caucasus, Central Asia, and Siberia.

Russian companies reached their maximum size in the early 1870s, as all the selected percentiles shown in Figure 2.7, except one, the 75th, stood lower in 1914 than in 1874. Because railroad companies consistently ranked among the largest in the empire, this decline in average size reflected the poor staying power of Russian railroads. The economic significance of corporate railroads relative to that of state-owned railroads gradually decreased, from 30 percent of total rail mileage in 1900 to 25 percent in 1913. The state's new lines may have helped to stimulate the Russian metallurgical and machinery industries, but, because they served almost exclusively "strategic," or military, purposes, they did little to solve the acute problem of insufficient railroad service for the civilian economy.[42]

The financial woes of railroad companies carried their survival rates to levels far below those for corporations as a whole (shown in Figure 2.8). Among railroads, rates of survival to 1914—16.7 percent (three of eighteen) from the quinquennium 1866–70 and 4.8 percent (one of twenty-one) from 1871–5, for example—compared unfavorably to those of corporations generally: 40.9 percent and 34.7 percent, in respective periods. Of the thirty-five railroad companies founded in 1866–75 that did not survive to 1914, seven were acquired by other lines, and at least twenty-five fell under state control. The state purchased no less than thirty-three railroad companies between 1887 and 1900, and others merged with the six largest companies, which owned between 2,112 and 4,112 versts of track in 1911. In the final flurry of incorporation (1908–13), more than two dozen new railroad companies received charters, but none of the new lines approached the size of the six giants by 1914.[43]

One of the most important features of the Russian economy just prior to World War I was the insufficient capacity of the railroad network. To be sure, in absolute terms the Russian Empire boasted the second-largest rail system in the world, greater in its total length than any except that of the United States. However, in terms of population and territory, the impressive length of the Russian railroad system dwindled to inadequacy because the empire encompassed one-sixth of the world's land surface. As early as 1879, the coal and iron producers of the Donets and Krivoi Rog regions rationed railroad cars among themselves, especially at harvest time, when grain shipments deprived mining companies of much of the existing rolling stock. Still, huge piles of grain stood unprotected from the weather at rural railroad stations.[44]

Small wonder, then, that the Russian railroad network failed to service either the domestic economy or the armed forces during World War I. On the eve of the war, French military experts considered the Russian railroad system insufficient to transport the requisite numbers of soldiers and equipment to the eastern border of Germany. In 1912, General Joffre pointed out the need for a rail network two or three times as large as the existing one. The French foreign minister and ambassador to St. Petersburg made the same point. The Russian government had a different concern: how to pay for these economically marginal railroad links at a time when increased expenditures for cannons and warships strained the military budget. Nicholas II and his minister of war, Gen. Vladimir A. Sukhomlinov, showed little interest in expanding the rail network in Russian Poland. Under pressure from French banks, Prime Minister Kokovtsov agreed in principle to launch a four-year program of railroad construction of 11,000 kilometers throughout the Russian Empire at a cost of approximately 220,000 francs per kilometer, for a grand total of nearly 2.5 billion francs. The capital was to be raised on the Paris Bourse by five bond issues of 500 million francs each, backed by the usual financial guarantees from the Russian government.[45]

Had World War I broken out in 1918 instead of 1914, Russian railroads might have met the colossal challenge, but the Franco-Russian agreement, concluded in December 1913, came too late to have a major economic impact. Paradoxically, imperial Germany and the other defeated powers avoided economic catastrophe during the war, but Russia, on the winning side, did not. The collapse of the rail network intensified the food supply crisis in the major cities of the empire, thereby contributing to the political upheaval that brought the Bolsheviks to power.[46]

Banks, like railroads, occupied such an important position in the corporate economy of the Russian Empire that their rates of formation and survival reveal much about the institutional structure of Russian capitalism. One of the limitations of the RUSCORP database is that it contains no information about the date of cessation of all corporations. Fortunately, such dates are available for all 91 commercial banks that received charters between 1864 and 1913.[47] Knowledge of the year of liquidation or merger with a larger company permits the use of several statistical tests that provide a clear picture of rates of survival from one year to the next.

Recently devised statistical tests also make allowances for the complications that arise when analyzing a population in which some units continue to exist after the end point of the study. Statisticians call such data sets "right-censored" because events after the cutoff date are ignored. The SAS program LIFETEST calculates rates of survival and hazard functions for right-censored populations.[48] In this case, the year 1914 marks the final point on the chronological spectrum laid out from left to right. (The liquidation of all corporations by the Bolshevik government lies outside the scope of this analysis.) The survival function shows the rate of survival over time, and the hazard function indicates the chance that a given entity will fail in a given period after its creation.

Like railroads, commercial banks felt the influence of governmental policies. (See Figure 2.10; dates of liquidation are known for only 99 of the 123 railroads chartered by the imperial government between 1836 and 1913, so the test for hazard functions cannot be performed on them.) In the first decade of corporate commercial banking (1864–73) in Russia, an extremely sharp S-curve indicated a significant boom. The ability of the economy to support over three dozen banks had obviously existed prior to 1864, but the concessionary system of incorporation had prevented their formation without the permission of the tsar. The restrictive essence of the concessionary system was never so clearly illustrated as in the first banking boom.

The capacity for banks remained fairly stable, as between thirty-two and forty-two banks existed for nearly three decades (1872–1910). This number did not reflect solely the rational calculations of Russian merchants. Bureaucrats in St. Petersburg limited the number of banks in the empire to the very minimum, always fearful that an excess of banking capacity might lead to undue competition among them, unsound loans, and, finally, massive defaults during a financial panic. The Ministry of Finance continued to exercise arbitrary power over the entire banking system, especially its geographical scope, to the very end.

From 1874 to 1914, approximately twice as many banks maintained their headquarters in St. Petersburg as in Moscow, and all the provincial cities together accounted for only between eighteen and twenty-eight bank headquarters. This geographical concentration can be attributed to the shortage of well-trained personnel in small cities and the minimal opportunities for commercial lending there.

Offsetting the tendency toward concentration were the policies of the Ministry of Finance, which refused for an entire decade (1872–82) to allow any new banks in cities where one already existed. This cautious policy limited competition in the major cities, to the benefit of existing banks, but it drove entrepreneurs to establish banks in small provincial cities. The meager financial opportunities there meant that bankruptcy often followed within a year or two. Of the twenty-two new banks founded between 1872 and 1879, six (in Kozlov, Rybinsk, Berdichev, Kerch, Kherson, and Kursk) did not begin operations at all, and three (in Kronstadt, Libau, and Kamenets-Podolsk) failed by 1882. Reutern's benevolence toward existing banks in the major cities implied indifference to the new banks in small provincial cities.[49] The final surge in the number of banks, in 1911–3, reflected the bureaucrats' renewed willingness to allow an expansion of the credit system as much as it did the desires of the would-be bankers themselves. As in the case of railroads, however, this late expression of enthusiasm came too late to transform the economy before the onset of the war.

The Russian industrialization drive in the 1890s impressed the entire world, but the boom ended abruptly in a sharp depression (1900–1903) that forced the liquidation of several banks. The weakness of the Russian banking network was evident in the fact that four of the nine banks liquidated after twenty years of operation met their demise in 1901–4, in the wake of the depression. The rapidly falling survival rate in early years of existence—"the liability of newness"—is typical for organizations in many times and places. A comparison of this curve for banks, in Figure 2.11, with those of all corporations in the seven cycles, in Figure 2.8, reveals that the overall survival rate of banks remained relatively high. Three-fifths of banks existed after twelve years of operation, and almost two-fifths survived for forty years and more, proportions far greater than those for the total population of companies, which lacked the solicitude of the Ministry of Finance.

The U-shaped hazard function of Russian banks, shown in Figure 2.11, departed from the normal pattern, according to which the function falls quickly at first and then approaches a low and stable level. Witte's depression at the turn of the century contributed to a rising hazard function for Russian banks in the third and fourth decades of their existence.

In the absence of biographical studies of leading Russian bankers, which would give insights into their intentions and capabilities, it is impossible to prove or disprove the contention that a laissez-faire policy by the Ministry of Finance would have strengthened the banking system. It seems reasonable to assume, however, that a dual policy of allowing new banks in the largest cities and of encouraging banks in the major centers to establish branch offices in small cities where no modern credit facilities existed would have allowed the banking system to develop more vigorously than it did.

Recent scholarship on tsarist economic policy has stressed its irrational and arbitrary elements, even under the stewardship of the vigorous Witte. However, the notion of the heavy costs of bureaucratic tutelage has met with some skepticism. For example, one of the foremost British scholars of the tsarist economy recently asserted that "capitalism had a way of side-stepping the corporate law," as "thousands of trading houses (*torgovye doma*), some of which enjoyed limited liability [for investors]," permitted Russians to create "non-corporate outlets for their energies."[50] By analogy, other arbitrary policies, such as subsidies to favored enterprises and restrictions on economic activity by members of ethnic groups who had much to offer in the way of entrepreneurship—Poles, Jews, and foreigners—could not prevent determined individuals from reaping profits in the early years of Russian industrialization.

Some of the biographical evidence in Chapter 3 lends support to this hypothesis. However, a plea for the liberalization of the banking law published by the Russian Banking Association (*Komitet s″ezdov predstavitelei aktsionernykh kommercheskikh bankov*) in 1917, shortly before the Bolshevik seizure of power, made a compelling case against bureaucratic restrictions on the banking system. The bankers alleged that the cautious policy of the Ministry of Finance had choked off the supply of credit for two decades, from 1875 to 1894. Only after Witte allowed banks to open numerous branch offices and relaxed other restrictions did industry enjoy an unprecedented boom, in the last half of the 1890s.

The bankers claimed that several indices of increased economic activity, including the number of new corporations and the amount of pig iron and cotton textiles produced each year, correlated strongly with the expansion of banking activity in the late 1890s. When banks contracted their activities, as in the "depression" of 1900–1908, industry likewise stagnated. Then, as banks resumed their expansion from 1908 onward, industry revived, new corporations proliferated, and existing companies issued a torrent of new stock. The "parallelism" in the movements of data in banking and industry, the bankers claimed, showed a causal relationship: "the development of banks in fact defines the development of economic activity."[51]

The various time series in the bankers' pamphlet of 1917 offer rich material for statistical analysis. The assertion of a cause-and-effect relationship between the state's restrictions on banks and economic stagnation finds some support in high positive correlations between the largest element of the commercial banks' liabilities, called the balance (*balans*), and data from RUSCORP on newly chartered corporations and their authorized capitalization for the forty years following 1874, the first year for which the bankers' pamphlet supplied the balance figure. The coefficient of correlation between the banks' total balances and new corporations was +.8362, and between the balances and total capital of new corporations, +.8575. Therefore, just one factor—the variation in balances—accounted for 69.9 percent and 73.5 percent of the variations in incorporations and authorized capitalizations, respectively. In both cases, the level of probability (p) reached the maximum, .0000.[52]

Of course, economic self-interest underlay the bankers' claim to occupy a crucial position in the national economy. Also, the failure of the four mature banks in 1901–4 might be interpreted as evidence that too many banks, rather than too few, had come into existence in the last quarter of the nineteenth century and that the bankers therefore had no grounds for complaint. Still, the argument that only commercial banks could amass the requisite investment capital of thousands of individuals appeared valid.

Apparently no one has yet evaluated the bankers' assertion, the strongest ever made in the Russian economic literature, that the government's control of the banking system crippled the entire economy for decades on end. Soviet scholars had every reason to ignore the pamphlet's thesis because they generally exaggerated the tempo of industrial development in the Russian Empire and the tsarist government's commitment to capitalism, the better to endorse the allegedly "socialist" nature of the Bolshevik Revolution of 1917, which would have been absurd without the industrial achievements of a previous capitalist phase in the Marxist teleological scheme.

Clearly, the bankers' critique deserves to be taken seriously as a promising hypothesis in Russian economic history, a corollary of the general thesis of the stultifying role of the tsarist government, first advanced by Arcadius Kahan and strongly supported by recent American research on tsarist economic policy and business history. The RUSCORP database provides additional preliminary support in trends throughout the empire as a whole in the last four decades before World War I. Another indication is the resort of the tsarist government on 103 occasions between 1870 and 1914 to European bankers for massive loans of investment capital for the construction and maintenance of the Russian railroad network. Of the foreign banks involved at least once in Russian railroad loans, fifteen were German, fourteen French, eight English, five Belgian, and three Dutch.[53] Russian banks simply could not amass the requisite amounts of capital. Thus, the constant financing of railroads by foreign capital provided yet another example of the essentially foreign character of capitalist institutions in Russia.

Finally, banks occupied a strategic place in the late imperial economy because of their role as de facto stock exchanges, especially in St. Petersburg.[54] Cash deposited in banks flowed into industrial enterprises, some of which fell under the influence of their sources of capital when members of bank boards and councils sat on the boards of the companies. Also, wealthy depositors exercised the right of borrowing cash from "on-call" (*onkol'*) accounts, in which collateral in the form of corporate stocks and bonds secured loans of cash for additional investments in stock, often for speculative purposes. In the industrial depression at the turn of the century, defaults on these on-call loans caused serious liquidity problems because the market for the collateral—corporate securities—collapsed at the same time. Financial intervention by the State Bank saved some banks, but others failed.[55]

Soviet historians, following Lenin, generally persisted in affirming the existence of a system of "finance capital," a stage in the inexorable evolution of capitalism to socialism. (The notion of "finance capital"—that the largest banks exerted operational control over whole groups of major corporations—is not the same as the bankers' claim that the condition of the banking system influenced the general environment of business activity.) Developed in 1912 by the Austrian Marxist Rudolf Hilferding in his monograph of that name and endorsed by Lenin in his pamphlet on imperialism four years later, the concept of finance capital became part of Marxist-Leninist orthodoxy. For example, in June 1917, Lenin had minimized the difficulty of harnessing the banks for the socialist cause:

> It would be enough to arrest fifty to a hundred financial magnates and bigwigs, the chief knights of embezzlement and of robbery by the banks. It would be enough to arrest them for a few weeks *to expose their frauds* and show all exploited people "who needs the war." Upon exposing the frauds of the banking barons, we could release them, placing the banks, the capitalist syndicates, and all the contractors "working" for the government under workers' control.[56]

Other scholars have viewed this formula with skepticism. Writing in 1927, before the advent of Stalinist ideological controls, Iosif F. Gindin criticized Hilferding for equating "financial control" with "control over production." "Because banks are specifically organs of capitalist financial control and are at the same time [simply] the circulation system [*krovonosnaia sistema*] of the capitalist economy, the seizure of the banks means, as 1917 showed, only the paralysis [*paralich*] of both its functions, and, with regard to the cessation of the second function, the paralysis of the entire capitalist economy." Gindin's frank criticism of "the famous phrase concerning the seizure of six banks" indirectly indicted Lenin's brash nationalization of the banks, a direct cause of the collapse of the Russian economy in 1918.[57]

Two decades after the Russian Revolution, an American economist posited three historical stages of corporate finance: the financing of expansion out of current profits; the use of banks during periods of rapid expansion or a scarcity of investment capital, as in Germany in the late nineteenth century; and a decline in the resort to banks. "The history of security capitalization indicates that control of the management of industry by banking capitalism is but a transitory phase."[58] Whatever the real importance of the largest banks in the tsarist economy in laying the institutional framework for the Bolshevik system, these phenomena underscored yet again the importance of the shortage of investment capital as a key element limiting the expansion and geographical diffusion of Russian corporations.

The Formation and Survival of Corporations in Ten Large Cities

The application of the theory of the population ecology of organizations to the RUSCORP database calls attention to the weakness of corporate development in the Russian Empire in comparison to that of Europe and North America. The second characteristic of Russian capitalism—the high degree of geographical concentration—becomes especially clear from an analysis of patterns of corporate development in the various regional economies of the empire. The phenomenon of concentration was already evident in patterns of incorporation in the ten largest cities of the empire, as shown in Figure 2.9. This pattern is likewise illuminated by eight quantitative indicators of corporate activity in the ten districts (*uezdy*) with the largest urban populations. (See Table 2.3.)

For convenience, this discussion of urban populations and corporations equates the ten cities with their respective districts. RUSCORP does not differentiate between cities and the districts in which they were located. In practice, very few corporations in a given district maintained headquarters outside the main city, the district capital. The only important category of corporations headquartered outside district capitals was that of beet-sugar refining, dominated by large landowners, mostly in the right-bank Ukraine, who maintained sugar refineries on their estates near the fields where the beets were grown and harvested. For example, in the entire period from 1821 to 1913, Lodz district contained eight new corporations with headquarters in Zgierz and one in Dabrowo; Rostov-on-Don district, one each in Nakhichevan-on-Don and Azov; and Riga district, one each in Schlock and Bolderaa.

As expected, corporate headquarters were concentrated in the ten most populous cities of the empire. Although they accounted for only 28 percent of the urban population of the empire in 1897, the year of the first comprehensive census, these ten cities accounted for almost three-quarters of all new corporations from 1821 through 1913, an almost identical percentage of all banks in 1914, and even higher proportions of corporate headquarters and managerial positions just before World War I. The degree of concentration was especially pronounced for large companies, as the ten cities accounted for seven-eighths of all corporate capitalization in the Russian Empire in 1914.

A precise demonstration of these patterns appears in a table of Spearman rank coefficients among the eight variables. (See Table 2.4.) Of the thirty-six correlations, twelve are significant at the .05 level, six at .01, and one at .005. Although the highest correlation, between the numbers of corporations and of managerial positions, comes as no surprise, some unexpected patterns emerge from a comparison of Tables 2.3 and 2.4. First, the size of the largest cities and their corporate populations varied not only in a highly correlated way but also in absolute terms, as the tenth-ranked corporate center, Rostov-on-Don, contained less than 12 percent as many inhabitants as the largest, St. Petersburg, and only about one-twentieth of the number of the northern capital's corporations in 1914. Second, the low coefficients of FIRST, only one of which was statistically significant, suggest that whatever patterns may have existed in the very early history of Russian corporate activity, in the eleven decades before 1815, had little relevance in the following century. Third, the importance of banking could be seen in the fact that half of the correlations for FBANK had statistical significance, but, except for St. Petersburg, Moscow, and Baku, the date of the first bank bore little relation to such key indicators as the total capitalization in 1914 because the other seven cities received their first bank charter in the short space of little more than six years, from June 1868 to August 1872.

Each city contained a unique combination of corporations that reflected not only geographical factors, such as proximity to trade routes and access to raw materials, but also cultural traditions of corporate founders and managers. A thorough exploration of these features would require a separate statistical analysis for each city. Suffice it to say that St. Petersburg remained by far the most important center of Russian corporate economy because technologically advanced factories and other key enterprises such as railroads and banks headquartered there enjoyed the advantages of access to foreign raw materials and markets, as well as massive financial support from the tsarist state.

Corporations in Moscow, the capital of the Central Industrial Region, tended to manufacture textiles and other mass-produced goods for the domestic market and also engaged in the trade of raw cotton from Central Asia. Warsaw served as the industrial, financial, and transportation capital of the Kingdom of Poland. Further south, the rich soil and relatively mild climate of the provinces surrounding Kiev led landlords to grow sugar beets and establish processing plants on their estates. Odessa, the leading port of southern Russia, exported raw materials, primarily grain, to Western Europe. Riga, a major Baltic port with a mercantile tradition dating from the Middle Ages, played an international economic role disproportionate to its small population. In the late nineteenth century, Kharkov became a major center of corporations in metallurgy and mechanical engineering in "South Russia," now Ukraine, where rich coal and iron deposits made possible the rapid growth of heavy industry behind the tariff wall erected in the 1880s. Toward the end of the imperial period, corporate entrepreneurs in Lodz, Baku, and Rostov-on-Don founded an impressive number of new corporate enterprises, primarily in textiles, petroleum drilling and refining, and foreign trade, respectively.[59]

The degree of geographical concentration of corporate headquarters remained remarkably consistent over time, as St. Petersburg occupied first place in all but one of the cycles, with slightly less than a third of all new companies. Moscow, which accounted for one-fifth of the total, claimed less than a third in its cycle of greatest influence, 1879–86, when it briefly surpassed St. Petersburg. After the first cycle, when Odessa garnered almost a quarter of the total with four charters, the highest percentage reached by any of the provincial cities was 8.7 percent in Cycle 5 for Warsaw, which had only 6.6 percent overall, and Riga had only 2.9 percent of the total. Except for Kharkov, in which one company was formed in 1838 to manage a sheep farm, none of the four latecomers ever accounted for more than 2.7 percent of new charters in any cycle.

These patterns support the notion of the immaturity of Russian capitalism. Entrepreneurs who petitioned for permission to launch new corporations remained concentrated in a handful of Russian cities. Faced with a shortage of competent managers, the imperial bureaucracy withheld corporate charters from enterprises that it considered unsound. The precise number of applications that were rejected by the tsarist state under the concessionary system of incorporation is unknown, but Table 2.3 suggests the advantage of entrepreneurs who located their corporations in St. Petersburg. The retention of the concessionary system thus reinforced the traditional geographical concentration of corporations, as St. Petersburg remained the primary source of governmental permission and funding, including what Gindin called "irregular loans" by the State Bank to individuals and companies favored by the emperor and his advisers.[60]

At the same time, however, the large variations in the totals and percentages for St. Petersburg underscored the baneful effects of corporate speculation by "wheeler-dealers" (*del'tsy*) in the northern capital. In contrast, the gradual rise of corporate numbers in Moscow and their remarkable consistency in terms of percentages from 1851 onward, broken only by the brief preeminence in Cycle 5, reflected the caution and ultimate success of the Moscow merchants in family-owned firms.

The structure of corporate enterprises varied significantly from one location to another in response to both economic environments and cultural traditions. A corporate charter (*ustav*) entitled corporate entrepreneurs to issue shares to investors and to operate the enterprise on the principle of limited liability for both shareholders and managers. This legal status differentiated corporations from trading firms, which took the form of full partnerships (*polnye tovarishchestva*), in which all partners assumed personal liability for the debts of the firm, or limited partnerships (*tovarishchestva na vere*), in which managing partners bore liability, but nonvoting investors did not.[61]

Charters generally referred to the corporation by one of two names: *obshchestvo* or *tovarishchestvo*. (The name *kompaniia*, from the French *compagnie*, appeared in some charters, primarily before 1861, but the number of new *kompanii* gradually dwindled to insignificance thereafter.) An *obshchestvo* typically issued shares called *aktsii* and was formally known as an *aktsionernoe obshchestvo*, literally "joint-stock company," whereas a *tovarishchestvo* issued shares called *pai* and assumed the formal legal name of *tovarishchestvo na paiakh*, literally "share partnership."

Although Russian law treated both kinds of corporations equally, the terminology revealed important differences in the approaches of various groups of entrepreneurs in Russia to corporate enterprise. The term *aktsionernoe obshchestvo* represented a direct translation of *société par actions*, the French name for corporation, also known as the *société anonyme*, "anonymous" in the sense that all participants enjoyed limited liability. In contrast, the phrase *tovarishchestvo na paiakh* drew on the Russian words for "partner" or "comrade" (*tovarishch*) and "share" (*pai*), the latter borrowed from the medieval Tatars.

The European and Asiatic etymologies signified real structural differences, as Russian corporations with *aktsii* tended to take different forms from those that issued *pai*. (The two words for "share" are used here to analyze structural differences. So few *obshchestva* issued *pai* and so few *tovarishchestva* issued *aktsii* that if the two words for "corporation" served as the basis for the dichotomy instead of the two words for "share," the statistical results would be similar. These computations ignore the handful of tiny membership organizations, operated for profit, that appeared at the very end of the tsarist period.) New corporations with *aktsii*, here called Type A, generally predominated, with 65.1 percent of the total between 1821 and 1913, while those with *pai* (Type P) constituted only 34.3 percent, but the proportions varied significantly over time.

Cycles of incorporation for Type-A enterprises closely followed the general pattern, as a linear regression of the annual totals for all corporations and Type-A companies yielded a significantly higher coefficient of correlation (+.989358; r^2 = 97.9 percent) than that of the total and Type-P corporations in the same period (+.899258; r^2 = 80.1 percent). From 1851 to 1913, the period of greatest fluctuations, the difference was even clearer, as the first coefficient rose to +.990361 (r^2 = .98.1 percent) and the second fell to +.884637 (r^2 = 78.3 percent; p = .00000 in all four cases). In the atypically gentle Cycle 5 (1879–86), distinguished by its low peak, corporations with *pai* consistently outnumbered those with *aktsii*. (See Figure 2.12, which compares three-year moving averages of totals of both types.)

Geography accounted for much of this variation. In Moscow, the center of light industry, corporations with *pai* outnumbered enterprises with *aktsii* in every cycle. This pattern occurred only rarely in the other cities: in Rostov-on-Don in Cycle 4, in Kiev in Cycles 4 and 5, and in St. Petersburg in Cycle 5. (See Figure 2.13.)

Cyclical patterns, especially the predominance of Type-P corporations in Cycle 5, reinforced the culturally determined preferences of entrepreneurs in the ten major cities, except in Lodz and Baku, where Type-A corporations accounted for between 90 and 100 percent of the total. In most other cities, the percentage of Type-A corporations inscribed a U-shaped curve with a low point that came in Cycle 5 (1879–86), a period of relative stagnation. The differences in percentages were striking. Warsaw, St. Petersburg, Odessa, Riga, and the other provincial centers showed a marked preference for Type-A corporations despite the decline in the 1880s, with averages ranging from 100 percent in Lodz to 56 percent in Kiev. Moscow, where only 36 percent of new corporations issued *aktsii*, remained the bastion of the share partnership. The strong tradition of German mercantile practice in Riga produced a more gradual change than in Odessa, where various ethnic groups contended for primacy in this period.[62] The reasons for the unique pattern in Kiev—a steady rise in Type-A corporations from 20 percent in Cycle 4 to 75 percent in Cycle 7—remain unclear, but they may include a gradual shift away from small, family-owned enterprises in light industry, especially beet-sugar production founded and managed by landowners of Polish extraction, toward a more diverse group of corporations led by Jewish merchants at the end of the imperial period.[63]

Another structural indicator, the amount of basic capital, contributed to the dichotomy. In all but seven instances (in Warsaw and Kharkov in Cycle 5, in Kiev and Baku in Cycles 6 and 7, and in Riga in Cycle 7), the median capitalization of new Type-A corporations exceeded that of new Type-P enterprises; in four cases, the medians were identical: 500,000 rubles. Founders of Type-A corporations generally sought to raise large amounts of share capital. Medians of such companies founded in each city ranged from 246,000 to 7.97 million rubles, while corporations with *pai* had modest figures of median capital, ranging from 150,000 to 750,000 rubles, with the exception of the single share partnership founded in Kharkov in Cycle 5 at 1.25 million rubles.

Likewise, the median price of *aktsii* in all ten cities from 1821 to 1913 held to a narrow range, between 100 and 500 rubles. Such low prices facilitated the circulation of shares among the public, while the median price of new *pai* ranged from 250 to 4,000 rubles because founders tended to distribute the shares among themselves and utilized high prices to exclude the purchase of shares by outsiders. In no cases did the median price of *aktsii* surpass that of *pai,* although in Warsaw and Riga they were identical in three cycles. Shortly before World War I, supplementary issues of stock in share partnerships occasionally bore a low price, such as the 100-ruble par value of *pai* issued in 1913 by the G. M. Lianozov's Sons Petroleum Company, headquartered in St. Petersburg, six years after its founding. The low prices were apparently intended to facilitate sale on the stock market. However, these exceptions did not alter the general pattern of cheap *aktsii* and expensive *pai* in the charters.

The percentage of corporations with par share values set at less than 1,000 rubles in 1914 provided a clear indication of the extent to which the stock market was accessible to the public. Baku, the latecomer and center of the capital-intensive petroleum industry, led with 91 percent, followed by the most important corporate centers in the western regions of the empire: Warsaw (89), Petersburg (84), and Riga (84). Managers of family-centered corporations in light industry strove to avoid selling shares to the public in Moscow (39) and Kiev (49). Elsewhere, in the less important industrial centers, percentages ranged from 73 in Kharkov and Lodz to 65 in Rostov-on-Don and 61 in Odessa.

Newly chartered corporations in Moscow and St. Petersburg also differed according to the newness of their operations. In a sample quinquennium, 1906–10, fully 84.7 percent of the 176 Type-P corporations founded in Moscow had previously existed before incorporation, generally as trading firms. In St. Petersburg, the percentage was lower but still significant: 64.0. In both cities, the percentage of foundings of Type-A corporations on the basis of previously existing firms fell below that for Type-P companies: 53.4 in Moscow and 41.6 in St. Petersburg. Chi-square tests for both samples—42.4 in Moscow and 28.2 in St. Petersburg—are significant at the .01 level. (This analysis excludes the few charters that authorized existing firms to undertake new activities upon incorporation.)

Thus, new railroads, banks, metallurgical plants, and other enterprises that anticipated major expenditures for heavy equipment tended to take the form of corporations called *aktsionernye obshchestva*, characterized by large capitalizations and cheaply priced shares, especially in St. Petersburg and other cities where European commercial practices had made an impact. In contrast, corporations called *tovarishchestva na paiakh* generally grew out of existing family firms, particularly those of the merchant dynasties in light industry, primarily engaged in the manufacture of textiles and food products, in Moscow.[64] Although the most advanced Moscow manufacturers used modern equipment imported from England, costs generally remained lower than those of a railroad or metallurgical plant. In addition, the Muscovites preferred to finance expansion out of current profits instead of issuing stocks and bonds, the better to maintain financial control over their enterprises.

These patterns of incorporation emerged even more strongly from data of survival, both throughout the empire and in the ten major cities. As before, the data suggest the immaturity of Russian capitalism and wide divergences according to geography, which in turn reflected cultural traditions of the leading entrepreneurial groups in each city. (See Figure 2.14.) The benefits of proximity to state power for existing enterprises, especially banks, railroads, and machine companies in St. Petersburg, appeared enormous. Corporations in the other nine leading centers also continued to specialize by function. Although St. Petersburg held first place in five of the six years for which survival data are available, the relatively high rate of survival among the small but hardy companies headquartered in Moscow led to a slightly higher number (184) than in St. Petersburg (164) in 1892, after two decades of weak growth in the corporate population.

Likewise, a comparison of the data in Figures 2.9 and 2.14 reveals that companies headquartered in Moscow constituted a larger percentage of surviving corporations at the end of the tsarist period (23.4 in 1914) than the percentage of the total recently chartered (19.3 in Cycle 7, 1906–13). Warsaw, Kiev, Riga, Lodz, and Baku also had higher-than-average survival rates at the end of the tsarist period. In contrast, the percentages in St. Petersburg indicated a lower rate of survival than would be expected in light of the percentage of new charters: 29.8 percent of survivors in 1914, compared to 35.2 percent of new corporations in Cycle 7. Low survival rates also occurred in Odessa, Kharkov, and Rostov-on-Don.

Although no clear pattern of corporate size according to location may be discerned in the first three years for which survival data are available (1847, 1869, and 1874), by 1892 two patterns did emerge. First, the median capitalization of corporations in all cities except Moscow and Kiev declined between 1892 and 1914, as medians for all companies fell from 1 million rubles in 1892 to 800,000 in 1905 and rose only slightly, to 840,000, in 1914 (Figure 2.7). Also, a strong positive correlation existed between the number of corporations headquartered in a given city and the size of its median capital amount in 1914: (+.908977; r^2 = 82.2 percent; p = .00176) among eight cities. (Lodz and Baku, two latecomers on the periphery of the empire, had few companies—45 and 34, respectively—but relatively high median capital amounts of 1.5 and 1.1. million rubles, which reflected the high concentration of industrial enterprises in textiles and petroleum, respectively.)

Thus, the median capital amount in St. Petersburg declined gradually from 1.405 million in 1892 to 1.282 million in 1905 and 1.2 million rubles in 1914; similar patterns were evident in Moscow (1 million, 900,000, and 1 million rubles) and in Warsaw (1 million, 750,000, and 750,000 rubles). This slight decline in the median capital amount reflected the increase in the share of small corporations in all cities as the total number of corporations grew over the decades. Likewise, the low numbers of existing corporations and median capital amount in Odessa in 1914 served as symptoms of that city's general economic malaise. Not only did its 38 companies place it far below Riga (57) and barely ahead of Baku and Rostov-on-Don (34 each), but its median capital amount fell steadily, from 1 million in 1874 to 498,000 rubles in 1914, far below the next lowest: 600,000 in Kiev and Kharkov. In contrast, the median capital amount in Riga actually rose, from 225,000 (1869) to 325,000 (1874), 500,000 (1892), and 930,000 (1905) before emulating the general pattern with a slight decline to 840,000 rubles—the empire-wide median—in 1914. Again, the high levels of commercial skill among the Riga merchants contrasted favorably with the somewhat more lax practices of the corporate elite in Odessa.

Indications of relative success and failure also emerge from a comparison of overall survival rates in 1914 and the percentage of new Type-A corporations in Cycle 6. (See Figure 2.15.) Each of the ten major cities had its own unique pattern, so that no significant correlation exists between the percentages of new Type-A companies and survival rates to 1914. (The Spearman rank correlation was a mildly negative −.2553, but the significance level, .4437, far surpassed the customary threshold indicating statistical significance: .05.) So many corporations of both Type A and Type P were founded in St. Petersburg that it is difficult to attribute the inverse relationship between the high percentage of Type-A corporations (79 percent) and the low survival rate (43.7 percent) to the speculative practices of entrepreneurs in the northern capital. Clearly, however, the inverse relationship worked in favor of the typically small, solid share partnerships in Moscow (36 and 47.5). Entrepreneurs in Kiev also showed the same success (61 and 50.5), despite the gradual move away from share partnerships, revealed in Figure 2.13. Likewise, Rostov-on-Don, which scored second-lowest in the percentage of Type-A corporations (53 percent), ranked first in survival (52.6 percent). The inverse relationship between the percentage of Type-A corporations and the survival rate was strongest in the two cities with the lowest survival rates: Odessa (85 and 20) and Baku (100 and 37.5).

The major exceptions to this inverse pattern occurred in the two Polish cities. In Warsaw, fully 98 percent of all new corporations issued *aktsii,* but the rate of survival, 46.4 percent, surpassed those of St. Petersburg, Kharkov, Baku, and Odessa. In Lodz, where all new corporations issued *aktsii,* the survival rate (52.0 percent) was second only to that of Rostov-on-Don. Clearly, the Polish, German, and Jewish entrepreneurs in the two corporate centers of Russian Poland demonstrated no less business acumen than did the cautious textile manufacturers of Moscow.[65]

These data suggest two patterns of corporate enterprise, "Western" and "Russian," as they might be called, typified by the predominance of joint-stock companies in Warsaw and Lodz and of share partnerships in Moscow. There is no need to take sides in the bitter dispute that divided these corporate elites along ethnic and regional lines.[66] Both forms of corporate enterprise could foster prosperity, as in the cities with the highest rates of survival—Rostov-on-Don, Lodz, Kiev, Riga, and Moscow; corporate founders could abandon one for another without sacrificing success, as in Kiev; but neither form made managers immune from economic decline, as in Odessa and Baku, the two cities with the lowest rates of survival to 1914.

This examination of major trends in the history of Russian corporations raises several issues, of which the most complex is this: To what extent did Russian capitalism embrace the legal and structural attributes common to other economies dominated in the nineteenth century by corporations, and to what degree did it remain Russian, displaying features unique to its cultural and geographical environment on the eastern periphery of Europe? Much statistical analysis remains to be done on the RUSCORP database, but this brief survey permits the drawing of several tentative conclusions.

The impression of the weakness of Russian corporate capitalism emerges not only from the aggregate data but also from statistics for the largest cities. Corporate enterprise remained geographically concentrated in a very few cities in the Russian Empire. The corporation came to Russia as a foreign institution, one in which non-Russians, especially Germans, Poles, and Jews, played a role disproportionate to their percentage in the population at large, as shown in Chapter 3. When ethnic Russian merchants, especially those in the Moscow region, embraced the corporation, they opted in most cases for small, closely held companies called share partnerships, formed on the basis of already existing family-owned partnerships. The preference of non-Russians for the joint-stock company, modeled on the French *société anonyme*, highlighted this cultural dichotomy within the corporate elite of the empire, especially in Poland and Baku.

After many decades of barely perceptible growth, the number of Russian corporations increased more than thirtyfold between 1847 and 1914. The environment encouraged heterogeneity in geographical location, function, and size, but trends in this direction remained uneven. High rates of growth occurred in some sectors and periods, with significant sectoral differentiation by 1914. The Russian Empire bequeathed to the Bolshevik regime the fifth-largest economy in the world. Its vast infrastructure permitted impressive growth rates in the 1920s (higher, indeed, than those of the First Five-Year Plan), once the chaos of war, revolution, and civil war had ended.[67]

In international terms, however, trends in Russian corporate development and survival over time appear mixed. Railroads performed poorly, in marked contrast to their leading institutional role in western Europe and the United States. Most importantly, corporations encountered considerable instability and turbulence in sectors that were sensitive to the world market and to arbitrary changes in the policies of the tsarist bureaucracy. Despite several periods of rapid growth, the overall pace of corporate development remained slow, especially in per capita terms.

Numerous riddles of macroeconomic policy and economic performance remain unsolved. Perhaps the most curious is the reason for the early occurrence, in 1871 and 1873, of the highest ratios of new corporate capital to population ever recorded in a single year: 3.9899 and 3.7231 rubles per capita, respectively, in Figure 2.3. Only in 1912 and 1913 did this ratio again surpass 3.0. Thus, the flurry of incorporation in the era of the Great Reforms (1861–74) witnessed the founding of some of the largest corporations ever chartered by the tsarist regime, but these giant enterprises failed to establish an institutional structure capable of maintaining the momentum of corporate development into the reigns of the last two emperors. The most prominent failure occurred in railroads, by far the largest of all corporations.

Paradoxically, the most capable ministers of finance—Reutern, Witte, and Kokovtsov—failed, at crucial moments, to accommodate tsarist economic policy to the needs of the corporation. Reutern and Witte drafted reforms of the outmoded corporate law of 1836 but refused to implement them. Reutern abandoned his reform bill because the crash of 1873 shook his confidence in an autonomous corporate economy. In particular, he perceived a threat, not an opportunity, in the enthusiasm for corporate entrepreneurship that seized Russian society in the early 1870s. His highhanded treatment of commercial banks and his rejection of corporate law reform exemplified the familiar bureaucratic methods of tutelage and arbitrariness at a crucial moment in the history of the imperial economy. Witte, who remained "skeptical of free enterprise" and "imbued with nationalism and statism, in the Russian bureaucratic and historical tradition," rejected incorporation by registration because the reform would have limited his ability to grant exceptions to laws restricting landholding rights of corporations in which Jews, Poles, and foreigners owned stock or served as managers and employees.[68]

For his part, Kokovtsov failed to inspire confidence among the shrewdest foreign capitalists. When, in 1910, B. A. Kennedy of International Harvester expressed an interest in requesting financial aid from the Russian government, he received a somber warning:

> Alexander Bary, an American who had lived and worked in Russia for thirty years, told him the government was "absolutely unreliable." Kokovtsov, though the "brightest" of the ministers, "had no regard for his word and would break it as easy as he would make it." In addition, Bary was "very strong" in warning Kennedy against asking for [financial] concessions. If International Harvester accepted any, the government "would oblige [it] in such a way that [it] would be in trouble for ever afterwards."[69]

Unlike Europeans, American bankers showed little interest in the Russian market, both because they disapproved of the tsarist government's discrimination against Jews and because they disliked the many institutional impediments to capitalist activity there.[70]

The role of the tsarist state and its effects on corporate enterprise therefore appeared negative to the very end. Gerschenkron's notion that the industrial surge of 1908–13 depended not on direct state sponsorship, as in the 1890s, but on private activity coordinated by the big St. Petersburg banks has been challenged recently by Gatrell, who found that "armaments took over from railways as the motor of growth before 1914." The armaments industry, much of which remained under direct state administration, accounted for over 4 percent of industrial production in 1913, a far larger share than in France (1 percent) and Britain (1–2 percent). Its percentage of the net national product, 4.1 percent, surpassed that of Germany (3.6), Britain (3.8), and France (3.9) and stood almost double, at 7.1 percent, after the subtraction of nonmonetized peasant consumption of food from the net national product. Likewise, Gregory found that the devotion of government spending "primarily to defense and administration (and not to health and education)" made the tsarist state's "share of final expenditure (8 percent) . . . the highest of the countries for which data are available."[71] On the very eve of World War I, the tsarist state remained true to the military-autocratic tradition, despite its high costs in terms of efficiency.

Should not some responsibility for the poor performance of Russian corporations be borne by the merchant elite? The familiar stereotype of the Russian merchant as a creature wedded to low standards of honesty and a penchant for short-term profits appeared to justify repressive laws and the state's manipulation of the market, at least in the eyes of tsarist bureaucrats. In a characteristic criticism, a tsarist bureaucrat chided Russian merchants in 1847 for their lack of "corporate entrepreneurship" (*obshchestvennaia predpriimchivost'*). Despite massive state spending on canals, highways, and the Petersburg-Moscow railroad, he claimed, "not a single corporate enterprise" had come into being to take advantage of new opportunities in transportation. The Tsarskoe selo Railroad, founded in 1836, remained the sole viable company in its category, the Volga-Don railroad company having published no accounts and offered no shares for sale on the exchange in the four years since its chartering. (It failed in 1849.) A plan proposed in 1831 to introduce a shipping line on the Tsna River, capitalized at one million assignat rubles, apparently failed to receive a corporate charter and disappeared, leaving "no information since that time."[72] Toward the end of the century, another economic bureaucrat wrote that "the apathy and crass ignorance that afflict our merchants" kept the consultative organizations created by Reutern in 1872 "from exerting all the beneficial influence that had been expected of them."[73]

The monographic literature already suggests that corporate founders and managers from various regions, ethnic groups, and social strata performed according to patterns that reflected their cultural values. A handful of outstanding individuals achieved substantial success despite the repressive tsarist legislation.[74] Although the present survey cannot accommodate comprehensive biographical portraits, patterns of entrepreneurship in the RUSCORP database strongly reinforce the findings of geographical diversity, institutional immaturity, and foreign influence evident in the statistics of corporations. Like restricted credit and the effects of governmental regimentation, entrepreneurial ability constituted a key element in the Russian corporate ecology.

As for the role of the state in promoting or hindering the cause of Russian economic development, much empirical work remains to be done, especially in the period of the Great Reforms. For the time being, it is sufficient to point out that the bureaucrat's condescending statement about the apathy of the merchants revealed the attitude that legitimized the government's refusal to embrace economic reform. As an American visitor to Russia observed at the beginning of our century:

> the capitalist, as such, has no more influence in Russian legislation or administration than has the laborer; and neither one of them, as such, has any influence.... So the government does not regard the capitalist as a partner in affairs of state; it regards him as a subject of the state.... The weakness of this whole system, of course, is that no matter how good the intentions of the government may be, it is impossible for it to intervene in even a small number of instances among all the enterprises of a people and an empire larger and more numerous than any on the globe.[75]

According to the sociologists who pioneered organizational ecology, "research at the population level leads naturally to a concern with history" because trends in "population dynamics" often can be perceived only in the long term. One of the greatest challenges facing students of population ecology is to "show how quantitative analysis can be applied to the study of social processes operating over long periods of time—that is, to social history."76 By revealing patterns of corporate entrepreneurship and management, the RUSCORP database helps to illuminate the social history of Russian capitalism in its personal as well as its mathematical dimensions.

3

Corporate Entrepreneurs and Managers, 1821–1914

> *The function of the historian is akin to that of the painter and not of the photographic camera: to discover and set forth, to single out and stress that which is of the nature of the thing, and not to reproduce indiscriminately all that meets the eye. . . . What matters in history is the great outline and the significant detail; what must be avoided is the deadly morass of irrelevant narrative.*
>
> Sir Lewis Namier[1]

Whatever the accuracy of the bureaucratic criticism of merchants' feeble entrepreneurship in the period of minimal corporate activity prior to the Crimean War, the perennial lack of sympathy typified by those remarks deserves attention because of constant allegations in the Soviet historical literature of a close partnership between business and the tsarist state. This essentially polemical assertion inspired suspicion on two counts. First, it merely reiterated the common criticism of capitalism that filled the prerevolutionary Bolshevik and Menshevik press. It also rested on a weak empirical foundation, Soviet historians having produced little in the way of enterprise histories and biographies of business leaders.

This neglect stemmed from more than the methodological bias of Marxist social science against biography and in favor of the inexorable logic of impersonal economic forces. In Soviet Marxism, the polemical style of political debate and ideological pronouncement suffused the social sciences, so that a dispassionate analysis of a millionaire's career, rendered in various shades of gray, would have seemed unduly favorable. Also, the political infighting that swept dozens of historians from academic positions in the poisonous atmosphere of high Stalinism inspired adherence to the stale dogmas laid down by the Institute of the History of the USSR. Although these doctrines evolved over time, especially in the Khrushchev period, the Soviet historical profession left unresolved and even unexplored a host of major issues. For example, it proved easier to trace the evolution of tsarist economic policy, as reflected in the ministerial records, than to evaluate its impact on the economic behavior of manufacturers and financiers.[2]

Tensions between business and government in late imperial Russia have received attention elsewhere.[3] One aspect of the problem requires special analysis: the contradiction between the accusation of entrepreneurial lassitude and the opposite argument, that bureaucratic strictures prevented Russian corporate entrepreneurs from pursuing economic opportunities more aggressively than they did. The weaknesses of Russian entrepreneurship prior to the nineteenth century were clear to scholars, despite a paucity of statistical data.[4] The tiny number of corporations chartered between 1704 and 1820 supported this impression. The prospects of the emergence of a competent corporate elite from the ruins of the command economy in the 1990s, an urgent question of economic and social analysis in our own time, is discussed in Chapter 6. A preliminary statistical analysis of RUSCORP data reveals complex patterns of entrepreneurship and management from 1821 to 1914 that complement the trends of relatively limited corporate formation and survival in this period.

Patterns of Entrepreneurship

Despite the enormous difficulties of assigning an unambiguous ethnic label to the approximately 14,000 persons named in the corporate charters, even this preliminary effort to categorize the Russian corporate elite by ethnicity yields some significant patterns. (See Table 3.1.) The most obvious conclusion to emerge from these data is that only a tiny fraction of the population participated in corporate entrepreneurship. For example, during the last corporate boom, the names of only 857 founders appeared in corporate charters in 1913, when the population of the empire (minus the Grand Duchy of Finland) stood at approximately 169 million. To be sure, in all countries where capitalism became the dominant form of economic enterprise by 1914, the corporate elite constituted a small percentage of the population. However, these data reinforce the impression of the weakness of Russian capitalism reflected in the tiny number of corporations and the relatively small amount of capital marshalled by companies in the transportation and credit systems, in comparison to the leading role of the tsarist state.

The dramatic cyclical variations demand explanation as well. Episodes of enthusiasm for corporate enterprise occurred in 1856–60, 1871–5, 1896–1900, and 1911–3. Especially striking were fluctuations in the average number of founders per charter. The high points, in 1866–70 and 1871–5, reflected the extraordinary enthusiasm for corporations that marked the era of the "Great Reforms." The fad reached ridiculous proportions in a handful of banks and shipping companies that attracted dozens of founders. The otherwise insignificant Linda Steamship Company, chartered on August 1, 1881, in Reval (now Tallinn) with a modest capitalization of 300,000 rubles and liquidated before 1892, took the prize, with 654 founders. (In this case, the compilers of the RUSCORP database entered only the first ten names so as not to introduce statistical anomalies into the general pattern.) Equally significant was the steady decline in the average from 1881 onward to a rate of approximately two and one-half for almost a quarter-century before World War I, a rare example of routinization in the history of Russian corporate capitalism.

What can be said of the managerial qualifications of the many men (and the few women, mostly wives and widows of merchants who owned existing enterprises) who became founders in the era of the Great Reforms? The effort to create an entire complex of capitalist institutions, including banks, railroads, and manufacturing plants, in the aftermath of the Crimean War appeared daunting in the absence of a large and vigorous Russian middle class. China and Japan, when faced with the challenge of adopting the corporate form of enterprise, could draw on a native entrepreneurial tradition that extended back through the centuries. Could enthusiasm compensate for the lack of expertise in Russia?

The effort to affix ethnic identifications to corporate founders, despite the enormous difficulties and resulting imperfections, yielded some preliminary answers to this question. Like the small numbers and geographical concentration of corporations, the ethnic composition of founders and managers testified to the essentially foreign nature of the corporation in the tsarist economy. Certain groups occupied positions in the corporate elite out of proportion to their numbers in the population at large: foreigners (including foreign Jews and Germans), Jews and Germans who held Russian citizenship, and Armenians.

Comparisons with the first comprehensive census of the Russian Empire in 1897 reinforce this pattern. Besides comparing census numbers to founders in each city, it would also be preferable to employ biographical research for the purpose of eradicating errors in ethnic identification and reducing the unknowns—6.9 percent overall—to an absolute minimum. (The lack of names in some charters makes it impossible to identify all individuals.) Still, the remarkable rise to prominence of corporate founders from ethnic minorities such as Germans and Armenians points to the importance of cultural determinants, such as high literacy rates and the long history of family-based commerce, that prepared individuals for careers in corporations once the new form of enterprise arrived from Western Europe.

Poles, Jews, and foreigners achieved special prominence among corporate founders. From the 1860s onward, the tsarist government sought to bolster the declining economic position of ethnic Russian peasants and landlords in the western provinces by restricting the rights of non-Russians to purchase landed estates there. Fearing that members of these three proscribed groups might form corporations to obtain rural land denied to them by law as individuals, the government gradually extended the restrictions to corporations in which Poles, Jews, and foreigners acted as directors, employees (such as real-estate managers), and stockholders. Thus, the relatively high percentages of individuals from these three groups might well have been even higher had legislative restrictions on corporate landholding not existed.

The steadily increasing percentage of Jewish entrepreneurs after 1861 appeared especially impressive. It was precisely in the last half-century before World War I that the ethnic restrictions imposed by the bureaucracy increased in severity. In their triumph over adversity, the Jews and other minorities demonstrated their superior ability in the corporate arena. To the extent that these groups resorted to figureheads who were Russians— and the existence in the Russian language of the term "straw man" (*podstavnoe litso*) provided good evidence that the phenomenon did exist— the real percentages stood even higher. The explanation of this rise to prominence will require a series of empirical investigations to take account of the distinctive talents and capabilities of each group. Definitive statistical results may well elude us because of the ineffable nature of ethnic prejudice and its psychological effects on all parties concerned, but the general outlines of the evolution of the Russian corporate elite may already be discerned.

Some of these patterns related directly to geography. For example, the percentages of Armenians among founders in each quinquennium from 1861 to 1913 correlated strongly with the percentage of new corporations headquartered in Baku (coefficient = +.8528; r^2 = 72.7 percent; probability level, or p = .00085). A slightly weaker correlation existed for the percentages of Germans and of new corporations chartered in Riga, where the German mercantile tradition dated from medieval times (+.7050; 49.7 percent; and 0.1539, respectively). In contrast, the same test revealed weak correlations between Poles and Warsaw (+.5755; 33.1 percent; and .06396) and between Jews and Kiev (+.2990; 8.9 percent; and .3255), despite the relatively prominent role of Poles as corporate founders in Warsaw and of Jews in Kiev by the end of the tsarist period.

The interplay between ethnicity and geography in percentages of founders from each major ethnic group in the ten largest corporate centers is clear from an analysis of data from two periods of corporate activity separated by more than half a century, in 1856–60, immediately after the Crimean War, and in 1911–3. (See Tables 3.2 and 3.3.) The absence of any new corporations in four of the ten most important cities in the crucial quinquennium following the trauma of the Crimean War reveals much about the weak development and geographical concentration of Russian capitalism in mid-century. In contrast, at the height of the last and most impressive cycle of corporate entrepreneurship before the war, the pattern of heterogeneity revealed in Table 3.1 for the empire as a whole became clear in the ten major cities as well.

By 1911–3, the patterns only vaguely suggested in the late 1850s had become clear. In seven of the ten cities, one ethnic group accounted for half or more of corporate founders. In Moscow, Warsaw, Riga, and Lodz, the preponderance of Russians, Poles, Germans, and Jews, respectively, came as no surprise, but several developments in the previous half-century testified to the entrepreneurial ability of Russians and Jews. Russians led other groups in five of the ten major cities, and the percentage of Russians in St. Petersburg and Rostov surpassed the already high levels of the late 1850s. Even more impressive was the emergence of Jewish entrepreneurs to leadership in Kharkov and to absolute majorities in Odessa and Lodz.

A statistical examination of entrepreneurial activity according to the social origins of corporate founders entails a variety of conceptual problems. First, the quality of these data was marred by the large number of unknown status identifications: above 15 percent in seven of the nineteen quinquennia between 1821–5 and 1911–3 and almost 40 percent in 1866–70. Unlike the unknown ethnic identifications, the missing status identifications are not likely to be removed in the course of future research, except in cases when an individual might be identified by biographical information drawn from other sources.

Organizations included zemstvos, trading firms, banking firms, and the like. Although several ambitious zemstvos launched railroads and other enterprises, primarily in the 1860s and 1870s, the vast majority of organizations that acted as corporate founders were trading firms represented by a senior partner or two.

More serious than the statistical difficulties were conceptual ambiguities inherent in these data. A regional analysis might well show the predominance of certain social groups in some cities and not others, for example merchants in Moscow and holders of bureaucratic and military ranks in St. Petersburg, but the value of such a statistical overview would be limited by the effects of cultural traditions in each of the ten major cities. Whereas the ethnic categories examined in Tables 3.2 and 3.3 were few and distinct, the cultural connotations of the word "merchant" varied from city to city, and the number of social categories, defined by official categories of social estate (*soslovie*) and by occupational function, made the task of analysis complex in the extreme. A comprehensive effort to sort out these difficulties cannot be attempted in the limited space at our disposal. The solution to these problems lies in a series of biographical studies, the lack of which has crippled serious research in Russian history until now. A general chronological survey, combined with some biographical details, suffices to indicate the complexity of the subject and the immense possibilities for future research.

Unlike the variations in entrepreneurial behavior according to ethnicity, those of corporate founders from the main social groups remained remarkably stable over time. (See Table 3.4.) Another indicator of this pattern is the fact that, whenever individuals named in the charters bore two or three status titles, in almost all cases the additional titles corresponded to the main group of the first. For example, a prince or count often held a military rank or a position at the imperial court, whereas a

Manufacturing Councilor (*Manufaktur-sovetnik*) with more than one status identification typically bore the title of honorary citizen (*pochetnyi grazhdanin*) or merchant (*kupets*). (In all cases, the status title used for this analysis was the highest in rank or prestige, as best this could be determined by the compilers of the database.)

Although commercial-industrial and professional men, together with their organizations, accounted for more than half of all founders, aristocrats, the gentry, and holders of bureaucratic and military ranks accounted for almost a third of founders overall and over a quarter of them in the early twentieth century. These patterns buttressed the familiar impression of the low level of urbanization in Russia under the tsarist regime and the correspondingly small size of the nascent urban groups, which hardly deserved the name "middle class" because of their cultural heterogeneity.

The decline of the agrarian elite and the rise of the urban elite—the main story of European social history from the Middle Ages to the modern age and an axiom of Marxism and modernization theory—might seem evident here to an observer seeking to place Russia within the allegedly universal scheme. However, a close examination of these data inspires caution, not certainty. Indeed, the most salient development was the sharp rise of individuals who represented none of the four major social groups from the 1890s (less than 1 percent) to 1911–3 (10 percent). Perhaps corporate entrepreneurs were emerging from a greater variety of social groups than before. The collapse of the entire system in World War I and the Bolshevik Revolution prevents our knowing whether this phenomenon foreshadowed a major reduction in the role of nobles within the corporate elite in later years. At this point, the familiar notion of "the decline of the gentry and the rise of the merchants" appears inadequate to account for many aspects of the story.

The task of combining the ethnic and status patterns into a coherent explanation of corporate entrepreneurship in Russia requires attention to the complexities of biography. A modest contribution to this vast project is given in Table 3.5, which lists leading entrepreneurs named in the corporate charters in each cycle. Several preliminary conclusions can be drawn from it. First, the most active corporate entrepreneurs operated across the spectrum of the Russian economy. They tended to base their operations in Petersburg, Moscow, and Warsaw, the three leading corporate centers, but the enterprises that they founded ranged from huge railroads and shipping lines to small beet-sugar plants in the villages of the southern and western provinces. The importance of light manufacturing and small-scale credit was especially visible during Cycle 5, when government policy discouraged the formation of railroads and large banks. This pattern supported the generalizations about sectoral activity in the various cycles discussed in Chapter 2.

Second, the staying power of the bureaucratic elite was clear from the fact that all the leading entrepreneurs but one in the last cycle held gentry or bureaucratic status and all but one based their operations in the imperial capital. However, this pattern did not necessarily connote the persistence of economic domination by the traditional agrarian elite. It is necessary to make a distinction between bureaucrats without significant incomes from agriculture and the largest landowners themselves. Bureaucrats devoted to the traditional military-autocratic form of political and social organization must also be separated from those who embraced a reformist attitude, based largely on exposure to European ideas. St. Petersburg occupied a contradictory place in Russian culture as both the center of the bureaucratic machine and as the city most susceptible to European ideas and economic practices. In other words, the high level of participation in corporate foundings by eminent bureaucrats in St. Petersburg in the last cycle of incorporation (1906–13) did not necessarily signify the retention of economic power in the hands of persons allied politically to the tsarist regime, an aspect of what Arno J. Mayer has called "the persistence of the old regime": the alleged maintenance of political power, especially in civil and military bureaucracies, by agrarians and aristocrats in western and central Europe to the very eve of World War I.[5] Proximity to the tsarist government, a high level of education, and years of experience in business affairs evidently facilitated prominence in corporate enterprise at the end of the imperial period. Still, the attitudes of each of these corporate leaders cannot be inferred simply from their high rank.

For example, Mikhail M. Fedorov, after serving as acting minister of trade and industry in Witte's short-lived cabinet in 1906, proved a far more dynamic entrepreneur in railroads and heavy industry than the typical Russian merchant. Educated at St. Petersburg University in physics and mathematics, he worked in the Central Statistical Committee, for which he published, with A. K. Veselovskii, a survey of zemstvo insurance. In 1883, he moved to the Ministry of Finance, where he edited the ministry's highly respected journals *Vestnik finansov, promyshlennosti i torgovli* (Herald of Finance, Industry, and Trade) and *Ezhegodnik Ministerstva finansov* (Yearbook of the Ministry of Finance) in 1891–3 and *Torgovo-promyshlennaia gazeta* (The Commercial and Industrial Newspaper) in 1893–7. For the Central Statistical Committee and the Ministry of Finance, Fedorov edited a book devoted to Russian corporations: *Aktsionernoe delo v Rossii* (1895). Two years later, he assumed the editorship of *Russkoe ekonomicheskoe obozrenie* (Russian Economic Survey), one of the most informative periodicals of its kind, for which he wrote analyses of foreign capital in Russian industry (1898–9) and the Russian grain trade (1902). The Petersburg Telegraph Agency, established in 1904, grew out of a telegraph office that Fedorov had created in 1902 to disseminate commercial information.[6]

Having served as chief of the Department of Commerce in the finance ministry, Fedorov became vice-minister of trade and industry when the new ministry came into being in October 1905. During his brief term as acting minister in early 1906, Fedorov endorsed a reform of the corporate law of 1836, including the introduction of incorporation by registration, and endorsed the concept of "a state based on the rule of law" (*pravovoe gosudarstvo,* a direct translation of the German *Rechtsstaat*). In so doing, he endorsed the main rallying cry of Russian liberals in the aftermath of the Revolution of 1905 and of liberals in the Soviet Union during the era of glasnost eighty years later.

In the period of semiconstitutional rule after 1905, before turning to corporate activity, Fedorov wrote for the newspaper *Slovo* (The Word), the organ of the liberal Party of Peaceful Renewal. He appeared at the "economic dinners" sponsored by the liberal Moscow industrialist Pavel P. Riabushinskii, where intellectuals and commercial-industrial leaders sought common ground, after centuries of mutual distrust. At the Second Congress of the Association of Industry and Trade, in May 1907, he called for the creation of a national network of elected chambers of commerce and industry, a reform never implemented by the tsarist regime because it threatened to grant too much latitude to the principles of free election and local autonomy. In the fall of 1916, he hosted a meeting of liberal politicians called by the Kadet Party leader, Pavel N. Miliukov. In emigration, Fedorov opposed the Bolshevik government as vice president of the Russian National Committee, which included such prominent Russian businessmen as S. L. Poliakov, James Whishaw (Dzhems Vishau), A. N. Rat′kov-Rozhnov, and G. E. Veinshtein.[7] Despite his career in the bureaucracy, therefore, Fedorov's education, business acumen, and devotion to liberal political principles would have qualified him, in Europe, for the title of *bourgeois*.

Further empirical spadework on the leading corporate founders in Cycle 7 may well reveal that other holders of high rank did not necessarily endorse the reactionary political and economic policies of the tsarist bureaucratic machine. It suffices to note in passing that Sirotkin's title, Commercial Councilor, denoted a distinguished career in business, and that his base in Nizhnii Novgorod, a traditional center of merchant culture, set him apart from the others. Likewise, Tishchenko, who held gentry status but no high rank, apparently owed his prominence to his industrial activities, not to a career in the government.

The significance of the persistently prominent role of nobles, bureaucrats, military men, and gentrymen in the corporate charters of the late imperial period remains to be ascertained. On the one hand, the fact that approximately a third of all corporate founders came from the traditional elite might suggest that capitalism in Russia remained too weak to break free of the power of the state and its main ally in society, the gentry. The failure of founders from urban social backgrounds to dominate the corporate elite by decisively high percentages would support the general argument, advanced in Chapter 2, that Russian capitalism in the tsarist period remained weakly developed, largely because of the heavy-handed tutelage of the tsarist state. According to this interpretation, capitalistically minded bureaucrats like Fedorov remained rare and atypical.

On the other hand, the strong showing of founders from agrarian and bureaucratic social origins might be interpreted as a sign of a successful adaptation by the traditional elite of Russian society to the dynamism of the new capitalist economy, on the model of the English landed aristocracy, which, like others, made the transition to production for the market in the early modern period. As Barry Supple noted: "In spite of the relative nature of this importance the aristocratic entrepreneur has escaped much historical attention rightly his due. Land, financial need, and social prominence could be strong incentives to undertake entrepreneurial activity. Enterprise did not necessarily recognize class barriers."[8]

The landlords need not have implemented commercial agriculture on their own estates; a limited transition, which included the use of political measures to extract a surplus from the peasantry, occurred elsewhere in the world, as in East Elbian Germany and in Meiji Japan. There, governmental power buttressed the economic interests of the agrarian elite, which in turn showed at least minimal sensitivity to the needs of the new industrialists, junior partners in an antidemocratic condominium that formed by the end of the nineteenth century.[9] Industry in Japan and Germany developed so successfully that the tsarist military machine met defeat twice in the early twentieth century, first from the Japanese in 1904–5, then from the Germans in World War I.

The failure of the Russian gentry to make the transition to commercial agriculture, unlike the English landed aristocracy, is clear from the historical literature. Did the largest landowners in Russia participate in the emerging capitalist economy in another way, namely by taking a major role in the creation of corporations? The hypothesis that wealthy landlords occupied a leading place in Russian corporate entrepreneurship can be tested by a review of statistics in a richly detailed study by Liudmila P. Minarik, published in 1971, and of corresponding corporate and biographical information in the RUSCORP database. Minarik found that 155 individuals in 102 leading landowning families at the turn of the century (1890–1905) held a total of 16 million desiatinas of land, or approximately one-quarter of the 65 million desiatinas owned by members of the gentry and merchant estates. Four clusters of intermarried families accounted for 11.6 million desiatinas, or over 70 percent of the total. According to her, they also were active in manufacturing.

Minarik's case for a high level of industrial development on the estates of the 102 families finds some support in data on mining, metallurgy, distilling, beet-sugar production, and other processing of raw materials. However, she pushed the evidence too far in reiterating the familiar Leninist formula that the magnates led the agrarian elite in corporate entrepreneurship typical of mature capitalism around the world. "As capitalism made the transition to its highest stage, imperialism, representatives of the landlord class, chiefly its leadership [*verkhushka*], were bound ever more closely to corporate and monopoly capital. . . . Many of the largest landowners entered joint-stock enterprises in various fields of industry, mainly mining and sugar production."[10] Minarik named individuals who founded corporations, served on boards, or owned stock in Russian and foreign companies. However, these biographical facts from the history of several dozen families did not prove that the landed magnates, as a group, led the transition to capitalist exploitation of their lands.

In fact, preliminary statistical tests yielded no meaningful correlations, positive or negative, between the size of a family's landholdings and its corporate entrepreneurship, as measured by the total capitalization of the new corporations that it founded. The first was a test for correlation between the amount of land owned by individuals in the 102 families and the total capitalization of corporations founded by those persons or their parents or children. Minarik drew her data on landholding from the period 1890–1905, but she occasionally consulted reference works published as early as 1874 and as late as 1913. To give her case the strongest possible statistical basis, this analysis included all corporate foundings by persons on her list in the period 1871–1913. The correlation is measured simply, by a regression of one group of numerical values on the other set. The most common forms of regressions are linear, in which a straight line connects points defined by the formula $Y = a + bX$, and multiplicative, in which a curved line is produced by $Y = aX^b$. In neither the linear nor the multiplicative regression did Minarik's data produce a correlation coefficient in excess of .15, positive or negative. Thus r^2—the square of the coefficient, showing the amount of variation in corporate capital explained by patterns of landholding—amounted to approximately 2 percent.

The second set of tests, which compared the rankings of each family according to its landholding and capitalization total, on the one hand, and its corporate activity, on the other, produced an even lower correlation coefficient: below .07. In both sets of tests, the probability level (p) remained far outside the zone indicating statistical significance: .05 and below.

Ranking the landed elite by size of landholdings and then dividing the list by deciles into ten approximately equal groups (with eleven in categories one and six, as automatically accomplished by the Statgraphics statistical program) makes clear the lack of a direct relationship between landholding and corporate entrepreneurship. (See Figure 3.1.) Six of the ten groups founded only a few corporations, between three and six each. In contrast, the remaining four groups of families—the third, fourth, seventh, and ninth—founded between thirteen and nineteen companies each.

Total capitalizations likewise varied greatly, as the seventh group founded nineteen companies, with an aggregate capitalization of almost 109 million rubles, two and one-half times the total capital of the next most active tenth, group four. Various statistical tests fail to produce significant coefficients of correlation among these data. Considered both as families and as groups of ten or eleven families ranked according to the size of their landholdings, therefore, large landowners did not enter the corporate arena in 1871–1913 in a way that directly reflected the amount of land that they owned.

Several patterns do appear significant, however. Categorization of the 102 family groups of major landowners according to the number of companies founded by them in 1871–1913 yielded seven sets of data, some of which showed strong relationships, both positive and negative. (See Table 3.6.) The data in the first two columns suggested a strong inverse relationship between the number of companies founded by each family and the numbers of families that founded new corporate enterprises. In contrast, the average capitalization appeared to increase with the number of companies founded, and the total landholdings of each category of families varied according to the number of families in each category. Coefficients of correlation measured these relationships precisely. (See Table 3.7.)

All these correlations are linear; that is, they inscribe a straight line when plotted on a two-dimensional graph, according to the formula $Y = a + bX$. For example, the strong negative relationship ($-.7758$) between COS and TLAND appears in a regression graph as a line sloping downward from left to right as it passes as closely as mathematically possible to the seven points. Squaring the coefficient yields an r^2 of 60.2 percent; that is, the variations in TLAND account for slightly more than three-fifths of the variations in COS. The probability level (p) in this case (.0403) falls within the area typically considered significant by statisticians: below .05. This negative correlation contradicts Minarik's claim that ownership of land varied positively in relationship to the founding of new corporations. The linear correlation between FAMS and TLAND is also strong ($+.9935$: $p = .0000$), but this high correlation is irrelevant to the issue at hand: the relationship between landholding and corporate entrepreneurship.

Other patterns in these data appear to show that a family's corporate activity increased somewhat with the extent of its landholdings. For example, for the forty-three families that founded at least one company, a strong linear relationship existed between TLAND and TCOS (correlation = $+.920268$; $r^2 = 84.7$ percent; $p = .00928$). Thus, the elimination of the least active category of landowners—those who founded no companies—changed a fairly strong negative relationship ($-.6119$ in Table 3.7) to one in which the variation in aggregate landholdings accounted for more than four-fifths of the variation in the founding of corporations. However, this strong statistical relationship resulted from comparing totals of land and companies within each category in FAMS in Table 3.6, not within families. Both sets of data, TLAND and TCOS, were primarily determined by the number of families in each category of FAMS, and so it was to be expected that the twenty families in the second category would have owned more land and founded more companies, as a group, than the two families in categories six and seven, which, despite their individually large holdings, owned less land in the aggregate than the twenty families in category two. More significant was the average amount of land owned by each of these forty-three families. In Table 3.7, the relationship between ALAND and COS is not particularly strong and is negative to boot.

The elimination of category one—families that founded no companies—produced a slightly positive correlation (+.3085), but both these correlations remain so far above the .05 probability level—$p = .1442$ and .5519, respectively—that they fail to carry statistical significance. Thus, no meaningful correlation exists between ALAND and COS, with or without the category of families that refrained from corporate entrepreneurship.

Use of the multiplicative formula, which produced a curved regression line based on the equation $Y = aX^b$, yielded a high negative correlation (coefficient = $-.921461$; $r^2 = 84.9$ percent; $p = .00901$) between COS and TLAND among the six categories with one or more corporate foundings. In this case, the curved line accounted for the variation better than the straight one. (The multiplicative test does not accept zero values, so the fifty-nine families without any corporate foundings must be excluded from this test.) At first glance, this excellent fit provides a better refutation of Minarik's hypothesis than the weaker, but still significantly negative, linear correlation between COS and TLAND. That is, the greater the total amount of land owned by families in each category, the smaller the number of corporations founded. Again, however, this high negative correlation resulted from the aggregation of land within each category in the first column of Table 3.6. No significant correlation exists between the number of new companies (COS) and the average amount of land per family in each category (ALAND).

Minarik named several individuals who served on the boards of mining, beet-sugar, and similar companies, but this information constituted only anecdotal evidence. Indeed, the fact that well-to-do landowners diversified their portfolios by purchasing stock in a variety of corporations should come as no surprise. Without massive amounts of new data on the extent of corporate stock ownership and board membership by landed magnates in the early twentieth century, Minarik's assertion remains an interesting working hypothesis, but nothing more. No one has done the requisite biographical research to settle the issue.

Nor did Minarik's stress on noncorporate industrial activity on landed estates prove the alleged accommodation between large landowners and corporate capitalism. Indeed, wealthy Russian landlords had produced flour, liquor, metals, paper, glass, bricks, textiles, and other commodities on their estates since the seventeenth century. Aristide Fenster specified sixty-two families of great landowners, consisting of fifty-six from the aristocracy and six holders of gentry status from merchant origins, who were active in at least two of the seven main branches of industry in the eighteenth century: salt, potash, liquor, metals, glass, textiles, and "other."[11] (Only seven individuals belonging to families in this list of sixty-two appeared in the RUSCORP database; they founded a total of seven corporations in the eighteenth century.) Thus, the Marxist-Leninist stage theory appears irrelevant to her data.

Biographical data drawn from RUSCORP also undermine Minarik's hypothesis that the leading landowners participated in a significant number of existing corporations. Because the focus of this study remains the population, rather than individuals or separate companies, a handful of representative cases must suffice to make the case. Only 11 of the 102 families named by Minarik appeared in the corporate directory for 1905, and only 1 of them, Poklewski-Koziełł, appeared in two companies, as Vikentii A. served on the board of the Volga-Kama Bank, capitalized at 12 million rubles, and Władysław V., apparently his son, managed a small gold-mining company in the Ural mountains, capitalized at only 400,000 rubles. Two sons of Aleksei I. Musin-Pushkin managed a small beet-sugar plant capitalized at 500,000 rubles. Other big landowners in corporate management in 1905 included Vladimir V. Meller-Zakomel'skii of the Kyshtym mining company (8.61 million rubles). The linear correlation between landholdings of families in Minarik's list and the capitalization of the twelve corporations in which family members served as managers is quite high (coefficient = +.887351; r^2 = 77.7 percent; p = .00027), primarily because two families with over 200,000 desiatinas of land, the Poklewski-Koziełłs and the Meller-Zakomel'skiis, contributed managers to the large bank and the mining company. However, 91 of Minarik's 102 families contributed not a single person to managerial positions. This fact alone indicates the weak role of the largest landholding families in the corporate elite of the Russian Empire in the early twentieth century.

Additional research is necessary to reveal the fate of the forty-three corporations in which Minarik's large landowners participated as founders. Did these companies tend to stay in the hands of the family or not, and did their rate of survival surpass that of corporations generally or fall below it? In view of the unimpressive performance of most of Minarik's landholding families in the fields of corporate entrepreneurship and management, these are questions of only secondary interest. They do not pertain directly to the evolution of the great mass of corporations or the largest and most important companies.

Minarik's work opened up dozens of promising lines of inquiry, including the extent of the managerial role of her 155 individuals in surviving corporations, both those founded by them and in others in 1905 and 1914. Enthusiasm born of curiosity must be tempered, however, by the warning of a weary economist against excessive manipulation of statistics to produce patterns tending toward perfect correlation: "If you torture the data long enough, nature will confess."[12] At this point, it is sufficient to advance a cautious negative conclusion. The data in Tables 3.6 and 3.7 and Figure 3.1 do not support the contention that the wealthiest landowners in the Russian Empire moved energetically and in great numbers into large corporations or even into those that produced raw materials on their own land. In fact, the level of participation by the wealthiest landed magnates appears low, as a majority of the 102 families named by Minarik founded no corporations at all, and the most active launched only six each in the forty-two years from 1871 to 1913. Nor did individuals belonging to these landowning families figure prominently among managers of existing corporations in 1905 and 1914.

Statistics and biographical information on entrepreneurship illustrate the simultaneous action of two somewhat contradictory processes in the corporate economy of the Russian Empire, both of which underlined the essentially foreign nature of the corporation under the tsarist regime. On the one hand, the leading role of the state, perhaps the central theme of Russian political and economic history, encouraged highly placed bureaucrats to participate in the creation of new corporate enterprises. The lack of European business expertise in the largely agrarian Russian society, itself a consequence of the low level of urbanization throughout the centuries; the vast scope of projects to be undertaken in finance, transportation, and manufacturing to meet the economic challenge of the West, following the humiliation of the Crimean War; the access to the corridors of power enjoyed by educated and capable bureaucrats, gentrymen, and retired military officers in St. Petersburg; and the autocratic government's tendency to stimulate corporate enterprise by granting favorable financial incentives to entrepreneurs with connections to the imperial court and the ministries in St. Petersburg—all these factors contributed to the huge advantage of ambitious men with impressive bureaucratic titles. One need not subscribe to the Slavophile doctrine that Peter the Great and subsequent Russian monarchs, many of German descent, constituted an alien regime of occupation to recognize that favorites of the tsarist state, by virtue of their European education and personal contacts with influential bureaucrats, held some of the most prominent positions in the corporate elite.

On the other hand, modern capitalism opened the way to many new forms of enterprise, some of which at least implicitly challenged the agrarian basis of the Russian autocracy. Although many bureaucrats adapted corporations to the traditional patterns of court patronage and favoritism that pervaded the tsarist system to the very end, it was the much larger group of entrepreneurs steeped in the cultural traditions of European capitalism that formed the core of the corporate elite in Russia. A significant minority of these individuals held foreign citizenship, and many more belonged to minority ethnic groups in the Russian Empire (especially in the major cities): Jews, Germans, Poles, and Armenians. Of the two contradictory patterns—the economic advantages of social privilege and the challenge posed by talented outsiders—the latter appeared the more familiar, given the prominence in the economic literature of foreigners, immigrants, and outsiders in entrepreneurial activity the world over. Those with little to lose from failure in nontraditional social roles—from Jews in Europe and North Africa from medieval times onward to Huguenots in France under the Edict of Nantes, Chinese in the Indonesian archipelago, and Koreans in contemporary American cities—often led the transition to a market economy, not least because ties of trust to family members abroad allowed access to firm lines of credit at reasonable interest rates and secure business deals sealed only by a promise.

In general, the most active entrepreneurs in Russian corporations were not members of the wealthy nobility but outsiders who, because of the paucity of entrepreneurial talent, found it possible to achieve predominance by applying ordinary European standards of efficiency in commerce and industry on the eastern periphery of European civilization. Some of these men eventually received the traditional trappings of imperial prestige for their service to the cause of economic development. Most commonly, the title of baron fell to outstanding bankers, as in the cases of the court banker Stieglitz, a German, in Cycle 3, and the Jewish banker, Goratsii I. Gintsburg, toward the end of the tsarist period. Likewise, the career of the unusually energetic Franz Wachter in Cycle 7 can best be understood in this light. Other foreigners and members of minority nationalities in the western and southern borderlands of the empire also figured prominently among the most active founders of corporations: Fehleisen, Bekkers, Rafalovich, Mscychowski, Zawadski, Kunitzer, Mantashev, Rothstein, and Lianozov. Even in Moscow, "the heart of Russia," as it was fondly called by Slavophiles and other patriots, the German firm of Wogau and Company stood at the center of the corporate network.[13] Other cultural outsiders in the Moscow corporate elite in Cycle 4 included the textile manufacturers Morozov and Soldatenkov, prominent in the Old Believer religious movement that had persisted, despite persecution, among Russian peasants and merchants since the late seventeenth century. Likewise, Gubonin, an Old-Believer serf who purchased his freedom in 1858, grew wealthy as a railroad contractor and gained hereditary gentry status in 1872 as a reward for generous philanthropic donations.[14]

Among entrepreneurs belonging to the various foreign nationalities, Germans figured the most prominently in Russian corporations. Many German firms incorporated branch enterprises in Russia, for example, Siemens and Halske, chartered in 1896 in St. Petersburg by three Germans and Adolph Rothstein, a Jewish subject of the kaiser, and the Bayer Chemical Company, chartered in 1912 in Moscow by three German citizens. Other foreign corporations, such as BASF, active in Moscow from 1874 onward, operated under special conditions granted by the Ministry of Finance. Technical expertise and up-to-date methods of business management often outweighed the purely financial contribution of German corporations, as Siemens and Halske's capitalization stood at only 5.6 million rubles and Bayer's, only 3 million, in 1914.[15] Thus, whatever their rank—and some of the most energetic entrepreneurs were simply merchants, Honorary Citizens, or "urban residents"—foreign citizens and members of ethnic and religious minorities in new corporations gave Russian capitalism a decidedly foreign complexion.

Statistics on the 262 foreign corporations in Russia in 1914 provide yet another indication of the essentially foreign nature of capitalism under the tsars. (See Table 3.8.) Foreign corporations active in Russia in 1914 comprised a substantial percentage, 10.8 percent, of the total: 2,429 (262 foreign and 2,167 domestic). The slightly smaller share of basic capital accounted for by foreign companies (8.2 percent) and their smaller average capitalization (2.478 million rubles, compared to 3.334 million in Russian companies) apparently resulted from the huge capitalization figures of railroads and banks chartered under Russian law, which forced the average upward. As previous research has shown, foreign corporations in Russia led in the application of high technology in Russia. Companies headquartered in Belgium excelled in machine production and streetcar installation and management; British companies predominated in petroleum drilling and refining; French, in mining and metallurgy; American, in the production of farm machinery; and German, in machine production and electrical engineering. Only five countries maintained corporations larger than the average: the United States (owing to the huge capitalization of International Harvester in Russia), Austria, France, Sweden, and Britain. Germany, the leading trading partner of the Russian Empire, occupied fourth place, down from third behind Belgium and France in 1907,[16] as British companies moved into second place, primarily because of their activity in the oil fields of the Caucasus region. Still, the German presence remained strong because of the leading role of Germans in corporations chartered under Russian law, as shown in Tables 3.1, 3.2, and 3.3.

Corporate Managers in 1905 and 1914

A conventional dichotomy, at least as old as Schumpeter's influential work, defines entrepreneurship as skill in creating new combinations, in contrast to managerial ability in essentially routine administrative work. The arbitrary changes in economic policy that emanated from the chanceries of St. Petersburg may have introduced so much uncertainty into the everyday life of corporate managers as to blur the distinction. In any case, the corporate directories published in the early twentieth century supply adequate data for a composite profile of the managerial elite in 1905 and 1914.[17] A comparison of these data with those of corporate founders reveals qualities associated with success, as defined by survival to 1905 and 1914.

Unfortunately, however, the RUSCORP database does not contain adequate information about the social status of managers. Scattered biographical information of this kind appeared in lists of merchants in separate cities, but these data had no direct relationship to corporations. The corporate directories for 1905 and 1914 provided little information about the status and occupational titles of managers. Instead, a smattering of aristocratic titles (prince, baron) and those related to the traditional merchant elite (merchant or Honorary Citizen) appeared in the directories. This deficiency rendered meaningless any tabulation of data on social status.

Evidence from the memoir literature sufficed to make two essential points about the social origins of successful managers. First, the corporations that survived to 1905 and 1914 at higher than the average rate in Moscow (discussed in Chapter 2) contained many founded by merchants, especially Old Believers of Russian ethnicity. Typically, the shares of such companies remained in the hands of a single family for decades. Indeed, one branch of the Morozov family refused to part with shares of the Nikol'skoe cotton-textile corporation (*tovarishchestvo na paiakh*) for ten years after a definitive sale to an outsider.[18] By financing expansion of the enterprise with cash from current profits, these cautious managers avoided the risk of financial loss or collapse due to abrupt fluctuations in the interest rate.

In contrast, the managerial abilities of persons drawn from the old imperial elite, primarily in St. Petersburg, often left much to be desired. Inexperience and a lack of financial caution on the part of former bureaucrats and military men occasionally drove large corporations into bankruptcy.

Two episodes from the history of banks in Moscow demonstrate the contrast between cautious merchants and irresponsible aristocrats. In the flurry of bank incorporations in Moscow in the late 1860s and early 1870s, the allure of easy profits attracted not only experienced men of commerce and industry but also members of the gentry whose bureaucratic careers had left them no time to learn the intricacies of high finance. At one extreme stood Nikolai A. Naidenov, the prominent textile manufacturer who founded the Moscow Bank of Trade in 1871 and managed it until his death in 1905. As the president of the Moscow Exchange Society from 1877 to 1905, Naidenov personified the cautious merchant industrialist from peasant origins. At the other extreme stood an official of the Ministry of Interior, Actual State Councilor Danilo D. Shumakher, who led a group of bureaucrats in the creation of the Moscow Commercial Loan Bank in 1870. A few prominent merchants sat on the council of this bank, but its board of directors, under the presidency of Shumakher, included, according to Naidenov's turgid memoirs, "in part his close friends from the bureaucratic world and in part persons to whom, although poorly prepared for the business, it was desired to give a job." In October 1875, during Shumakher's term as mayor of Moscow (1874–6), the bank suddenly became the first in Moscow to collapse. A scandal erupted when it was learned that Shumakher, no longer a member of the board, had withdrawn his money and that of his nephews from the bank shortly before the crash. A trial acquitted him, but the scandal forced his resignation from the mayor's office and his bureaucratic post. The failure of his bank also caused a financial panic that damaged other banks in Moscow.[19]

Forty-five years later, Octave Homberg, a French banker with vast business experience in tsarist Russia, recoiled in disgust at the dishonest dealings of his fellow managers of the Moscow Union Bank. The president of this bank, Count Tatishchev, belonged to an important family with many connections at the imperial court, the Ministry of Foreign Affairs, and the Ministry of War. Although an intelligent man, Tatishchev lacked scruples. Homberg took particular offense at the count's carousing in Paris and his habit of recommending for positions in the bank various persons "of exceptional honesty." Finally, Homberg announced that he would be content to hire men who were "simply honest," not exceptionally so. He resigned from the council of the bank soon after the managers voted themselves annual bonuses of 50,000 rubles each, in defiance of the bank's charter.[20]

Homburg's remarks underscored the importance of corruption in the Russian corporate economy, a consequence of the weak legal tradition and of the enormous power of bureaucrats to extort illegal payments in exchange for the granting of permission for economic activity. To the extent that Tatishchev and other bureaucrats used their personal connections in the government to win lucrative posts on corporate boards, their presence constituted a symptom of political and cultural backwardness, not of successful adaptation to the techniques of modern enterprise.

By its very nature, corruption cannot be measured accurately. Two cases define the range of possibilities in the late imperial period. A Soviet account drew incriminating evidence from the personal papers of Konstantin A. Skal'kovskii, head of the Mining Department in the early 1890s. An anecdote revealed both his venality and his famous wit. A prominent petroleum industrialist once requested special permission to buy a plot of oil-bearing land in the Caucasus that should have remained in reserve. "'One hundred thousand rubles for you, my dear friend, and no one will know!' 'Three hundred thousand,' he replied calmly, 'and let all Petersburg know.'" After retiring from state service in 1896, Skal'kovskii sat on several important corporate boards, where he obtained sensitive information that he passed to French bankers in exchange for generous gifts.[21]

In contrast, the leading Frenchman in high finance in St. Petersburg declared in his memoirs that Finance Minister Witte and his talented staff remained free of corruption and that Vladimir N. Kokovtsov, his successor, maintained the tradition of honesty within this ministry. Many foreigners expected to encounter requests for bribes and often gave them to self-styled intermediaries, such as the reactionary Prince Meshcherskii, publisher of *Grazhdanin* (The Citizen), for help in gaining permission to establish industrial operations in Russia. However, these payments were not really necessary. "Black sheep [*brebis galeuses*] existed especially in the entourage of highly placed persons in the imperial family and the court and the offices subordinate to them; in the Ministry of Finance, [however], there were none to speak of."[22] In this regard, as in many others, the personality of the minister set the tone for the behavior of subordinates within each bureaucratic unit.

Many of the difficulties that hindered the effort to ascertain status indicators of corporate managers in 1905 and 1914 did not exist in the assignment of ethnic labels. The inclusion of first and middle initials instead of full first names and patronymics, as in the corporate charters, reduced the value of the directories as sources of information on the ethnicity of managers. Fortunately, however, problems of ethnic identification could be overcome in large measure by referring to the full names in the charters in the many cases when founders acted as managers of a given company, often many years after the date of incorporation.

The RUSCORP data show a high degree of correlation between ethnic patterns of founders and managers, not only in the Russian Empire as a whole but also in each of the ten major cities. The rate of participation of individuals from various ethnic groups in corporate management varied widely, from Russians, who comprised more than a third, to Ukrainians, who accounted for only about 1 percent. (See Table 3.9, columns D and E.) The rank order among the various groups remained remarkably stable from 1905 to 1914, even with the inclusion of the categories of "other" and "unknown." The only dramatic change occurred in the case of foreign citizens, whose share declined by almost half in less than a decade, from 10.5 percent in 1905 to 5.7 percent in 1914, so that they fell to sixth place behind Poles, whose smaller decline did not prevent them from rising to fifth place. (See Tables 3.10 and 3.11.) All the other important groups maintained their relative place order despite a 54 percent increase in the number of managerial positions. This stability in rank orders inspired confidence in the methodology used to categorize individuals by ethnicity.

A better indication of the participation of the various ethnic groups in the corporate economy was found in systematic comparisons of these percentages with those of each group in the population of the empire. Unfortunately, the only comprehensive census of the Russian Empire took place in 1897. Although the relative percentages of ethnic groups in the Russian Empire probably changed little from one year to the next, comparisons with RUSCORP data for later years entail some loss of statistical validity, depending on the chronological disparity. Still, the available data provide an unprecedented statistical index of corporate activity by the major ethnic groups in the Russian Empire. Dividing the percentage of each group in 1897 into the percentage for each set of corporate founders in the contemporary quinquennium (1896–1900) and of managers in 1905 and 1914 yields crude indicators, or what might be called "quotients of entrepreneurial and managerial activity" for each ethnic group. A composite quotient, the average of the three separate scores based on the population as a whole and three others based on urban population percentages, appears to be the most meaningful statistic. A quotient above 1.000 indicates that the group's share of entrepreneurs or managers surpassed its relative share in the population at large; conversely, a quotient below 1.000 shows that it did not participate at a rate that would have been expected from its share in the population. (See Table 3.9, column L.)

In the future, it might be possible to trace the rise and fall of entrepreneurial quotients for each group over time. For the time being, the lack of available data on managers before 1905 prevents the calculation of managerial quotients before that date. In any case, the decisive role of Germans, Jews, and Armenians as corporate entrepreneurs and managers mirrors the conclusions reached in the previous section of this chapter regarding the crucial importance of the relatively few non-Russian corporate founders.

Especially impressive is the high quotient for German subjects of the Russian emperor, a quantitative indicator that appears consistent with the leading role described on the basis of biographical information later in this chapter. In contrast, the marked disparity between the performance of Armenians in entrepreneurship, on the one hand, and management, on the other, resulted from the contrast between the flurry of incorporation in Baku at the end of the nineteenth century and the modest number of corporations headquartered there, coupled with the devastation wrought by the depression in the petroleum industry in the 1905, phenomena reflected in figure 2.15. Still, the Armenians' overall quotient surpassed those of Jews, Russians, and Ukrainians.

However crude and preliminary, these quotients help to clarify patterns already clear from the memoir literature. The composite score, in column L, shows the negligible role of Ukrainians in the corporate elite and the large disparity between the percentage of ethnic Russians in the population at large and in corporate positions. In contrast, German subjects of the empire occupied more than eleven times the number of positions that would have been expected had all groups participated to the extent of their percentage in the population. Other ethnic groups that far surpassed their expected share were the Poles, with almost five times the expected number of positions (4.98), and Armenians, with over two times (2.17). The many restrictions on residence imposed by law on Jews, combined with their high percentage in the urban population, reduced their overall quotient. However, the effects of governmental persecution and various forms of ethnic prejudice, which remain too subtle to be captured by statistical analysis, did not prevent Jews from occupying almost twice the corporate positions (1.81) than would have been expected in light of their numbers in the population.

The calculations based on urban percentages illustrate the variety of possible analyses that lie ahead. They also focus attention on the importance of the major cities of the Russian Empire, where corporate activity tended to concentrate. The vastly different roles of the various ethnic groups in corporate management in the early twentieth century are reflected clearly in Tables 3.10 and 3.11.

In 1905, Russians constituted the largest ethnic group of corporate managers, but they made up a majority only in Moscow and outnumbered the next largest group in only three of the other nine cities. The high quotients of Germans, Armenians, and Poles in Table 3.9 are consistent with the high percentages of managers from these ethnic groups in key cities. Particularly impressive is the prominence of Germans, who comprised only one-fifth of all managers (and little more than 1 percent of the total population) but outnumbered all other ethnic groups in three of the ten largest cities. The existence of a remarkably similar pattern in 1914 provides some assurance of the reliability of the two sets of statistics.

In 1914, Russians made up only three-eighths of the corporate managers and led other groups only in the same cities as nine years before:

Moscow (with an absolute majority that decreased after 1905), St. Petersburg, Kharkov, and Rostov-on-Don. In only one city, Odessa, did the leading role pass from one group to another. Whether this statistical change reflected instability within the corporate elite during that city's well-known economic decline or from imperfections in the categorization system used by the compilers of the RUSCORP database is a question for future research.

Although the percentages of ethnic groups for the empire as a whole in 1914 are not available, it might eventually be possible to construct a managerial quotient for each of the groups in the ten cities in that year, using local census data published shortly before the outbreak of World War I and the percentages drawn from Table 3.11. Such a detailed analysis would require separate graphs for each ethnic group or city. It seems likely that the resulting patterns would bear out the general theme of ethnic diversity among the corporate elite of the Russian Empire, especially the higher than expected rates of participation of Jews, Armenians, German subjects of the tsar, and foreigners.

This statistical exercise could also be extended to the creation of entrepreneurial and managerial quotients of the various social groups, as well, if adequate status identifications, missing in the corporate directories, could be supplied from other sources. The effort should begin by creating tables for 1905 and 1914 showing the most prominent corporate managers in these years, on the model of Table 3.5, which named the most active corporate founders. The goal would be to ascertain the relative weight, within the corporate elite, of the two main groups that predominated in the corporate charters—members of the gentry estate, bureaucrats, and former military men, on the one hand, and representatives of the merchant estate and urban professionals, on the other—in light of their percentage of the population at large.

Anecdotal evidence already shows that many bureaucrats and former military men used their connections in the ministries and at court to acquire lucrative managerial positions in some of the largest Russian corporations. As noted in the earlier discussion of corporate entrepreneurship, these men gained access to the peak of the corporate pyramid not because they excelled in industrial or financial management but because they commanded the requisite administrative skills and made the most of their personal contacts within the tsarist bureaucracy. For example, Nikolai N. Sushchov made a fortune drafting corporate charters and sitting on corporate boards after his dismissal from the Ministry of Justice for unethical behavior. In his memoirs, Witte accused Vladimir M. Vonliarliarskii, a former colonel of the imperial guards, of selling his Chukchi Peninsula gold-mining concession to foreigners, in defiance of his outspokenly nationalistic views, in order "to pocket a substantial amount of unearned profit."[23] (Vonliarliarskii and his supporters denied the charge.)

In his recent analysis of corporate directories at the end of the tsarist period, Aleksandr N. Bokhanov identified the social status of approximately two-thirds of all managers and calculated the percentages of corporate managers from two main social groups that supplied members of the corporate elite: merchants and Honorary Citizens (about 60 percent) and high bureaucratic and military officials and titled aristocrats (about 33 percent). These percentages resembled those for corporate founders in 1911–13: 49.5 for managers with professional and commercial-industrial status and 28.1 for nobles, bureaucrats, military men, and gentry, as shown in Table 3.4. Bokhanov argued that these two groups had coalesced by 1914 into a united "big bourgeoisie."[24] However, the memoir literature testified to the persistence of regional, sectoral, and ethnic tensions that weakened the cohesion of corporate managers as a social group and prevented the formation of a genuine Russian bourgeoisie. Bokhanov apparently accumulated the mass of new biographical information on note cards, not a computer, so his statistical results took the form of percentages in the empire as a whole. Perhaps for this reason, he paid little attention to regional patterns of corporate development.

The negative findings from Minarik's data and the complex social and ethnic composition of the Russian corporate elite cast additional doubt on Bokhanov's notion of a united bourgeoisie. Important political implications of the fragmentation of the Russian commercial-industrial elite are also worth exploring in future research. As is well known, the German and Japanese elites from agrarian and commercial-industrial backgrounds cooperated in restraining radical challenges from workers and peasants during the social transformation brought about by modern industry, to the detriment of democratic institutions in the century before 1945. To the extent that the Russian agrarian and industrial elites remained socially and economically separate and culturally diverse, they lacked the ability to close ranks against the workers and peasants and thus failed to restrain the revolutionary upheavals that finally shattered the politically inflexible tsarist system in the early twentieth century.

These and other considerations suggest that the statistical patterns of corporate entrepreneurship in the RUSCORP database may well become an important subject for business historians of Russia as they seek to build a bridge between sociology and biography. For the moment, it appears that success in corporate business came to those who were flexible in their choice of opportunities, had access to capital at reasonable interest rates, and benefited from a network of close relatives and friends, within social and ethnic groups, that sometimes extended across national boundaries. Foreigners clearly acted as catalysts of corporate activity.

Despite the occasionally pejorative connotation of the word *colony* in the twentieth century, it is appropriate to analyze the activities of foreigners in terms that they themselves employed. Indeed, a brief English account in the late nineteenth century actually referred to "the British colony in Russia."[25] In this discussion, the word is used in a value-neutral sense to indicate a group of mostly foreign-born inhabitants of Russia who remained culturally distant from the indigenous population, even after many decades of residence there.

The most important single group of non-Russians, as shown in Tables 3.10 and 3.11, was composed of Germans. Some Germans living in Russia remained citizens of the kaiser, so that a certain portion of the 10.5 percent of corporate managers who held foreign citizenship in 1905, and of the 5.7 percent in 1914, should be also added to that number, for a German total of well over 20 percent.

This computation excludes the men, generally of foreign origin, who managed the agencies of the 262 foreign corporations active in Russia in 1914 under special "conditions" (*usloviia*) separate from the charters granted to domestically incorporated companies. Of the 262 foreign corporations operating in the Russian Empire, 64 maintained their main agencies in St. Petersburg, 27 in Moscow, 13 in Warsaw, and 2 in Kiev. Thus, the four most important centers of Russian corporations attracted foreign corporations in approximately the same pattern of geographical concentration as domestically chartered companies.

Other evidence of the strong foreign presence in Russian manufacturing at the turn of the century emerged from a survey of managers in all forms of factories and plants, corporate and otherwise, in 1903. Of 16,400 managers, fully 8.7 percent were foreign. Concentrations higher than the average occurred in St. Petersburg (16.3) and Kiev (9.4), with extremely high percentages in the mechanical engineering shops of St. Petersburg (25.5), Kharkov (24.6), Kiev (20.9), Moscow (20.8), and Warsaw (14.5). Certain fields of industry in the five major cities and the Volga region witnessed even higher percentages: the cotton-textile mills of St. Petersburg (62.8), and sugar refining in Moscow (57.1), for example. The most prominent foreign groups were those of Germans (49.2 percent) and Austrians (14.6). English managers and foremen were concentrated in the cotton-textile mills of St. Petersburg (58.8 percent) and Moscow (51.5); Belgians in the machine plants of Kharkov (56.0); and Austrians in the sugar plants of Kiev (41.0). Although foreigners had generally higher educational levels than Russians, almost a quarter (23.0 percent) of the foreigners, or 2 percent of all managers, spoke no Russian, and in some industries and cities this percentage was far higher: 48.8 percent in St. Petersburg and 30.0 percent in Warsaw. This lack of knowledge of Russian was somewhat mitigated by the ability of 7.6 percent of all managers in Poland to speak Polish, but the concentration of foreigners without Russian in the highly visible cotton and machine industries of the northern capital contributed to the general impression that foreign managers were poorly integrated into Russian society.[26]

Anders Henriksson's recent analysis of the German colony in St. Petersburg has shown that not all bearers of German names identified strongly with German culture or ethnicity. Businessmen who used Russian in their everyday affairs tended to adopt the Russian language and the

Orthodox religion more easily than Baltic German aristocrats in the imperial bureaucracy, for example. Despite the variety of outlooks conditioned by "social class, gender, occupation, regional origin, marriage, politics, and personal ambition," the relatively large German community in St. Petersburg clearly enjoyed a prominent role in the Russian corporate elite. It also became the target of discrimination and abuse from both the imperial government and its political rivals, the liberal and radical movements.[27]

Henriksson's study of St. Petersburg buttressed the major theme of the present chapter: that capitalist institutions in Russia bore the heavy cultural imprint of foreigners and ethnic minorities and, for that reason, attracted antipathy from Russians on many points on the political spectrum. As data in Table 3.11 show, four of the ten leading cities—St. Petersburg, Warsaw, Odessa, and Lodz—had significant minorities of Germans, ranging from almost 20 percent in St. Petersburg to over 44 percent in Lodz. In Riga, the high proportion of Germans among corporate managers—three out of four—came as no surprise because of the strong tradition of German culture in that city.[28]

The memoir literature suggested the existence of several related patterns. First, Germans demonstrated an amazing degree of flexibility in seizing new economic opportunities in Russia. Second, they strove to accommodate themselves to local customs, such as the stereotypical nonchalance of the Russian industrial worker and the fabled avarice of the Russian bureaucrat. Finally, subtle connections within family groups, including access to investment capital at reasonable rates of interest, which the rudimentary Russian banking system could not provide, maintained the Germans' sense of community within a separate "colony" in Russia, even after they had mastered the intricacies of its economic and political systems.

Success came most of all to those experts who fully understood Russian culture: Wogau, Amburger, and some non-Germans as well: Jules Goujon in Moscow, who held dual French and Russian citizenship; and Emmanuel Nobel, the Swedish petroleum and machinery magnate who was universally respected as the voice of enlightened business in St. Petersburg. Corporations based in Europe, such as the French and Belgian companies that created the coal and iron industry of "South Russia," encountered more difficulty in finding capable "bicultural Western technicians" than did the trading firms managed by transplanted Germans.

> Thus foreign entrepreneurial groups often learned to spread their talents thinly by attaching them to leading firms or banks, either in the Donets or at St. Petersburg, from which they traveled for investigations or emergency consultation. These men could also screen new entrepreneurial opportunities at minimal cost. . . . While Russians handled commercial affairs and bureaucratic negotiations, . . . it was hoped that the foreign but acculturated engineer would assure the honest direction and the technical expertise which remained essential to the whole general strategy of entrepreneurship. . . .

Generally this effective balance, which definitely prevailed in the prewar years, was achieved with difficulty over time.[29]

Shortly after World War I, after years of commercial experience in Russia, a German-Swiss merchant, Dr. Ernst Jenny, published a thorough commentary on the role of Germans in the Russian economy. In his opinion, Russian merchants and workers lacked the business skills that had emerged gradually in Europe in the preceding millennium. Because Russia had never experienced feudalism, the Renaissance, or the Reformation, it remained, in his view, "Asiatic, Byzantine, despotic, and Orthodox." Allegations by patriotic Russians of "the German assault" (*deutsche Vergewaltigung*) and "the German yoke" (*deutsches Joch*) before World War I simply reflected, in his opinion, "envy and jealousy" toward Germans who enjoyed economic success in the Russian Empire. "German tenacity and German diligence" (*deutsche Zähigkeit und deutscher Fleiss*), not unfair business practices, were the keys to prosperity.[30]

Jenny accused Russian merchants of apathy and dishonesty. Like a spider in its web, most Russians simply waited for opportunity to arrive, he claimed. Others committed outright fraud. In one case, a Russian merchant grew rich by producing sturdy plows for the peasant market, but after fifteen years he decided to reduce the width of the plows by several millimeters in order to decrease production costs. His plows still sold "like hot cakes," but if his customers learned his secret and became angry, he said, "then I'll just spit [*dann spuck' ich drauf*] because we have already feathered our nest." His business, once worth a million rubles, rapidly declined. To this opportunist, Jenny contrasted the firm of Ransome, Sims, and Jefferies, which prided itself on manufacturing sturdy agricultural implements since 1779. In the second case, a tobacco firm was transformed by Russian merchants into a corporation, only to be "eviscerated" (*ausgeweidet*) by its new owners. The merchants planned to reduce the quality of the cigarettes, turn a profit two or three times the amount of the basic capital, and then sell the factory buildings at a loss after the public realized the swindle. Jenny saw in this attitude "the character of a grasshopper" (*Heuschreckennatur*). Evidently borrowing stereotypes from children's stories, he implied that the typical German resembled the frugal ant, in contrast to the Russian, who behaved like the lazy spider and the irresponsible grasshopper.[31]

Russian workers also made a negative impression on Jenny because of their alleged lack of a sense of pride in their craft. Although capable of hard work under close supervision, the Russian tended "to lose all self-control" (*raspuskat'sia,* in Russian) without it. Jenny compared the typical Russian worker to a docile cow that gave abundant milk but suddenly kicked over the bucket.[32] Some evidence in the specialized historical literature contradicted the stereotypes repeated by Jenny and many others. For example, Carl Glaser, the manager of the dye plant operated by BASF in Moscow, held Russian workers in high regard. "Certainly they got drunk from time to time, but there were also many who were content with tea."33

As these contrasting assessments suggest, the degree of German entrepreneurs' assimilation varied within and among the various European colonies in each Russian city. At one end of the spectrum stood the Amburger family of St. Petersburg, for generations a leading force in the oldest insurance company in the country. According to Erik Amburger, the distinguished historian born into this family ten years before the Revolution, his relatives all spoke German with a strong Russian accent.34 Likewise, a German immigrant who achieved prosperity producing sheet metal in St. Petersburg wrote his memoirs in Russian, though he inserted numerous elegant sentences in various European languages.35 The family of Alfred Swann, an Englishman who worked for the Russian timber magnate Beliaev and the Russian-American Triangle Rubber Company, succumbed to both Russian and German cultural influences in St. Petersburg. The family retained its British citizenship, but Swann's son recalled in his memoirs that he learned English only at age 16:

> My father was a typical example of those who became part of German Baltic society. He married into a Danish-German family and sent his children to a German school. At the same time, we spoke Russian among ourselves and tried to assimilate Russian customs and habits. Yet Father also tried to maintain his links with his native country. He would say grace in English before dinner, though he would then immediately lapse into German or Russian.36

At the other extreme, the prominent English merchant James Whishaw sent his children home to southern England for their education, lest they develop too strong an attraction to Russians or to the textile foremen from Lancashire, Yorkshire, and Scotland in "the English colony" in St. Petersburg. Whishaw and his wife sought to keep their children from becoming "what we termed 'St. Petersburg' English, and I am glad to say that none of my daughters spoke with the curious accent acquired by even purely English people who rarely left the country. The accent was a peculiar one, being of a sing-song nature: I have only heard it amongst Anglo-Russians."37

Likewise, the Germans of Moscow constituted a close-knit colony. The prominent Moscow merchant Robert Spies took Russian citizenship in 1846 only because the law required this action. He resumed his Prussian citizenship with his whole family when permitted to do so by the government of Emperor Alexander II. During his entire business career in Russia, he always intended to return to Germany after amassing a fortune. In 1874, he indeed took his entire family back to Dresden. Robert Spies dealt mainly with the other German businesses in Moscow—Knoop, Wogau, Bansa, Marc, Prowe, Zenker, Aschenbach, and Stucken—and the French merchant Catoire. Before 1850, few German merchants took the trouble to learn Russian well. According to Spies, the "German colony" in Moscow included several major families that had intermarried: Wogau,

Bansa, Spies, and Rabeneck. After the increasingly nationalistic Russian government made Russian the official language, Germans used it in their everyday affairs, and their children studied German as a foreign language. They also celebrated the kaiser's birthday, the holiday "that united the entire German colony" (*das die ganze reichsdeutsche Kolonie vereinigte*). However, after he dismissed Bismarck, their "hero," they felt little devotion to the kaiser.[38]

Georg Spies left a fascinating rumination on the cultural distance between Germans and Russians in the Moscow business world. The separation resulted primarily from the low social status of the merchant estate, a situation that persisted until the end of the nineteenth century. Even the wealthiest Moscow merchants commanded so few of the social graces common to polite European society that they felt obliged to hire a general to give the toast at ceremonies, family gatherings, and weddings. Such was the case until the new generation of educated Moscow merchants emerged shortly before 1905 to take an active role in public life. With some exaggeration, Spies wrote: "All in all, the life of the foreign colony [*Kolonie*] in Moscow in my parents' time, and even in mine, until the end of the century, appeared the same as that of an English colony in India or China."[39]

This feeling of ethnic solidarity coexisted, however, with a certain cosmopolitanism within the German families, the result of occasional intermarriage with non-German Europeans. An uncle of Georg Spies, a Swedish transport engineer from Finland named Knut von Stjernvall, had participated in the construction of the railroad between St. Petersburg and Moscow. Although one of his sisters married Hugo von Wogau, a member of the most solid firm of the "Moscow Germans," Georg Spies married Henriette Clason, the daughter of a prominent German merchant in Liverpool.[40]

Similar colonies of foreign business managers existed in Warsaw. The chronicler of the Rau family noted that, after years of residence in Warsaw as entrepreneurs in steel, machinery, coal, railroads, and sugar, the family still retained its identification as Germans. "The Raus valued Poland and Russia only from the economic point of view but never felt at home there [*sich aber nie dort heimisch gefühlt*] and remained tied to their German nature and homeland [*Art und Heimat*]." Wilhelm Rau the elder returned to Breslau in 1853 and to Brussels in 1862, despite having married the daughter of a Polish-Jewish banker, von Laski, in 1841. His brother, Heinrich, and his nephew, Karl Jakob, also left Poland for Germany, lest their daughters marry in the East. Even the indefatigable Johann Wilhelm Ellis Rau, who distinguished himself as one of the most active corporate entrepreneurs in the Russian Empire (see Table 3.5), settled in Frankfurt/Main in 1887, although he maintained a residence in Warsaw thereafter.[41]

As in Moscow, this attitude did not bespeak a narrow devotion to German culture itself but coexisted with a cosmopolitan toleration of family ties with prominent merchants of other European nationalities. Like the Spies family, the Raus intermarried with "influential Belgian, Rhine, and Westphalian industrial families: Cockerill, Pastor, Suermondt, and Haniel." The wedding of the daughter of Wilhelm Ellis Rau to Robert Suermondt in 1879 carried this tradition onward. Until World War II, the Rau family maintained business interests in Poland, for example in the Ostrowiec metal company, founded with the Rau family's capital by Georg Pastor in 1885.[42]

The adaptability of German business leaders in Russia typically did not proceed so far as to obliterate the sense of separateness, as happened, for example, in some Baltic German families who became more or less Russified after several generations of service at the top ranks of the tsarist bureaucracy and, in many cases, conversion to Russian Orthodoxy. The Moscow Germans and members of other foreign colonies in Russia, despite their entrepreneurial success, adaptability, and family ties, therefore remained foreigners in their adopted Slavic land. The biographer of one English family noted that "in sixty years not one of the Smiths of Moscow married a Russian."[43] According to a British diplomat, the "local British colony" in Moscow had few contacts with Russians outside of business hours. "Many of the local English, in fact, regarded the Russians as good-natured but immoral savages whom it was not safe or proper to introduce into their home circle." To the "pious horror" of the English ladies, for example, one female Russian millionaire had lunch and a bridge party every Sunday with her husband and two former husbands.[44]

For their part, few Moscow merchants could bridge the cultural gap. Georg Spies praised Pavel and Sergei M. Tret'iakov, creators of the magnificent gallery devoted to Russian art. One of the brothers, whom Spies did not name, appeared "a highly educated, well-adjusted" man with "a rare quality: a combination of West-European, especially German culture [*Kultur*] and the Russian delicacy of soul [*Seelen-Zartheit*] in wonderful harmony."[45] Such words of praise occurred rarely in the memoirs of foreigners active in Russia.

Despite his low opinion of Russians, Ernst Jenny looked optimistically toward the future. In the aftermath of World War I, he claimed, Germans and Russians should resume the economic "symbiosis" that had taken shape in the imperial period. More than any other group of foreigners, he wrote with some exaggeration, Germans had become integrated into the Russian economy. "This can be observed clearly down to the present day in the fate of German families and German enterprises. Unlike them, French or English settlers always remain strictly isolated from the Russian people and usually return to their old homeland with their accumulated riches." Germans, he admitted, tended toward excessive pedantry, but they made a useful contribution in exerting discipline over the Russians' "expansive character" (*breite Natur,* the celebrated *shirokaia dusha* of the stereotypical Russian). "It will become clear from all this how much the German's steadfastness, devotion to business, and capability supplement the personal submissiveness of the agile but feeble and volatile Russian." According to Jenny, even Russians grudgingly admitted the Germans' superior technical and organizational ability, saying "Nothing is possible without a German!" (*bez nemtsa nel'zia!*).[46]

However self-serving, these notions of national character achieved wide acceptance in Europe. The contrast between the tender-hearted but impractical Oblomov and his close friend, the dynamic and ambitious half-German Stolz, in Goncharov's great novel, published in 1859, is only the most famous stereotype in Russian literature of the impractical Russian and the enterprising German.[47] Eventually, the simplex dichotomy took on a life of its own, as it engendered much ill will on both sides. The opposite side of this cultural divide—the Russians' resentment of stereotypical foreign capitalists—is discussed in Chapter 5.

Russian Entrepreneurship in Comparative Perspective

The high rates of participation by foreigners, Russian Germans, Poles, Jews, and Armenians in Russian corporations require explanation. Why did Russian society not generate its own cadre of accomplished corporate managers in the era of the so-called Great Reforms? A glance at the careers of some of the most prominent Russians who leaped with more enthusiasm than expertise into the dangerous world of corporate high finance reveals the weakness of what might be called their cultural conditioning. Comparisons with recent scholarship on the phenomenon of entrepreneurship in other cultural settings not only throws into relief some of the reasons for the widely divergent patterns of economic behavior among persons from different cultural backgrounds in the Russian case but also provides an opportunity to make a modest critique of the theories of entrepreneurship in light of evidence from imperial Russian history.

In the past half-century, historical scholarship on entrepreneurs has undergone an impressive evolution. A recent contribution to the literature neatly summarized the achievements and shortcomings of previous theories of entrepreneurial behavior. Schumpeter's emphasis on the creative individual who combined factors of production in new and more productive ways than before despite the resistance of tradition offered a useful corrective to equilibrium theory. Then A. P. Usher and N.S.B. Gras examined successful businesses and laid the foundations of business history at the Graduate School of Business Administration at Harvard University, where the *Business History Review* is still published. The landmark collection of essays edited by Hugh Aitken, *Explorations in Enterprise,* summarized the findings of the Harvard school. During the Cold War, when American social scientists sought formulas that would promote non-Communist modes of economic development, attention turned from Europe and North America to the poorest countries in the world, where entrepreneurial impulses appeared relatively weak. Already, Thomas C. Cochran had begun examining the influence of cultural tradition on entrepreneurship in Latin America. Psychological barriers to entrepreneurship were identified by David McClelland in *The Achieving Society* (1961). At the same time, Everett Hagen sought to explain entrepreneurial success by pointing to the necessity of community solidarity and hard work on the part of minorities, whether religious or ethnic, as a means of fighting discrimination; his examples included dissenters in England, Protestants in France, samurai warriors in Japan, and Jews in Europe.[48]

Recent research has focused on why some ethnic groups adapt more successfully than others to a given economic environment. Examples of successful entrepreneurial groups include Chinese and Indian shopkeepers in Seychelles, who preserve strong, patriarchal families with high rates of savings, emphasize the education of children, and maintain family ties with relatives abroad, in Southeast Asia and India, respectively. In contrast, the families of Creole shopkeepers in the same villages in Seychelles lack solidity, and their businesses consequently suffer from poor access to credit, as well as a lack of unpaid labor of family members.[49]

The most intriguing facet of this recent work has been the effort of researchers to transcend the abstractions of social science in favor of flexible theories drawn from Darwinian biology. As two pioneers of this methodology explained it,

> an appreciation of the role of the entrepreneur requires that we seek the selective factors that determine the fate of entrepreneurial innovations. In the framework of the new metaphor, the entrepreneur introduces variant behavior into a community; but the ultimate historical significance of his activities is the result of the selective process. It is only if an innovative act is copied, and its frequency increased, or has secondary effects, that it appears as a patterned regularity, or institution in the community. . . . In the populationist view, both successes and failures can be viewed as individuals seeking new or modified ways to obtain goals. Theoretically they are the source of both social pattern and its change.[50]

Likewise, Janet T. Landa recently offered an analysis of "ethnically homogeneous middleman groups"—Jews in Europe since the Middle Ages, Chinese in Southeast Asia, Indians in East Africa, and Lebanese in West Africa—in an effort to discover links between ethnicity and entrepreneurship. She followed other social scientists in defining ethnic groups according to the usual criteria of shared origins, common values, a sense of separateness from other groups, and visible signs of distinctiveness. She also stressed, however, that a comprehensive definition of ethnicity must include a provision for the transmission of shared values from one generation to the next; "the cultural traits of ethnic groups are treated as a group inheritance that is transmitted most often, but not exclusively, through family upbringing."[51]

By examining entrepreneurship in a global context, Landa was able to offer a useful corrective to the theory of Oliver E. Williamson, who accounted for the rise of firms in his analysis of three kinds of economic interactions: through markets, the vertically integrated firm, and long-term contracts among firms. Williamson's typology lacked explanatory power in poor countries, where such capitalist institutions did not exist:

> The particularistic kinship/ethnic trading networks are the dominant form of economic organization in non-Western LDCs [less-developed countries]. As such, particularistic trading networks may be considered a fourth kind of economic organization in which relational contracting takes place between traders linked by particularistic ties of mutual trust. . . . [They] may be considered to be an *intermediate* form of economic organization, lying *between* markets (contracts) and hierarchies (the vertically integrated firm). They are an efficient form of economic organization that emerged for the protection of contracts, given the conditions of contract uncertainty and the historical-institutional context in which these ethnic middlemen-entrepreneurs operate.[52]

Landa's findings found support in research on entrepreneurs in a variety of other historical settings. Among Norwegians in rural Wisconsin between the world wars, for example, "a common ethnicity seemed to increase the probability that the person would honor obligations of trust." Likewise, in Latin America in the 1970s,

> kin-based groups linked together by social networks . . . provided the paths for the flow of information, including information about the reliability of information and consequently the reliability of those kin groups and associated social networks that supplied the information. The ideology of kinship assured that members of kinship groups—and participants in their networks—would fulfill the obligations without the need to appeal to formal sanctions.

Finally, in Nicaragua, business groups that controlled "a great variety of enterprises in different sectors of the economy" provide a key ingredient of economic success: "financial intermediation in which the group facilitates both the making of investments for members with excess savings and the securing of credit for members with net capital needs."[53]

These patterns had analogies in the Russian Empire before 1914, where the rudimentary contract and bankruptcy law provided little defense against unscrupulous debtors, suppliers, and customers. Several of the ethnic groups prominent in Russian corporations resembled Landa's ideal type of ethnic middlemen. The statistics suggest that Germans and Jews conformed most closely. Although the parallels between Puritans in England and Old Believers in Russia has been drawn in the historical literature, and although several Old Believers distinguished themselves in corporate entrepreneurship, among them Petr I. Gubonin, Timofei S. Morozov, and Koz'ma T. Soldatenkov in Cycle 4 (See Table 3.5), their corporations remained restricted to textiles and related banking operations or occasionally to railroads, not to the kaleidoscopic variety typical of the Moscow Germans.

Vasilii A. Kokorev, one of the many Old Believer merchants imbued with enthusiasm for economic nationalism after the Crimean War, showed unusual energy as he launched grandiose corporate plans in international trade, railroad and steamship transportation, insurance, banking, petroleum, and agriculture. However, he lost his fortune as easily as he gained it. Although his Old Believer coreligionists may have contributed some funds to his schemes, Kokorev always acted alone, as a gambler whose impetuosity alarmed his more cautious associates. In particular, he failed to convince the tsarist government of the cogency of his plan to finance the emancipation of the serfs and the construction of a railroad network by the proceeds of a reformed vodka tax-farming scheme. After the collapse of his railroad and petroleum ventures, he owed his financial recovery to the State Bank, which rescued him from bankruptcy and forgave millions of rubles' worth of debts to the state.[54]

In this respect, the shortcomings of the older literature on entrepreneurship become evident. The Old Believers may have provided a good example of Hagen's theory of entrepreneurial activity as the defensive response of a minority group to governmental repression, but that explanation had no relevance to Europeans who became wealthy in Russian corporations under the last three Russian emperors. Knoop, Rau, Spies, and Whishaw owed their superior business abilities to their mastery of the merchant traditions of Germany and England. Jewish and Armenian entrepreneurs may have developed their entrepreneurial expertise as a defensive strategy, but they did so in communities that had reached cultural maturity outside the power of the Russian state, long before it absorbed them in the late eighteenth and early nineteenth centuries. In this case as well, Hagen's explanation adds little to our understanding.

More promising is the factor of "relationships of confidence and trust" among business partners, a general phenomenon explicitly stressed by Greenfield and his colleagues. Each successful group of entrepreneurs "seems to have a characteristic group or network of persons on whom he can depend and whom he can trust. From the members of this unit he is able to mobilize the kinds and quantities of resources needed to carry out the new combinations. Just who constitutes this trusted coterie in any particular case varies widely."[55]

As Landa noted, trust is most often cultivated among members of a family network or an ethnic group. Both the intimate knowledge of subtle messages among persons who share a similar cultural background and the distrust of outsiders contribute to the feeling of loyalty that is essential to reducing or eliminating what economists call opportunistic behavior: the cheating of one party by another in the absence of effective incentives or sanctions. In a large corporation, the complexity of managerial functions and the relatively large number of persons unrelated by family ties render supervision more difficult than in a small firm. The need for trustworthy personnel becomes all the more important.

The colonies of German, French, English, and other ethnically distinct merchant groups in the major Russian cities depended on trust within each group to carry out economic operations. Trust and friendship among merchants occasionally bound individuals from vastly different cultural backgrounds. According to a letter from Ludwig Knoop to his brother, several Russian merchants figured prominently among his closest friends. In the words of one biographer, Knoop "enjoyed unlimited trust; the Russian merchants were satisfied with Knoop's verbal assurances in the largest contracts, and only in later years did they begin to adopt developed forms of business relations."[56]

Likewise, trust occasionally operated across ethnic lines among Swedes, Russians, Armenians, and Azeris in Baku, where capitalist institutions developed very late. Hagelin, a Swedish technician in the employ of the Nobel Brothers Petroleum Company, once sealed with a handshake a promise to process oil from a gusher owned by an Azeri named Shamsi, who eventually collected over a million rubles in royalties from the Nobel corporation without ever asking to audit its records. A Russian merchant once explained to Hagelin his willingness to buy fuel oil from Nobel Brothers at slightly higher prices than those set by other suppliers: "With Nobel there are always forty pounds [*funty*] in a pud." Thus, Nobel's reputation as an enlightened European businessman sufficed to build bonds of trust in the notoriously lawless and violent frontier town of Baku. Access to investment capital and modern technology played crucial roles, but superior entrepreneurial ability, including the ability to inspire trust among customers, also appeared to be an essential factor in determining the survival of corporations. Trust also proved crucial among the Azeris of Baku. Of a prominent Azeri oil producer who loaned money at high rates of interest to fellow Moslems without written contracts, Hagelin wrote: "It was profitable for him to be honest. Besides that, according to Moslem concepts, trust was binding [*doverie obiazyvalo*]. A written contract could be evaded. A contract indicated a lack of trust. Trust, based on one's word, was always sacred."[57]

Without attempting a contribution to the theory of entrepreneurship, this chapter has offered new statistics and biographical data from the history of corporate capitalism in Russia in an effort to identify leading entrepreneurs and managers and the cultural determinants of their economic success. Among the key patterns were the tiny size of the Russian corporate elite and its heavy geographical concentration. In some important sectors and regions, Russians gradually displaced foreigners, but this trend proceeded slowly.

These findings raise further questions about the cultural and political causes of the slow pace of corporate development in the Russian Empire. As noted in Chapter 1, the most interesting topic for further investigation is the disappointing performance of capitalist institutions in the era of the Great Reforms, from the early 1860s to the mid-1870s. The most likely reasons appear to be the weak entrepreneurial tradition in Russia before the Great Reforms; the complexities of the new projects in rail transport, shipping, and heavy industry, which overwhelmed all but the most skilled entrepreneurs, among whom foreigners, Jews, Poles, Armenians, and Old Believers figured prominently; and the inability of the landed elite to embrace modern business techniques instead of relying on traditional connections at court, the arguments of Minarik and Bokhanov notwithstanding.

The failings of Russian corporations in the 1860s contrasted sharply with the successes of Japanese businesses under the Meiji restoration. There, the efficient state bureaucracy pioneered the creation of enterprises in heavy industry and then transferred successful enterprises to an equally efficient managerial elite drawn not only from displaced samurai warriors but also from a long tradition of merchant enterprise. These two sources of domestic entrepreneurship—an enlightened bureaucracy and a vigorous native merchant class—barely existed in Russia. Under the tsarist regime, merchants had endured centuries of discriminatory legislation; and the state's own economic program under the last three emperors consisted of restrictions on banks, a large number of state-owned enterprises that competed directly with corporations, and, eventually, state control of railroads. The tsarist bureaucracy gave only the slightest support for technological innovations outside industries tied to the military, traditionally the state's highest priority, as in efforts of the imperial army and navy to discover military uses of electricity from the late 1860s to the early 1880s, before it became commercially viable.[58]

Thus, statistics and the memoir literature reiterate three of the main characteristics of Russian capitalism under tsarist rule: its institutional immaturity, its geographical concentration, and its foreign nature. These features emerged once again in the brief period of reform at the end of the Soviet period, when, just as before 1917, they contributed to the creation of resentment against foreign and domestic capitalists.

4

Perestroika and the Failure of Soviet Capitalism, 1985–1990

There is no alternative to the transition to a market economy. World experience clearly testifies to the viability and effectiveness of the market economy concept. In our society, the switch to the market economy is necessitated predominantly by people's needs; its aim is the establishment of an economy conscious of social needs, an economy serving the consumer, an economy without shortages and humiliating lines, an economic mechanism ensuring entrepreneurial freedom for citizens and creating beneficial conditions for diligence, creativity, initiative and high productivity.

Transition to a market economy in no way contradicts the socialist choice made by our people. It is only the market, in tandem with the humanistic orientation of all society, that will be able to satisfy people's needs, ensure just distribution of wealth, safeguard social rights and guarantees, and consolidate such values as freedom and democracy.

Mikhail S. Gorbachev (1990)[1]

Historians of the era of perestroika (1985–91) may well conclude that, like the tsarist regime before it, the government of Mikhail Gorbachev fell because it failed to solve the problem of economic productivity. The collapse of the railroad system and the bread shortages that faced the tsarist ministers in December 1916 far exceeded the gradual dissolution of the economy seventy-five years later. Still, Gorbachev's reluctance to implement market reforms on a scale commensurate with his rhetoric contributed directly to the economic crisis that doomed his regime.

To his credit, Gorbachev legalized individual enterprise in November 1986, promulgated legislation on cooperatives in 1987 and 1988, and authorized the creation of genuine corporations in June 1990. At every stage and at all levels of the Soviet administration, however, opponents of market reforms slowed the progress of reform. The autocratic party-state, even in its attenuated form, proved far more inimical to the market than the tsarist bureaucracy on the eve of World War I. Capitalism for Soviet ideologists signified not only the international threat, as under the tsarist regime, but also the class enemy, according to Marxist ideology.

Moreover, perestroika retained a host of irrational restrictions on economic activity. The law on cooperatives sought to resurrect the mixed economy of the New Economic Policy (1921–8), which rested on the political autocracy of the Communist Party. Only at the very end, in 1990, did Gorbachev opt for the corporate form of enterprise, and even this was modeled largely on the tsarist pattern, with some concessions to modern European practice. Gorbachev himself bore major responsibility for the slow pace of his economic reforms. As the epigraph shows, he hoped to introduce a free market that would not undermine the "socialist choice" made by the Bolshevik party in 1917. The legalization of corporations in 1990 therefore came too late to halt the downward spiral of the economy. Why, then, did Gorbachev wait more than five years before embarking on this major reform?

Cooperatives and the Culture of Communal Envy

The Soviet decree on cooperatives, promulgated in February 1987 and superseded by a comprehensive law in May 1988, sought to promote economic efficiency but imposed so many restrictions out of a deference to collectivist ideology that the economic effect remained minimal. To those versed in Soviet history of the 1920s, the law on cooperatives had a familiar ring. In January 1923, Lenin had announced, with undue optimism, that "the system of civilized co-operators is the system of socialism."[2] From a Marxist-Leninist point of view, cooperatives posed no ideological threat to the Soviet regime. Their small size and cooperative essence prevented them from posing a threat to the state, and their ability to respond to local market opportunities actually promised a pragmatic economic benefit.

Nikolai I. Bukharin, the chief theoretician of the Soviet Communist Party until Stalin's consolidation of power at the end of the 1920s, kept in place the major concessions granted by the Bolshevik government in 1921: the abolition of forced requisitions of grain, the free market in foodstuffs, and the limited use of hired labor by individuals. Although committed to the eventual creation of a planned economy, Bukharin saw the wisdom of limiting direct state control to the key sectors—heavy industry, transport, banking, and foreign trade—and, even in them, sought to maximize the comparative advantage of the Soviet Union by inviting foreign concessions to prepare raw materials such as timber, gold, and manganese for sale on the world market. Bukharin, of whose dedication to Communist ideals there could be no doubt (he edited the party newspaper, *Pravda,* from 1917 to 1929) viewed agricultural cooperatives as a halfway house from capitalism to socialism, a useful school for the inculcation of communal virtues in the long and difficult transformation of the human soul from the individual to the collective mentality.[3]

Stalin's imposition of hypercentralized economic planning and his destruction of voluntary cooperative farming during the forced collectivization drive in 1929–30 represented an abandonment of the confidence expressed by Lenin and Bukharin in the capacity of Soviet citizens to grow to socialist maturity under the benevolent tutelage of the party-state. Although the collective farms (*kolkhozy*) retained the outward forms of cooperative activity, they fell under the control of Machine Tractor Stations (1930–58) and other new bureaucratic mechanisms. The regimentation and impoverishment of the peasantry constituted the introduction of a new form of serfdom less than seven decades after its abolition by the tsarist regime.

Gorbachev resurrected Bukharin's concept of the cooperative as a flexible tool of economic reform within the framework of the Communist Party's monopoly of power. Stalin's destruction of voluntary cooperatives prevented our knowing whether Bukharin's dream of prosperity under a Soviet autocracy without mass terror would have been possible in the absence of a much greater concession to capitalism than he was prepared to grant, including Soviet corporations capable of bringing raw materials to the world market. Gorbachev's abdication in 1991 likewise left unclear the implications of his modest economic reforms of 1986–8. What seemed most interesting about this limited experiment in cooperative economic activity was the storm of protest that it raised.

Like the law on individual enterprise, the legislation on cooperatives strictly restricted the scope of the enterprise's activity. First, because members of cooperatives did not enjoy limited liability unless their charters explicitly granted that privilege, these new enterprises could hardly aspire to large size. Second, the law required that anyone who withdrew from a cooperative forfeited his or her investment unless the enterprise was dissolved. Thus, shares were not subject to sale or transfer. Finally, despite the right to found cooperatives by the procedures of simple registration with local authorities, officials often refused to comply.[4] Gorbachev's legalization of cooperative economic activity simply failed to protect the new enterprises from fierce resistance from conservative Communists at all levels of government and from the public itself.

However, because the law authorized the activity of unlimited numbers of persons, at least three, the size of a cooperative could surpass that of an individual repair shop or tutoring service. Soon two major forms became evident. At the most rudimentary level, cooperatives sprang up in public services. Especially prominent were restaurants that offered fast service and high-quality products at correspondingly high prices, in contrast to the notoriously inefficient, grimy, and uncomfortable state-run cafeterias. At the opposite extreme, in state enterprises, some shrewd managers converted subsidiaries into cooperatives in order to reap the twin advantages of access to raw materials within the planned economy and the right to charge high prices for the cooperative's products on the free market.5

The number of cooperatives mushroomed in the late 1980s from a negligible number in mid-1987 to over 180,000 enterprises employing over five million individuals in mid-1990.6 These data inscribed an S-curve somewhat like that of banks in the Russian Empire in the 1860s and 1870s. One researcher noted, however, that cooperatives flourished in the late 1980s only because Soviet law permitted no other appropriate form of private enterprise. Throughout the world, cooperatives tended to cluster in agriculture (37 percent), credit (29 percent), and consumer purchasing (10 percent), but in the USSR they flourished in cities and in construction, light manufacturing, and services, with few in agriculture (2 percent) and none in consumer credit. "This indicates that cooperatives in the USSR today are only the tentative name given to the majority of legally operating small businesses (roughly 80 percent according to my estimate) that have donned the cooperative 'hat.'"7

As in the Russian Empire, new capitalist institutions developed according to a clear pattern of geographical concentration. In January 1990, the ratio of cooperatives to the total population varied widely among the fifteen republics of the USSR. (See Figure 4.1.) Armenia's ratio was nearly four times that of the USSR as a whole (6.7 per 10,000), and all three of the Baltic republics plus Georgia also had double-digit ratios. In contrast, the ratios in the predominantly Turkic and Iranian republics along the southern border of the Soviet Union—Azerbaijan and the five Central Asian republics—ranged from 3.6 to 5.9 per 10,000, well below the national ratio. This unevenness resulted from a variety of factors, including the level of development of markets and the cultural traditions of the various nationalities. (This is not to imply that all the cooperatives in a given republic were managed by members of the titular national ethnic group, but for the purposes of this preliminary analysis the large nontitular minority populations, such as ethnic Russians in Estonia, Kazakhstan, and Ukraine, can be considered of secondary importance.) A multiplicative regression of this ratio on the rate of urbanization in each republic produced a fairly strong positive correlation (coefficient = +.68586; r^2 = 47.0 percent; p = .00476). Elimination of the Armenian case, which constituted an outlier (a point far removed from the curve), produced an even better fit (+.707914, 50.1 percent, and .00461, respectively). Other social indicators in the various republics, such as average levels of education or the extent of ownership of foreign goods, might well have been more highly correlated with the propensity to form cooperatives, but a single indicator, the rate of urbanization, proved significant, as it accounted for almost half of the variation in ratios of cooperatives to population in all fifteen republics and over half after the removal of the Armenian outlier.8 This pattern recalled the uneven geographical distribution of corporate headquarters and the high index of entrepreneurial and managerial activity by Armenians in the imperial Russian economy before World War I, discussed in Chapters 2 and 3.

The rapid proliferation of cooperatives reflected two features of the economy under perestroika: the highly developed system of black marketeering, which immediately took advantage of the legalization of commerce; and the strong geographic concentration of cooperatives, which echoed prerevolutionary patterns. In the Brezhnev period, according to one expert on crime, black marketeers plied their trade with special zeal in Moscow, Leningrad, Riga, Vilnius, Odessa, Tbilisi, Baku, and Tashkent. Five of these eight cities had ranked in the top ten as centers of corporate management in 1914. (Warsaw and Lodz no longer qualified for this list because they lay outside the Soviet state after World War I.) As Hedrick Smith aptly described the process, "Entrepreneurs came out of the woodwork, especially in the Baltic republics, in Soviet Georgia, and in big cities such as Moscow and Leningrad, where illegal enterprises had been concentrated."[9]

As had happened 120 years earlier in the case of commercial banks, the explosion of new enterprises so alarmed the government that it responded by imposing restrictions that temporarily drove down the number of existing enterprises. The upward trend resumed by mid-1990, but until the end of the Soviet period cooperatives did not pose an institutional threat to the planned economy, as they accounted for only 4 percent of economic activity in ruble terms in late 1989. "Their role in causing inflation and shortages was infinitesimal compared with the role played by production problems in the state sector and by government fiscal and wage policies."[10]

As a member of the Central Committee told Smith in early 1990, cooperatives encountered opposition in a variety of forms: "ideological, economic, and personal." Besides the Communist Party, the labor unions, and nostalgic Stalinists who opposed the market on ideological grounds and out of fear of losing political power, the opponents included those who felt their economic interests to be threatened, from workers to managers and planners.[11] Officials opposed to cooperatives quickly tried to discredit them with accusations of criminal activity on the part of the new enterprises.

The case of the Tekhnika (Technique) cooperative clearly revealed the effectiveness of this smear campaign. Created by Artem Tarasov, the so-called honest millionaire, this cooperative worked closely with the Soviet Ministry for Foreign Economic Relations to import computers from the West in exchange for exported raw materials and scrap metals. So efficient was Tekhnika that it sold the imported computers and its own software to dozens of customers, including the space research agency and the State Committee for Supply (Gossnab), at half the price charged by the state's own agencies. Although the cooperative made impressive profits, which it duly deposited in the State Bank, the bank refused to allow Tarasov to withdraw his deposits on demand. Additional audits led the authorities to accuse him of having sold strategic material abroad. Its assets frozen, Tekhnika failed to meet all its contractual obligations and suspended operations.

In late 1990, the State Arbitration Agency (Gosarbitrazh) ruled in favor of Tekhnika,[12] but Tarasov's fortunes continued to decline. In early 1991, a presidential decree authorized "unannounced searches" of any cooperative or corporation. As an American reporter noted, "People involved in business say that the authorities cannot—or will not—recognize the difference between a capitalist and a crook and that well-intentioned deals and dealers are becoming the victims of ever-changing laws and ideologies." Tarasov, having created Tekhnika as "a kind of laboratory for new inventions," also established the Istok (Source) cooperative, which arranged commercial deals between Soviet manufacturers and foreign suppliers. Without specifying the nature of the charges against Tarasov, who held a seat in the Russian Parliament, the Soviet authorities spoke "conspiratorially and sketchily about Tarasov business associates leading a nationwide network involving weapons and currency violations and murder." This harassment caused Tarasov to lose faith in perestroika by the spring of 1991. "Once I thought I could help change this country. Now I feel like a superfluous man."[13]

Early in 1991, Tarasov flew to "self-imposed exile" in Paris, and within a year, from an office in London, he was helping Russian businessmen export cash to avoid governmental controls. The capital thus diverted from the Russian economy to safe havens in the West was estimated to exceed eight billion dollars, the entire amount of Western aid sent to Russia in 1992.[14]

Despite the apparently legal nature of Tarasov's operations before his departure, Soviet officials who alleged criminality on the part of cooperatives in order to disparage them often had some justification for doing so. A notorious case of illegal activity by a cooperative caused "a major foreign trade scandal" in early 1990. The cooperative called ANT (Avtomatika-Nauka-Tekhnika, or Automation-Science-Technique) earned large amounts of foreign currency by exporting heavy equipment under a special authorization from the chairman of the Soviet Council of Ministers, Nikolai Ryzhkov, without the usual import and export licenses. Large crates supposedly filled with earthmoving machinery turned out to hold a dozen T-72 tanks bound for a member of the NATO alliance (presumably France), in violation of Soviet law. According to the official version of events, "only the vigilance of the KGB prevented a major breach of national security." For their part, ANT officials claimed to be victims of an artificial scandal that the authorities created to provide a pretext for closing the cooperative.[15]

Anatolii Sobchak, then a liberal member of the Congress of People's Deputies, at first considered the scandal an attack orchestrated by the "Stalinists," led by Ivan Polozkov, "to discredit Gorbachev while at the same time smearing the whole cooperative movement." The opponents of ANT referred to it "as a cooperative venture rather than a state-run concern, a swipe at the democrats who were promoting the co-op movement." Eventually, however, Sobchak obtained access to documentation of ANT's illegal dealings. An unnamed economic expert explained that the enterprise's exemption from customs inspections gave it "virtually unlimited opportunities for conducting barter transactions and the unlicensed export of raw materials. . . . The ANT is in no way a phenomenon of the market economy, but an offspring of the bureaucratic class, who use state-run channels for personal enrichment. . . . The state-run channels of raw materials allocation are being used by the state bureaucracy as sources of personal wealth." Sobchak's parliamentary investigation of ANT's illegal exports embarrassed Prime Minister Ryzhkov.[16]

It is difficult to ascertain whether such speculation and criminal activity by cooperatives justified what one observer called the "general witch-hunt atmosphere." There is little doubt, however, that the inefficiencies of the planned economy opened up multiple opportunities for quick profit-taking by unscrupulous cooperative managers:

> The most profitable ventures have typically involved, to one degree or another, arbitrage profits from the diversion of state resources at low or negligible prices to the private sector. Perhaps the most profitable and popular activity of Soviet cooperatives is to pump (*perekachat'*) money illegally from earmarked blocked investment funds into cash through the cover of a contract between a cooperative and a state enterprise. A state enterprise pays the cooperative out of its blocked investment funds or earmarked bank credit, which the latter organization can withdraw as cash. A serious argument can be made that activity in the private sector has generally contributed to the current economic crisis. Efforts have been diverted away from value-adding activities to arbitrage and tax evasion, which has polarized income distribution. As [legal] market activity has expanded in the USSR, it has tended to take the form that [illegal] market activity took in the past: personal ties and income hidden from the government.[17]

Profitable relationships between state enterprises and cooperatives did not necessarily entail corruption or illegality, however. Because of lax legislation,

> firms in the private sector have much more opportunities for price setting and conversion of money from bank accounts into cash. On this basis a mutually beneficial symbiosis of state enterprises and private firms emerges. Private firms receive access to cheap resources through state enterprises; state enterprise managers, in their turn, receive opportunities to redistribute income to salaries through private firms. A large number of cooperatives and joint ventures are organized on the basis of state enterprise and use their resources, equipment, and workers for the fulfillment of orders which they receive from the same enterprises. . . . Expenditures remain state, while profit becomes private.

Moreover, cooperatives used "industrial espionage" to acquire and sell various inventions and other forms of intellectual property created by state enterprises.[18]

Allegations of criminality thus had some validity. Abundant evidence shows that organized crime used the cooperatives as a vehicle for the legalization of previously illegal activities and as a convenient camouflage for continued theft. However, many cooperatives fell easily into the opposite role, that of victims of organized crime, which saw in legally constituted cooperatives a rich new source of extorted capital. "The Soviet criminal mafia—'racketeers' in current Soviet parlance—singled out cooperatives as a target for attack, on the assumption (often correctly) that large sums of cash were there for the taking."[19] Knowing full well the negative attitudes of local officials and the weak development of the rule of law in Soviet political culture, the "mafia" found it easy to demand "protection money" or outright participation in cooperatives. (The untranslated word *mafiia* entered the Russian language from the Italian at this time.)

For their part, cooperative managers faced the choice of capitulation or risking arson, physical assault, kidnapping, or murder. Although some cooperatives hired guards, often unemployed veterans of the ill-fated Afghanistan campaign, the danger added major costs to the already risky ventures. According to one source, 20 percent of cooperative managers had bodyguards. The police proved helpless to curb criminal attacks on cooperatives. In fact, according to one manager, "The police do not much care; in a way, the racketeers are doing their work, as they repress the [alleged] cheats."[20]

Accusations of criminality on the part of cooperatives smacked of hypocrisy for several reasons. First, illegality had permeated the Soviet political and economic bureaucracy for decades before Gorbachev launched his reforms. A recent analysis of crimes committed by members of the Communist Party of the Soviet Union in the quarter-century following the fall of Khrushchev in 1964 found evidence in the Soviet economy of an "extremely high level of informal and illegal entrepreneurial activity," including hoarding, exaggeration of procurement requests, false accounting procedures, and the use of "expediters" (*tolkachi*) to locate essential raw materials. Perpetrators received light punishments because such crimes facilitated the production and delivery of goods in short supply. In contrast, embezzlement and other crimes that enriched the criminal instead of promoting the operations of the enterprise or the ministry earned harsh punishments. Aware that routine corruption would alleviate the bureaucratic irrationalities of the autocratic system, the Soviet government condoned "the development of a number of informal institutional arrangements that were perceived by the Soviet leadership to perform positive functions for the Soviet state" despite their formal illegality. Some political scientists have applied to this kind of corruption the label "functional dysfunctionality." "Illegal activities based on the pecuniary self-interest of the Soviet official were punished more often and more severely than those illegal activities of Soviet officials aimed at rationalising the irregularities of the formal Soviet institutions."[21]

Third, the specter of crime served as a useful rhetorical device but cannot be considered the main reason for bureaucratic repression of the cooperatives. The danger posed by cooperatives to the entrenched elite lay elsewhere: in the threat to the bureaucracy's political monopoly. Using the pretext of illegality of cooperative enterprise, the Soviet ministries imposed all sorts of restrictions, ranging from a ban on all publishing not related to "advertising and information" (a prohibition evaded by strange combinations of pornography and advertisements—for cooperatives—in the same periodical) to the right of local soviets to prohibit cooperatives from purchasing raw materials in retail or wholesale markets. Such prohibitions had the unexpected effect of driving cooperatives into close alliances with powerful state enterprises.[22]

Local officials showed special enthusiasm in the repression of cooperatives. Although the law of May 26, 1988, required the "automatic" registration of any cooperatives created to pursue a legal function, local authorities often "added demands that went beyond those outlined in the law." Interviews with cooperative managers revealed that delays in obtaining permission commonly ranged from six to eighteen months, often on the false pretext that no premises were available for the new enterprise. Bribery became "the only recourse" in such cases.[23]

Thus, the traditional struggle between the state and market had become, by 1988, a three-way rivalry between the reformist center, the conservative ministerial and local elites, and the wary public.[24] The situation grew especially murky as local officials joined criminals in extorting bribes from cooperatives. The bureaucracy thereby contributed to crime instead of to its reduction. One Soviet newspaper quoted an unidentified "millionaire" who denounced the "bureaucratic racket" that preyed on the cooperatives:

> Of each ruble that we earn, we spend 40 kopeks to buy raw materials, 5 to 10 on wages; then we pay 15 kopeks to the boss of the enterprise that supplies us, 5 kopeks to its workers, and 5 kopeks to the police so that they will close their eyes. For us, there remains a profit of 15 to 20 kopeks to reinvest. Of every ruble that we earn, we would prefer to pay 30 kopeks directly to the state if it could protect us from corruption.[25]

A quarter of the profits illegally purchased benevolence from the two forces that held potentially fatal power: suppliers and the police. To gain such security legally would be worth an additional 5 percent, but the level of legality deteriorated, rather than increased, as time went on.

One manager of a construction cooperative responded to the inhospitable environment with a clever trick: the creation of two separate cooperatives, one in ceramics, the other in metal stamping. These he alternately opened and closed in order to evade confiscatory taxes: 25 percent of gross revenues, 13 percent of the manager's salary, and 12 percent of each worker's pay, for social security. Having two cooperatives allowed him to neglect the affairs of one at any given moment, so that it amassed a small profit and therefore bore a small tax burden. Despite this clever ruse, he still found it necessary to hide some of his income; otherwise, his labor would produce no net profit. Thus, tax evasion continued to pervade the cooperative sector. The general picture remained a somber one. A French scholar concluded her account, based on numerous interviews with cooperative members, with the sad observation that "a completely honest cooperative member certainly does not exist because he would not be able to survive."[26]

By 1988, the processes of official repression and illegal maneuvers by cooperative managers had taken on the familiar shape of a vicious circle. The official campaign to cripple the cooperatives gathered momentum in December of that year, when the Council of Ministers banned cooperatives from certain kinds of activity: the management of private schools, the making or selling of videocassettes, the operation of broadcasting networks, the provision of certain kinds of medical care (cancer treatment, drug production, and surgery), and the manufacture of weapons, ammunition, alcohol, narcotics, and jewelry composed of precious metals.[27] Equally harsh were the special tax schedules imposed on cooperatives at the end of the decade. The Presidium of the USSR Supreme Soviet, acting on a suggestion of the Ministry of Finance, began the campaign in March 1988. The lenient income tax on cooperatives as institutions (2–3 percent in the first year, 3–5 percent in the second year, and 10 percent in the third year) remained unchanged, but the ministry set highly progressive rates for members of cooperatives: 50 percent on monthly earnings above 700 rubles, 70 percent above 1,000 rubles, and 90 percent above 1,500 rubles. As Shmelev and Popov commented wryly, "There is probably no example of such a sharply graded income tax in economic history." (Under NEP, rates had remained far lower: 30 percent on income over 24,000 rubles per year, roughly equivalent to 70,000 in the late 1980s.) The "public outcry" that greeted this decree led the Supreme Soviet to refuse ratification.[28]

Suspended in July, the decree was eventually annulled, but early in 1989 the Ministry of Finance authorized each republic to set its own tax rates. It also gave local soviets the option of reducing or eliminating the tax burden on the gross income of individual cooperatives (excluding production expenses but not wage and salary costs), but since the taxes collected by the local soviets were to be spent by them, they had little incentive to grant such tax relief. Following the promulgation of widely varying tax rates at the republic level, some of which appeared confiscatory, the Supreme Soviet set a maximum income tax rate at 23 percent for cooperatives that set their prices at or below those of the state, and 35 percent for others. Higher rates were permitted for cooperatives that had received the brunt of official and public scorn: those in commerce, food service, entertainment, and business mediation. The republics promulgated new rates in the fall of 1989. Finally, all enterprises, whether cooperative or state-owned, became subject to maximum tax rates—45 percent of profits—in June 1990, effective January 1991. Again, enterprises in commerce, food service, and entertainment could be subjected to higher rates.[29]

On the local level as well, the campaign of local officials against cooperatives forced many vulnerable enterprises to close. Others withdrew from public scrutiny and ensured stable supplies of raw materials by strengthening their ties with state enterprises. "By mid-1990 the proportion of cooperatives attached to state enterprises had reportedly increased to 86%." By mid-1990, the official persecution had affected the sectoral distribution of cooperatives. Those in consumer services, trade, and restaurant management declined in response to the heavy burden of income taxes and a resolution of the Supreme Soviet in October 1989 that prevented cooperatives "from purchasing goods from state stores or wholesale trade and then reselling the goods."[30] At the same time, the number of cooperatives in construction grew rapidly and those in other fields continued their modest increase. (See Figure 4.2; not shown in this graph are the numbers of cooperatives in medicine and recycling, which hovered near 3,000.)

Cooperatives in consumer goods production, retail trade, and restaurant management proved vulnerable not only to criminal extortion and official harassment but also to violent attacks from the public at large. The official campaign against cooperatives therefore drew support from significant groups in Soviet society. Although the term "public opinion" had little meaning in the era of party-state controls, the relaxation of censorship under Gorbachev permitted open discussion of major issues to an extent unprecedented in Soviet and Russian history. It is impossible to ascertain precisely the ideological and economic sources of the public disapproval of cooperatives. To some extent, they appeared to pose an economic threat to the potential losers in the new market-driven economy: unskilled workers, pensioners, students, and others who derived some benefits from the Soviet policies of full employment and subsidized prices for food and shelter, however poor the quality. As Shmelev and Popov noted in 1988, the prospect that a free market might require workers to endure lower wages, to find a new job, a new place to live, or even a new occupation, or—worst of all—to face the nightmare of extended unemployment, unknown in the previous six decades, all raised the level of public concern. They warned that if Gorbachev's reforms did not show "something substantial" by way of improved economic conditions "in the next year or two, the fate of *perestroika* could be in jeopardy."[31]

By 1990, of course, the economic situation had deteriorated, not improved. Cooperatives bore little responsibility for the disintegration of the Soviet economy, a phenomenon that Marshall I. Goldman called "a supply-side depression" because it resulted from the collapse of the old system of centralized command and control. A Soviet expert analyzed the economic crisis in terms of its most important components: the disruption of imports, the decrease in production of fuel and raw materials, the decline in employment, the deterioration of fixed capital, high levels of military spending, and mushrooming budget deficits. Significantly, he placed no blame on the cooperatives.[32]

Chronic shortages forced everyone into the black market to some extent. A major effort at quantification, based largely on data provided by émigré Soviet citizens in the late 1970s, showed the considerable proportion of illegal activity to which ordinary people resorted in their search for income and purchases.[33] Like the political scientists who employed the term "functional dysfunctionality" to explain the pervasiveness of officially sanctioned crime, an astute American journalist resorted to an oxymoron in an attempt to explain the general public's ambivalence toward economic crime two years before perestroika began:

> Because so much of ordinary life is enveloped in vast areas of illegality and because "speculation" is vilified in the official press as bourgeois, nearly anti-Soviet, this synthetic crime of private buying and selling becomes both serious and light, grave and ubiquitous. It stirs both revulsion and a sly, winking envy. And the concept of crime thus becomes blurred, disorienting, until synthetic crime and genuine crime fade in and out of one another, melting into a vague mash of disreputable acceptability.[34]

Although virtually everyone traded on the black market, the constant barrage of official condemnation in the state-controlled media continued to undermine the respectability of private gain once the laws on private economic activity and cooperatives made it legal. Vitalii Korotich, editor of *Ogonek* (The Little Fire) magazine, sought in 1990 to legitimize the phrase "private property" (*chastnaia sobstvennost'*), which included not only "personal property" (*lichnaia sobstvennost'*), such as clothing, furniture, and books, but also real estate and workshops: the means of production. "We have used it in our articles about the struggle for independence. . . . Without private property you can't have independence." For his outspoken journalism, including his exposure of brutality in the ranks of the Soviet Army, Korotich received death threats.[35]

Smith, reporting from the Soviet Union at the height of perestroika, employed a colorful phrase to portray the depth of popular resentment against cooperatives and the nouveaux-riches in Soviet society under perestroika: "the culture of envy." In this, he followed the terminology of Shmelev, who wrote in 1988 that "the blind, burning envy of your neighbor's success . . . has become the most powerful brake on the ideas and practice of *perestroika*. . . . Unless we at least damp down this envy, the success of *perestroika* will always be in jeopardy." For her part, the eminent sociologist Tat'iana Zaslavskaia attributed such envy to the dictatorship of Stalin, which had "turned the Soviet worker into a robot" and created a state structure that "literally dwarfed the individual." Before cooperatives became legal, she wrote, "family contract teams in agriculture" had been allowed to perform designated tasks for a negotiated fee and often, through hard work, derived considerably high returns, but this form of labor often encountered fierce resistance from peasants on collective farms. Cooperatives faced the same resentment under perestroika.

> This shows that many Soviet people quite simply regard a high income as a negative phenomenon irrespective of whether serious and creative work was done to obtain it and whether it brought great benefit to society. As a survival of the ideology of the 1920s and 1930s, this kind of wariness in respect of high earnings does not reflect the interests of our society and undermines the possibility of a more rapid pace of social and economic development.[36]

A French expert likewise saw in the public's resentment the effects of sixty years of Soviet indoctrination in the values of egalitarianism. "For some, the secret of happiness consists not in personal success but in lowering of their neighbor to the same level." The quest for profit appeared "a suspicious desire to separate oneself from the collective." In her opinion, considerable time would be needed for Soviet citizens "to relearn how to work."[37]

However severe the Stalinist repression of individual initiative, the situation appeared more serious than these analysts implied. It was not a matter of six decades but of centuries. Smith recognized that this attitude had roots in the prerevolutionary past, long before the Soviet government had begun to preach the evils of social and economic inequality. "The Russians are a long-suffering people who can bear the pain of their misery, so long as they see that others are sharing it. The collective jealousy can be fierce against those who rise above the crowd." This "culture of envy," the product not only of the ideological controls of the Soviet state but also of "the deep-seated collectivism in Russian life, . . . has turned rancid under the misery of everyday living" in the 1980s. In a gruesome example of this mentality, Anatolii Sobchak, the reformist mayor of Leningrad, related the parable of God's offer to give a Russian peasant anything he desired, on condition that his neighbor receive twice as much. Torn between greed and envy, the peasant finally opted for the latter: "Strike out one of my eyes."[38]

The collectivist mentality of Russian peasants long before 1917 has, of course, received attention from ethnologists and historians. The Slavophiles saw in this mentality evidence of a generous Christian spirit untainted by European rationalism, but their view was excessively tinged by a romantic nationalism that exaggerated the peasantry's devotion to Christian morality. Far more persuasive was Edward L. Keenan's anthropological explanation, which located the roots of communal values—the need to share both the rewards and the burdens of life—in the harsh northern climate and the limited productivity of the soil. Only if all members of the community utilized their land, animals, and labor to the maximum extent would the desolate environment of the Eurasian plain yield a surplus. A widow would be obliged to marry a bachelor farmer for the sake of the village as well as her children, lest her labor power and that of her meager livestock go unused. Conversely, a healthy husband and wife blessed by fate with a large family and a cow or two would be expected to bear the responsibilities of providing charity for the destitute or of representing the village to the hostile forces of the outside world: the landlord, the tax collector, and the recruiting agent.

Communal constraints promoted not the realization of a concept of justice, nor economic progress, nor even

> "the preservation of a way of life," but the preservation of life itself—human life, the life of vital livestock, the life of life-giving field cultures. And the most significant autonomous actor in peasant life was not the individual (who could not survive alone in this environment), and not even the nuclear family (which, in extended form, was marginally viable, but still too vulnerable to disease and sudden calamity), but the village, to whose interests all others were in the end subordinated.

The economic consequences were clear. Unlike the capitalist mentality, which accepted a certain amount of risk for the sake of a potentially large gain in the future, the bleak realities of the Russian village encouraged the opposite: "the minimization of risk." "If innovation offered short-term improvements in the standard of living at the cost of an increased risk of possible disaster, it was rejected. If the interests of an individual reduced the potential viability of the group, they were denied." A strong and competent individual who grew moderately prosperous but refused to share his resources with his fellow villagers represented a threat to "the tenuous continuity of village life."[39]

The negative effects of this communal mentality on the development of Russian capitalism attracted the attention of most observers in the era of perestroika. However, Keenan's analysis of the traditional collectivism of the village was value-neutral. Indeed, attitudes that partisans of capitalism found to be selfish and inimical to economic progress in the 1980s were precisely those that had permitted the village to survive over the centuries.

Keenan's general account has been supplemented by recent research that illuminates important regional variations of this pattern, changes over time, and evidence of the commune's flexibility in the face of new and demonstrably superior technology. Esther Kingston-Mann, for example, concluded that communal landholding in the decades after Emancipation did not necessarily stifle technological innovation. "The commune sometimes provided a convenient mechanism for the implementation of community-wide innovation; its powers of compulsion were used to compel change as well as to block it." She also observed that the poverty of the Russian village could not be attributed solely to the allegedly stifling incentive system maintained by the commune because any innovations in peasant agriculture had to be carried out within unfavorable "geographical and political constraints." The northern climate imposed severe limitations on the fertility of the soil and the length of the growing season; and the tsarist government bore primary responsibility for insufficient land allotments, high redemption payments, and the heavy tax burden, all of which limited the peasants' prosperity.[40]

In the six centuries that elapsed between the rise of the Muscovite state in the fourteenth century and the relaxation of the Soviet autocracy under Gorbachev, individualism and its eventual economic concomitant, market-based capitalism, remained weak in Russian culture. Traditionally, Russians equated trade and industry with pure greed. Of aristocratic origin, the stereotype of the "dirty" or "filthy" (*griaznyi*) merchant[41] figured prominently in the dramas of Aleksandr N. Ostrovskii, who depicted the Moscow merchants in the mid-nineteenth century as coarse, venal, proud, and domineering. Although this image faded toward the end of the tsarist period as leading merchants became patrons of high culture and participants in municipal and national politics, the negative stereotype lived on in literary portrayals of provincial merchants, such as the miserly grain miller who begrudged his aged mother twenty kopeks in Anton Chekhov's short story "At the Mill" (1886).

Bonds of communal solidarity began to loosen as market forces entered the Russian village toward the end of the tsarist period, but Stalin's revolution from above during the First Five-Year Plan (1928–32) wiped out the modest gains of the 1920s and prevented peasant entrepreneurs from reaping the benefits of their labor. At the same time, the "peasants" and "sons of peasants" who rose by the millions into positions of power "in politics, in art, in literature, in science" imparted to the entire Soviet system its peculiarly communal nature as they "practiced the traditional habits of risk-avoidance and the subjection of the individual will and impulse—including one's own—to the interests of the group."[42] To the three categories of opposition to cooperatives already mentioned—the ideological, economic, and personal—must therefore be added a fourth: the communal.

The prospect of market reforms filled most Russians with horror in the late 1980s. The market threatened massive unemployment and social inequality, or at least a more public inequality than that created by Stalin and maintained in the secret system of privileges enjoyed by the Soviet party-state elite between 1930 and 1985. As a reformist economist complained, no one wished to live without subsidized prices. "This is the kind of 'market' that we have imagined. Like a rose without thorns. But such a plant does not exist in nature. The market is a rose with thorns." Only in the Soviet Union, he noted with exasperation, or perhaps Albania, did such "strong 'anti-market' feelings" exist.[43]

A service worker in Volgograd in the mid-1980s denounced the wealth of her neighbor as eloquently as any Russian peasant alive in the past seven centuries: "I don't want to live like her. I want her to live like me."[44] Spontaneous resistance to the market based on this culture of communal envy took the form of random violence against cooperatives.

"Throughout the USSR, cooperative enterprises became the object of envy, and many were damaged, burned down, or destroyed by 'indignant citizens.'" In a typical case, in Balashikha district near Moscow, a cooperative pig farm that had begun to prosper by selling meat to the new restaurants in Moscow encountered hostility from local peasants. Ignoring the foul odor of the city dump, the peasants complained about the smell of the pig farm and asked for compensation in the form of meat at low prices. "It was a pure case of blackmail." An investigation showed that the farm produced no excessive noises or odors. However, after the owners of the cooperative persisted in their refusal to provide cheap meat to their neighbors, fires broke out. Eventually, the farm burned to the ground. *Moscow News* reported that the peasants "openly rejoiced at the fire and, making no secret of it, feel like the victors of the conflict with the cooperators. This is the most distressing and disturbing thing."[45]

To make matters worse, some cooperative managers became the object of spontaneous violence not only because of their wealth but also because of their status as ethnic minorities in some of the Soviet republics. "Much of the violence against cooperatives in Central Asia had an ethnic undercurrent; special targets for attack were cooperatives run by traders from the Caucasus," presumably Armenians and Georgians, whose unusually high rates of participation in cooperatives were suggested in Figure 4.1. During ethnic riots in Turkmenistan in May 1989, cooperatives received special attention. In Novyi Uzen, Kazakhstan, the following month, mobs destroyed twenty-seven cooperatives and killed eleven of their workers, prompting the authorities to close all commercial and food-service cooperatives in the region.[46]

By 1990, the cooperative movement had reached a plateau. Threats of intimidation from criminals and the harassment of officials and envious neighbors drove many cooperatives out of business. As under the tsarist regime, managers of cooperatives complained that "the chief problems they face arise from inconsistent and unstable government regulation."[47] The population ecology of cooperatives in the USSR displayed two structural features of corporate ecology in the tsarist period: numerical weakness and geographical concentration. Gorbachev's attempt to resurrect Bukharin's sixty-year-old vision of the cooperative as a stepping-stone to socialist communal solidarity had failed.

According to one expert's estimate in mid-1992, half of all cooperatives had gone bankrupt in the economic turmoil that followed the abortive coup and the disintegration of the Soviet Union. "Certainly, the private sector has suffered while the state sector was able to get benefits from the government," declared Evgenii Iasin, head of economic research for the Russian Union of Industrialists and Entrepreneurs.[48] The importance of the cooperatives lay elsewhere: they served as the first step in the revival of a capitalist market, weak though it may have been in 1991. In their definitive study of Soviet cooperatives, Jones and Moskoff cited the prediction of a leader of the cooperative movement to the effect that cooperatives would cease to be the dominant form of enterprise soon after the legalization of all forms of private business. He estimated that half of the cooperatives would take the form of "purely private businesses," and one-third, presumably the largest, would become corporations, leaving only about one-sixth as cooperatives. "If this were to occur, then the cooperative movement would have had a relatively short life-span, but its importance historically would have been enormous. The energy, initiative, and perseverance of the nation's first true entrepreneurs in sixty years enabled the Soviet Union to embark on the road to a new economy."[49]

By 1990, Gorbachev had realized the shortcomings of the experiment in cooperatives and had resolved to introduce the corporate form of enterprise, complete with the legal principle of limited liability and the implied diminution of the scope of state planning. In response to the new legislation, entrepreneurs shifted their attention from cooperatives to corporations. However, Gorbachev's effort to employ the corporate form of enterprise met with little success in the brief period between the legalization of corporations in mid-1990 and the disintegration of the Soviet Union at the end of the following year.

Corporations and Exchanges

Gorbachev first attempted to invigorate large-scale industry and trade by a timid half-measure: the Law on the State Enterprise, which took effect in January 1988. Only after the deterioration of the economy had reached serious proportions, in June 1990, did his government issue a genuine corporate law. Shortly thereafter, in December 1990, the Russian Republic, led by Boris N. Yeltsin, set legal norms far less stringent than those of the Soviet law. The government of Lithuania had already implemented a sweeping reform in June 1990. By mid-1991, just a few months prior to the collapse of the Soviet Union, banks and corporations had begun to proliferate. However, the patterns of incorporation at the end of the Soviet period echoed those of the tsarist period: tiny numbers, geographical concentration in the capital (now Moscow), the heavy influence of state bureaucrats in new corporations, the weakness of legal norms regulating corporations and exchanges, and the shortage of investment capital. The Soviet flag over the Kremlin came down for the last time at the end of 1991, but the debilitating struggle over economic reform between Yeltsin and his parliament, the Congress of People's Deputies, continued even after the ratification of the new constitution and the election of the bicameral legislature in December 1993. A glance at the capitalist institutions that had emerged by that date serves to underline how little Gorbachev had accomplished by 1991.

The Law on the State Enterprise, promulgated in 1987, had heralded Gorbachev's intention to abandon Stalin's policy of hypercentralization. However, in the three years that elapsed between January 1988 and the end of the USSR in December 1991, the law had failed to solve the economic dilemmas of incomplete monitoring and ineffective incentives. It allowed managers to make contracts with suppliers and customers outside the plan, but it reserved a substantial share of output—70 to 85 percent, according to some reports—for state orders (*goszakazy*) under the old system. It turned out that managers found state orders less risky to fulfill than others because they lacked experience in market relations.

Even those managers who complied with the main thrust of the law paradoxically contributed to the breakdown of the Soviet distribution system. The law sought to improve efficiency by adopting "full cost-accounting" (*polnyi khozraschet*), under which managers sought to place their enterprises on a firm financial foundation by obtaining profits from contracts with other enterprises, thereby reducing the role of state financing. However, managers who shifted to profitable lines of production tended to ignore the need of traditional customers for inexpensive products. In an effort "to finance all expenditures out of revenues, including wages, replacement of fixed capital and net investment," they stressed the maximization of profits in the short term. They also neglected not only the needs of their former customers but also the long-term financial health of their own enterprises as they reduced investment in equipment, placed a low priority on job safety and training, and discriminated against workers deemed less productive than average: the young, the handicapped, and women of child-bearing age.[50] Despite these efforts to reduce production costs, the new system offered no solution to the endemic problems of faulty data and weak incentives in the economy at large. One expert characterized as a form of "serfdom" the state's continued controls over enterprises, epitomized by articles in the law that imposed mandatory state orders, budgetary restraints, and assignments of specific customers to manufacturers.[51]

One astute analyst concluded that the fatal flaw in Gorbachev's program of perestroika, exemplified by the Law on the State Enterprise, consisted in its attempt to employ "so-called 'market mechanisms,' but without the actual introduction of a market, predicated, as the latter must be, upon exchange between independent commodity producers." This reluctance to embrace the market revealed, in turn, the Soviet policymakers' ultimate concern: to reduce any threat to their "hold on power, which could no longer be guaranteed under a system of private ownership of the means of production." The provisions of the law calling for a thorough democratization of each enterprise, including the election of the manager, recalled the socialist verbiage of the early Bolshevik era but appear not to have been implemented. At the end of 1989, only 8.5 percent of Soviet enterprises had made the transition to full cost-accounting and only another 4 percent operated on the basis of leases. Although these percentages were expected to grow in 1990, and although "some enterprises used the new system to good advantage, achieving considerable improvements in quality, productivity, and wages, often with substantial redundancies" (firings of employees), the economic situation deteriorated rapidly. Gorbachev's partial price liberalization and the weakening of central control—the planning and administrative mechanisms that had held the economy together since the inauguration of the five-year plans—began to cause distortions. By mid-1990, massive budget deficits and shortages had triggered strikes in coal mines, and a general malaise.

Only at this point did Gorbachev resolve to embrace the quintessentially capitalist institution. In mid-1990, he issued what amounted to a capitulation to capitalist ideology: the legalization of the corporation. As one expert observed: "It was clear that an attempt at a complete transition to the market, and the restoration of some form of capitalist economy which this inevitably would entail, was unavoidable. *Perestroika,* at least in its original conception, was over."[52]

The Soviet corporate law of June 4, 1990, officially called the Law on Enterprises in the USSR, attempted to blend two fundamentally opposed principles: that of production and commerce for personal profit and the opposite notion of the satisfaction of all basic needs of the larger society and the work force under the traditional Soviet ideology.[53] The law and Gorbachev's policy address of October 1990 offered abundant evidence that he saw no contradiction between these two facets of the law. Article 1, Section 2 specifically allowed economic activity by enterprises for the purposes of "profit." These provisions demonstrated an accommodation to market principles that no previous Soviet leader had dared to make since the 1920s.

In several respects, Gorbachev's corporate law followed the tsarist corporate law, as in the dual terminology for company (*obshchestvo*) and partnership (*tovarishchestvo,* Art. 2, Sec. 1) and words for charter (*ustav,* Art. 9), securities (*tsennye bumagi,* Art. 12), council (*sovet*), and board of directors (*pravlenie,* Art. 18). However, on the crucial issue of registration of a new enterprise, the law abolished the high administrative threshold—incorporation by a separate legislative act for each new enterprise—that had characterized Russian corporate law in the centuries before 1917 and in the 1920s. After registration with local authorities, each enterprise was to be recorded in a national "state register" within ten days. Officials could refuse to register an enterprise only if its articles of incorporation failed to comply with existing laws. "Refusal of state registration of an enterprise on grounds of the inadvisability of the enterprise shall not be permitted" (Art. 6, Sec. 3).[54] Indeed, the founders of an enterprise had the right to take action in court in cases of refusal that they considered "groundless." With these two sentences, Gorbachev's government broke with centuries of bureaucratic arbitrariness in the administration of the corporation.

Many articles of the law granted an important role to existing Soviet institutions, including state-owned enterprises. Several provisions of the law proceeded logically from the Law on State Enterprises of 1987: that every enterprise should endeavor to operate on the basis of full cost-accounting, meaning a lack of state subsidies; that enterprises could be owned not only by individuals, families, cooperatives, and corporations but also by "a state Union enterprise, a state Republic enterprise (of a Union Republic), a state enterprise of an Autonomous Oblast or Autonomous Okrug, or a state municipal enterprise"; and that enterprises had the right to combine into "associations [*ob"edineniia*] according to branch, territorial, or other principles for the coordination of their activity" (Art. 1, Sec. 1; Art. 2, Sec. 1; and Art. 3, Sec. 1). The latter provision appeared especially dubious because the Soviet government had encouraged enterprises to amalgamate into ever larger associations since the 1960s in a vain attempt to improve productivity.[55]

The seven decades of Soviet rule left their mark in other ways. The law specified that enterprises existed to satisfy "the needs of society" and to serve "the social and economic interests of the workers' collective" as well as those of "the owner of the enterprise's property" (Art. 1, Sec. 2). This sentence therefore hinted that the claims of society and the workers took precedence over those of owners. The tsarist and Soviet tradition of state control lurked in the cryptic reference to the "special permission (license)" (Art. 1, Sec. 3, reiterated in Art. 8), that might be necessary if a corporation sought to engage in certain types of economic activities, to be defined by the laws of the USSR and its republics. A particularly ominous provision appeared in the list of grounds for liquidation. These included not only bankruptcy and the invalidity of the corporate charter but also decisions made by political authorities: "on other grounds specified by legislative acts of the USSR and Union and Autonomous Republics" (Art. 37, Sec. 2).

Strong echoes of the Marxist-Leninist ideology persisted as well in the provisions for worker self-management, which denied the absolute value of the principle of private ownership. "The management of the enterprise shall be carried out according to the charter by combining the principles of self-management of the workers' collective and the rights of the owner to the economic use of his property" (Art. 14, Sec. 1). Several provisions (Arts. 14–17, 29) enumerated the rights and responsibilities of the workers' collective, including its role in deciding issues of safety, medical insurance, and vacations for workers. Another bit of nostalgia for Stalinist tutelage appeared in the explicit reference to the many social services that Soviet enterprises had routinely furnished to workers under the five-year plans: "the enterprise may provide material support for workers in medical, child-care, cultural, educational, and sports institutions, in public cafeterias, and in organizations that provide services for the workers' collective [of the enterprise] but do not work for it" (Art. 29, Sec. 6). A crucial difference lay in the fact that these services became optional instead of mandatory, as in the past.

Later that month, on June 19, the Soviet government issued a second law on enterprises specifically directed at corporations: the Regulations on Joint-Stock Companies and Limited Liability Companies.[56] Compared to the legislation of the tsarist state and the Soviet Union during NEP, this law introduced principles of unprecedented liberality. It reiterated the right of founders to create a corporation for any lawful purpose and prohibited the rejection of a corporate charter on the grounds of the "inadvisability of the establishment of the company" (Art. 10). The principle of limited liability appeared in Art. 30: each corporation was liable only to the extent of its property, and "stockholders shall bear losses only to the limit of the value of the shares that belong to them."

Other provisions specified the usual features of a corporation: the division of the basic capital (*ustavnyi fond*) into a certain number of shares (*aktsii*) of equal par value (Art. 30); the establishment of reasonably low minima of 500,000 rubles for basic capital (Art. 30) and 100 rubles for a share (Art. 31); the issuing of shares by name (*imennye aktsii*) or to bearer (*aktsii na pred"iavitelia*) (Art. 33); the possibility of restrictions on the sale of shares, including the requirement to obtain the consent of the company, when specified in the charter (Art. 34); the option to issue preferred shares, representing up to one-tenth of the basic capital, which gave owners a prior claim on dividends but carried no voting rights unless explicitly granted by the charter (Art. 35); and the right to issue bonds (*obligatsii*), by name or to bearer, in an amount up to one-quarter of the basic capital (Art. 36). If a company failed to sell at least 60 percent of its initial share offering within six months of chartering, it was required to return all cash contributions to shareholders within thirty days (Art. 42).

The structure of decision making also conformed to the usual European pattern, embodied in the tsarist corporate law of 1836. Ultimate power lay with the general assembly of stockholders (*obshchee sobranie aktsionerov*), in which persons representing 60 percent of the voting rights constituted a quorum (Art. 49). A three-quarters majority vote was required to establish a corporation, to elect the initial council and board, to amend the charter, and to liquidate the enterprise or its subsidiaries. Other matters, such as the election of officers, the setting of salary levels, and the approval of contracts with third parties, were to be decided by a simple majority vote (Arts. 49, 50). One share gave one vote, and proxies were allowed (Art. 52).

The general assembly had to meet at least once a year, unless the charter specified otherwise, and a special meeting had to be held when requested by shareholders representing more than 20 percent of the voting rights (Art. 53). The supervisory council (*nabliudatel'nyi sovet*) set general policy guidelines (Art. 54) and hired the board of directors (*pravlenie*), the executive organ that managed the day-to-day affairs of the enterprise (Art. 55). The audit commission (*revizionnaia komissiia*), to be composed of elected stockholders and workers, examined the company's records. An audit had to be conducted whenever requested by the general assembly, the council, the commission itself, or more than 10 percent of the stockholders. Furthermore, "members of the audit commission [were] entitled to participate with an advisory vote in the meetings of the board" (Art. 57). The separation of powers, which included a prohibition on simultaneous membership in both the council and the board by any individual

(Art. 54), was designed to minimize fraud. Additional share issues had to be offered to shareholders before sale to the general public (Art. 58).

Article 63 referred in passing to "an open corporation, the shares of which are distributed by open subscription." Each open company had to publish an annual report no later than the first quarter of every year, including the findings of the audit commission; and all corporations and their executive officials were liable for the truthfulness of the report under Soviet law. Although the law did not mention the obvious corollary, the "closed corporation," some enterprises took that form by distributing shares among founders and acquaintances, not to the public at large. Article 63 implied that closed corporations need not publish an annual report.

Besides the ease of incorporation, the only departures from prerevolutionary Russian practice in the Soviet corporate law of June 1990 came in occasional intrusions of Soviet lip service to the ideal of workers' control, as in Article 57 on the participation of workers' representatives in the audit commission. Likewise, Article 54 stated: "The supervisory council may include representatives of the workers' collective, labor unions, and other public organizations." The optional character of this provision constituted an admission, however, of the weakness of the socialist ideal of decentralized industry functioning under the control of workers' councils, an ideal that faded quickly in the chaos of the Bolshevik Revolution and Russian Civil War and never again led the list of priorities of the Soviet Communist Party and the weak Soviet trade unions. The brief mention of the myth of workers' control, which had no intrinsic relationship to the concept of a corporation as an economic unit subject to control by its stockholders, appeared as something of an afterthought inspired more by ideology, or more precisely an echo of ideology, than by practical considerations. (This principle found wider application in a capitalist country, postwar West Germany, in the form of *Mitbestimmung*—the representation of workers on corporate boards—than in the Soviet Union.) If its purpose was to stimulate the allegiance of the Soviet working class to the ideals of corporate capitalism, it failed. (See Chapter 5.)

A special provision (Art. 46) allowed existing state enterprises to transform themselves into corporations if the pertinent ministry and the workers' collective agreed to do so. The task of establishing the value of the basic capital lay with a commission to be composed of representatives of the ministry, the workers, and "financial organs." Needless to say, the valuation of the enterprise would prove difficult in the absence of a genuine market, all the more so because the commission had every incentive to undervalue the enterprise for the benefit of its workers and managers, who would profit from buying it at a low price. Any unsold shares would remain in the hands of the ministry. Because its role in the deliberation of the general assembly of stockholders would reflect the quantity of its shares, this provision ensured a major role for ministries in formally privatized corporations.

This expression of the awesome power of the state constituted more than a form of historical continuity with the Soviet system. The provision for ministerial representation recalled the structure of many Russian railroad companies before 1917, namely those that had fallen into debt to the state. Having obligated itself in the corporate charter to ensure a steady return (usually 5 percent) on all stocks and bonds of the enterprise, the tsarist regime took a special interest in perennially unprofitable railroad companies. Once the debt to the state reached a substantial sum, the ministries of finance and transportation assigned their own representatives to the council of the railroad company, presumably to protect the state's interests.

Whether Gorbachev knew of this arrangement between the tsarist ministries and loss-making railroads is not certain. In any case, this provision, like the law on cooperatives, also recalled the Soviet economic system of the 1920s. Gorbachev seemed to be attempting a resurrection of the economic system of the New Economic Policy, when state control over large enterprises organized as joint-stock companies (*aktsionernye obshchestva*) took the form of shareholding enterprises owned by various ministries and other governmental entities. Market relationships existed among enterprises, each of which was expected to turn a profit by the end of the fiscal year, but the state's monopolies on foreign trade, banking, transportation, and heavy industry created a dense network of price controls. The extent of Gorbachev's indebtedness to NEP—particularly his efforts to encourage cooperatives, to increase the efficiency of state-owned enterprises under the principle of full cost-accounting, and to foster a network of joint-stock enterprises owned largely by ministries, managers, and workers—remains to be determined.

The law of June 19 also legalized the creation of so-called limited-liability companies (*obshchestva s ogranichennoi otvetstvennost'iu*), which issued shares like corporations but, unlike them, generally had few stockholders and undertook restricted operations in keeping with the modest size of their basic capital. (Unless specifically mentioned, all the features of the corporation, such as decision making in accordance with the number of shares owned, also appeared in this section of the law.) In contrast to corporations, which had a basic capital of at least 500,000 rubles (Art. 30), limited-liability companies enjoyed a much smaller minimum capitalization: 50,000 rubles (Art. 66). The principle of limited liability of small enterprises had a long pedigree in Europe. It began in Germany with the legalization of the GmbH (*Gesellschaft mit beschränkter Haftung*) in 1892 and reached France in the form of the SARL (*société à responsabilité limitée*) in 1925. Neither the tsarist nor the Soviet regime had allowed this form of enterprise.

The limited-liability company combined the advantages of both the small firm and the large corporation: flexibility and trust among investor-managers on the one hand and limited liability from financial loss on the other. Its structure, simpler than that of a corporation, vested ultimate authority in the owners themselves, meeting as a group in the "assembly of participants" (*sobranie uchastnikov*), "or their designated representatives" (Art. 74). Shareholders enjoyed the right of first refusal whenever another shareholder desired to sell his or her share (*dolia*) (Art. 67). In the event of the death of a participant (or the dissolution of an organization that acted as a participant), the heirs or successors received the right to join the company, subject to the permission of the company. If either party refused, the heirs or successors received the appropriate portion of shares in cash or kind, and the basic capital of the company was reduced by that amount (Art. 70). This article strongly suggested that family groups were expected to opt for this form of company. Similarly characteristic of the intimate nature of the firm was the necessity of a unanimous vote, with all participants in attendance, on decisions to determine the nature of the enterprise's activity, to amend its charter, and to exclude a participant for having hindered the operations of the enterprise; decisions on all other issues required only a simple majority vote (Arts. 75, 81). Any participant had the right to raise an issue for discussion providing he or she gave twenty-five days' notice (Art. 76). Participants' meetings were required at least twice a year unless otherwise specified in the charter (Art. 77).

Owing to the simplicity of the structure of the enterprise, the executive was to be composed of either one person (a director) or several (a directorate). Responsibility for periodic inspection of the books fell to an audit commission, composed of elected participants and representatives of the workers' collective, as outlined in the charter (Art. 79).

The distinction between two kinds of shares (*doli* and *aktsii*) and shareholders (*uchastniki* and *aktsionery*) in the Soviet corporate law of June 19, 1990, had not previously existed in Russian or Soviet law. *Dolia*, the term specific to the limited-liability company, connoted portion or part, appropriate to a relatively small and simple enterprise; and *uchastnik* meant participant, in the sense of both an investor and a manager. In contrast, *aktsiia* and *aktsioner*, the traditional words in the corporate law of the Russian Empire and the Soviet state, continued the use of familiar financial concepts borrowed from the French in the early nineteenth century.

This terminology appeared significant in two respects. First, the introduction of an entirely new word—*dolia*—into the Russian financial lexicon suggested that the Soviet legislators modeled their new limited-liability company on an existing European institution and simply translated all the key terms. (A close comparison of the law of June 19 with various European laws of the early 1980s would probably reveal which country provided the model.) Second, the most striking feature of the law was the absence of the term *pai* (share) and the various derivatives of that word: shareholder (*paishchik*) and share partnership (*tovarishchestvo na paiakh* or *paevoe tovarishchestvo*). As noted in Chapter 2, the structural distinctions between joint-stock companies and share partnerships in pre-revolutionary Russia had cultural, not legal bases. The tendency of many small, family-centered firms to take the form of share partnerships evidently convinced the tsarist ministers that the limited-liability company, on the model of the GmbH in Germany before World War I, was not needed in Russia.

The theme of workers' participation in management appeared once more in Article 74: "The participants' meeting may include one representative, or, if otherwise provided in the foundation documents, a greater number of representatives, of the workers of the company." As in Article 54, which pertained to workers' representatives on the councils of corporations, Article 74 expressed this notion as an option. Whether or not any limited-liability companies included it in their charters remains an interesting empirical question.

Because the law of June 19 granted founders considerable discretion in defining the internal structure of each new corporation and limited-liability company, it is reasonable to expect that enterprises of all possible sizes would have come into existence had this law remained in effect for long. Among small companies, it might have been possible to find some closed corporations that shared most of the attributes of a limited-liability company. Among medium-sized companies, the largest closed companies might well have resembled the smallest open companies. In other words, the law granted limited liability to a far greater variety of potential enterprises than had the tsarist law.

In comparison with previous Soviet legislation, the law of June 19, 1990, represented a major relaxation of state controls. However, the tide of reform that swept the USSR at that time made Gorbachev's law seem timid. The two features of corporate law that had traditionally served to restrict the foundation of new enterprises under the tsarist and Soviet regimes—high financial minima and restrictive procedures for registration—no longer appeared in the law of June 19, but the new laws of the Russian Federation and of the Lithuanian republic, then in the process of demanding secession from the USSR, went significantly beyond it. (See Table 4.1.)

The Russian law of December 1990 contained only sketchy provisions for limited-liability companies, but the enormous latitude granted to founders of corporations made detailed guidelines unnecessary. In the words of the foremost American analyst of Soviet business law, "the lack of a clear law on the limited liability company creates no practical problems because it is possible to draft a corporate charter under the Russian provisions for a closed joint-stock company that creates the virtual economic equivalent of a limited liability company."[57]

Likewise, the Lithuanian law allowed great flexibility, especially to founders of small companies. By mandating that local governments register all new corporate charters unless they violated laws of the republic, Article 7 opened up the economic field to an unprecedented number of corporate enterprises. So-called public corporations, counterparts of the Soviet and Russian open corporations, had the usual structural components—the General Meeting of Stockholders, the Council of Observers, and the Board of Directors—but in a company with less than two hundred employees and fifty shareholders no council was required. Closed companies, defined as those with between twenty and fifty stockholders and no public sale of stock, had the right to dispense with the board, in which case the tasks of management devolved upon the General Meeting and the hired managers (Arts. 2, 3, 17). Strangely enough, the Lithuanians' campaign for secession did not entirely inhibit their acceptance of traditional Soviet ideology, as the law reserved one-third of the seats on the Council of Observers for workers' representatives. Only closed companies with fewer than two hundred employees received the right to dispense with this provision (Art. 23).[58]

A comparison of numerous minor provisions in these laws would reveal much about the subtleties of corporate legislation in its nascent forms. More relevant for our purposes are the patterns of population ecology in 1990 and 1991. They require examination at this point because they provide vivid evidence of the rudimentary nature of late Soviet capitalism. Two sets of data on the newly emerging capitalist institutions in mid-1991—the fifty largest corporations in existence on April 30 (out of seven hundred registered by that date) and the hundred largest banks in existence in July—suffice to demonstrate the emergence of patterns of the population ecology of capitalist institutions in the USSR similar to those of corporations in the Russian Empire in the mid-nineteenth century. (See Figure 4.3.)

These data suffer from several shortcomings, including the incompleteness of information available to the state register and the lack of a distinction between corporate and cooperative banks. Still, at this early date, approximately a year after the legalization of corporate banks and more than a year before the inauguration of the privatization voucher system in October 1992, the familiar patterns of prerevolutionary Russian capitalist institutions were already clear: weak numerical development, geographical concentration, and foreignness.

The striking predominance of Moscow resulted, of course, from its role as capital of both the Soviet Union and the Russian Federation. Many banks sprang up in small cities where none had been headquartered in 1914—three in Sverdlovsk (Ekaterinburg) and two each in Saratov, Samara, Briansk, Volgograd (Tsaritsyn, later Stalingrad), Krasnodar (Ekaterinodar), Perm, Ufa, Krasnoiarsk, Barnaul, Novosibirsk, Irkutsk, and Alma-Ata (the capital of the Kazakh Soviet Republic, formerly Vernyi, now Almaty), for example—but only one in Riga, then the capital of the Latvian Soviet Republic.

Likewise, the two largest corporations far outstripped the next largest enterprises in size. The KamAZ Automobile Company in Naberezhnye Chelny, transformed into a joint-stock company in June 1990 by decree of the USSR Council of Ministers, had a work force of 140,000 and a massive basic capital of 4.7 billion rubles, which accounted for 40.5 percent of the entire corporate capital of the fifty largest companies. The second giant, the Mezhkniga publishing and bookselling company of

Moscow, had 4 billion rubles in basic capital, an advantage that apparently existed only on paper, as it soon went bankrupt. Far smaller were the next largest enterprises: the Chasprom watch company of Moscow (464 million rubles) and the Plemkonesouiz cattle-breeding company of Moscow (341.7 million rubles). As before World War I, basic capital constituted the only convenient measure of the size of a corporation in this period.

At the other extreme, the single company headquartered in Leningrad, with only 0.2 percent of the total capital, contrasted sharply with the large number of corporations based in St. Petersburg (its original name, adopted once more in the fall of 1991) in the tsarist period. The four companies in the southern industrial center of Krasnodar, the three companies in the industrial center of Sverdlovsk in the southern Ural mountains, and the two in Alma-Ata all testified to the high degree of geographical dispersion of heavy industry in the years of Soviet power.[59] The rise to prominence of cities in Siberia and Central Asia did not, however, necessarily indicate that corporate enterprise had made great progress throughout the Soviet Union in its first two years. To be sure, the broad geographical scope of large corporations reflected in Figure 4.3 would have been unthinkable in the tsarist period, when corporations tended to grow in the very largest cities in the empire, especially those in the western regions. However, the gross disparity between the percentage of corporate headquarters in Moscow and the next most important cities suggested the opposite: a high degree of geographical concentration characteristic of an immature population. To a degree that remains to be ascertained by statistical tests, this geographical dispersion may have resulted from the high literacy levels attained by the Soviet population and the possibilities of economic integration offered by communications technology.

Shrewd bureaucrats, having grasped the inevitability of decentralization, had begun to establish new economic enterprises that seemed capitalist in form. Close examination revealed, however, that they retained the essential nature of bureaucratic institutions. The list of the hundred largest banks, for example, included some created by giant enterprises for the purpose of providing much-needed investment capital for themselves alone: Aeroflot (ranked 29), Avtovazbank (38), and Surgutneftegazbank (85), to cite only the most obvious cases. As one expert noted, "The scope for insider lending abuse is obvious." As in the 1920s, the main shareholders of the new banks were typically not individuals but institutions, such as the State Committee for Material Supply (Gossnab), the USSR and Russian state insurance committees, the Soviet Ministry of Aviation, and the state insurance agency (Gosstrakh), all of which took major positions in Tokobank. Founded in December 1989 with a basic capital of 57.7 million rubles, Tokobank had increased its capital to 163 million by the end of 1990, a sum that permitted it to earn a profit of 21 million rubles in 1991.[60]

How real were such profits in a system where many banks charged no interest at all, where "banks have sprung up faster than regulations to control their activities," and where ownership remained in the hands of "the regional communist institutions and hierarchy," subject to all manner of political pressures? Although the law on banking deregulation, promulgated by the Soviet government on December 11, 1990, opened the field to any institution or group, its provisions encountered criticism from bankers. On the one hand, the law suffered from vagueness, which left wide scope for arbitrary action; on the other, it lacked flexibility, as in the requirement that all defaulting enterprises be liquidated.[61]

One expert explained the simultaneous emergence of new corporations and banks under the control of influential bureaucrats in these pessimistic terms:

> Typically, this [privatization] takes the form of transforming a state enterprise [SE] into a joint-stock company with the shares held by other state enterprises and institutions (ministries, local authorities, banks, workers' collectives). Usually enterprises and ministers together found a commercial bank in the form of a joint-stock company and use it later as a shareholder of the transformed SE. This cross-ownership structure is typical of a form of spontaneous privatization taking place in the Soviet economy.... Controlling, through this cross-ownership structure, a large amount of state capital, [managers of state enterprises] have a good opportunity for privatizing the SE's profits.... This spontaneous privatization ... is characterized by the short-term orientation of the new owners, corruption, and large-scale stealing of state property.[62]

Experts named these maneuvers "*nomenklatura* buy-outs" because "the old hierarchy assumes controlling positions in the new enterprise, and at the same time secures inputs at (subsidized) state prices."[63] The *nomenklatura*, literally a list of nominees, constituted the key officials in all governmental agencies, hand-picked by the Communist Party of the Soviet Union since Stalin's time to ensure compliance of the state bureaucracy with the general party line. The clearest indication of this was the huge concentration of new corporations in Moscow, the bureaucratic nerve center.

At the end of 1991, the largest industrial associations acted as "extremely powerful cartels" that monopolized between 80 and 99 percent of production in Russian petroleum, natural gas, nickel, coal, machine tools, and agricultural machinery. "They have survived the demise of the Soviet Union and still comprise the umbrella organizations of a very substantial part of the Russian industry" and "may be a serious obstacle to privatization" in the 1990s.[64]

The slow emergence of stock exchanges likewise testified to the rudimentary nature of corporate capitalism in the USSR. No real stock exchange existed in the strict sense of the term in 1991. Numerous commodity exchanges (*tovarnye birzhi*) proliferated in the form of corporations under the liberal Soviet laws of 1990, and a few of these evolved into stock exchanges (*fondovye birzhi*) with periodic sales of small blocs of shares. The first, the Moscow Stock Exchange (*Moskovskaia fondovaia birzha*), emerged in November 1990, barely one month after Gorbachev announced the right of Soviet citizens to buy "stocks, bonds, and other securities as part of his plan to switch from central planning to a market economy." Despite announced plans for branch offices in Frankfurt, New York, Tokyo, and Singapore, the Moscow Stock Exchange set no date for its opening.[65]

The lack of a comprehensive securities and exchange law made the new market in securities a treacherous one. As one survey noted,

> With patchy legislation and the absence of laws on bankruptcies, mortgage, and securities, and with an underdeveloped legal culture, it is possible to establish phony joint-stock societies. These "dead souls" may issue public shares, accumulate capital, and then simulate bankruptcy. This type of affair will primarily affect the interests of ordinary people involved in the exotic process of buying shares.

The recommended remedy against fraud—that "citizens are advised to consult the United State Register, an official register of all joint-stock societies"—hardly seemed adequate in the absence of an agency to enforce laws regulating the sale of securities.[66]

This gap in the institutional structure reflected the general lack of economic legality in the Soviet system under Gorbachev, as in previous centuries:

> All in all, the Soviet leadership has made essentially no progress in establishing economic legality, which is a prerequisite for creating incentives that could support a healthy market. On the contrary, as the continual policy reversals and economic decline of recent years have undermined the credibility of the leadership, it may be that the reform movement in the USSR [led by Gorbachev] has actually moved farther away from the institutional prerequisites necessary to support a market economy.[67]

To conclude the analysis of the capitalist institutions that had emerged in the Soviet Union by 1990, it is necessary to recognize the extreme anxiety that they inspired, even in their nascent form and apart from the connection to Europe and America. Many economists, including those most committed to radical reform for the sake of economic efficiency, agonized over the deleterious social consequences of market reforms, particularly the gross inequalities of income that seemed inevitable: massive unemployment, especially during the transition to market-based systems of production and distribution, and potential abuses of power within enterprises by the new owners of the means of production. This is not to suggest that the Soviet system had ever achieved income equality or equity in the workplace; but many of the economic injustices of the Soviet period had remained hidden or at least unmentioned in the censored press.

The most enlightened of economists under perestroika, Nikolai Shmelev, resisted embracing capitalism in the form of large corporations. He warned that the public would resort to violence in opposition to the inevitable negative effects of private enterprise, including inequality of rewards and the threat of mass unemployment:

> I don't see anything objectionable in the idea [of a stock market] from an ideological point of view. It would be efficient and advantageous for the Soviet economy because of all the unused savings lying around and because there is so little to buy. . . . It would allow state and cooperative enterprises, in industry and agriculture, to raise tens of billions of rubles. [However, private enterprise] is a problem, not so much with small family businesses but if there were to be large private firms that hired labor and started issuing stock. Not only are official bureaucrats and ideologists against this, but the man in the street wouldn't accept it either.

Further than Bukharin's mixed economy Shmelev was not prepared to go:

> Purely in terms of economic efficiency, yes, we ought to have such a private sector, as there was under NEP. But we have to take into account people's psychology, which is a legacy of the last sixty [sic] years. For them, a private enterprise hiring a lot of labor would mean exploitation and they might burn it down. . . . [To have] a thousand people working for one person is clearly immoral. When a skilled professional hires three students, I don't see a moral problem. But I don't know what people are prepared to accept.[68]

Shmelev correctly anticipated the eruption of workers' criticisms of corporations. In April 1990, the Central Council of Trade Unions addressed a strong appeal to the Soviet Council of Ministers, warning of the deleterious consequences of abrupt market reforms: intensified inflation, massive unemployment, and "the deterioration of the living standards of a vast majority of the population." Although the labor leaders expressed support for economic reforms, they demanded that the state "guarantee full employment of the population" and maintain "mandatory insurance of the subsistence minimum and a regular compensation for the growth of prices" (indexing of state payments), especially for those most vulnerable to inflation: pensioners, war veterans, citizens with large families, and students. The statement ended with a veiled critique of reforms from above and an appeal for delay pending some sort of public referendum: "such a turn can and must be effected only on the basis of nationwide concord, having received a mandate of people's trust on the entire complex of questions of accelerating the switching over the economy to market relations."[69]

Massive opposition to privatization existed in 1991. Asked what form their enterprise should take in the future, more than two out of five workers favored the current system of state ownership and fewer than 5 percent preferred a joint venture with foreign capital, a corporation, a private enterprise with an unknown buyer, or a cooperative.[70] A concrete example of workers' resistance to the corporate form of economic enterprise erupted in Togliatti when the council of the labor collective (STK) at the huge Volga Automobile Plant (VAZ) opposed the managers' plan to convert the enterprise into a joint-stock company with the possibility of foreign ownership of a portion of the shares. Although the plan eventually went forward, "the controversy sparked the formation of a rank-and-file movement against privatization that has spread to much of heavy industry."

For example, workers at the KamAZ automobile plant, which became a corporation in mid-1990, resented the 25 percent maximum of shares allowed to workers under the new enterprise law. In December 1990, a new organization called the Union of Councils of Labor Collectives and Workers' Committees came into being, principally organized by automobile workers from VAZ, KamAZ, ZIL in Moscow, and Kirov in Leningrad. The union sought to oppose the new enterprise law, which dramatically weakened the STKs. Perhaps recognizing the inevitability of the demolition of the state planning system, the union endorsed "the full-scale introduction of the market" but took "a militant stand in favor of collective workers' self-management and against private managerial ownership of state enterprises."[71] These were precisely the issues of economic power and privilege that had to be resolved as unemployment increased in the transition to the new market, although the political deadlock between the president and the legislature delayed the resolution of the problem of wasteful state subsidies and credit to loss-making enterprises until the election of the new Russian legislature in December 1993.

By itself, the fear of mass unemployment and other inherent problems of unplanned economies would have sufficed to cause unprecedented anxiety among Soviet workers. The prospect of losing the many subsidies traditionally provided by the Soviet state became even more fearful, however, because the principles of capitalism appeared to be essentially foreign not only to the ideals of Marxism-Leninism but also to Russian culture itself, so weak had capitalism remained under the tsarist regime. VAZ workers vehemently opposed the prospect of even partial foreign ownership of their plant. This impulse, mentioned in passing by various analysts of the debate over markets in the period of perestroika, reached back into centuries of Russian history. It lost little of its momentum as the various republics of the former USSR faced the painful consequences of integration into the world economy.

5

Capitalism and Xenophobia in Russia

"You are a very learned man of the greatest intellect and the pride of your country, but the Germans have ruined you. Yes, the Germans! The Germans!" Since leaving Dorpat, where he had studied medicine, Samoilenko had rarely seen Germans and had not read a single German book, but, in his opinion, everything harmful in politics and science stemmed from the Germans. He himself could not say where he had gotten this opinion, but he maintained it firmly. "Yes, the Germans!" he repeated again. "Let's go have tea."

Anton Chekhov, "The Duel" (1891)[1]

If the significance of the Russian Revolution of 1917 lies less in its closure of an era of rapid economic development, according to the Leninist teleology, than in the traditional violence and xenophobia with which workers, peasants, and the radical intelligentsia assaulted the agrarian bureaucracy, the gentry, and the essentially foreign system of corporate enterprise recently transplanted from European soil, then the question of Russian capitalism takes its rightful place as an aspect of the perennial debate over the relationship between Russia and the West. The identification of corporate capitalism with the foreigner—the Briton, Frenchman, German, Jew, Pole, or Armenian—carried special cultural importance because of the residual power of Russian xenophobia: fear and hatred of foreigners. According to this interpretation, the long tradition of anticapitalism that manifested itself in the late tsarist period, the Russian Revolution of 1917, and the late 1980s constituted a major cultural obstacle to the expansion of the market in the 1990s.

Radical and Reactionary Critiques of Capitalism under the Tsarist Regime

A distinction must be drawn between three closely related phenomena in Russian culture: hostility toward capitalism based on a low regard for behavior essential to success in the marketplace, such as calculation, saving, deferment of gratification, and the like; the impulse toward economic nationalism, which at times lacked a specifically xenophobic component; and the xenophobic rejection of capitalism, the theme of this chapter. The first of these attitudes was so pervasive that a comprehensive analysis of it would require a separate monograph. It suffices to cite one example, recorded by the factory inspector Ivan I. Ianzhul, of a petition of local officials in Orel province in the early 1890s. They called for the abolition of savings funds in the public schools on the grounds that encouraging Russian children to save "would only inculcate in them an exaggerated idea of the importance of money and develop 'egoism' and selfishness," cultural traits generally considered "typical of the German petty bourgeoisie, and not of the broad Russian nature!"[2] Although only expressions of fear and hatred of foreigners deserved the label of xenophobia, all three attitudes reflected the sense of a deep cultural gulf between Russia and the West. On the one side stood a kind of moral innocence and lack of competitiveness attuned to the predictable rhythms of village life; on the other, a legalistic individualism that, while it might produce wonders of economic efficiency, appeared to Russians as excessively materialistic.

Xenophobia resides, of course, in attitudes, not sociological statistics such as those in Tables 3.2, 3.3, 3.10, and 3.11. Hostility to foreign capitalists figured prominently in the outlooks of four separate groups in Russian society under the tsarist regime: industrial workers, radical intellectuals, reactionary intellectuals, and—strange though it may seem—some capitalists, primarily ethnic Russian merchants in the Central Industrial Region. All these groups made crucial ideological contributions to the greatest upheaval in Russian history, the Bolshevik Revolution of 1917. The complexity of the revolutionary process requires that the description of these arguments remain schematic and the documentation suggestive rather than exhaustive. The quotations that follow suffice to convey the xenophobic content of revolutionary and reactionary rhetoric.

Sporadic strikes from the 1880s onward testified to the spontaneous anger of industrial workers who felt unfairly exploited by low wages while industrialists and bankers lived in luxury. A German economist stressed that peasants took work at factories only out of "extreme need. . . . They hate and despise the factory—a phenomenon that is always observed among a native agricultural population."[3]

Recent studies of Russian workers' attitudes and behavior suggest that their violence often lacked a specifically Marxist content. For example, in the strikes that broke out in the printing industry in St. Petersburg and Moscow from 1903 onward, the workers' "expressions of class protest were often imbued with a moral ethos, an emotional faith in the righteousness of the cause." As one socialist agitator admitted, more than half the workers who joined the political strike in St. Petersburg in October 1905 did so "purely instinctively, feeling that here is truth and justice [*pravda*], but not understanding the connection between politics and economics." Workers tended to call their employers not "capitalists" but "tyrants" and "bloodsuckers," words that resonated with a moral fervor and dramatized the struggle between "good and evil, light and darkness, honor and insult."[4]

Some workers ignored the ethnic issue completely. The memoirs of Sergei I. Kanatchikov expressed no particular bitterness toward his foreign employers: List, Maxwell, Siemens-Halske, and Bering.[5] Thousands of workers, however, recalled mistreatment by German or English foremen. Many Russian corporations, having purchased advanced machinery from England, Belgium, or Germany, routinely hired foreign-born managers and foremen to supervise the use of this equipment. In the coal mines and metal plants of the Donbass region, for example, "foreigners were to be found in significant numbers, and they experienced privileged living conditions, received large salaries, and wielded a great deal of authority."[6] Beatings, sexual molestation of female workers, and other outrages by foreigners constituted major sources of workers' discontent.[7]

A French banker reported: "A good Russian director is virtually a mythical beast and therefore foreign engineers supervise the coal mines and are paid 10,000 rubles a year." For example, in 1911 the monthly pay for Donbass coal miners, almost all of Russian ethnicity, ranged from 14 to 35 rubles, while chief engineers and technical managers of coal companies, almost all foreigners, received up to 833 rubles and from 1,250 to 2,500 rubles, respectively. These huge differentials aroused resentment among Russian workers.[8]

The Revolution of 1905 witnessed many episodes of labor violence against foreign capitalists. A xenophobic content may be detected in the outbursts of unskilled workers in the coal and iron industries in the Dnepr and Donets region of South Russia, where, in October 1905, workers rioted one day under the socialist banner but shortly afterward vented their fury on "administrators and staff at mines and railroad stations as well as local Jews."[9] A French banker warned in 1907:

> One must remember that the mass of workers has been heavily indoctrinated in these last years and their nationalism has been over-excited. The consecutive assassinations of several plant managers have shown this all too clearly. In such conditions one cannot even dream of directing Russian workers except with their countrymen, or with French engineers understanding completely their very special mentality. Such men are very rare, and when found they very often draw back from the grave personal risks involved.

John P. McKay tersely explained why European engineers commanded high salaries in Russia. So many foreign businessmen had been "killed, maimed, and threatened," especially in 1904–8, that talented engineers from Europe felt entitled to "hardship premiums for work in Russia. The boredom of the Donets was one thing; a bullet in the back was another."[10]

Such hostilities flared again on the eve of World War I. Mass demonstrations swept the country in the wake of the killing of two hundred workers, in April 1912, by soldiers at the Lena Goldfields, owned by a prominent British company. In St. Petersburg in 1913, workers struck the New Aivaz Company to protest the introduction of time-and-motion studies developed by Frederick W. Taylor in the United States. The strikers condemned "the savage extremes of the American system," which allegedly threatened to turn their factory into "a 'workhouse' with its horrible bondage; it will be a brutal laboratory of human exploitation, where the latest work in technical science will be bought at the price of hunger, humiliation, sweating, illness, and premature death." This relatively large company, chartered on November 2, 1911, with an authorized basic capital of 1.2 million rubles, was founded by a Jewish merchant named Iakov M. Aivaz, who shared managerial tasks with two Russians in 1914.[11]

These outbursts reflected the cultural traditions that workers brought to the factory. Unskilled workers in particular found it difficult to shed their peasant habits, which included an irregular tempo of work, indifference to precise notions of time, passive resistance toward authority, and occasional episodes of violence against perceived injustices. Historians have found that workers' violence took many forms, only one of which was really revolutionary in the Marxist sense.[12] Xenophobia may therefore account for much of the extraordinary anger that eventually burst forth in 1917.

Public endorsements by Russian industrialists of massive foreign investments reinforced the identification of capitalism with foreigners. Nikolai S. Avdakov, president of the Association of Industry and Trade, welcomed an English delegation in 1912 with the warmest of salutations. Speaking in the name of "all industrial and commercial institutions in Russia," he announced that "England will always be the model for us, worthy of imitation in its concern for the national economy." The head of the English delegation saw in Avdakov's attitude "a sign of economic maturity,"[13] but the advantage of hindsight allows the historian to perceive in Avdakov's remarks an insensitivity to Russian xenophobia.

Like workers, Russian radicals tended to lapse into xenophobia as they attacked the evils of capitalism. When, in midcentury, Aleksandr I. Herzen created the ideology of Russian agrarian socialism, he idealized the traditional peasant commune as the moral basis of an egalitarian society in Russia. His condemnation of Europe reflected both his aristocratic contempt for the bourgeoisie and his ethnic prejudice. In his letters to Ivan S. Turgenev in the early 1860s, Herzen expressed an aristocratic disdain for the clothing, music, art, and even the cigars of the European bourgeoisie. Although he referred mockingly to his own "still fermenting brew of

Slavophil socialism," he staunchly refused to consider "the *bourgeois* system as the final form of Russian society. . . . It is time to stand on our own feet. Why is it absolutely necessary to take to wooden legs because they are of foreign make?"[14]

Disillusioned with Europe from 1847 onward, Herzen rejected the European principles that he had revered in his youth—individualism, progress, and republicanism—in favor of a new ideal: an anarchistic socialism rooted in the traditional peasant commune of Russia. The socialist theories of foreigners—both the Frenchman Babeuf and the German Marx—appeared to him excessively repressive.

> Herzen carefully continued to distinguish his revolutionary nationalism from the conservatism of the Slavophiles. But it was nationalism none the less; for the Russian commune represented everything that he maintained Europe was not, and was vainly striving to become. The commune by its very nature was incompatible with the Roman and Western notion of the state. . . . The Russian's instinctive reaction to the law and the courts was not respect, but evasion and noncooperation. . . . The Russian peasant knew neither the institution nor the idea [of] private property.[15]

Because Herzen based his socialism on moral imperatives, aesthetic judgments, and ethnic stereotypes, it is difficult to define clearly his opinion of European capitalism as an economic system. Never blind to the coarseness of peasant life, he consistently criticized the commune for its tendency to stifle individual liberty. However, his contempt for the Western legal tradition implied a rejection of capitalism because of the central place of law and private property in it.

Petr N. Tkachev added a note of urgency to this conception. Capitalism, gathering strength in the West, threatened to undermine the peasant commune, the foundation of the future socialist society in Russia. A ruthless vanguard acting in the name of the people (but not with its consent) must act soon or forever let slip the revolutionary opportunity. As Andrzej Walicki paraphrased Tkachev's call to action in 1874: "Today the Russian bourgeoisie is weak and Russian capitalism is still in its initial stage; tomorrow it might be too difficult to eradicate [the] bourgeois weed from the Russian soil."[16] Here again, capitalism bore a European physiognomy.

Anti-Semitism proved a powerful rhetorical tool as well. In 1878, the radical group "Land and Freedom" condemned "our joint-stock swindling enterprises" for their alleged exploitation of cheap labor, endorsed and encouraged by the tsarist autocracy. The inclusion of the names of several prominent Jewish capitalists—"Gorvitses, Poliakovs, and Kogans"—heightened the emotional impact of this denunciation of nascent Russian capitalism.[17]

Similar episodes of opposition to European economic and cultural influences have been common in world history, from German romantic nationalism and the Boxer Rebellion in China to the *négritude* movement in Africa and the current trend to define Islam in terms of contrasts with the West: "peaceful, not aggressive; spiritual, not materialistic; compassionate, not exploitative; prim, not vulgar." Faced with the choice between "a future without authenticity and authenticity without a future," a Moroccan schoolgirl preferred the latter because "at least Muslims will be on firm ground."[18] Poverty and weakness became proofs of spiritual superiority over the adversary, whose superior technical or military power masked moral decadence. A comparable sense of pride in an agrarian civilization, even one based on slavery, coupled with the rejection of prosperity founded on industry, constituted a key element in the ideology of the Confederacy during the American Civil War.

Liah Greenfeld detected this same combination in the works of late-eighteenth-century Russian intellectuals who admitted their country's "absolute impotence in the competition with the West" but insisted on "the rejection of the West because it was evil," despite the persistence of serfdom in Russia long after it had died out in Western Europe. Through an "intellectual somersault," Russian patriots "turned backwardness into a guarantee of greatness." They "connected the abomination of reason to too much civilization—a curse they were spared—and interpreted the latter as separation from vital, primeval forces, of which they had to spare."[19] Andrzej Walicki called this aspect of the Russian populist ideology "the privilege of backwardness."[20]

The Marxist stage theory constituted an internationalist, global vision, in which a capitalist phase awaited all countries in the European economic orbit. By the late nineteenth century, Russian Marxists welcomed the growth of modern industry and the working class created by it. Although they agreed that capitalism represented a crime against the poor, they considered their prediction of the future more scientific than that of the agrarian anarchists. Long before he seized power in 1917, however, Lenin gave his arguments a most unscientific nationalist tinge. In 1902, for example, he accused the minister of finance of surrendering the natural wealth of the Russian Empire by offering state property as collateral to European capitalists in general and Jews in particular:

> The autocracy is slowly but surely going bankrupt because it is impossible to keep raising taxes endlessly and the French bourgeoisie will not continue to come to the rescue of the Russian tsar forever. . . . In fact, only one European country, Turkey, has ever used government property as collateral for state loans. And this naturally allowed *foreign creditors to take control* of the property that was used to guarantee the repayment of the borrowed money. The economy of "Russia, the great power," under the control of agents of Rothschild and Bleichröder: such is the brilliant vista that you unveil for us, Mr. Witte![21]

Marx himself, never free of nationalistic emotions, clashed repeatedly with the leading Russian anarchists, Herzen and Bakunin, who responded with anti-German insults. According to Greenfeld, Marx also employed anti-Semitic rhetoric, a conventional tool of German romantic nationalism, in his condemnations of Jewish capitalists. She stressed Marx's early debt, in "Introduction to the Contribution to the Critique of Hegel's Philosophy of Right" (1843), to German romanticism. "While the proletariat was the metamorphosed Germany, Capital was the metamorphosed West. Both retained all the qualities of good and evil, respectively, of the Romantic nationalist scheme."[22] Lenin apparently remained ignorant of these details of German intellectual history and blended Russian socialist and nationalist ideas for his own tactical purposes.

The radical journalist Vlas M. Doroshevich likewise attacked the "exploitation of Russia by outsiders," particularly British capitalists. He also ridiculed the *burzhui* (a term of contempt derived from a mispronunciation of bourgeoisie, *burzhuaziia*) for its support of the State Duma in 1906 and other alleged political sins, although he did not, apparently, attack Russian capitalists as tools of foreign business interests. Louise McReynolds correctly noted the logical connection between industrial development and Russian xenophobia at the turn of the century: "As the nation began to industrialize, the presence of Westerners in Russian commerce became more conspicuous, especially because Western Europeans controlled many major Russian industries and manufactories."[23]

On the reactionary side of the political spectrum, the expression of Russian nationalism varied widely according to geographical location and the educational level of citizens. However, it was sufficiently widespread to bear a distinctive, if curious, name: "kvas patriotism" (*kvasnoi patriotizm*). Kvas, a slightly fermented brown beverage made from rye bread, symbolized the simplicity of Russian peasant life. The significance of kvas and wine as beverages of peasants and nobles, respectively, was clear in Tolstoi's *War and Peace* (vol. 3, part 3, sec. 29), where officers of the invading French army in Moscow disparaged kvas as "*limonade de cochon.*" In this scene, cultural divisions cut across national antagonisms, even in wartime, as a French officer and the Russian Prince Bezukhov shared a bottle of wine, while their servants, French and Russian, drank kvas.

The term *kvas patriotism,* coined by Pushkin's close friend, Prince Petr A. Viazemskii, had become common by midcentury. Whether or not Russian intellectuals ever seriously contrasted the virtues of home-made kvas to the shortcomings of French champagne and Bavarian beer remains an open question, but sophisticates employed the term to ridicule reactionaries who praised backward Russia for its alleged moral purity before the rich but allegedly decadent West. For example, shortly after Karakozov's abortive attempt on the life of Emperor Alexander II in 1866, Petr A. Valuev expressed disgust at a series of hyperpatriotic speeches delivered at the Gentry Assembly by "demagogues" and "kvas patriots who play on the balalaika of Russian folk phrases, like Chizhov."[24]

The repeated use of the word alien (*chuzhoi*) and the frequent resort to anti-Semitism by writers on the reactionary end of the political spectrum blurred the distinction between Russian nationalism and racism. In the first decade of the reign of Alexander II, conservative ideologists warned of the evil power of the "princes of the stock exchange" and bemoaned the rise of a hereditary working class, the embodiment of social revolution. This fear of capitalism acquired a specific ethnic content at this time, as in the first important pogrom against Jews in Odessa in 1871. "The anti-industrialism of the Russian intelligentsia and the use of anticapitalist arguments to justify vandalism against Jews introduced Jewish intellectuals to a new factor that they were ill-prepared to confront." In late imperial Russia, according to one astute historian, "the symbolic meanings of Germany and America became more negative" as the two industrial giants posed an ever greater economic threat, and "stereotypes of Jews and Poles became similarly linked with the bad values of capitalism and thus were perceived and often portrayed as anti-Russian."[25]

The polemics of the great novelist Fedor M. Dostoevskii appear interesting to the historian because, as a politically unsophisticated person, he articulated in his journalistic columns ideas shared by much of the educated Russian public. Following the Slavophiles, Dostoevskii blended anti-Semitism, devotion to Russian Orthodox Christianity, and hatred of capitalism into a principled rejection of European culture. He perceived an incompatibility between Christianity and what he called the *"idea of the Yids,"* allegedly represented by the materialism of the European bourgeoisie. To him, capitalism meant "mercilessness to the lower masses, the decline of brotherhood, [and] the exploitation of the poor by the rich." At one extreme stood "materialism, a blind, carnivorous lust . . . for *personal* accumulation of money by any means"; at the other, "the Christian idea of salvation only through the closest moral and brotherly unity of people." In 1881, he blamed railroads, the largest of Russian corporations, for "destroying our agriculture."[26]

Dostoevskii's devotion to the supposedly superior spiritual qualities of the Slavic people led him to equate European culture with simple greed. "Nations live by great feelings and by great ideas that unite all and illuminate everything, by solidarity with the masses of the population . . . and not by mere stock-exchange speculations and concern for the value of the ruble." He feared that Catholicism and Protestantism could not stem the rising tide of social revolution in Europe:

> The fourth estate [working class] . . . does not want the old ideals; it rejects every existing law. It will not agree to compromises or concessions; the edifice cannot be saved by shoring it up. Concessions will only inflame the fourth estate; it wants everything. Something will come to pass that no one can even conceive. All this parliamentarianism, all the civic theories now being expounded, all the accumulated wealth, the banks, the sciences, the Yids—all of it will collapse in a moment, without a trace—except for the Yids, who will then find ways to carry on, so that this work will even be to their advantage.[27]

The Christian utopianism of Dostoevskii seemed incompatible with the secular and anarchist socialism of Herzen, but later conservative thinkers sensed the essential notions that both thinkers shared: the promotion of Slavic power at the expense of the Germanic and Latin peoples of

Western and Central Europe and the identification of the evils of capitalism with European civilization. Like Herzen, the reactionary literary critic Nikolai Strakhov ignored economic theory, but in his belligerent commentary on Russian and European literary trends, "The Struggle against the West in Our Literature," he praised both the Slavophile journalist Ivan S. Aksakov and the anarchist Herzen for their rejection of European values. In his obituary of Aksakov in March 1886, Strakhov identified himself as a Slavophile. Although he spoke pessimistically of the chance that "our religious, political, intellectual, and artistic life" would triumph over the increasingly influential "European culture," he followed the Slavophile tradition in denouncing both the radical and liberal tendencies in European politics and literature. Equally repugnant to him were the Paris Commune, the philosophers John Stuart Mill and David Strauss, and two French scholars whom he called "historians without principles": Ernest Renan and Hippolyte Taine.[28]

Conservative agrarians, both in the tsarist government and outside it, failed to block the spread of capitalist institutions in Russia, but their plans for action gave some indication of how they identified the enemy. An ideologist of gentry interests, N. A. Pavlov, proposed to a congress of the United Nobility in November 1910 an economic union to provide "cheap, flexible credit" to landowners and peasants and to organize the trade in grain and other products "without the use of exchanges, agents, petty grain traders, commission agents, etc." Because Jews predominated in the grain trade and flour-milling industry of the Russian Empire, his condemnation of "middlemen" carried unmistakable anti-Semitic overtones.

Especially significant was the German model on which Pavlov and his friends based their plan. In late 1892 and early 1893, some 350,000 Junker landlords in Prussia had created an agrarian credit union that eventually published a newspaper in 400,000 copies and amassed a treasury of over 200,000 marks. If the Junkers could organize for the defense of their *Heimat,* why should the Russian gentry not act in "self-defense" against the international danger, what Pavlov called the "peaceful, non-revolutionary and non-bloody but constant conquest of power by the proletariat, by socialism, by the street, by city-dwellers"?[29] Like their political enemies, the Marxists, conservative agrarians viewed capitalism, imported from Europe, as the first step toward socialist revolution.

Pavlov's plan for an All-Russian Chamber of Agriculture received the tsar's confirmation on November 15, 1912. Despite an ambitious publicity campaign, however, few landowners or local agricultural societies joined the organization. This attempt to link producers of agricultural goods by a noncapitalist mechanism thus carried more ideological than economic significance. The failure of Pavlov's plan owed much to the preference of the United Nobility to work informally with the tsarist bureaucracy. Consequently, it never mastered the techniques of independent public activity. Although the agrarians defended the principle of private property against the socialist program of expropriation, they opposed the free exercise of the power of capital in commerce, industry, and finance on the European model. Even before the Russian Revolution, Sir Donald MacKenzie Wallace gave a brilliant description of the ideology of agrarian foes of capitalism, "who have, strange to say, more influence in Russia than in any other country."[30]

Reactionaries in the tsarist bureaucracy did not, of course, reject industrial development entirely. Some industry was essential, if only to supply the huge military machine. In the tradition of Peter the Great, however, they preferred direct state ownership of cannon factories and shipyards. This method of economic administration had little in common with capitalism because it rejected the spontaneous workings of the free market. In 1917, shortly after the collapse of the old regime, the Russian Banking Association complained that the refusal of tsarist bureaucrats to reform the Russian banking system along European lines in the course of two decades, from the 1870s to the 1890s, had stemmed from a reactionary prejudice: hatred of the so-called rotten West (*gnilyi Zapad*).[31] (This colorful term was coined by the Slavophile theorist Aleksei S. Khomiakov prior to the Crimean War.) In the words of the economic historian Kornelii F. Shatsillo, autocrats from Peter the Great to Stalin preferred to rule the economy by fiat: *skazano, sdelano*.[32] The standard translation of this Russian saying in English, "no sooner said than done," exaggerates, however, the efficiency of the tsarist and Soviet bureaucracies in their notoriously arbitrary administration of the economy.

Grievances against European bankers, managers, and foremen easily blossomed into a rejection of capitalism itself, especially when anti-Semitic prejudice added an element of irrational fervor to the economic debate. Many reactionaries considered Witte a traitor for opening up Russia to European economic influences. There is, however, no evidence of his disloyalty to the tsarist regime. Far from serving as a pliant tool of foreign business interests, he drove hard bargains on behalf of the Russian economy and occasionally uttered unflattering remarks about foreign Jewish bankers. For his part, Witte offered a cynical explanation for the economic xenophobia of the Russian nobility: "There are some ultranationalist, self-styled 'true Russians,' largely from the nobility, usually nobles who have lost their fortunes and have gone into commerce and industry, who are not particularly in favor of the importation of foreign capital unless it is to their personal advantage, for example, by providing them a place on the board of directors of some company."[33] Witte's own ambivalence toward capitalist institutions was examined in Chapter 2. We shall never know whether an enlightened policy favorable to foreign and domestic corporations would have provided sufficient industrial development to forestall the economic collapse and social revolution that overwhelmed Russia during World War I. No quantitative methods exist to measure the precise cost. What is certain, however, is that the regime deliberately refused to embrace such a policy and paid a high price in lost entrepreneurial opportunities.

Throughout Russia, the proliferation of agricultural cooperatives and other noncapitalist economic institutions, including local savings banks, demonstrated a widespread desire to avoid the market. One Briton noted the xenophobic implications of this anticapitalist attitude in 1914:

> In addition to these grievances [over German diplomacy in 1912–14], there has always been the aggravation as to loss of business to the German, always ready to secure any opportunity for exploitation of the agriculturalist. It has recently been said that Germany carries on business as if it were war, and Russians think that the competitive methods of Germans are very unfair, and the establishment of co-operative societies, so widely adopted, is an endeavour to break up the power of the German export houses, and it may have some effect in that direction.[34]

The memoirs of Aleksei A. Ziablov, a mechanical engineer, testified to the bitterness that many Russians, even those of cosmopolitan culture, harbored against foreign capitalists. The son of a lieutenant colonel, Ziablov received an education in engineering, devised improvements in steam locomotives, and managed several machine plants. In the course of his career he rose from chief mechanic to member of the board of directors of the famous Kolomna Machinery Company, which produced some of the best Russian locomotives. However, he resented the company's German managers for their reluctance to appoint qualified Russian engineers to high positions and their humiliating searches of workers and foremen at the plant's gates. At the beginning of World War I, Ziablov warned the Russian government that the empire's entire supply of injectors, crucial to the construction and repair of locomotives, came from a plant in Warsaw owned by the A. Friedmann firm of Vienna, which merely assembled the injectors in Poland. Only when the disruption of the supply of injectors caused a severe shortage in late 1914 did the tsarist government seek a domestic supplier. The first batch emerged from Ziablov's small plant in July 1917, too late to avert the collapse of the railroad system.

Ziablov perceived in these economic difficulties evidence of a plot aimed at "German domination" (*nemetskoe zasil'e*): a conspiracy to make Russian industry dependent on German and Austrian equipment, the better to cripple the economy in wartime. To some degree, perhaps, this accusation reflected his upbringing in a military family and his high bureaucratic status. (He retired with the rank of State Councilor and a St. Anna medal, second degree.)[35] However, years of technical work in cooperation with German technicians in Kolomna, St. Petersburg, and Reval had not weakened his suspicions concerning the economic conspiracies of which foreigners were capable.

Thus, prejudice against foreigners and capitalist institutions pervaded Russian society, from the highest bureaucrats to the lowliest workers and from the anarchists to the reactionary monarchists. The major liberal party in 1905–17, the Constitutional Democrats (Kadets), occupied a special place on the political spectrum. In an effort to stand "above class," the

Kadets refused to embrace the political and economic demands of either the industrialists, the landed gentry, or urban professionals, although many of their leaders had close personal and cultural ties to the two latter groups. In the First and Second State Dumas, the Kadets' proposals for "compulsory alienation of certain portions of privately owned nobles' land" with compensation below market prices placed their agrarian program closer to socialism than to capitalism. As Pavel N. Miliukov, the Kadet leader, announced at the founding congress of the party in October 1905: "[W]e are unalterable enemies of [both] bureaucratic centralization and the Manchester school [of unfettered capitalist competition]." At the same time, however, Miliukov, perhaps the most cosmopolitan of Russian politicians, harbored no prejudice against European culture in general or capitalism in particular. His closest friend in the United States was the Chicago manufacturer Charles R. Crane.[36]

It must also be admitted that Russian resentment often lay hidden for decades. An optimistic London journalist noted that many British businessmen in Russia prospered with little or no bureaucratic interference. In the oil fields of Baku, for example, British entrepreneurs found conditions "perfectly satisfactory in every respect, and instead of 'difficulties' they had encountered [from government officials] nothing but courtesy and goodwill." (The superficiality of his understanding of Russian economics and politics was suggested by his unwarranted assessments that Nicholas II "must be regarded as one of the most liberal of the Tsars" and that "as trade and industries expand the dangers of internal dissentions in Russia will decrease.")[37] During wars or in the wake of wars (1812, 1855–60, 1914–17), capitalists, both foreigners and the Russians who worked with them, tended to be regarded as having primary loyalties outside of Russia.

Slavophile Capitalism

Where and when did the identification of Europe with the evils of capitalism first appear? Isolated instances of economic xenophobia occurred throughout the centuries. As a coherent point of view, however, economic xenophobia in Russian culture sprang not from radical socialists or reactionary landlords but from Russian capitalists themselves.

Soon after the Napoleonic Wars, some Russian manufacturers expressed resentment against low tariffs and their consequences, massive imports of European manufactured goods. The phenomenon became politically significant in the late 1850s. Threatened by inexpensive European imports in the wake of the Crimean War, textile manufacturers in the Moscow industrial region turned to the Slavophiles for aid in petitioning the state for tariff protection. This "merchant-Slavophile alliance," led by the leading Moscow manufacturers and two prominent Slavophiles, Ivan S. Aksakov and Fedor V. Chizhov (the latter identified as a "kvas patriot" by Petr A. Valuev in 1866), elaborated powerful slogans of economic nationalism that won favorable policy changes from the bureaucrats in St.

Petersburg. Schulze-Gävernitz, a perceptive observer of Russian society, stressed the ideological affinities between Russian industrialists and the Slavophiles. The alliance began to erode in the last quarter of the century, when the high tariffs demanded by the Moscow merchants in cooperation with their intellectual allies had called forth industries that undermined the precapitalist communes and workers' cooperatives (*arteli*), beloved by the Slavophiles.[38]

The term *Slavophile capitalism* might seem a contradiction in terms. Weber's six-part definition of the elements of capitalism, cited in Chapter 1, stood in opposition to the ideal of Russian romantic nationalism and its religious overtones. In the middle of the nineteenth century, however, the program of economic nationalism had not yet revealed its internal contradictions, and the merchants found in the Slavophile ideology precisely the sort of emotionally powerful rationale for economic development that legitimized their struggle with European capitalists. The term is useful, therefore, as a means of identifying the peculiar ideological rationale of economic nationalism in the Moscow region at that time.

Slavophile capitalism had three distinct ingredients. The first was the myth of the benevolence of employers toward their workers, modeled on the identical agrarian notion of hierarchical trust and love between landlord and peasant. According to the leading memoirist of the Moscow merchants, Pavel A. Buryshkin, the manufacturers in the Central Industrial Region saw the wisdom of treating their workers well and maintaining hospitals and schools within the factory complex. In contrast, workers in factories owned by foreign companies or Russian corporations under the control of the great St. Petersburg banks allegedly fared more poorly because their managers preferred high prices of shares on the exchange to the long-term health of the enterprise. The novels of Charles Dickens, which dramatized the squalor of English cities during the Industrial Revolution, no doubt reinforced this mythical dichotomy.

Buryshkin also contrasted the Moscow merchants' sense of public duty to the allegedly more mercenary motives of European and American businessmen. In Moscow, factory owners "looked on their activity not only and not so much as a source of wealth but as the fulfillment of a mission entrusted [to them] by God or fate." The general disdain for wealth among not only revolutionaries but also "the urban intelligentsia" in general impelled successful merchants to apply their wealth to useful projects. In his opinion, the fabled philanthropy and art patronage of the Moscow merchants demonstrated that in Russia the "'cult' of wealthy people, which may be seen in western countries," did not exist.[39]

This attitude may have prevailed among the most sophisticated and generous of Moscow merchants, but the historical record suggests that it constituted wishful thinking when applied to Russian manufacturers as a group. The corps of factory inspectors, created soon after a huge strike at the Morozov factory in Orekhovo-Zuevo in 1885, documented complaints of mistreatment by workers and occasional outbursts of violent protest in the most patriarchal of factories.⁴⁰ The struggle between factory owners and workers grew out of quite different notions of fairness and justice as well as objective economic conflicts over working conditions and rates of pay. For their part, merchants persisted in regarding the participants in the enterprise as a sort of family in which the owners exercised tutelage (*opeka*) over the workers. Such paternalism, which corresponded to the Slavophile notion of rural harmony between the kind landlord and loyal peasants in years gone by, eventually engendered resentment among workers.

By claiming to care for their workers as a father cared for his children in a tradition that had for centuries endorsed physical violence against children for the sake of discipline, the Moscow merchants could reject the accusation that their factories represented the poverty and squalor of capitalism in Europe, which served as the sources of revolution in the teeming cities. In this portrayal, the paternalism that allegedly motivated Moscow merchants, free from the greed and violence that infected the West, would save Russia from revolution. To admit the existence of economic antagonism within the factory would have deprived the Moscow manufacturers of the last vestige of the Slavophile myth. To be sure, the late nineteenth century marked a change from paternalism to formal and antagonistic relationships in the Central Industrial Region. The labor violence of 1905 prompted the most enlightened merchants to call for a frank and open struggle against the workers' unions. Numerous employers' associations sprang to life after 1905 to counter the labor movement with blacklists, lockouts, and other tactics, especially in St. Petersburg, where employers had no use for the Slavophile myth. Still, the self-congratulatory notion of the benevolent factory owner persisted until the very end in the Moscow region.⁴¹

The second element of Slavophile capitalism, economic xenophobia, grew directly out of the struggle to protect Russian industry, especially textile manufacturing in the Central Industrial Region, against the fatal threat of European imported goods. The Moscow merchants and their Slavophile allies resorted to classic kvas patriotism in their campaign against foreign capital. For example, Chizhov denounced the European bankers who mismanaged the construction of the Russian railroad network in the early 1860s as heartless exploiters "to whom Russians and redskinned Indians are just one and the same."⁴²

Likewise, the most influential merchant in Moscow expressed contempt for the advocates of free trade whom he encountered in the debate over tariff protection in 1868: the Warsaw banker Juliusz Wertheim, who spoke no Russian; Sachert of Lodz; Haffenberg of Riga; Fronstein of Rostov-on-Don; and Goldenberg of Odessa, "a wily Jew and former smuggler." These non-Russians, who owed their prosperity to close economic relations with Europe and thus opposed industrial protection, appeared to the Muscovites as economic traitors.⁴³

The ultimate origins of the economic xenophobia of the merchants and Slavophiles must be sought far back in Russian history. As part of the general repudiation of foreign influences after the reign of Peter the Great, Russians expressed indignation against the financial abuses of the chief of Russian mines, a mining expert from Saxony. His attempt, in 1740, to found a company that would have assumed control of the state-owned iron foundry "is considered by most Russian historians as a sellout of Russian interests to foreigners and therefore an act of national betrayal."[44]

Medieval historians have documented the impulse even earlier, before the emergence of corporate capitalism in Europe. It apparently began shortly after the first English merchant, Richard Chancellor, reached Russia via the White Sea in 1553 and a group of London merchants established the Russia Company. The "mistrust and scarcely veiled hostility with which nearly all Russians regarded foreigners" owed much to "the profound sense of difference from the west produced by the existence of the Orthodox church in Russia,"[45] but economic conflict intensified the tension. In 1563, Tsar Ivan IV angered Russian merchants by permitting William Garrand, a governor of the Russia Company, to trade freely throughout Muscovy without paying duties. Nine petitions submitted to the tsar between 1627 and 1667 expressed the Russian merchants' "commercial backwardness and psychological feelings of inadequacy in the presence of foreigners." An impassioned petition from the Assembly of the Land (*zemskii sobor*) of 1648–9 complained that English and Dutch merchants evaded customs payments on foreign goods and sold them illegally throughout Muscovy, so that Russian "merchants have perished completely because of them." Smuggling and other forms of "trickery" by the English in evading restrictions on trade meant that "the royal customs revenue suffers harm and great loss." (The attempt to identify the merchants' economic interests with those of the Russian state recurred regularly in the following centuries.) The petition requested that foreigners be confined to Archangel and Pskov.[46]

From his exile in Tobolsk in the 1660s, the Croat scholar Iurii Krizhanich, imbued with a vision of Slavic unity, eloquently reiterated the Russian merchants' complaint:

> If everyone is allowed to trade with foreigners, or if foreigners receive permission to live among us, the people suffer greatly; they take our wealth away from us and we starve, while they consume the fruit of our land before our eyes. . . . All of our Slavic people are so cursed that everywhere they look they see Germans, Jews, Scotsmen, Gypsies, Armenians, Greeks, and merchants of other nations sucking their blood.

The merchants' campaign "for the restriction of all foreigners to trade at the country's frontiers" ended in success with the passage of the New Trade Charter in 1667.[47]

The Old Belief (*staroobriadchestvo*), the fundamentalist pre-Petrine Orthodox religion that embraced between a tenth and a fifth of the ethnic Russian population, including many important merchant clans, from the mid-seventeenth century onward contributed important ideas and attitudes to this outlook. The British journalist Donald Mackenzie Wallace called the Old Belief "the origin of the Slavophile sentiment," though not its formal philosophical "doctrine." The Old Believers condemned the innovations of Nikon as errors of the Western church, transmitted via Constantinople. Future research on the merchant-Slavophile alliance of the mid-nineteenth century might well focus on who influenced whom.[48]

The reactions of foreign capitalists who encountered this hostility in Russia remain unclear. On the one hand, as discussed in Chapter 3, a handful of foreigners occupied positions of great influence in the Russian corporate elite. After years of honest conduct in business, they apparently convinced their closest partners and customers among the Russian population of the falsity of the notion of the evil foreigner. Still, their habit of referring to their own groups as "colonies" and their tendency to leave Russia after years of residence made it clear that the cultural tension never dissipated. This hostility was typified by the angry denunciation, by a minor character in Goncharov's great novel *Oblomov* (1859, part 4, sec. 3), of shares (*aktsii*) as nothing but "a German invention!" By issuing worthless pieces of paper, he complained, clever swindlers fleeced gullible "fools."

Major contributions to the cause of Russian economic development did not suffice to insulate foreigners from xenophobic abuse at the hands of business associates or the public at large. The distrust of the Russians toward even the most useful of their German business partners became clear by the end of the century. In 1895, shortly after the death of Ludwig Knoop, his sons' firm became the target of criticism in the liberal Moscow newspaper *Russkie vedomosti* (Russian News). The dispute raged over the fate of the Lapino Manufacturing Company, a small cotton-textile enterprise outfitted and supplied by the Knoops. (The company, founded in 1877 by five Russian merchants, including a father and two sons named Klopov, took the usual structural form of a share partnership in light industry in the Central Industrial Region: a small capitalization of 600,000 rubles divided into 600 shares called *pai* with a relatively high price of 1,000 rubles. The factory, in the village of Lapino, in Moscow district, was managed from the corporate headquarters in the city of Moscow.)

Russkie vedomosti claimed that the Knoops held the enterprise in "bondage" (*kabala*) because it had supplied not only the equipment in the factory and the raw cotton processed there but also the English foremen who supervised the workers and maintained financial control over the company. The Knoop firm granted credit to the company by accepting bills of exchange that could be presented for immediate payment at any time and, to prevent the sale of shares without permission, held the book listing shareholders in the firm's own office safe. When the company began to lose money, the "cotton kings" allegedly forced the company into bankruptcy, "to teach the Russian merchants a lesson," rather than settling accounts amicably. The newspaper called for "legislative measures" to weaken the financial stranglehold of Germans over Russian industry.⁴⁹

An article in a St. Petersburg technical journal, published separately as a pamphlet, reprinted this account from *Russkie vedomosti* and alleged that the Knoops had engaged in many other unfair business practices. These included the delivery of substandard raw cotton; the creation of "a whole colony" of English foremen in the Moscow region; the importation of English machinery that was "very much out of date"; and an attitude of "complete contempt" for textile machines manufactured in Russia. What Schulze-Gävernitz and Spies had praised in the Knoops—their success in outfitting 122 Russian factories with the best English equipment and establishing a stable price structure for the entire Russian textile industry at the annual fair at Nizhnii Novgorod—the anonymous author castigated as the evil power of foreigners over defenseless Russian merchants. The pamphlet's many objections to the hiring of English foremen and to their lack of expertise, their haughtiness, and their alleged brutality toward workers suggested that the anonymous author was a Russian engineer jealous of restricted opportunities in an industry controlled by foreigners. The rest of the pamphlet alleged substandard design of factory buildings, faulty construction techniques, careless installation of machinery, and physical abuse of workers by English foremen under the Knoops' supervision.⁵⁰

Germans saw the matter differently. To Schulze-Gävernitz, Knoop had acted honorably in closing down the Lapino company. Virtually every Moscow textile mill owed its very existence to Knoop and his sons because they had provided essential inputs: machinery, raw materials, foremen, and even construction materials for modern factories, all on easy credit terms available from no one else in Russia. At any moment, Knoop could have ruined any of his Russian customers, but he refrained from doing so because in the long run he profited from their continued purchases.

The Germans accused the manager and main stockholder of the Lapino company, a second-guild merchant named Nikita F. Sergeev, of dissolute and incompetent management. In desperation, he tried to extricate himself from debt by arranging to steal the share book of the company from the Knoop firm's safe. Only then did the Knoops deny the company further credit, thereby dooming it to bankruptcy. (Sergeev was apparently found guilty of theft at this trial, and the Lapino factory eventually fell under the control of the Franz Rabeneck Company, managed by Georg Spies, one of the leading "Moscow Germans," in the 1890s.) The Russian press called the Knoops' action a vindictive persecution, but Schulze-Gävernitz justified it as a response to a criminal act. He admitted the accuracy of the Russians' complaint that Knoop exercised a form of "benevolent tutelage" over his customers but argued that Knoop's "activity was beneficial for Russia" because "his clients also became wealthy."⁵¹ Schulze-Gävernitz did not deign to respond to the accusation that the Knoops forced Russian merchants to purchase substandard machinery and cotton.

The lack of adequate empirical spadework on the lives of the Knoops in Moscow prevents our knowing precisely how this public denunciation of German capitalism affected their personal relationships with their closest business partners among the Moscow merchants. The unusually candid memoirs of Georg Spies suggested, however, that even the closest affinity could not erase these partners' suspicion that foreigners abused their superior economic power over Russians. A "splendid, clever, loyal" man from peasant stock from the Viatka region far to the northeast of Moscow, Afinogen Stepanovich Isergin managed one of the many vicuna textile factories to which Spies supplied dyed yarn. Spies recalled that Isergin regarded "European culture with fear mixed with wonder." In the old Russian style, he displayed a strangely contradictory outlook comprised of both "deep piety" and "an antipathy [*Abneigung*] bordering on hatred for everything European. It was the instinctive emotion of the semi-Asiatic (for the Russians must be called that) against the power of the West, which was [allegedly] undermining the Russian-Oriental culture; this feeling dominated [the thought of] Dostoevskii as well." Isergin had never visited St. Petersburg and felt such "antipathy" toward Poland because of its Catholic religion that he refused to travel to the firm's factory in Poland until ordered to do so by his superiors in the company. "Because he had taken a great fancy to me, he expressed his sorrow that I was a Protestant. For I was destined someday to suffer the horrible torments of hell, while he, as an Orthodox Christian, dared to hope that he would go to heaven. The certainty that he would not encounter there so beloved a friend as me caused him deep sadness."[52]

The provincialism of Orthodox Russian merchants and peasants seemed to lack any specifically economic or political content. Isergin hated the West primarily because he perceived in Catholicism and Protestantism a threat to his beloved "Holy Russia." However, it was a small logical step to proceed from the identification of foreigners with a repugnant religion to the condemnation of the vast economic power that they wielded in Russia. As the criticism of the Knoop firm in the liberal *Russkie vedomosti* showed, successful sponsorship of Russian industrial development by Europeans did not protect them from accusations of enrichment at the expense of weak and gullible Russians. Even the most honorable of foreign merchants, like Spies, who furnished lucrative employment to hundreds of Russians and won their genuine friendship and admiration on a personal level, appeared, in their opinion, to be destined for eternal damnation.

Having blossomed in the 1850s, Slavophile capitalism remained strong among the Moscow industrialists into the twentieth century. The career of a minor journalist, Sergei F. Sharapov, revealed the reactionary potential of this ideological pedigree. Sharapov claimed to follow the example of the leading Slavophile publicist, Ivan S. Aksakov. Having learned the rudiments of economic xenophobia as the secretary of the Moscow Branch of the Russian Industrial Society, funded by the most prominent merchants of the Central Industrial Region, Sharapov attacked

German industrialists in the Kingdom of Poland with rhetorical flourishes such as these:

> Germany offers us friendship and we can be assured of her sincerity. What sense is there in war, in taking by force what we give away with the kindest smile? But there is a terrible price to this friendship. It requires the complete renunciation of all economic independence and the complete opening of Russia to German wheeling and dealing [*khoziainichan'ia*]! Our huge, strong, and fresh state lies as if seized by paralysis. . . . Let us await with hope this moment of enlightenment, for only then will a new and radiant life begin for Russia!

In this speech, he advocated a ban on foreign ownership of land and factories in the western provinces of the Russian Empire.

Sharapov subsequently devoted his rhetorical energies to the plight of Russian agriculture and won fame as a critic of Witte's industrialization policies, which he considered too favorable to foreign capital. In 1902, he founded an agricultural implements company for the salvation of the Russian gentry and peasantry, but its tiny capitalization—100,000 rubles—made it the smallest joint-stock company (*aktsionernoe obshchestvo*) chartered in Moscow province between 1864 and 1908. He spent the last years of his life as an embittered defender of patriarchal agriculture and small-scale industry on the extreme right of the Russian political spectrum.

Heinz-Dietrich Löwe identified Sharapov as "the most important foster-father of the Russian radical right" and correctly stressed his identification of Jews with foreign capital. However, Löwe neglected the logical connection between Sharapov's early journalism on behalf of the Moscow industrialists and his later, more famous, attacks on Jews and Witte's economic policies.[53] The ease with which Sharapov moved from industrial to agricultural journalism illustrates the closeness of the Moscow merchants' ideology to that of the reactionary agrarians.

The notoriously conservative reign of Emperor Alexander III (1881–94) witnessed a variety of outbursts by Russian merchants and their spokesmen against foreign merchants in Russia. To be sure, the Moscow merchants' economic xenophobia found little resonance among the Russian merchants in St. Petersburg, who apparently accepted the benefits of close relationships with foreigners. The formation of the First Russian Fire Insurance Company in 1827, in which foreigners were not permitted to invest, had provided an early opportunity for merchants in St. Petersburg to show their determination to wrest the insurance business in Russia from English companies. However, this campaign of economic nationalism had little significance as an episode of xenophobia because several German subjects of the Russian emperor, including the banker Baron Ludwig Stieglitz, figured prominently among the founders of the company.[54] Six decades later, one clash did occur there. In 1888, merchants of the second guild complained that first-guild merchants, many of them foreigners, had chosen foreigners to fill eleven of twelve seats on the

Petersburg Exchange Committee, including the presidency, which was held by a British subject. The protest culminated in a demand that only "genuine [*korennye*] Russian merchants" be allowed to serve as president of the exchange committee.[55]

Moscow remained the center of Russian economic xenophobia. In the late 1880s, an obscure writer named D'iakonov sketched a somber picture of Jews, Armenians, and other non-Russian merchants who congregated in the Moscow Exchange. Borrowing religious rhetoric from the Book of Judges, he alleged that these outsiders, distinguished by their swarthy complexions and guttural speech, had transformed the exchange into "a temple of Baal," the ancient Canaanite god whose priests had presided over child sacrifice and ritual prostitution. Reiterating Dostoevskii's prejudice against railroads, he also castigated the "big shots" (*tuzy*), including not only the Germans Meck and Derwies but also Mamontov, a prominent Russian merchant based in Moscow, who had grown rich by building and managing railroads. He reiterated Sharapov's claim that the textile factories of Lodz prospered at the expense of those in Moscow. He also took credit for an article in favor of Russian industrial development published in 1885 in *Sovremennye izvestiia*, a journal edited by the notoriously nationalist writer Nikita P. Giliarov-Platonov. However, he offered neither a rational explanation of his distinction between evil non-Russian and good Russian capitalism nor any concrete suggestions as to how the economic position of Russian merchants might be strengthened.[56]

Such xenophobia was not confined to the reactionary fringe but remained strong among the Moscow merchants themselves. During the bitter tariff war between Russia and Germany in the early 1890s, the Muscovites' xenophobic rhetoric resounded with special ferocity. In 1893, Savva T. Morozov, the president of the Nizhnii Novgorod Fair Committee, demanded high import tariffs to prevent German industry from dominating the Russian domestic market. During this debate, another prominent Moscow textile manufacturer likened German-owned factories in Central Europe to "alien, poisonous little mushrooms and tumors" (*chuzheiadnye gribki i polipy*).[57]

In their campaign of economic nationalism just before the start of World War I, the leading Moscow manufacturers demanded state aid to meet the threat of the Germans, whom Pavel P. Riabushinskii characterized as "the ancient oppressors of Slavdom." In 1916, Pavel Riabushinskii's brother Mikhail spoke in the name of cultured capitalism, but used the old rhetoric of resentment and fear to warn against the new economic and cultural threat from the United States of America:

> The Americans have seized our money, have entangled us in colossal debts, and have amassed incalculable riches. The center of [international] payments is passing from London to New York. They have neither science, nor art, nor culture in the European sense. They buy from vanquished countries their national museums; they lure artists, scholars, and businessmen to their employ with huge salaries and create for themselves what they lack. The downfall

of Europe and the loss of its primacy in the world to another continent—after such heroism, genius, persistence, and intellect manifested by old Europe! The only hope [is] that Europe, having demonstrated such stupendous energy, will find within itself the strength for a new renaissance.[58]

Although the Moscow industrial leadership refrained from anti-Semitism, the mass of poorly educated Russian merchants in Moscow and the provinces figured prominently in the mobs of anti-Semitic and antiliberal Black Hundreds.[59] In the end, the reactionary and radical movements proved far more influential in Russian society than the weak liberal tendency, which taught ethnic toleration, free trade, and cosmopolitanism.

The third element of Slavophile capitalism, the notion that Russian industry constituted an essential tool in the defense of the fatherland against the economic threat from the West, also had deep roots in Moscow merchant culture. It represented a skillful use of Slavophile patriotism against the gentry, who often used other Slavophile ideas for their own reactionary purposes. As Buryshkin noted bitterly, "the idea, or rather the prejudice, that Russia was a purely agricultural country" persisted to the end in aristocratic circles. Such a belief, he opined, threatened to condemn Russia to eternal economic backwardness:

> However strange it may seem, right up to the revolution (and this notion survives even now in some cases amid "the debris of the wreckage"), in a certain part of so-called fashionable society and the upper bureaucracy there existed an unusually contemptuous attitude not only toward leaders of commerce and industry, who were in the great majority not of gentry status and often had recently emerged from the enserfed peasantry, but also toward industry and commerce themselves. Sometimes this idea was camouflaged by peculiar economic theories, such as that Russia allegedly was exclusively agricultural and had no need of industry.

Closely related to this idea was the theory that "Peter the Great, in inaugurating the creation of industry in Russia, had diverted the country from its historic path and that all misfortunes flowed from this." This "scornful attitude . . . was endured rather painfully in Moscow, especially by the most educated industrial leaders, who had contacts with the West and knew what a [great] role economic issues played in the modern state and what was being done [by industry and commerce] to raise and develop the productive forces of the country."[60] The merchants' defense of Russian industry proceeded from patriotic motives, not from a love of the West. Indeed, it was only by borrowing foreign technology, Russian industrialists argued, that they could defend the national interest against the threat of economic enslavement to the West.

It might be argued that the second and third rhetorical stances represented two chronological stages in the development of the Moscow merchant ideology: Slavophile denunciation of the evils of foreign capitalism in the second half of the nineteenth century and the notion of progressive industry in the early twentieth. However, merchants had criticized the doctrine that Russia was an exclusively agricultural country as early as the 1850s; and Pavel P. Riabushinskii articulated both these ideas simultaneously during the brief heyday of open political activity after the Revolution of 1905.

A vivid statement of Slavophile capitalism appeared in 1911 in an anonymous diatribe against the abuses of large corporate banks in St. Petersburg. Large transactions typical of a modern economy required credit, in the form of discounting thousands of bills of exchange, for which service the joint-stock banks charged a high fee. Having invested depositors' funds in the stock market, and using information not available to the public, the largest banks reaped huge profits. In terms as vitriolic as those of any Bolshevik, the author condemned the banks' "stock-exchange speculation: . . . the swindling and charlatanism of the mass of wheeler-dealers who strive to make money in the air, without any productive work." Because they accumulated huge amounts of deposits, for which they required profitable investments, the joint-stock banks allegedly were tempted to risk failure in pursuit of massive gains.

More fascinating than this article's bitter condemnation of capitalist speculation was its optimistic prediction of a bright future that lay just ahead. Less crass norms of economic activity would finally supplant individual and group ones. According to this Hegelian logic, which lacked any socialist content, the great banks constituted only the highest stage of capitalism yet in existence. The "machine period of capitalism is the highest development of capitalism, its last stage," which would inevitably give way to the triumph of cooperative economic activity, represented by mutual credit societies. Unfortunately, these new institutions grew slowly because they depended on the meager resources of small savers and suffered from bureaucratic constraints imposed by the State Bank and Ministry of Finance, which favored the big banks. Ultimately, however, the principle of democracy would prevail in the marketplace. The immoral swindling of the joint-stock banks would succumb to the productive lending policies of "the mutual credit society, based to a certain extent on public and social [*obshchestvennykh, sotsial'nykh*] principles, not those of the group or the individual." A harbinger of this happy future lay in the creation, in the previous year (1910), of a central bank to service the five hundred mutual credit societies that existed in Russia and to free them from dependence on the corporate banks.

Far from endorsing socialism, the author praised the Moscow manufacturers for their sane and honest business dealings. Certainly, many difficulties lay ahead, including "the struggle of the laboring masses with capitalist industrialists who treat labor unjustly." However, the article closed by celebrating the industrialists of Moscow, who had recently established several solid mutual-credit societies, symbols of what the author called the country's "social and economic renaissance."[61]

This article restated the familiar Russian resentment against the overly mechanistic aspects of European capitalism and reiterated the Moscow merchants' traditional feeling of moral superiority over the big banks and cartels based in St. Petersburg. On the eve of World War I, the prominent Moscow banker and philanthropist Aleksei S. Vishniakov considered the Taylor system of industrial management something of a joke.[62] This indifference stood in stark contrast to the determination of the St. Petersburg manufacturers to apply Taylorism in defiance of the workers' protests, as at the New Aivaz factory. The Moscow merchants' feelings of paternalism toward their workers and their alleged devotion to the motherland, to their traditional peasant culture, and to Russian Orthodoxy (or even to the fundamentalist Old Belief of the seventeenth century) combined to form a powerful economic vision rooted in a specifically Russian sense of national identity.

Slavophile capitalism—the notion that somehow Russian industrialists could create a capitalist economy free from the moral depravity of the West—proved difficult to export beyond its birthplace, the Moscow region. Paradoxically, the rhetoric of Slavophilism kept open the fissures that divided the Russian manufacturers along geographical lines. The Muscovites seemed all too eager to use the rhetorical weapon of economic xenophobia, originally devised in the struggle against Britain, France, and Germany, against their regional rivals, especially the manufacturers of Lodz and the bankers of St. Petersburg.[63]

Several appeals to economic nationalism appeared in the commercial-industrial press outside Moscow. One engineer in the normally cosmopolitan newspaper of the South Russian mine-owners calculated that foreigners enjoyed far greater returns on Russian industrial investments than at home: 25 million francs on a 10 million investment over ten years, for example, compared to only 6 million in France. "Thus it is not difficult to see who is enriching whom."[64] Even Avdakov, who praised England as a model for Russia in 1912, had resorted to fears of German economic control of the Russian metallurgical industry in his appeal for high tariffs on coal and iron two decades earlier. In 1896 he had led a successful campaign to bar from South Russian industry all foreign technicians and managers who were not fluent in the Russian language.[65] The Russian merchants of Archangel, in the far north, resented the tsarist government's eagerness to grant timber and trade concessions to foreigners along the coast of the White Sea. Although their prosperity depended on close commercial relations with Europeans, cemented in many cases by intermarriage, "a byproduct of the merchants' perception was xenophobia," which drew on the long tradition of North Russian "regionalism and xenophobia," deeply rooted in the local folklore. Witte gave a simple explanation for the Russian industrialists' hostility to foreign capitalists: their aversion to "competition from foreigners."[66] Just before World War I, an Armenian scholar published a general critique of foreign capital in Russia that reiterated the main arguments of the Moscow merchants.[67]

The Association of Industry and Trade, created in 1906, strove to forge unity among Russia's disparate commercial and industrial elites. To this end, it borrowed the rhetoric of Slavophile capitalism in its denunciation of the foreign economic threat. Some of the AIT's leaders were pillars of Moscow industry. However, regional differences and rivalries among various commercial, industrial, and financial interest groups persisted until the end, preventing the emergence of a united "Russian bourgeoisie."[68]

The sharpening of rivalries among the commercial-industrial elites in the various regions of the empire constituted only one of the negative consequences of this campaign of economic xenophobia. Another was the eventual use of anticapitalist rhetoric against the sons and grandsons of its creators—the Moscow manufacturers—by their political rivals in the early twentieth century. A major paradox of Russian economic thought lay in the fact that the rich armory of rhetoric created by the Moscow merchants eventually served the revolutionary socialists who swept capitalist institutions from the scene in 1917.

War and Revolution: The Origins of Economic Xenophobia in Soviet Ideology

World War I placed the very survival of the Russian state in jeopardy. Charges and countercharges of treason filled the air as liberals, reactionaries, and radicals portrayed their domestic enemies as tools of foreign interests. During the diplomatic crisis in early August 1914, the British consul in Moscow sensed the mercurial mood of the Russian population toward foreigners. "Strong hands passed me over the heads of the crowd to the entrance [of the British consulate], while a thousand Russian voices thundered: 'Long live England.' A bearded student kissed me on both cheeks. England had declared war on Germany. Another day's delay, and the demonstrators would have smashed our windows."[69]

Less than a year later, he stood horrified as the crowd attacked German property:

> On June 10th [1915] vast anti-German riots broke out in Moscow, and for three days the city was in the hands of the mob. Every shop, every factory, every private house, owned by a German or bearing a German name, was sacked and looted. The country house of [the late Baron Ludwig] Knoop, the great Russo-German millionaire, who more than any other man had helped to build up the Russian cotton [textile] industry by importing English machinery and English managers, was burnt to the ground. The mob . . . cared nothing that its victims were Russian subjects and in many cases men who, in spite of their names, could speak no German. . . . Hooligans sacked the leading piano store of Moscow. Bechsteins, Blüthers, grand pianos, baby grands and uprights, were hurled one by one from the various stories to the ground, where a high bonfire completed the work of destruction.[70]

In his famous "Stupidity or Treason?" speech to the State Duma on November 1, 1916, the leader of the liberal Kadet party, Pavel N. Miliukov, branded the royal family and Foreign Minister Stürmer as agents of the kaiser. Although the historian Sergei P. Mel'gunov found "that Miliukov was wrong on most counts," his speech marked the beginning of the revolutionary upheaval of 1917.[71]

Liberals and moderate socialists, horrified by Lenin's opposition to World War I, attributed his "defeatism" to the power of "German gold." Lenin, as a self-professed Marxist, bore an ideological burden as well. When Archangel rebelled against the Bolshevik dictatorship in April 1918, Chaikovskii, a prominent socialist, castigated the "outdated German ideology" of Marx.[72] For their part, Bolsheviks and Left Socialist Revolutionaries criticized the Provisional Government for its allegedly mercenary devotion to the Allies. The proliferation of these rhetorical appeals suggests that all the major parties detected a xenophobic temperament in the public and hoped to derive political benefit from it.

Liberals who upheld the country's diplomatic obligations to the Allies lost public support as the economic deprivations of war became unbearable. Although hatred for the Germans remained strong, resentment among workers and peasants against the Allies increased as the war dragged on, much to Lenin's political benefit. Mikhail I. Tereshchenko, the liberal sugar manufacturer and last foreign minister of the Provisional Government, justified the war effort on the basis of national economic interest. "Our enemy [Germany] looks upon Russia as a market for its products. The end of the war will leave us in a feeble condition, and with our frontier open the flood of German products can easily hold back for years our industrial development. . . . I say openly and frankly: the combination of forces which unites us to the Allies is *favorable to the interests of Russia*."

This selective use of economic xenophobia, directed against the Germans but not the Allies, strengthened Lenin's case that Russian liberals willingly served as agents of Allied "imperialism." Still more provocative was the willingness of the liberals to turn to foreigners in hopes of quelling the unruly Russian masses. The petroleum magnate Stepan G. Lianozov, for example, called upon "foreign powers" (apparently the Allies) to suppress social revolution "as one would intervene to cure a sick child, and teach it how to walk. Of course it would be more or less improper, but the nations must realize the danger of Bolshevism in their own countries— such contagious ideas as 'proletarian dictatorship,' and 'world revolution.'" After the Germans seized Riga and began marching toward Petrograd, some merchants there reportedly expressed a preference for the rule of the kaiser to that of the Bolsheviks or even the provisional government.[73]

The importance of xenophobia as an element of Bolshevik ideology contradicts the familiar concept of the Russian Revolution of 1917–21 as a conflict among social classes. As is well known, Lenin called for an international revolution of workers and peasants against the capitalists and landlords of the world in the spirit of the famous slogan of Marxism, "the working men have no country."[74] His strategy, as laid out in the "April Theses" of 1917, envisioned a revolution of workers and peasants of all nationalities, including minorities oppressed by the tsarist regime, against all landlords and capitalists. The challenge of demonstrating the importance of xenophobia in the Russian Revolution is great; some might call the effort presumptuous. However, this interpretation is not intended to diminish the importance of social hostilities in the Russian Revolution. Its purpose is to show that the class conflict derived much of its emotional force from the powerful strain of xenophobia in Russian culture, a tendency far removed from Marxian socialism and insufficiently recognized as a component of the various revolutionary ideologies in 1917.

Mikhail Agursky, an émigré Soviet historian, has demonstrated that the Bolsheviks' success owed much to their ability to graft traditional Russian nationalism onto Marxist internationalism.[75] In addition, recent studies in Russian social history provide new evidence in support of this thesis.

Identifying Russian capitalists with foreigners served the Bolsheviks' political ends perfectly. For example, in early May 1917, during the diplomatic and political crisis over the provisional government's war aims, Lenin attacked the ministers for their alleged submission to the will of European capital.

> The point is that [the ministers] Guchkov, Miliukov, Tereshchenko, Konovalov represent the capitalists. And the capitalists need the seizure of foreign lands. They will get new markets, new places for the export of capital, new profitable jobs for tens of thousands of their sons, etc. The point is that at the present moment the interests of the Russian capitalists are identical with those of the English and the French capitalists. . . . The capitalists are intent on robbing Turkey, Persia, China. If, in order to accomplish this purpose, it be necessary to slaughter another ten millions or so of Russian muzhiks,—why worry?[76]

To be sure, Lenin attacked the British and French capitalists as capitalists, not as foreigners. He paid lip service to the ideal of proletarian and peasant internationalism in his condemnation of European and Russian imperialism in Turkey, Persia, and China, and his denunciation of the carnage of war from a socialist perspective echoed the impassioned rhetoric of the French radical Jean Jaurès, whose opposition to chauvinism cost him his life on the last day of July 1914. However, Lenin's sarcastic portrayal of Russian capitalists as tools of foreign imperialists, like his attack on Witte, Rothschild, and Bleichröder in 1902, contained an unmistakable xenophobic component.

In June 1917, Lenin condemned European capitalism in terms that resonated with xenophobia:

> The basis of the foreign policy of the politically conscious [Russian] proletariat is no separate peace treaty with the German capitalists and no alliance with the Anglo-French capitalists. . . . The foreign policy of the [Russian] capitalists and the petty bourgeoisie is "alliance" with the imperialists, that is, disgraceful dependence on them. The foreign policy of the proletariat is alli-

ance with the revolutionaries of the advanced countries and with all the oppressed nations against all and any imperialists.[77]

The "revolutionaries of the advanced countries" whom Lenin praised included only those of the Zimmerwald Left, who strove to transform World War I into a civil war pitting labor against capital in each country. As Robert Service noted in passing, Lenin condemned Prime Minister Aleksandr F. Kerenskii for allegedly submitting to the influence of "Anglo-French and Russian capital" by allowing the German army to capture Riga. Thus, "Lenin, the unbending internationalist and harrier of all professed patriots, was simultaneously standing forward as the only sure defender of Mother Russia."[78]

Just a week before the Bolsheviks seized power, Miliukov ridiculed Lenin's revolutionary program by stressing its ideological affinity to the utopian dreams of the Slavophiles. "The noble Lenin only imitates the noble Kireevskii when he holds that from Russia will come the New World which shall resuscitate the aged West, and which will replace the old banner of doctrinary Socialism by the new direct action of starving masses—and that will push humanity forward and force it to break in the doors of the social paradise." (An eminent historian of Russian culture, Miliukov had written the article on Slavophilism for the Brokgauz-Efron encyclopedia.) He then provided the Bolsheviks with yet another example of the Russian liberals' admiration of Europe: "Long live the light of humanity, the advanced democracies of the West, who for a long time have been traveling the way we now only begin to enter, with ill-assured and halting steps! Long live our brave Allies!"[79]

Agursky's analysis of Bolshevik ideology focused on Lenin's rivalry with German socialists over leadership of the international revolutionary movement. Although committed in theory to cooperation with non-Russian labor leaders, Lenin insisted that the Bolshevik Party, having come to power in Moscow, had full right to assume control over the socialist movement that bore Marx's name. He branded as "social-chauvinists" (socialists in word but chauvinists in deed) all, including German Marxists, who refused to follow the Bolshevik lead. They became virtual allies of German capitalism, according to the Leninist demonology. This impulse soon had worldwide consequences, as he subordinated the Third International or Comintern (1919–43) to the tactical needs of Soviet foreign policy.[80]

Lenin's implicit nationalism apparently derived from his intellectual and emotional ties to revolutionary populism, with which he had become acquainted in his youth at Kazan University in 1887, and his reading of the radical literature of the 1860s and 1870s after the execution of his older brother that year for participation in illegal political activities. The devotion of Lenin and his followers to the essentially Blanquist organizational tactics first proposed by Tkachev in the mid-1870s is well known to historians. For example, Richard Pipes stressed Lenin's emotional ties to the pre-Marxist agrarian revolutionaries generally known as "populists." Although there is no "direct evidence of Lenin's having been influenced by Tkachev in the 1890s," the young Lenin "was surrounded by social revolutionary Jacobins; he absorbed their ideas and thus no doubt was indirectly influenced by Tkachev." Likewise, Bertram Wolfe pointed out the similarities between Tkachev's and Lenin's doctrines regarding revolutionary tactics, such as the notion that only a disciplined minority could lead a social revolution in Russia.[81]

The parallel between Lenin's xenophobic attitudes toward European capitalism and those of Tkachev, examined earlier, has not attracted the notice of historians, however. An important hint came in quite another context, in a casual comment by Lenin's wife, Nadezhda Krupskaia, to her mother in a letter from Krakow in 1912, describing his devotion to classics of nineteenth-century Russian literature and art. "Volodya is a terrible nationalist. He wouldn't go to see the works of Polish painters for anything, but one day he got hold of a catalogue of the Tretyakov Galleries . . . and he frequently becomes absorbed in it." Thus, Lenin's artistic tastes turned out to be identical to those of the merchants Pavel and Sergei M. Tret'iakov, who had acted as the major patrons of the nationalist trend in nineteenth-century Russian painting.[82] As prominent textile manufacturers and public figures—Sergei served as mayor of Moscow from 1876 to 1882—the Tret'iakov brothers held conservative nationalist attitudes forged in the era of Slavophile capitalism.

Lenin's xenophobia, although subtle and perhaps unconscious until 1917, apparently strengthened his political appeal to the Russian workers and peasants in the revolutionary upheaval of 1917–20 even as it undermined his pretensions to Marxist internationalism. This logical contradiction probably worked to the Bolsheviks' advantage as the predicted world revolution receded steadily into the realm of the improbable and the need increased for secure domestic support in the face of foreign military threats during the Russian Civil War. Ironically, the revolutionary thinker who gained immortality for raising "conscious" revolutionary activity to the status of a political dogma in opposition to the merely "spontaneous" striving of the labor movement for incremental reforms rode to power on one of the greatest spontaneous outbursts of nationalist passion that Russian society had ever witnessed. Having appealed to this elemental power, Lenin perhaps remained oblivious to its effects, for he never renounced his faith in the ability of the Bolshevik Party to mold the inchoate striving of the masses according to the famous dichotomy in "What Is To Be Done?" (1902). Given the enormous emotional appeal of Russian economic xenophobia, however, Lenin may have owed his victory to his unconscious ability to harness this mighty political force.

In the 1920s, Lenin's cultural commissar, Anatolii Lunacharskii, explicitly embraced traditional Russian nationalism. Without it, he warned, the Bolsheviks "could find themselves in the situation of a band of conquerors in a foreign country." Citing Dostoevskii with obvious approval, Lunacharskii claimed for the Soviet state the leadership of the oppressed peoples of the world in their struggle against international capitalism as exemplified by the United States. Dostoevskii's monarchism and Orthodox Christianity had nothing in common, of course, with the Bolsheviks' atheistic socialism, but the claim of universality provided a crucial element of ideological continuity across the decades and the Russian political spectrum. To the allegedly crude, "industrial-commercial" soul of Americans, Lunacharskii contrasted the allegedly "more profound, elementary" Russian soul. Thus, "the Russian working class was able, bleeding and offering enormous sacrifices, to rise from the depths of autocracy and barbarism to the position of the avant-garde of humanity, in spite of all its awkwardnesses, which, however, were . . . recompensed by barbarian freshness and by the ability to be captivated by grand slogans—in other words, by its inclination toward active realistic idealism."[83]

To demonstrate conclusively that the Bolsheviks' xenophobic appeals actually drew the masses to the revolutionary banner would require an enormous effort of historical research. Several pieces of evidence support this hypothesis. The first was offered by a former Soviet historian who recently admitted that the violence of the Russian workers and peasants in the October Revolution of 1917 found no justification in Marxist ideology: "[T]heir antibourgeois moods and aspirations were not at all equivalent to socialist views, let alone conviction."[84]

The second episode indicating that economic xenophobia existed among the masses and that it eventually redounded to the Bolsheviks' benefit concerned the issue of foreign policy. Lenin gained enormous political support from workers and peasants, including thousands of soldiers, disgusted by the immense sufferings caused by World War I. In Moscow in March 1917, the Kadet slogan of "War to the Victorious Conclusion" received no endorsement in workers' resolutions, while many statements demanded a clarification of war aims, and a substantial minority demanded peace negotiations "or an outright end to the war."[85]

Third, the Russian Civil War called forth spontaneous hostility of the Russian masses toward the capitalists, both Russian and foreign. In her perceptive analysis of the war, Sheila Fitzpatrick observed that "outbursts of antisemitism, xenophobia, anti-intellectualism (*spetseedstvo*), and mob violence against individual *burzhui* and their wives and property" by Russian workers did not fit the official Bolshevik stereotype of the "conscious" worker in the great industrial centers of Russia. These lapses into what the Bolsheviks called "peasant" behavior in fact derived from the workers' experience in the cities, not solely from peasant traditions. Moreover, the official "disapproval was not absolute, since the cruder forms of class intimidation and resentment sometimes served revolutionary purposes." Xenophobic attacks against foreign capitalists, "particularly vulnerable and easy to defeat" in many factories, therefore "may have been a more typical part of Russian working-class *mentalité* than is usually acknowledged—perhaps even a part of the 'proletarian consciousness' that the Bolsheviks tapped or encouraged among their supporters."[86]

Throughout the Civil War, Bolshevik posters portrayed the Whites as tools of the evil imperialists in Europe and America. Four posters made graphic appeals to xenophobic sentiments. Viktor N. Deni's "League of Nations" (1919) portrayed the French, American, and British heads of states as pot-bellied, cigar-smoking tyrants, indifferent to the suffering of the oppressed masses of the world and seated on huge thrones before a row of hangman's nooses, above which fluttered a banner that read "Capitalists of the World, Unite!" Deni's "Capital" (1919) showed a pig-faced millionaire, dressed in the obligatory tuxedo and silk top hat, with four diamond rings on his fingers, waist-deep in a pile of gold coins. Dem'ian Bednyi's poem beneath the design called attention to the "steel spider web" in the background, symbol of the capitalist's claim to be "the conqueror of the world." Nikolai Kochergin's "Capital and Co." (1920), accompanied by another poem by Bednyi, depicted Capital as an obese green monster, draped in an ermine robe and served by the claw-fingered Entente leaders, Clemenceau, Wilson, and Lloyd George, and an odd assortment of enemies, foreign and domestic, including the Japanese, Poles, and Germans and Russian priests, kulaks, and anarchists.

In "Labor" (1920), D. S. Moor portrayed the Russian Revolution in cartoons and rhymed quatrains. Oppressors of the workers and peasants included not only priests and bureaucrats but two capitalists in their stereotypical tuxedos and silk hats. One, enthroned near a heap of money bags, symbolized world capitalism.

Capital, idol of all countries,	*Kapital, vsekh stran kumir,*
Has subdued the entire world.	*Pokoril sebe ves' mir.*
And into his pocket has flowed	*I v karman ego tekli*
All the treasures of the earth.	*Vse sokrovishcha zemli.*

The other rich man clutched a bag marked "1000 rubles." His round nose and thick lips left no doubt that the artist meant to conjure up in the viewer's mind the negative stereotype of the Jewish capitalist.[87]

It might be objected that Lenin's appeal to the Russian workers, within five months of the October revolution, to "Learn from the Germans!" undercut the xenophobic impulse. However, he meant only that the Soviets must borrow advanced technology for the sake of the revolution. Likewise, his emphasis on the massive gains in efficiency to be derived from Taylorism under Soviet rule indicated his belief that technology could be neutral in political terms once Soviet power had prevailed.[88] Neither the appeal to apolitical technology nor the many formal references to the international aspirations of the Marxist-Leninist revolutionary movement in Soviet posters diminished the significance of xenophobic metaphors in Bolshevik propaganda.

The social base of Bolshevism may account for the success of these appeals. Although Lenin appealed primarily to the workers, a large and amorphous group in which he included the poor peasants, recent research by Daniel T. Orlovsky has stressed the crucial revolutionary role of "the lower middle strata," composed of salesclerks, teachers, agronomists, paramedical workers, employees of the postal service and railroads, and the like. Far removed from the experience of factory labor, these groups became fully radicalized and pressed for democratization in the workplace in 1917. Orlovsky correctly concluded that, although not all these unions supported the Bolsheviks, "the occupations and state-building skills represented by all the white-collar unions were part of the fabric of revolutionary politics." Counterparts of these groups in France and Germany occasionally "wavered between left and right" before supporting "right-wing movements that promised to curb the excesses of capitalist development, restore 'old values', and promote a 'healthy' nationalism."[89] Their role in the rise of Hitler is well known. The degree to which Russian white-collar unions accepted xenophobic notions that eventually fused with the Soviet ideology remains an interesting empirical question.

Episodes of cooperation between anti-Bolshevik military forces and European powers during the Civil War reinforced the xenophobic demonology. For example, in Archangel, the socialists who overthrew Bolshevik power in August 1918 found it impossible to win the loyalty of peasants opposed to World War I. "The lack of a popular base and institutionalized links created a dependence on foreign [Allied] troops in a region with a long history of foreign war and xenophobia." Workers' demonstrations against alleged "English imperialism" in early 1919 opened the way to the eventual reassertion of power by the Bolsheviks in the Russian North.[90]

Likewise, managers of the Volunteer Fleet, a steamship agency heavily subsidized by the tsarist government to maintain a Russian presence in the Black Sea, the eastern Mediterranean, and the northern Pacific, obliged Lenin by behaving according to the stereotype of Russian capitalists as junior partners of world imperialism. They aided Denikin, Wrangel, and the French interventionists in the Crimea; mortgaged ships to the French in order to raise twenty million gold rubles; and flew the French flag in an effort to prevent the Russian Federation and the Far Eastern Republic from asserting control over the fleet's vessels in the Black Sea and Pacific Ocean.[91]

At the height of the foreign intervention, crews of ships belonging to the Volunteer Fleet in the Russian Far East declared their allegiance to the local Bolshevik government as the defender of the Russian "native land" against interventionists. The Union of Sailors in Vladivostok declared in early 1920 that "the intervention of foreigners, which has caused internal discord and bloodshed and destroyed the well-being of our people, ... consciously tightens the deadly noose [*soznatel'no zatiagivaet mertvuiu petliu*] around the neck of the Russian people." The sailors pledged to "employ all our skill and labor to promote the immediate evacuation of the interventionists for the welfare of the Motherland and our merchant fleet."[92]

Soviet propaganda conveniently ignored the existence of significant political tensions between the Whites and the Allies during the Russian Civil War. A persistent theme in the émigré literature was the alleged abandonment of the White cause by halfhearted European politicians. In any case, it appears likely that, if the Bolsheviks had not won the Civil War, an authoritarian Russian government under a military dictator, with or without the sanction of the Romanov dynasty, would have drawn political strength from the anti-Western mood of the masses, including the "lower middle strata" examined by Orlovsky, so weak was the liberal and cosmopolitan tradition in Russian society. In the absence of World War I, which caused the economic chaos that finally opened the way for the Bolshevik seizure of power, radical and liberal political tendencies would most likely have remained too weak to prevent the victory of a "a nationalist, but not legitimate [monarchist] regime" once the discredited Romanov dynasty had fallen.[93]

The vilification of foreign capitalists as enemies of Russia fitted all too comfortably into Soviet Marxism in the decades after the revolution. John M. Thompson referred in general terms to the revolution's "growing undertones of anti-Westernism, of a revulsion against Russia's inferiority, of a resentment against Russia's military and economic subservience to the West, of a hatred of foreigners as being chiefly responsible for the debacles of the war and, in fact, for all of Russia's woes." Likewise, Hugh Seton-Watson characterized the ideology of the new Bolshevik elite as a unique combination of "residual Marxism, Great Russian or Soviet chauvinism, and a type of esthetic, literary philistinism"; of these three elements, he noted, the tradition of "Great Russian chauvinism" remained particularly strong after five decades of Soviet power.[94]

These xenophobic tendencies eventually permeated Soviet ideology under Stalin, whose mediocre education in a provincial Orthodox seminary imbued him with the familiar rhetoric of kvas patriotism. With characteristic emphasis on the continuities of Russian cultural history, James H. Billington described Soviet culture under Stalin as "the revenge of Muscovy," replete with "masochistic and chauvinistic impulses." Long before the rise of Stalin, however, "the belief that Russia was destined to provide ideological regeneration for the decaying West had been propagandized by conservative as well as radical theorists. . . . For this dream people proved willing to die resisting the counterattacks of the old order during the Civil War." Thus, Stalin found some elements of xenophobia in the original Bolshevik ideology. Jeffrey Brooks detected in the mass consciousness an unwillingness to accept the official ideology of synthetic xenophobia in the 1920s.[95] In view of the pervasive identification of capitalism with foreigners before 1917, however, this dichotomy appears unduly sharp.

The self-proclaimed Marxist regime that ruled the Soviet state for seventy-four years so intensified the anticapitalist mentality that few Soviet citizens, historians included, found it possible to contemplate capitalism with any degree of intellectual objectivity. By the time Gorbachev legitimized economic initiative from below, no one understood the functioning of a mature capitalist economy. This ignorance provided a fertile field for the resurrection of nationalist (as opposed to Marxist-Leninist) critiques of capitalism at the end of the Soviet period.

A general critique of modernity emerged in Russia in the 1970s and grew stronger in the following decade. Writers known as the "partisans of renaissance" (*vozrozhdentsy*), including émigrés of the stature of Aleksandr I. Solzhenitsyn and Igor Shafarevich and novelists and artists in the USSR such as Valentin Rasputin, Vasilii Belov, and Il'ia Glazunov, called for a return to Russian traditions and a rejection of both Soviet internationalism and American capitalism. Their attacks on the negative aspects of American life—the alleged "secret dictatorship of capital," the narrowness of the political spectrum under the domination of two parties, the "psychedelic and sexual revolutions," and "the devouring spirit of mercantilism"—echoed the puritanical and anticapitalist rhetoric of the early Bolsheviks and, indeed, the prerevolutionary Russian xenophobes, both radical and reactionary. Most importantly, the partisans of renaissance rejected capitalism on religious grounds even before it had begun to reappear under Gorbachev. Feliks Karelin wrote in 1981 that capitalism was destroying Christianity in western Europe and the United States.[96] This attitude drew heavily on the long tradition of Russian anger against humiliation at the hands of foreigners, a major theme of the immensely popular nationalist writer V. Pikul', whose historical novel *Slovo i delo* (Word and Deed) chronicled the alleged "dominance of foreigners" (*zasil'e inozemtsev*) typified by the "rule of Bühren" (*Bironovshchina*) in the reign of Empress Anna Ivanovna (1730–40).[97]

The xenophobic current grew stronger during the general crisis of confidence that swept through Russian society during the era of perestroika. Under glasnost, various opponents of reform resorted once again to the familiar caricature: domestic enemies serving the interests of foreign enemies. The leaders of the conservative wing of the Soviet Communist Party—Egor K. Ligachev, Vladimir A. Kriuchkov, and Valentin S. Pavlov—warned against cooperation with Western businessmen on the grounds that they acted as spies and threatened Soviet society with the contagion of capitalism. Anders Aslund stressed that Ligachev's devotion to socialist morality was "intertwined with vivid anti-western sentiments. . . . He seems fascinated by the competition between the Soviet Union and the West, between socialism and capitalism, between collectivism and individualism." To the economic historian, perhaps the most striking aspect of these accusations, apart from their preposterous exaggeration, was the strong element of continuity with the prerevolutionary xenophobia of the Slavophile capitalists. When in late 1989 the Communist Party leader Ivan K. Polozkov attacked the newly legalized cooperative movement as "a social evil, a malignant tumor" that must be extirpated, by illegal means if necessary, he echoed the rhetorical condemnation of foreign capitalism as an alien force enunciated by the Moscow merchants nearly a century before.[98] (The resort to the identical image of poisonous and malignant tumors in the 1890s and 1989 demonstrates the emotional power of biological metaphors characteristic of reactionary nationalism worldwide.)

The concept of capitalism as an essentially foreign phenomenon continued to fuel popular resentment against the new forms of Russian capitalism that emerged under Gorbachev. Considerable resentment against newly arrived corporations, including McDonald's, Rank Xerox, and Coca-Cola, became evident even before the collapse of perestroika. Joint ventures, which often limited their activities to the extraction of Soviet raw materials because of currency restrictions, became, in Marshall Goldman's words, the targets of "critics and nationalists" who saw in such concessions "the foreigners' rape of the Soviet Union."[99]

Under a banner that proclaimed "Russia: My Motherland," several thousand nationalists in Moscow in 1990 cheered Nina Andreeva, a leading defender of the Stalinist legacy. She identified twin evils: the "counter-revolutionary and anti-people" policy of perestroika and the mortal threat from the West, which was allegedly "'infecting' the 'Russian motherland' with everything from AIDS to pornography." In her famous defense, two years before, of Stalin's alleged achievements, Andreeva warned of the danger posed by "potential Soviet millionaires" and other entrepreneurs, "demolishing young people's spiritual world with masterpieces imported from 'the other side', or home-grown imitations of mass culture."[100]

With similar exaggeration, Lt. Col. Viktor Alksnis, chairman of the reactionary "Union" (*Soiuz*) faction in the Soviet legislature, defended Stalin's economic dictatorship on essentially nationalistic grounds. "'You cannot blame everything on the command system,' he was quoted as saying in late 1990. 'Whatever its obvious minuses, it enabled us to restore our ruined economy in the five years after World War II.'" (The closely related argument that the Soviet economy, despite its inefficiencies, at least prepared the country to meet the onslaught of the Nazis in World War II, appeared often in both journalism and the specialized literature, even in the West. This example of the philosophical fallacy *post hoc, ergo propter hoc* received definitive refutation in a recent quantitative study.)[101]

The most extreme strains of reactionary nationalism and anti-Semitism emanated from bands that bore the name Pamiat (Memory), the organizational history of which included a series of splits and mutual recriminations typical of fringe groups everywhere. Factions of Pamiat explicitly denounced multinational corporations as tools of the alleged international Jewish conspiracy directed at Russia. The most outspoken contingent, led by a leather-jacketed photographer, Dmitrii D. Vasil'ev, appeared "not so much politically as socially and culturally anti-Western."

Like the Nazis, whom they resembled in their thuggery, black shirts, and "red flag with a white circle in it," Vasil'ev and his followers rejected capitalism as spiritually rotten.[102]

Vasil'ev explained the origins of the Russian Revolution in prose devoid of scholarly moderation. Jews and European governments had conspired to bring the Bolsheviks to power, he claimed. "Having sown panic among the deceived masses by means of a beastly terror, the representatives of the Jewish nation led the criminal coup [*perevorot*] in Russia according to the world-wide conspiracy, in which the Entente [Western powers] participated." The horrors of the Russian Revolution, including the overthrow of tsarism, the repudiation of Stolypin's land reform, and the ultimate mass murder of the Russian peasantry, represented "a deliberate crime [designed] to annihilate a great power and its mighty people; to turn our country into a colonial producer of raw materials for transnational corporations controlled by Zionist capital; and to impose unprecedented exploitation, which reduced nations to slavery."[103]

Vasil'ev attacked the restoration of capitalism in Russia, allegedly controlled by Jews; denounced all cooperatives that exploited workers; demanded reparations for Russia from Israel and "Jewish-owned multinational corporations and banks of the entire world"; and rejected Gorbachev's political reforms, which allowed democratic parties to triumph, allegedly with massive financial support from cooperatives. In a tape-recorded statement on August 16, 1990, Vasil'ev claimed that Zionists had inflicted National Socialism and World War II on the world.[104]

The appeals of such conspiracy theories were strong throughout Eastern Europe in the wake of the collapse of the Soviet empire. Post-Communist Romanian nationalists resorted to precisely this mixture of "xenophobic, anti-Semitic, anti-Gypsy, and anti-Hungarian rhetoric, inflaming public opinion against other nationalities. They also adopt the time-honored language of opposition to Europe, used since the nineteenth century all over the region to resist both penetration by western capital and the dislocating introduction of western political forms." By inculcating fear and hatred of "class enemies, saboteurs, or traitors" and blaming all problems on "external 'aliens'," the Communist regime in Romania "produced specific conditions in which scapegoating has emerged as an effective political tactic." The new nationalist rhetoric linked Gypsies to theft, illegal commerce, and unearned income from trade and Jews to the principles of private property, international capitalism, and democracy.[105]

The persistence of the idea of Russian moral superiority was evident in a statement by Mikhail F. Antonov, a leading Russian nationalist, in 1990: "Let other countries surpass us in the technology of computer production. . . . But only we can provide an answer to the question: Why? For whose sake? We are the only legitimate heirs to the great, spiritual Russian culture. The saving of the world will come from Soviet Russia." An American journalist paraphrased the economic views that flowed from this attitude in these terms: "Russian nationalists are against free markets, wealthy entrepreneurs and free trade zones that they believe will make Russia a colony of multinational corporations. They are against the 'video-player culture'." The residual anticapitalism of Marxism-Leninism found a sympathetic audience among angry workers organized by the Leningrad Communist Party: "speaker after speaker railed against 'millionaires' and Westernizers [in] an orgy of populism with Russian nationalist overtones."[106]

So powerful had this tendency become that Gorbachev himself resorted on occasion to the familiar rhetoric of xenophobia. In an angry outburst against the newspaper *Glasnost'* (Public Discussion), which called for the democratization of Soviet society at a pace too rapid for Gorbachev's taste, the Soviet leader claimed that the paper's editor, Sergei Grigor'iants, "is tied not only organizationally but also financially to the West, that his constant visitors and guests are Western correspondents. Therefore, people think of him as some kind of alien phenomenon in our society, sponging on the democratic process." In terms that could have come from *Pravda* in 1937, Gorbachev resorted to a familiar but sinister biological metaphor: "There are such parasites living off healthy organisms and attempting to harm them."[107]

Thus, the complex of ideas labeled here as "economic xenophobia" grew out of the long tradition of xenophobia in Russia and Eastern Europe, not only in the recent Soviet past but also in centuries of imperial history prior to World War I. The ease with which the opponents of perestroika resorted to the specter of evil foreign capitalism is understandable in view of the prominence of what we may call "political xenophobia" in Soviet culture. For example, Andreeva's speech of March 1990 equated evil forces in Soviet society with the external enemy. This attitude appealed to virtually all social groups in Soviet society, from the workers, peasants, and entrenched Communist bureaucracy to the anti-Semitic right. Needless to say, economic xenophobia constituted a major obstacle to the emergence of a democratic and capitalist society in the last decade of the twentieth century.

6

Conclusion: Varieties of Russian Capitalism

Path dependence means that history matters.
Douglass C. North[1]

Before examining the institutional patterns that seem likely to determine the evolution of Russian capitalism in the future, it is appropriate to review the four main patterns in the development of corporations in Russia under the tsarist regime and in the late Soviet period. First, despite the familiar Leninist formulas of "finance capitalism," "monopoly capitalism," "state-monopoly capitalism," and the like, capitalism remained weakly developed in Russia. The small numbers of corporations, especially on a per capita basis in comparison to the major European countries before 1914, reflected the ambivalence of the imperial government toward the intrinsic dynamism of capitalism. Although the tsarist government granted favorable treatment to large companies in the form of high import tariffs, massive financial subsidies to railroads, and lax enforcement of laws against cartels, it refused to allow incorporation by registration and maintained bureaucratic tutelage over all the key capitalist institutions: corporations, exchanges, and business organizations.

Second, capitalist institutions tended to cluster in the largest cities of the empire. Huge factories in cities and industrial villages held within a small space thousands of workers capable of violent action, while the vast majority of the population of the empire had no direct experience of the operation of corporations, either as workers or as managers.

Third, the corporation came to Russia as a fully mature institution, having evolved over the centuries in the distinctive cultural environments of Amsterdam, London, Paris, Hamburg, and New York. Capitalism in Russia wore a foreign face. The weakness of the native tradition of entrepreneurship, except in small and unincorporated enterprises such as textile workshops, meant that leading positions in the most dynamic sectors tended to be occupied by managers trained in the culture of European capitalism—foreigners, Jews, Germans, Poles, Armenians, and only occasionally Russians—or by former bureaucrats, military men, and courtiers, a significant percentage of whom turned their contacts in the imperial ministries to fraudulent ends. The ease with which unscrupulous corporate managers cheated stockholders and customers appeared to justify the maintenance of restrictive legislation, at least in the minds of bureaucrats, such as Reutern and Witte, who insisted that economic growth and corporate development remain under strict governmental supervision.

These patterns emerged once more in the brief period of reform under Mikhail Gorbachev in the late 1980s. Cooperatives proliferated in 1987–90, but the total reached only 193,400 in mid-1990, and the corporate law of 1990 came too late to permit the proliferation of corporations before the USSR collapsed. Cooperatives and corporations developed according to clear geographic patterns. As in the tsarist period, corporations clustered in the capital and other large cities to avail themselves of three rare factors found there: bureaucratic sponsorship, investment capital, and managerial expertise. The essentially foreign nature of production and distribution oriented toward a free market—a weak tradition in Russia before 1914 and an illegal one for more than fifty years after 1932—meant that the Soviet corporate elite would be drawn from the ranks of former criminals in the underground economy and former bureaucrats, few of whom evinced any respect for legality or the ethical norms of modern capitalism. Indeed, the strongest parallel between the tsarist and late Soviet periods consisted in the prominent role of former bureaucrats in the corporate elite, a feature unusual in the history of world capitalism outside the Third World in our century.

Finally, the numerical weakness, geographical concentration, and foreignness of corporations in both periods produced a predictable cultural impact: widespread revulsion against what appeared to many subjects of the tsar and the Soviet regime as an insidious economic threat from the West, aided by a handful of compliant Russians. Capitalism spurred resentment among millions of Russians who disapproved of the great wealth of corporate managers, considered corporate economic power morally suspect, or feared that corporations threatened their economic survival. Under torture, thousands of victims of Stalin's purges confessed to the crimes of espionage and plotting to break up the Soviet Union, allegedly at the behest of European intelligence services. These confessions reinforced the identification of alleged enemies of the Soviet regime with agents of international capitalism.

To the official Soviet condemnation of capitalism Marxism contributed important ideological elements. These included the allegedly scientific reasoning of nineteenth-century economics and the utopian claims of socialist morality. Still, to the cultural historian of Russia, the most striking feature of the political ideology of the late Soviet regime was its enormous debt to the Russian xenophobic tradition. From the refusal of the tsarist bureaucracy to relinquish the concessionary system of incorporation to the great anticapitalist riots that swept through the cities and villages of Russia in 1917, resentment of corporate capitalism *because of its alien nature* pervaded all segments of Russian society, except the most cosmopolitan members of the tiny liberal intelligentsia and the few thousand persons who comprised the corporate elite.

New corporations had barely begun to emerge under Gorbachev before the collapse of the Soviet state in 1991. Since then, economic and political institutions inherited from the past have evolved so rapidly that it is difficult to predict how the institutional environment will affect the development of corporations. Cultural inheritances from the past, particularly ideological notions of Russia's place in a hostile world, promise to exert a significant effect, however. Just as Japanese capitalism, even under the American occupation after World War II, retained cultural features specific to that island nation in previous centuries, so Russian capitalism will inevitably bear the mark of its past as managers, workers, and peasants remain imbued with distinctive values common to both the tsarist and Soviet ideologies.

The Russian economy now has considerable scope for change in a variety of directions, but the importance of ideology promises to remain great in the near future. In their analysis, foreign observers must resist the temptation to prescribe a given economic or political model rooted in the distinctive historical circumstances of other countries, an intellectual exercise both presumptuous and futile. As Ralf Dahrendorf recently observed, "American-style capitalism is only one way forward; few countries anywhere have opted for it." Within a system of constitutional liberties, "there are a hundred ways" to organize a society, "a nightmare for the conceptual purist."[2] At the other extreme, however, economic and moral relativism offers no clearer guide to the future than does ethnocentrism. Some paths of evolution entail more economic waste, political repression, and needless human misery than others. Without attempting to prescribe or predict the precise form that capitalist institutions will take in Russia in the decades ahead, the economic historian can distinguish several likely directions of evolution.

Daniel Yergin and Thane Gustafson recently examined these possibilities. Their description of "Capitalism Russian-Style" in the early twenty-first century, congruent with the analysis given here, stressed the likelihood of uneven development among sectors and regions, the persistence of a large underground economy, continued dependence on the state for subsidies and credits, and ambivalence toward the West.[3] Although Yergin and Gustafson did not use the term, their scenarios embodied to some extent the concept of path dependence elaborated by North. The ultimate inspiration of the tripartite analysis offered here is the elegant Weberian analysis of the Soviet system laid out four decades ago, shortly after the death of Stalin, by Barrington Moore, Jr.[4] No system in the Russian past, whether that of Witte in the 1890s or of Bukharin in the 1920s, inspires confidence as a model of exceptional economic dynamism or efficiency. However, patterns of economic behavior that predominated in the near or distant past deserve consideration as possible models for the future.

The historical weakness of Russian capitalism stemmed largely from the failure of the tsarist state to create a hospitable legal environment, one that would protect rights of property, enforce contracts, and reduce the level of bureaucratic corruption, for example. Heirs to the autocratic tradition, the rulers of the post-Soviet Russian state have failed so far to create a firm system of legality. Securities and exchange laws, for example, scarcely exerted any influence, and no central statistical index existed to reflect the state of the stock market in the early 1990s. The legacy of Marxist-Leninist contempt for bourgeois legal norms remained strong despite the collapse of the Soviet regime.

To make matters worse, the venality of the bureaucracy of the late Soviet period, which continued the long tradition of Russian corruption, intensified as rampant inflation in the early 1990s destroyed the purchasing power of paltry state salaries, to the point that "low salaries encourage bureaucrats to over-regulate, so as to be bribed." The reduction of wholesale corruption appeared to be a major prerequisite for the flourishing of a modern corporate culture, the more so because businessmen from the United States were forbidden by U.S. law from paying bribes in foreign countries, but no diminution of the phenomenon appeared likely. Equally ominous was the extortion inflicted on fledgling corporations by organized crime syndicates, which routinely resorted to murder and arson to extract protection money and policymaking positions on corporate boards. In 1993, ninety-four entrepreneurs were murdered, presumably in connection with extortion at the hands of organized crime. Early the following year, one Russian agency estimated that three-quarters of all businesses paid between 10 and 20 percent of their earnings to organized crime and that 150 gangs controlled 40,000 private and state companies and most of the 1,800 banks.[5]

The institutional environment inherited from the past, particularly the lack of firm legal norms, can be expected to evolve only slowly. In a recent analysis of the economies of North America and South America after their liberation from the political control of Britain and Spain, respectively, North noted that the two areas evolved along highly divergent paths despite the resemblance, in purely formal terms, between the constitution of the United States and those of the newly independent South American states. "In the case of Latin America, an alien set of rules was imposed on a long heritage of centralized bureaucratic controls and accompanying ideological perceptions of the issues." Gradually, bureaucratic controls smothered "federal schemes and efforts at decentralization" in Latin America. The bureaucratic environment produced "neither political stability nor consistent realization of the potential of modern technology." In these and other Third World countries, North noted, the existing institutional structure

> tends to perpetuate underdevelopment. With insecure property rights, poorly enforced laws, [high] barriers to entry, and monopolistic restrictions, the profit-maximizing firms will tend to have short time horizons and little fixed capital, and will tend to be small scale. The most profitable business may be in trade, redistributive activities, or the black market. Large firms with substantial fixed capital will exist only under the umbrella of government protection with subsidies, tariff protection, and payoffs to the polity—a mixture hardly conducive to productive efficiency.[6]

Precisely this pattern took shape in the successor states of the Soviet Union in the early 1990s, as entrepreneurs found it impossible to pursue their dreams and lapsed instead into speculation. In early 1992, a Russian businessman bitterly told of his failure to produce classical music recordings, his recent passion:

> "I don't make records anymore," he said matter-of-factly. "Now I'm a trader. I export timber, and in France and several other countries I buy chocolates and perfumes—whatever I think will sell in Moscow. This is the only kind of business that can succeed here now. . . . My case is very typical," he continued. "There is only one form of business that makes money now in Russia: speculation, not production."[7]

How the institutions of Russian capitalism will develop in the new political environment is impossible to predict, but three distinct paths of evolution appear possible. These can be called the *reformist, reactionary,* and *statist* varieties of future Russian capitalism. The goals of these three ideal types of capitalism are so different as to be mutually incompatible. The distinctions among them are based on real historical experience, not imaginary criteria, so that an evolution in one direction requires the weakening of the other two.

The rivals for control of economic policy in the early 1990s were the reformers, led by Egor Gaidar, Anatolii Chubais, Boris Fedorov, and Grigorii Iavlinskii; the reactionary politicians, of whom the Liberal-Democratic leader, Vladimir V. Zhirinovskii, became the most prominent as a result of his strong showing in the parliamentary elections of December 1993; and the partisans of continued state control, led by Prime Minister Viktor Chernomyrdin and the most prominent spokesman for heavy industry and the military bureaucracy, Arkadii Vol'skii of the Civic Union party and the Union of Entrepreneurs. Which of the three tendencies eventually predominates will depend on the institutional environment, in Professor North's terminology, that emerges as a result of political decisions made in the next few years by the Russian president, his advisers, and the contenders for political power in the bicameral legislature elected in December 1993.

Differences between these tendencies become intelligible when seen in comparison to the two varieties of Russian corporations that prevailed in the late tsarist period, those of the joint-stock company and share partnership. (See Table 6.1.)

The first two rows recapitulate the main features of Russian corporations at the end of the nineteenth century, discussed at length in Chapters 2, 3, and 5. Although the notorious arbitrariness of the tsarist legal system and the many restrictions on the mobility of peasant labor imposed by the Emancipation Statute of 1861 limited the possibilities of capitalist enterprise in both forms, managers of joint-stock companies adopted those aspects of capitalism that the bureaucratic state could not restrict— economic calculation, modern technology, large capital investments, and the public sale of stock—more readily than did the merchants, who preferred share partnerships as a means of perpetuating their generally family-centered businesses.

Post-Soviet reformists appeared eager to embrace all six elements of Weber's definition of capitalism. In contrast, the reactionaries scored even lower in 1990 than did the managers of share partnerships a century before. The statists, who stood midway between the other two, exhibited an ambivalence toward all aspects of modern capitalism, except modern technology.

The reformists sought a high degree of integration into the world economy. To attain it, they favored policies aimed at deriving maximum benefits from comparative advantage in the international division of labor. This required an effort to create and maintain a convertible currency despite the considerable hardships that fiscal and monetary discipline would inevitably impose on much of the population. In contrast, reactionaries sought the maximum possible restriction of the effects of corporate capitalism for the sake of economic xenophobia. They demanded legislation to limit contacts with the outside world and to favor Russians at the expense of foreigners and members of ethnic minorities in the former Soviet Union. Finally, statists endeavored to buttress the traditional economic power of the state and favored traditional forms of its tutelage over labor, management, the military, students, and pensioners. Although the statists expressed less hostility to non-Russians on purely ethnic grounds than did the reactionaries, the statist approach entailed the retention of many bureaucratic controls on key industries, strategic raw materials, and the transport system, all of which were typical of the tsarist regime and the Soviet state of the 1920s.

The reformers derived substantial advantage from the collapse of the Soviet censorship system and other reforms of the era of perestroika. The foreign nature of the corporation appeared to pose less of an obstacle than in the past because of the generally high level of literacy in the Russian population inherited from the Soviet period. Also, the adoption in 1990, for the first time in Russian history, of the principle of incorporation by registration boded well for the proliferation of new corporations and other enterprises. The appearance of new business schools modeled on those in the West also presaged a rapid increase in the number of managers trained to current international standards. However, the lack of a corporate business terminology in Russian indicated the great dimension of the challenge. Also, whether the skills of corporate entrepreneurship could be rapidly taught in the context of general corruption and the weak legal tradition remained to be seen. Although some corporate managers invented the rudiments of rational-legal procedures on the enterprise level,[8] the absence of national legislation conducive to corporate enterprise posed immense obstacles. The reformist score in Table 6.1 was therefore less than perfect.

Another aspect of the post-Soviet economy also favored the reformers: the capacity of Russians to adapt to foreign ways. Some precedents already existed. Pepsi-Cola, introduced from the United States more than two decades before, had become a familiar sight on Russian tables. Other American foods, such as Coca-Cola and Snickers candy bars, which seemed so alien as to prompt fears of foreign contamination in 1993, may well gain acceptance.

Still, foreign corporate managers faced the challenge of demonstrating to suspicious Russians that integration into the world market need not entail gains for foreigners at the expense of long-suffering Slavs. Particularly unwelcome was the kind of arrogance expressed by the German-Swiss businessman Ernst Jenny in 1919: "Just as the Varangians were once summoned, so it is still true today: 'The Russian land is great and rich, but there is no order in it!' The German is the organizing and productive intelligence [*der ordnende und fördernde Geist*] in Russia and will remain so. Nature is stronger than the obstinacy of the jealous masses."[9] Referring to the Varangians, who arrived in the Novgorod region from Scandinavia in the ninth century A.D. and took a leading role in the creation of the first Russian state, Jenny quoted a famous sentence from the Novgorodian chronicle. However, the notion of simple Slavs incapable of governing themselves without the assistance of Germans was an eighteenth-century stereotype based on notions of nationalism that did not exist in early Russian history.

The need to avoid obnoxious stereotypes while making accommodations to the realities of Russian culture has a direct application to the recruitment of both workers and managers. Historical experience may prove relevant for foreign managers seeking to overcome cultural disparities between the Western corporation and the Russian work force. Prior to the revolution, the managers of International Harvester, the largest foreign company operating in Russia, discovered a way to overcome the notoriously low productivity of the semi-peasant work force. In 1910, International Harvester obtained a geographically remote industrial site, the former factory of the New York Air Brake factory at Liubertsy, twelve and one-half miles east of Moscow, on the Moscow-Kazan Railroad.

There, the company recruited unskilled workers directly from neighboring villages, paid a slightly higher wage than normal, and trained workers in American techniques.[10]

This pattern reappeared in the early 1990s, as managers of new enterprises "agreed that teaching new skills is easier than breaking old habits." Capable workers could be found, and productivity could reach European standards, but only if managers offered suitable training, high wages, clearly defined incentives, and good working conditions. The key to a productive work force in Russia, according to the director of a Russian-Canadian joint venture, lay in avoiding experienced workers. "We hire only people who have never worked for the state. And they *must* be under forty. Everyone else has learned bad work habits which are almost impossible to correct." His counterpart, the manager of a joint venture with Germany, concurred in the negative assessment: "The generation of people over forty is lost for enterprise."[11]

As for managers, the way to mutually beneficial cooperation may well lie in the recruitment of experts like the "old Russian hands" employed by leading European corporations before 1914. These men brought to their positions not only proficiency in engineering techniques but also "great Russian experience, a profound knowledge of the country, and a mastery of the Russian language." Few foreign industrialists in the Russian Empire possessed this rare combination of skills. In the several decades that were required for Russian managers to gain expertise in European techniques, French and Belgian corporations assigned their own experts to the boards of Russian banks, cartels, and large companies, primarily those headquartered in St. Petersburg. There, having become "largely assimilated into Russian [economic] life," these experts gradually worked out "the solution to the challenge of effective management" with inadequate managerial talent: "widespread use of Russian personnel under a tiny handful of experienced top foreign directors. This gave the foreign firm the necessary balance."[12]

Third, the introduction of principles of business behavior capable of creating prices that reflected real opportunity costs appeared to depend on a major break with the tsarist and Soviet policies of economic tutelage by the state. In this regard, foreign capitalists can make a crucial contribution.

However, European, American, and Japanese corporations contemplating operations in the post-Soviet economy would do well to ponder the depth of Russian xenophobia, particularly its implications for resistance to foreign capitalism. An opinion poll of managers and workers in state, privatized, and private enterprises in four Russian cities in mid-1992 revealed that few—between 1 and 18 percent—would have preferred to work in a cooperative and only slightly more—between 3 and 20 percent—favored corporations, even those that lacked foreign participation. A clear sign of change was that a significant minority, above one-fifth, preferred to work in some kind of joint venture, meaning one with a foreign partner.[13] Taken as a whole, however, these data suggested that the corporate form of business remained unfamiliar and therefore exotic and distrusted. Even Anatolii Sobchak, the liberal mayor of St. Petersburg and a partisan of economic reform, predicted that corporations in his city would eventually be owned not only by private individuals but also by "banks and local government bodies," which would seek to balance "the interests of society and the workers" in keeping with the tradition of "Russian idealism and collectivism."[14]

Finally, it is essential to recognize that economic processes themselves have cultural consequences. As North observed, "fundamental changes in relative prices will gradually alter norms and ideologies, and the lower the costs of information, the more rapid the alterations."[15] The sudden exposure of the post-Soviet economies to the harsh realities of the world market has threatened for all time the ideology of insularity that flourished under tsarist and Soviet autarchy and buttressed it in turn. Historical examples can be found for the gradual fading of xenophobic notions of victimization by foreigners, under the influence of mutually beneficial economic integration, as stressed by the Mexican historian Aguilar Camin:

> The élite is bilingual, ten per cent of our population lives in the United States, and . . . our greatest authors were weaned on United States authors. Perhaps the United States is the enemy, but is is also our big opportunity, and, while I think that with the free-trade treaty we will have more fights than ever with the United States, these will be about things like tomato and broom quotas, and not about the twisted rhetoric that for years had us saying fantasizing, idiotic things on the order of "They have the know-how, but we have civilization."[16]

The Russian-German relationship might well have evolved in this direction had World War I not intervened. A second opportunity now exists, as a recent survey of public opinion found that hostility toward the market was inversely correlated with youth and educational attainment.[17]

Interviewed in April 1992, Egor Gaidar, the deputy prime minister in charge of economic reform, insisted that Russians need not feel threatened by foreigners because

> Russia is very large. It is hard to feel threatened by a possibility that, say, Germany or France will buy up the entire country. . . . We can get large amounts of western investment. We are also different from East Europeans. We don't have so much xenophobia. The social and political problems connected with foreign investment are easier here than, for instance, in Poland, which is preoccupied with its relationship with Germany.

This optimistic view required qualification, however, especially in view of the brevity of Gaidar's own career as an economic reformer. Indeed, his enthusiasm for the allegedly universal benefits of free markets and private property recalled the devotion of Russian academic economists to the principle of free trade in the mid-nineteenth century.[18] Political dangers lurked in the government's frank admission of economic backwardness in both the tsarist and post-Soviet periods. Opting for a Western model of economic development required acknowledging Russian backwardness, a most unpleasant political and cultural action. Economic reformers encountered political resistance from the many Russians who refused to accept Western norms, including economic ones, out of a sense of cultural pride. The Slavophile tradition, for example, rejected the notion of Russian backwardness and instead praised the uniqueness of Russia. As we have seen, the tsarist government's adoption of economic policies, especially low import tariffs, based on the precepts of classical economic theory aroused intense opposition among Russian manufacturers, who borrowed from other foreign theorists, such as the American Henry C. Carey and the Germans Wilhelm Roscher and Friedrich List, the polemical tools that undergirded Slavophile capitalism in the Moscow region. Most Russians resisted even this attempt to base economic development on a selective borrowing of Western institutions. Economic austerity for the sake of modernization demanded too high a price in taxes and wounded pride, to say nothing of the diminution of political power that faced the traditional agrarian elite as capitalism developed in the late tsarist period. The post-Soviet bureaucracy faces a similar threat to its legitimacy today.

The tradition of Russian economic xenophobia, which combined elements of the Slavophile and Stalinist ideologies, remained powerful in the early 1990s. As the Soviet Union disintegrated, the specifically Marxist elements of Soviet communism lost their appeal to all but the most conservative diehards loyal to the memory of Lenin and Stalin. Opposition to capitalism no longer took a Marxist form because Marxism had been discredited by the regime's failure, in the seven decades following 1917, to realize the socialist paradise predicted by Marx and Lenin. However, nothing in Soviet culture prevented resentment against the market from taking the familiar xenophobic turn. Industrial workers and their sympathizers resorted to xenophobic rhetoric, which, as has been argued here, always constituted an important element of Soviet Marxism. At the 1992 May Day parade organized by the Moscow Federation of Trade Unions, loudspeakers resounded with a slogan drawn directly from this tradition: "Privatization: a foreign word for a foreign process!"[19]

The partisans of reaction articulated a clear vision of their preferences for the Russian economy. The impulse of Russian politicians to heed the appeals of industrialists for special tariffs and other mechanisms to protect weak "infant industries" from lethal foreign competition appeared to pave the way for the emergence of what may be called "neo-Slavophile capitalism," especially as managers stressed their identity as ethnic Russians. Neoclassical economic theory teaches that high import tariffs for industry, the favorite economic weapon of the Moscow merchants in the era of the Great Reforms, cannot soon resolve the problem of Russian economic backwardness because, by raising prices artificially, they reduce the purchasing power of the very population that they purport to aid.[20] Still, economic xenophobia may well gain the ascendancy in the wake of the humiliation of Soviet Russia in the late 1980s, as it did after the defeat of imperial Russia in the Crimean War.

An indication of this potential appeared in a pamphlet entitled "The Path to Russia's Rebirth (A Nationalist and Orthodox View)," by the Metropolitan of St. Petersburg, Ioann. This high official of the Orthodox Church called for a middle way of "economic diversity" (*mnogoukladnost' khoziaistva*) to avoid what he called the extremes of "barracks socialism" and "savage capitalism." He expressed these seemingly innocuous platitudes in the familiar rhetoric of Slavophile capitalism. For example, labor should be considered "a service having a lasting moral worth, and not as a means to earn money, become wealthy, or satisfy one's whims." Like all reactionary theorists, the metropolitan praised "the production of essential goods and products" while condemning "the commercial intermediary, who makes a profit by reselling without having produced anything." He also warned against unnamed "forces hostile to the Russian people." Condemning the moral and intellectual tradition of the European Enlightenment, he called for "a categorical rejection of the recognition of the legality of 'the rights of man', which have exerted a fatal influence on society." The extreme nationalism of this statement was also reflected in the church leader's insistence that the Russian (*Rossiiskoe*) state return to "its natural boundaries," especially by pursuing "the gradual, voluntary [*sic*] return of Ukraine and Belorussia" to a union with the Russian Federation.

Lest the reader miss the implicit condemnation of certain ethnic groups that had occupied the role of commercial middlemen in Russia and had, in that capacity, attracted hostility in the course of centuries, the advertisement for *Russkii vestnik* on the back cover of the pamphlet listed among the themes of the newspaper "religion, politics, economics, Russian entrepreneurship [*national'noe predpriminatel'stvo*], the rebirth of the Cossack people [*vozrozhdenie kazachestva*], Orthodox education in the family, and Russian martial arts [*russkie boevye iskusstva*]." Elsewhere in this journal, monarchist splinter groups debated the merits of various contenders for the throne of the Romanovs and argued whether or not the murder of the royal family in July 1918 was carried out according to Talmudic ritual. Already in 1990, Dahrendorf sensed the emergence of factors favorable to the rise of fascism in Eastern Europe. "I hate to think of the combination of military leaders, economic planners, and racist ideologists which might be brought to power by dislocated and disenchanted groups" in the wake of the collapse of Soviet power.[21]

Zhirinovskii's Liberal Democratic Party developed many of these same reactionary themes.[22] Some statements in the party's campaign materials appeared to separate it from fascism: its claim to be "a center-right, moderately conservative party with a patriotic platform" (22/1); its pledge to refrain from violent means of struggle and to work within the parliamentary political system (22/1); and its formal endorsement of equal rights before the law for all persons regardless of ethnicity, ideology, or religion (22/2). However, its use of code words like "transnational interests" (8/1) for "Jews" and its contempt for the free market placed the party on the extreme right of the political spectrum.

Although he faulted the Soviet government for its division of the country's territory into nationally distinct republics, a strategic decision that allegedly exacerbated ethnic tensions and led eventually to the breakup of the Union (22/4), Zhirinovskii renounced anticommunism in a bid for support from ten million Russian Communists (22/1). At the same time, the front page of issue 3 featured an expression of good wishes from Patriarch Aleksii, leader of the Russian Orthodox Church. This apparently illogical appeal to Communists, Orthodox believers, and all groups in between rested, however, on a solid foundation of xenophobic emotion. In a typical tirade, Zhirinovskii portrayed the United States as the cunning enemy that had allegedly resorted to subversion, in the form of agitation among secessionist minority nationalities, to destroy the Soviet Union (9/1).

To restore control over the rebellious non-Russian republics, he called for harsh economic measures. For example, he advocated excluding independent Estonia from the old Soviet power grid, so that "clever Estonians" would be forced to "read their ancient Estonian books by the light of the moon" (9/1). He also claimed for the Russian Federation the traditional role of the Russian Empire as power broker in the Middle East, particularly as a Christian bulwark against Islam (11/4) and as the dominant economic power in Eastern Europe (22/2).

The theme of subordination of the individual to the all-powerful state pervaded the party's economic program. "The basis of morality now is becoming not religion or any moral code but the idea of the nation, to which everything must be subordinated. Then any anti-Russian religion or ideology will turn out to be immoral and amoral, and morality will be defined by only one criterion: the struggle for the freedom of the nation and the independence of Russia" (1/2). In foreign economic policy, Zhirinovskii called for government control of all exports and high tariffs for Russian industry in hopes of winning the domestic computer and video technology market away from foreigners (4/2), a fantastic dream, given the failure of Soviet science and industry to keep up with advances by the United States and Japan in this highly volatile field. In domestic policy, the Liberal Democrats called for the abrogation of the decree that authorized "free commerce," meaning trade without the payment of taxes, and castigated the resale of goods by speculators, which they considered harmful to the interests of the nation (10/4). In an appeal to both the land-hunger and anticapitalist fears of the Russian peasantry, Zhirinovskii affirmed the right of private ownership of land to those who worked it but not that of free sale, only the right to bequeath land to one's heirs (8/1).

Several echoes of Soviet policy could be discerned in this economic program. A state monopoly on foreign trade was needed to stem the outflow of valuable raw materials. "The government maintains supervision over [*kontroliruet*] key sectors of the economy and plans basic productive indicators." The state should set prices on key goods by manipulating the tax system and leaving to manufacturers the power to set all other prices;

"the activity of middlemen [*posredniki*] in setting prices is restricted" (22/4). The state should strive to maintain a vast system of social services. At the same time, however, the crushing economic burden of military spending must not be lightened. Indeed, Zhirinovskii called for an end to the conversion of military industry to civilian production (22/2). In general, private enterprise must serve as a "supplement" to the state-dominated economy and would be tolerated only if it pursued "national economic interests" (22/4), a phrase almost identical to "Russian entrepreneurship" in *Russkii vestnik*.

The identification of unfettered capitalism with evil foreigners, the core of Slavophile xenophobia, appeared clearly in the propaganda of Zhirinovskii's Liberal Democratic Party. One S. F. Dergunov, who invoked the memory of Nicholas II on the seventy-fifth anniversary of his death, called for the creation of a solid core of patriotic entrepreneurs "to struggle against the domination of foreign capital, the incipient comprador bourgeoisie [a Marxist term of abuse attached to Chinese agents of European businesses who served their own interests instead of those of the nation], and the [Russian state] bureaucracy that is selling itself to the West." Two kinds of capitalists and Yeltsin's government thus stood condemned on grounds of treason to the Russian nation. In contrast, "national capital," animated by a "moral code" based on patriotism, should pay high wages to workers, raise the standard of living to that of the late Soviet period within two or three years, "and achieve the prosperity of the country in the future" (7/2).

The solution to the crisis, Zhirinovskii claimed, lay in the resurrection of the powerful Russian state. The Liberal Democratic Party's intention "to introduce protectionist tariffs in defense of the Russian manufacturer and simultaneously to give tax breaks to enterprises in order to encourage exports" (13/4) recalled the tariff strategy of the tsarist government from 1822 to 1850 and from 1877 onward. Indeed, to the economic historian the most important antecedent of Zhirinovskii's economic program appeared to be the tsarist state, staffed by talented individuals of German, Polish, Finnish, and other nationalities, as well as Russians, and devoted to the maintenance of a military machine second to none. One of Zhirinovskii's supporters, M. P. Burlakov, put the Liberal Democratic economic program firmly within the old autocratic tradition: "Only patriotic forces, working with a nationally oriented stratum of entrepreneurs, can put an end to the tragedy and maintain the imperial order [*sokhranit' imperskii poriadok*]" (8/1). Whether Russian industry could rise to the challenge of world competition more successfully in the 1990s than it did a century before remained doubtful, however, owing to the lack of business skills among the population, a direct result of government repression in both periods, and the intrinsically stultifying effect of high tariffs on technological change.

In the last analysis, the details of the Liberal Democrats' economic program were less important than the belligerent tone in which Zhirinovskii cultivated the wounded pride of Russians. In perhaps his most extreme statement on economic issues during the parliamentary campaign of 1993, Zhirinovskii declared himself determined that Russians would gain a place of honor in the world,

> not sitting in tanks and eating out of pans, but dining in the proper manner in the grandest restaurants in Europe and America; that Russian firms would be the most powerful in Europe; that Gazprom would supply all Europe with our natural gas and that Agrozim would bury the world with our fertilizers; . . . that every black in Harlem would know that it was useless to compete with the Russian mafia; [and] that every girlie [*devchonka*] in Australia would feel physically aroused by the word "Russian" because she would know that Russians [*russkie*] are the liveliest, the wealthiest, [and] the most generous [men of all].[23]

Thus, Zhirinovskii viewed the large corporation not so much as an institution of productive economic activity than as a means of restoring Russian prestige in the world, the moral equivalent of a well-run criminal syndicate. His appeal to male youth, couched in the traditional xenophobic rhetoric of envy and pride and his own inimitable vulgarity, illustrated the vast distance between the economic program of the Liberal Democrats and the notion of modern capitalist rationality. The low scores in Table 6.1 assigned to the reactionary tendency, in both the religious and secular versions, expressed by Metropolitan Ioann and Zhirinovskii, respectively, reflect this disparity.

Strong parallels existed between the reactionary version of post-Soviet Russian capitalism—virtuous entrepreneurship, ethnic pride, religious devotion, family solidarity, and physical violence—and the similar ideological system articulated six decades before by the Nazis, which contrasted the allegedly healthy capitalism of Aryans to the dangerous capitalism of despised minority groups, especially the Jews. This is not to suggest that Metropolitan Ioann or Zhirinovskii endorsed genocide for non-Russians. The counterparts of the Nazi Party in post-Soviet Russia remained tiny fringe groups. Whatever the many differences between the Nazi and reactionary Russian ideologies, however, they shared a similar approach to economics. In both systems, the notion of a dichotomy between good capitalism and evil capitalism rested on purely arbitrary ethnic or political criteria, not the nature of the economic behavior itself. The reactionaries' coupling of archaic cultural norms and modern technology also recalled the Nazi ideology.[24]

The neo-Slavophile rhetoric exerted some appeal on the new post-Soviet entrepreneurs. In February 1992, the Congress of Civic and Patriotic Organizations, convened to create a new organization of the Russian right, the Russian People's Assembly (*Sobranie—RNS*), attracted the participation of Christian Entrepreneurs and the Merchants' Guild, as well as assorted monarchist, agrarian, and Cossack groups. "The meeting was financed by one of the new stock exchanges." Four months later, 1,100 delegates of "the right-wing alliance" included former Communists, nationalists, labor unions, and "the new capitalists," led by the head of the stock exchange in Nizhnii Novgorod. Although the Russian People's Assembly had in the meantime distanced itself from Pamiat and Zhirinovskii's party, it did not renounce their hostility to the free market and nostalgia for the imperial tradition, both tsarist and Soviet.[25] This program had no appeal for the most ambitious and capable of new capitalists, led by Konstantin Borovoi of the Economic Freedom Party, who threw in his lot with the reformers.[26] For small-scale entrepreneurs eager for public approval in the highly charged political atmosphere of national humiliation, however, the Russian People's Assembly offered a congenial ideological home. The social psychology of Russian entrepreneurs at ease with the rhetoric of neo-Slavophile capitalism constitutes a fascinating subject for future research.

The statists enjoyed the advantage of laying claim to the heritage of the powerful centralizing tendency in Russian politics and economics over the centuries, specifically the legacy of the Soviet command economy. To be sure, the degree of the state's economic control declined precipitously in the early 1990s, largely because of the privatization program directed by Anatolii Chubais in the initial years of Yeltsin's presidency. Widespread corruption also reduced the prestige of the old elite in the eyes of the public. Even before the inauguration of mass privatization through the voucher system in October 1992, many of the most lucrative enterprises or their constituent parts had passed into the hands of well-connected bureaucrats under the *nomenklatura* privatization. Thus, informal personal and professional ties persisted within the managerial elite, despite the formal privatization of state assets.

Edward L. Keenan stressed the continuities between the "traditional political culture" of the tsarist bureaucracy in the early 1890s and the Soviet party-state from the mid-1930s onward, which finally restored order after four decades of tumult occasioned by industrialization, war, and revolution. Both systems of rule remained remarkably "informal, corporate, conspiratorial, risk-avoiding, [and] guided by a pessimistic view of man and a sense of the nearness of chaos."[27] To the extent that the former Soviet elite strove to maintain its grip on the new levers of political power in the 1990s—a likely development, given the relatively high quality of education and executive experience that the *nomenklatura* brought to the new economic environment—the role of the state promised to remain strong in the post-Soviet economy. Indeed, because the political changes that began in 1985 did not entail a massive social upheaval, the transition under Yeltsin resembled less the Russian Revolution of 1917 than the reign of Peter the Great two centuries before, when a flood of regulations required the old Muscovite elite to adopt new styles of clothing, residence in St. Petersburg, and the European lexicon of government without, however, depriving it of the highest offices in the military and civil hierarchies.[28]

The most articulate representative of the statist strategy, Arkadii Vol'skii, rose from humble beginnings as an auto worker to positions of influence in the Communist Party and the military-industrial elite under Iurii Andropov. Vol'skii's profession of faith in the rule of law and equality of entrepreneurial opportunity placed him closer to the principle of rational-legal capitalism than to reactionary nationalism. In this spirit, he condemned the extreme rhetoric of the "Red-Brown" alliance and those he called "Communofascists," who circulated all sorts of conspiracy theories, including the claim that the CIA had masterminded the destruction of the Soviet state.

However, his party's economic program contained elements of economic xenophobia, as it called for "a socially oriented market economy" in contrast to "a violent revolution that would impose an alien experience and violate the traditions of our country." Vol'skii opposed "shock therapy" (as if it had really been tried) and rejected any reforms that might cause mass unemployment. Instead, he favored a huge state sector, a large military budget, and indexed pensions. His party boasted of the alleged accomplishments of the Soviet Union: "a mighty industry and progressive science, the exploitation of natural resources and the conquest of the cosmos, the victory over fascism and the struggle for democratic ideals." His endorsement of "stability and guarantees for the entrepreneur!" represented an understanding of the importance of firm legal norms in the capitalist system, but his opposition to the transfer of large enterprises to corporations and his dedication to wage and price controls kept the score of the statists in Table 6.1 below that of the most ambitious corporate capitalists a century before.[29]

In the early 1990s, neither the reformers nor the reactionaries had implemented a consistent policy, the former because of resistance from the legislature and its appointees at the Central Bank, and the latter because of insufficient electoral strength to capture the levers of state power. In contrast, the statists appeared to enjoy a crucial advantage in their resistance to reform: strong residual support among much of the population for the centuries-old tradition of bureaucratic control of the economy. At the same time, however, the erosion of President Yeltsin's power, a result of the crisis of legitimacy following the armed clash at the Moscow White House in October 1993, political factionalism in the State Duma, the military fiasco in Chechnia, and the inability of the central government to collect tax revenues, has prevented the Russian state from acting as the successor to the tsarist bureaucracy. Professor North's warning about corruption, monopolies, and the penchant of small-scale capitalists for quick profits in commerce under an economic system without firm guarantees for property and contracts fits the current Russian case all too well. Its professions of devotion to the principle of free international trade notwithstanding, the Russian government appeared willing in early 1994 to protect insolvent enterprises from bankruptcy for the sake of avoiding the politically unsavory plague of mass unemployment. The sorry spectacle of bureaucrats selling off choice mineral and timber rights to foreign corporations likewise has done nothing to endear the post-Soviet government to Russians concerned about sinking to the level of an economic colony of foreign capitalists.

The statists enjoyed a key strategic advantage in their struggle against the reformers and reactionaries: control of the credit system. Viktor Gerashchenko, who headed the State Bank until October 1994, pursued such a lax monetary policy that Sachs called him perhaps "the worst central-bank governor of any major country in history."[30] Gerashchenko and the managers of large enterprises whose interests he served preferred rampant inflation to the closure of factories and the mass unemployment that would follow.

The perennial shortage of investment credit in Russia made access to abundant credit at reasonable interest rates the key to economic survival. Just as in the decades before 1914, so in the early 1990s the purveyors of credit enjoyed great leverage. In 1906, George Greaves, an English manufacturer of agricultural machinery in Berdiansk, complained to the tsar than industrialists found it necessary to give customers from nine months' to two years' credit. Their large loan portfolios imposed financial difficulties, however, because banks, from which industrialists obtained loans, required repayment in four months, and neither the State Bank nor commercial banks would "discount the farmers' notes at a fair rate." Cash flow was thus "often insufficient to sustain factory operations." Similarly, in 1992, sociologists "were surprised to find that financing was more often a serious problem for respondents than either supplies or personnel."[31] Large enterprises with access to cheap credit—the Knoops in prerevolutionary Moscow and state enterprises recently favored with long-term loans from the State Bank—therefore enjoyed a crucial competitive advantage. In both periods, the tendency of wealthy Russians to seek safe havens for their capital in Europe deprived the economy of much-needed investment capital. The flight of capital amounted to a billion dollars a month in mid-1994.[32]

The immaturity of the capital market also allowed the new banks to use their control over scarce credit resources as a means of gaining power over industrial enterprises. By 1993, a familiar pattern of late tsarist capitalism had begun to emerge. The managers of two dozen large banks welcomed Finance Minister Fedorov's announcement that creditors in future bankruptcy proceedings could receive their unpaid loans in the form of bills of exchange. As the primary buyers of such bills, the banks would then enjoy priority in the division of assets in preference to shareholders. "Russia's leading banks thus have the means to take control of a large chunk of the country's assets; to be the main supplier of new capital; and to corner equity trading."[33] This trend held out the prospect of coordination of industry by banks on the German model. In any case, as in the tsarist period, the Central Bank remained the dominant force in the financial system, the ally of monopolies, especially in heavy industry, and the bane of small firms starved for investment capital.

A Finnish expert writing in late 1991 characterized as "slim indeed" the possibility of massive infusions of foreign investment capital capable of transforming patterns of post-Soviet "growth, competitiveness and technical progress during the next ten years." To the extent that "foreign investment concentrates only on blue-chip opportunities," which promise the greatest returns in a highly competitive global economy, "the higher will be the possibility of a public and political backlash. There is no easy way out of this dilemma." Thus, the notion that the post-Soviet economy might become "a locomotive of the world economy" appeared dubious in the extreme.[34]

The perennial weakness of capitalist institutions in Russia and the Soviet Union resulted largely from their overwhelming regimentation by the autocratic state. To the extent that state control of the economy wanes in coming years, the vigor of capitalist institutions may be expected to increase. However, the preponderant role of the state, despite the inherent inefficiencies of central control, flowed from two strong impulses in Russian political culture: the determination of the tsarist and Soviet bureaucracies to funnel a huge proportion of the country's wealth into a military machine capable of maintaining a multinational empire on the vast Eurasian plain; and, in the Soviet period, the universal yearning for security against unemployment and other forms of economic uncertainty. The breakup of the USSR unleashed numerous ethnic animosities in the region, and the popular demand for economic security persists.

Resistance to market reforms therefore remained strong in the mid-1990s. The weakening of anticapitalist attitudes instilled by centuries of tsarist and Communist autocracy—passivity, envy toward superiors and mistreatment of inferiors, and contempt for the rule of law—would require not a year or a decade, as some had hoped in the early days of glasnost, but whole generations; and the total eradication of such attitudes seems unlikely even in the distant future. Dahrendorf stressed the difficulties in bringing "civil society" to life: constitutional reform might take six months; economic reform, six years; but "sixty years are barely enough to lay" the "social foundations" of a firm constitutional order and an efficient economy.[35]

One path toward the resolution of these tensions may lie in the ways that foreigners approach the vast natural resources of the former Soviet Union. They can seek to turn to their advantage the massive environmental damage that resulted from decades of irresponsible Soviet industrial development, though the challenge is great. Russians who flocked to the banner of environmental protection often condemned both Soviet industry and its counterpart in the capitalist world. Conservative nationalists, like Rasputin and Solzhenitsyn, who rejected foreign principles, including international Marxism (originally a German ideology) and corporate capitalism, derived considerable prestige from their laudable devotion to the preservation of the threatened environment.

For example, in his angry letter to the Soviet leaders in 1973, Solzhenitsyn demanded that Siberia and the Russian North be saved from further depredation. "These spaces allow us to hope that we shall not destroy Russia in the general crisis of Western civilization." Apparently unaware that the Soviet government had granted numerous concessions to foreigners in the 1920s, he warned in apocalyptic terms:

> And what irony: for half a century, since 1920, we have proudly (and rightly) refused to entrust the exploitation of our natural resources to foreigners—this may have looked like budding national aspirations. But we went on and on dragging our feet and wasting more and more time. And suddenly now, when it has been revealed that the world's energy resources are drying up, we, a great industrial superpower, like the meanest of backward countries, invite foreigners to exploit our mineral wealth and, by way of payment, suggest that they carry off our priceless treasure, Siberian natural gas—for which our children will curse us in half a generation's time as irresponsible prodigals.

He also called for a ban on all vehicles in Russian cities, except those drawn by horses or powered by electric motors: a brilliant, if idiosyncratic, juxtaposition of the old and the new.[36]

In a reiteration of these warnings, in 1990, he warned of the danger posed by foreign corporations.

> Western capital must not be lured in on terms that are advantageous to it but humiliating to us, in come-and-rule-over-us style. There would be no rectifying this later, and we would turn into a colony. . . . Foreign investment must be permitted on the strict condition that the economic stimulation it introduces will be exceeded neither by the profits exported nor by the damage to the natural environment.

He specifically opposed giving corporations and cooperatives, especially those controlled by foreigners, the right to buy agricultural land and to lease it to farmers. Private property and economic initiative should be encouraged, but "there should be firm legal limits to the unchecked concentration of capital; no monopolies should be permitted to form in any sector"; and banks must not be allowed "to become usurious growths and the hidden masters of all life."[37] The disparaging reference to the Novgorodians' alleged invitation to the Varangians to "come and rule over us" came from the same medieval chronicle quoted by Ernst Jenny seven decades earlier. Likewise, the distrust of banks as incipient usurers reflected the powerful Russian tradition of animosity toward financiers.

The explicit xenophobia of these passages, reminiscent of the rhetoric of Dostoevskii, was tempered by the admission that foreign capitalism could, under some conditions, make a positive contribution to Russian economic development. Solzhenitsyn's eloquent plea for cooperation in the solution of environmental problems provided a hopeful basis for conciliation.

A cautionary note is essential, however. As Douglas R. Weiner, an expert on Soviet environmentalism, recently noted, the "hidden history" of movements to protect nature in Europe and the United States reveals that they were "closely tied to eugenics, right-wing nationalism, anti-modernism, Eurocentrism, and anti-Semitism." Stressing the "xenophobic Russian nationalism and anti-Semitism" of the "village writers" in the USSR in the 1960s, who prided themselves on their devotion to the environment, he concluded that "political neutrality in scientific discourse is a myth."[38] In 1993, Zhirinovskii claimed to oppose unlimited economic growth on ecological grounds and favored "environmentally safe development" in keeping with recommendations of the UN meeting in Rio de Janeiro the year before. However, his silence on the environmental degradation of the Russian environment at the hands of Soviet authorities, his criticism of the "rich capitalist countries" for their high levels of energy consumption, and his call for "a system of ecological restrictions and regulations" to prevent "anarchy" (a codeword for market forces) betrayed his opportunistic use of the ecological issue for xenophobic political purposes (1/4). The ecology page in Aleksandr Prokhanov's newspaper *Zavtra* (Tomorrow), the successor to *Den'* (The Day), suppressed in the aftermath of the failed uprising in Moscow in October 1993, likewise couched its attacks on Western economic prosperity in the familiar xenophobic rhetoric of the Stalin era.

It seems that the Germans currently lead the world in the application of "green" industrial technology, but Americans also have distinct advantages, particularly in computer hardware and software, that may well prove crucial in efforts to maximize economic efficiency, remove toxic pollutants from the manufacturing process, and design the nonpolluting industrial processes of the future. American corporate managers seeking to overcome hostility and distrust toward foreign capitalists in Russia must convince Russians that market reforms will bring more benefits of modern technology than detrimental effects. The environmental destruction wrought by the Soviet economic system, of which the Chernobyl disaster was only the most visible example, makes environmental remediation one field in which Western capitalists can make vital contributions.

One of the most lucrative fields of economic activity, however, promised the opposite. The efforts by American and British companies to manufacture cigarettes in the former Soviet republics and Eastern Europe struck entirely the wrong chord. The attachment of Russians and other former Soviet citizens to tobacco comes as no surprise, given the addictive nature of nicotine and the decades of state sponsorship of the sale of tobacco, which, like alcohol, provided significant revenues in the Communist period. The strong demand for cigarettes and the prospect of high profits attracted Western tobacco companies to the post-Soviet market. By mid-1992, Philip Morris had acquired three cigarette factories in former East Germany, and RJR had bought one in Kazakhstan. By the end of the following year, Philip Morris was planning a $60-million cigarette factory, Rothmans had chosen a manufacturing site, and RJR had created a joint venture, R. J. Petro—all in St. Petersburg.[39] However, the manufacture and distribution of tobacco products carried the danger of intensified xenophobic resentment, once the deleterious effects of tobacco consumption on public health became widely known, as they undoubtedly would in the absence of censorship on the subject of environmental carcinogens. The negative image of American capitalists pumping profits out of the Russian economy, already strong in the case of Coca-Cola and McDonald's, grew more intense as advertisements for American cigarettes proliferated in Russian cities. The political vulnerability of foreign tobacco manufacturers became clear in mid-1993, when the Moscow municipal government moved to ban cigarette and liquor advertisements from billboards, newspapers, magazines, and television.[40]

The contest between the three most likely paths of economic development—those of Gaidar's rational-legal economic enterprise, oriented toward high technology and the international division of labor; of Zhirinovskii's reactionary isolationism, tinged with traditional Russian imperialism; and of Vol'skii's state-monopoly tutelage—appears destined to last for decades. Whether corporate capitalism in the former Soviet Union will contribute to the political vision of democracy to which Max Weber aspired, contrary to his dark prediction in 1906, remains one of the great questions of the historical drama. Historians can offer no tidy agendas for economic progress, but the institutional history of Russian and late Soviet capitalism provides some insights into the complex path that has brought the Russians and their neighbors to their present historical turning point.

A

The RUSCORP Database

The database contains machine-readable profiles of 4,542 corporations chartered by the imperial Russian government from 1704 to the end of 1913 and their 14,338 founders. Most of the information is drawn from corporate charters published by the tsarist government. Supplementary files describe companies in operation in 1847 (68 cases), 1869 (186 cases), 1874 (433 cases), 1892 (614 cases), 1905 (1,354 cases; 5,243 managers), and 1914 (2,167 cases; 8,090 managers), excerpted from corporate directories issued in those years. Companies headquartered in Finland and outside the empire are not included, except for foreign companies in operation in 1914 (262 cases).

The six files, divided chronologically into fifty-two subfiles, contain the following information:

A. Master file. Charter number; date of founding; headquarters; and company name in English and Russian.
B. Corporations at time of founding. Charter number; type; functions; locations of operations; capitalization; number of shares; price of shares; option to issue bonds; and restrictions on property ownership and on ethnicity and citizenship of managers, staff, and stockholders.
C. Founders. Charter number; name; sex; ethnicity; citizenship; and social status.
D. Surviving corporations. Financial profiles in 1847, 1869, 1874, 1892, 1905, and 1914.

E. Managers. Data on managers of surviving corporations in 1905 and 1914, as in file C, except that the citizenship and social status fields seldom contain specific information because of inadequate data in the corporate directories.
F. Foreign corporations in 1914. Foreign and Russian names; function; locations of operations; total capitalization; capital allocated to operations in the Russian Empire; and name of agent.

In this relational database, files A through E are linked to each other by the number assigned to the corporate charter in the *Polnoe sobranie zakonov* (1649–1913). File F lacks such numbers.

Interested researchers may obtain a copy of the RUSCORP files and codebook from the Inter-University Consortium for Political and Social Research, P.O. Box 1248, Ann Arbor, Michigan 48106-1248. Institutional members of the consortium are entitled to receive the materials free of charge. The consortium's computer tape contains the database in a format suitable for use on a mainframe computer. The files can also be stored on twenty-three double-density $5^{1}/_{4}''$ diskettes, ten double-density $3^{1}/_{2}''$ diskettes, or a single Bernoulli cartridge.

In the future, the database can be expanded by the inclusion of additional information published in a variety of local, regional, sectoral, and national corporate directories from the 1860s to 1917. The RUSCORP manual describes the creation of the data files and some of the problems of determining correct ethnic identifications. In 1847, Nebol'sin ("Aktsionernye obshchestva," 24) noted the existence of several dozen gold-mining companies in Siberia, but only one of these, founded in 1842, appeared in the *PSZ,* indexed under "Siberia"! Such errors in the *PSZ* may have prevented the compilers of the RUSCORP database from tracing the establishment of all Russian corporations. After the Crimean War, however, the official publications routinely contained all corporate charters, and the indexes listed them in special sections for "joint-stock companies" (*aktsionernye obshchestva*) and "share partnerships" (*tovarishchestva na paiakh*).

The database reflects both the strengths and weaknesses of the charters and corporate directories on which it was based. The most serious flaw in the directories for 1905 and 1914 is the lack of information about railroad companies, which were subordinate to the Ministry of Transport, not the Ministry of Trade and Industry. The RUSCORP manual's Appendix G describes the techniques used to generate missing capital data for railroad companies. In the absence of information about railroad managers, one dummy entry, with unknown sex, citizenship, and social status, was included for each company.

B

Basic Capital as an Indicator of Corporate Size

Of the various quantitative values contained in the RUSCORP database, the most important was that of basic capital. In order to perform basic computations, including the plotting of trends over time and comparisons among geographical regions, the compiler of the database needed an unambiguous criterion to determine the size of corporations. Economists and historians use several such criteria, among them the number of employees, the value of the enterprise's assets, its annual gross sales or net profits, or the valuation of its stocks and bonds on the exchange. The rudimentary nature of the statistics available to the compiler ruled out the use of any of these indicators for the study of Russian corporations. The size of the labor force appeared in some of the corporate directories, but only in descriptions of industrial corporations, not banks and insurance companies, for example, and even then often in vague terms. The published balance sheets of corporations, containing statements of assets and liabilities, appeared only sporadically, as did annual reports of sales and profits, so it was impossible to compile meaningful time series embracing all corporations throughout the empire in the course of over two centuries. Also, the lack of a uniform system of corporate bookkeeping caused imprecision in data regarding profits (Gorbachev, *Tovarishchestva*, 225–35). Only a small percentage of Russian corporations issued stock that circulated on the exchange, and the aggregate value of these securities rarely appeared in print. No secondary literature exists on Russian stock-market trends.

An admittedly imperfect criterion formed the basis for all measurements of size in the database and subsequent computations: the basic capital of the corporation. Each corporate charter contained a statement of the authorized capitalization of the new enterprise. (For the few cases in which the charter lacked such a figure, the compiler generated an estimate based on comparisons with similar corporations founded in the same region at approximately the same time. These are presented, with the rationale for their computation, in Appendix F of the RUSCORP manual.) It became necessary to choose a standard ruble of account that would serve as a common denominator among the various rubles mentioned in the charters and directories (gold, silver, credit, or assignat), each of which had its own value at a given moment, so that totals in a given year and comparisons over time would be expressed in terms of a single monetary unit. (On these methods, covering the period from 1769 to 1914, see Owen, "Ruble of Account"; Appendix C of the RUSCORP manual contains the ruble conversion tables for the period 1801–1914.)

This system has several imperfections. First is the lack of any adjustment for inflation or deflation over time. In the absence of a readily available table of conversions, all ruble values in the database and the present study remain specific to a given year. Perhaps in future analyses in Russian business history it will be possible to make computations in terms of 1897 or 1913 prices.

Second, the ruble figures in the charters and corporate directories indicate only the authorized capitalization of each enterprise, not the actual value of its stock or of its marketed shares. Still, the capitalization figures in the RUSCORP database, drawn from thousands of charters and entries in corporate directories, appear valid because corporations with modest activities—restaurants, beet-sugar plants, and small manufacturing factories, for example—typically had low levels of capitalization, ranging from 100,000 to 500,000 rubles. In contrast, the most ambitious projects—railroads, steamship lines, coal mines, locomotive factories, and petroleum drilling and refining enterprises—were capitalized in the millions of rubles. This general impression derives additional support from the steady increase of capitalization figures in corporations that proved their solidity by surviving various hazards over the decades.

Several simple statistical tests buttress this contention. A linear regression of nominal capitalization on total assets of the twenty-eight largest manufacturing corporations in the Russian Empire in 1914—defined as those with at least ten million rubles in stock and bond capital—produced a high coefficient of correlation = $+.69432$; $r^2 = 48.21$ percent; probability level = .00004, indicating strong statistical significance. (Four additional large manufacturing corporations were excluded from this test because the corporate directories did not specify their total assets.) This coefficient appears especially high because it reflected capital and asset amounts in a variety of manufacturing sectors, including mechanical engineering, petroleum refining, and textile production, each of which can be assumed to have had a unique optimal ratio between capital and assets, depending on the specific technologies in use in the early twentieth century. The two largest capitalizations belonged to enterprises recognized in the economic literature as giants in their fields: the Singer Company, manufacturer of sewing machines (50 million rubles), and Nobel Brothers Petroleum Company (45 million rubles).

Similarly, a linear regression of capitalization on the size of the labor force in the oldest fifty-one corporations existing in 1905 for which labor force size was specified produced a slightly better result: coefficient of correlation = +.756132; r^2 = 57.17 percent; probability level = .00000. (Another sixty corporations founded in the same period, 1827–70, were excluded from this test because their employment figures were not available in the corporate directory. These included banks, insurance companies, and shipping companies; for the latter, only the number of laborers in machine shops, not the number of crew members, was specified.) The fifty-one corporations belonged to an even more diverse group of enterprises than the sample in 1914: all types of manufacturing enterprises and three gas-lighting companies, which had very small numbers of workers (between 95 and 348) but large capitalizations (between 924,000 and 4 million rubles), in keeping with the relatively large investments in specialized equipment.

The same type of test applied to railroad companies produced results that were even more significant. Although a strong linear relationship between capitalization and length of track existed in the nine largest railroad companies in the early twentieth century (+.947517; 89.78 percent; and .00010), a multiplicative regression curve fitted the data even better: coefficient of correlation = +.975745; r^2 = 95.21 percent; probability level = .00001. (Capitalization from Pushkin's directory, 1901; track length as of March 31, 1907, from Barrett, *Russia's New Era*, 116. Simultaneous data for both variables were not available.) The slightly curved multiplicative line indicated that the railroads with the greatest lengths of track had slightly higher ratios of capital to track than smaller companies.

Finally, in the financial sector, basic capital correlated highly with total assets among the thirteen largest banks on the eve of World War I. A linear regression produced significant results: coefficient of correlation = +.834377; r^2 = 69.62 percent; probability level = .00074. (Assets on January 1, 1913, from Girault, *Emprunts*, 502; basic capital in 1914 from RUSCORP.)

A third objection to the use of capitalization as an indicator of corporate size arises because historians have grounds for suspecting that managers might have set a high capitalization figure in order to exaggerate the real assets of the enterprise, the better to commit fraud at the expense of gullible investors. Fortunately, the tsarist corporate law contained powerful incentives for the founders to choose a capitalization figure that reflected fairly accurately the scope of their operations and the size of their assets. Most charters set a deadline for raising half the stock capital, usually six months. Also, the law required that any increase in the capitalization figure receive the approval of the tsarist bureaucracy. Thus, too high a figure in the charter would risk the failure of the entire venture at the outset owing to inadequate sales of stock; and too low a figure would risk bureaucratic complications in the future.

Still, it is essential to bear in mind the formal nature of the capitalization figure. As a measure of size, it specifies only the officially authorized capitalization, not the amount of investment or the actual productive capacity of a Russian corporation. As Arcadius Kahan correctly noted ("Capital Formation," 287), the capitalization figure did not measure real economic activity, as expressed in the number of workers employed, value of products manufactured, or puds of coal mined or transported. The correlations cited earlier, although high, are not perfect.

Likewise, Fred Carstensen pointed out that many incorporations occurred simply because the managers of previously existing partnerships sought to reduce their tax burden by transforming them into companies. "Incorporations often represented only a change in the legal status of existing firms," and "expansions of nominal capital were often the result not of new investments but of efforts to reduce the effective rate of taxation on business profits" ("Foreign Participation," 144). Such changes appeared common in response to increases in the tsarist corporate income tax in 1899 and 1906. "To reduce taxes, a company needed only to increase its capital," thereby decreasing the ratio between net profits and capitalization. Such a maneuver could bring savings because the tsarist corporate tax was mildly progressive; the higher the profit rate (net profit divided by capitalization), the higher the rate of taxation. Thus, nominal levels of capitalization "reflect more about the legal and tax environment than about real patterns and rates of investment" ("Foreign Participation," 145).

In one sense, Carstensen's point is well taken. Governmental reports specifying average corporate dividends in various sectors, although widely circulated and debated at the end of the imperial period (as in Barrett, *Russia's New Era,* 291–2), contained no indication of the inherent statistical distortions and therefore must be used with great caution. However, this objection does not entirely undermine the significance of the RUSCORP figures. By definition, the object of this study is the corporation. Any changes in capitalization that resulted from revisions in the tsarist tax code themselves constituted entirely valid subjects of investigation, however difficult it may be in practice to disentangle them from responses to economic trends unrelated to bureaucratic innovation. Also, running counter to the process described by Carstensen was the practice of some managers, especially those of Moscow textile factories, to reinvest significant portions of profits at the end of the year without increasing the number of shares or their face value. The merchants thereby expanded their productive capacity without diluting their financial control over the enterprise, which often remained within a narrow circle of family members and friends of the founder-manager for decades on end. In such cases, the nominal capital grossly understated the assets of the firm, exaggerated the profit rate, and caused a larger income-tax payment than would have otherwise occurred.

To balance these and other tendencies toward erroneous overstatement and understatement would require a review of the account books of every corporation in the Russian Empire. Unfortunately, the massive destruction of corporate records at the hands of negligent archivists in the early Soviet period, as described by Andrei Golikov ("K voprosu"), makes this an impossible task.

At this early stage in Russian business history, therefore, capitalization figures, despite their imperfections, appear far more useful than the dubious data regarding profit rates and dividends. To rely on nominal capital values as the only convenient indicator of the extent of a corporation's operations may make a virtue of necessity, but approximate statistics appear better than no statistics at all. Comprehensive data on the number of workers and total assets, the best indicators of the size of a corporation, simply do not exist. Perhaps the effort to ascertain corporate size through the imperfect indicator of basic capitalization will inspire other researchers to discover more accurate measures in the future.

C

Tables

TABLE 2.1 European and Russian Corporations on the Eve of World War I

Country	Date	Corporations in existence	Population (in millions)*	Corporations per million inhabitants*
United Kingdom	1913	60,754	36.778	1,651.91
France	1913	15,000*	39.331	381.38
German Empire	1913	5,487	67.494	81.30
Italy	1913	3,069	35.330	86.87
Russian Empire	1914	2,167	169.000	12.82

Sources: Data on European corporations from "Società," 1010; Russian corporate data from RUSCORP; population figures interpolated from data in Mitchell, European Historical Statistics, 30-34, 36.

*Estimated

TABLE 2.2 Profiles of Largest Corporations Founded in the Russian Empire, 1825-1855

Name	Date	Capital (in millions of rubles)	Fate
Russian Fire Insurance Co. (in 1914: First Russian Ins. Co.)	1827	2.681	Survived to 1914
Second Russian Fire Ins. Co.	1835	1.397	Survived to 1914
Russian Life Insurance Co.	1835	1.117	Survived to 1914
Vegetable Dye Co.	1837	1.127	Failed, 1871-4
Petersburg Water Co.	1837	1.901	Never functioned
Black Sea and Eastern Trading Co.	1839	3.429	Failed, 1842-7
Russian Maritime Insurance Co.	1844	3.000	Survived to 1914
Salamander Insurance Co.	1846	3.000	Survived to 1914
Petersburg Hope Insurance Co.	1847	2.000	Survived to 1914
Russian Livestock Insurance Co.	1848	3.000	Failed by 1869
Suksun Iron and Copper Co.	1848	1.800	Failed by 1869
Petrine Cotton Textile Co.	1851	1.200	Survived to 1914
Redeemer Cotton Yarn Co.	1852	1.200	Survived to 1914
Knauff Iron and Copper Co.	1853	1.225	Failed by 1869
Second Petersburg Water Co.	1853	1.005	Never functioned
Russian Lumber Co.	1853	4.020	Liquidated in 1858
Golden Fleece Gold Mining Co.	1854	5.310	Failed by 1869
Lower Dnepr Steamship Co.	1855	3.237	Liquidated in 1863

Source: RUSCORP database.

TABLE 2.3 Corporate Development in Ten Major Cities, 1700-1914

DIST	POP97	TCOS	COS14	CAP14	MAN14	FIRST	FBANK	B14
St. P.	1,265	1,410	646	3,347	2,786	1753	July 1864	12
Moscow	1,039	899	507	2,222	1,693	1711	July 1866	8
Warsaw	691	299	150	228	703	1857	Feb. 1870	7
Kiev	248	170	103	135	342	1868	June 1868	1
Odessa	424	161	38	28	129	1806	Mar. 1870	2
Riga	284	130	57	82	218	1750	Nov. 1871	1
Kharkov	181	90	41	51	146	1838	Mar. 1868	0
Lodz	333	79	45	113	174	1872	Aug. 1872	2
Baku	112	69	34	63	121	1886	Oct. 1899	1
Rostov/Don	148	62	34	54	116	1858	Dec. 1871	1
Totals	4,725	3,369	1,655	6,323	6,428	--	--	35
Empire	16,855	4,509	2,167	7,225	8,090	--	--	47
Tot/Emp	28.0%	74.7%	76.4%	87.5%	79.5%	--	--	74.5%

Sources: Population data from Russia, Tsentral'nyi statisticheskii komitet, Pervaia vseobshchaia perepis', vyp 4, and Entsiklopedicheskii slovar', supplementary vol. 4/d, "Rossiia," iii; other data from RUSCORP database.

Codes: DIST = District; POP97 = Urban population, 1897, in thousands; TCOS = New corporations, 1821-1913 (rank criterion); COS14 = Corporations in in existence, 1914; CAP14 = Capital of COS14, in millions of rubles; MAN14 = Managerial positions in COS14; FIRST = Year of first corporate charter; FBANK = Month of first commercial bank charter; B14 = Number of banks in 1914.

TABLE 2.4 Population and Corporate Development in Ten Russian Cities, 1700-1914 (Spearman Rank Coefficients of Selected Indicators)

	POP97	TCOS	COS14	CAP14	MAN14	FIRST	FBANK	B14
POP97	--							
TCOS	.8667**	--						
COS14	.8268*	.9119**	--					
CAP14	.6606*	.7212*	.8875**	--				
MAN14	.8182*	.9152**	.9970***	.8909**	--			
FIRST	.6364	.6242	.5471	.2485	.5273	--		
FBANK	.6364	.8303*	.7599*	.5030	.7455*	.6606*	--	
B14	.9034**	.7214*	.6859*	.7089*	.6838*	.3952	.4078	--

Sources and codes: same as in Table 2.3. (Signs for FIRST and FBANK are reversed to assign high ranks to early dates.)

*p < .05   **p < .01   ***p < .005

TABLE 3.1 Ethnicity of Corporate Founders, 1821-1913 (Percentages)

	First Year of Quinquennium									
Ethnic Group	1821	1826	1831	1836	1841	1846	1851	1856	1861	1866
RUS	76.9	43.2	23.0	39.4	50.0	49.1	30.0	54.5	34.5	50.7
UKR	0	0	0	0	0	1.8	0	0.5	1.5	0.9
POL	0	2.7	0	0	1.7	1.8	1.4	1.0	7.7	6.0
RGER	0	8.1	19.7	20.6	10.3	12.7	15.7	24.0	37.6	19.1
RJEW	7.6	0	0	1.8	0	0	1.4	1.7	1.5	6.4
ARM	0	0	0	2.9	0	0	0	0	0	0.1
OTH	0	2.7	1.6	1.2	0	9.1	0	0.7	0.5	1.6
FOR	0	2.7	13.1	15.3	12.1	5.4	30.0	12.2	11.9	12.4
UNK	15.4	40.5	42.6	18.8	25.9	20.0	21.4	5.4	4.6	2.8
N	13	37	61	170	58	55	70	409	194	671

(continued next page)

TABLE 3.1, continued

Ethnic Group	First Year of Quinquennium (Last = 1911-13)									1821-1913
	1871	1876	1881	1886	1891	1896	1901	1906	1911	
RUS	48.9	42.4	43.4	52.1	52.0	34.4	42.5	47.2	49.7	45.3
UKR	1.1	0.4	1.3	0.4	0.8	1.0	1.4	2.1	1.6	1.2
POL	6.4	7.0	7.9	6.3	8.6	10.8	8.4	7.4	5.7	7.2
RGER	12.4	17.9	18.5	16.5	13.9	20.3	13.1	10.0	11.6	15.3
RJEW	9.9	4.3	8.1	7.2	6.4	11.0	11.2	13.8	12.9	9.8
ARM	0.6	0	0.8	1.3	0.3	4.0	3.6	1.7	2.8	1.9
OTH	2.2	7.7	1.9	1.4	2.3	1.6	1.4	2.4	1.7	2.1
FOR	11.6	16.2	15.8	10.4	12.0	11.3	8.7	6.7	6.1	10.3
UNK	6.8	4.1	2.2	4.4	3.7	5.6	9.4	8.6	7.8	6.9
N	2,012	531	670	557	777	2,546	1,023	1,836	2,441	14,131

Source: RUSCORP database.

Ethnic codes: RUS = Russian or Russified; UKR = Ukrainian; POL = Polish or Polonized; RGER = German, subject of the Russian Empire; RJEW = Jewish, subject of the Russian Empire; ARM = Armenian; OTH = Other subject of the Russian Empire; FOR = foreign subject; UNK = Unknown. Note: Totals diverge from 100 percent because of rounding.

TABLE 3.2 Ethnicity of Corporate Founders in Ten Russian Cities, 1856-1860 (Percentages)

City	Ethnic Category									N
	RUS	UKR	POL	RGER	RJEW	ARM	OTH	FOR	UNK	
St. Petersburg	50.2*	0	0.9	24.0	1.3	0	1.3	15.6	6.7	225
Moscow	76.6*	0.9	0.9	10.3	0	0	0	7.5	3.7	107
Warsaw	0	0	0	25.0	25.0	0	0	50.0*	0	8
Kiev	0	0	0	0	0	0	0	0	0	0
Odessa	44.4*	0	11.1	22.2	0	0	0	0	22.2	9
Riga	3.6	0	0	89.3*	0	0	0	3.6	3.6	28
Kharkov	0	0	0	0	0	0	0	0	0	0
Lodz	0	0	0	0	0	0	0	0	0	0
Baku	0	0	0	0	0	0	0	0	0	0
Rostov-on-Don	66.7*	0	0	0	16.7	0	0	16.7	0	6
Empire	54.5*	0.5	1.0	24.0	1.7	0	0.7	12.2	5.4	409

Source: RUSCORP database.

Ethnic codes: same as in Table 3.1. *Largest percentage. Note: Totals diverge from 100 because of rounding.

Appendix C 183

TABLE 3.3 Ethnicity of Corporate Founders in Ten Russian Cities, 1911-1913 (Percentages)

City	Ethnic Category									
	RUS	UKR	POL	RGER	RJEW	ARM	OTH	FOR	UNK	N
St. Petersburg	53.9*	1.8	1.9	11.7	9.1	2.9	2.0	9.1	7.5	788
Moscow	63.5*	0.2	1.0	11.0	9.6	0.7	0	8.1	5.8	417
Warsaw	5.2	0	50.3*	8.7	20.8	0	0	4.6	10.4	173
Kiev	47.0*	0	8.8	5.9	11.8	5.9	0	2.9	17.6	34
Odessa	15.8	1.8	0	7.0	61.4*	0	3.5	7.0	3.5	57
Riga	0	0	0	50.0*	38.9	0	0	11.1	0	18
Kharkov	35.6	0	2.2	4.4	40.0*	2.2	0	11.1	4.4	45
Lodz	0	0	5.1	33.3	53.8*	0	0	2.6	5.1	39
Baku	42.3*	0	0	0	0	38.5	11.5	0	7.7	26
Rostov-on-Don	69.6*	5.4	0	0	8.9	1.8	5.4	3.6	5.4	56
Empire	49.7*	1.6	5.7	11.6	12.9	2.8	1.7	6.1	7.8	2,441

Source: RUSCORP database.

Ethnic codes: same as in Table 3.1. *Largest percentage. Note: Totals diverge from 100 because of rounding.

TABLE 3.4 Social Status of Corporate Founders, 1821-1913 (Percentages)

Social Status	First Year of Quinquennium									
	1821	1826	1831	1836	1841	1846	1851	1856	1861	1866
NBM	84.6	37.8	32.8	42.9	48.3	43.6	31.4	44.0	35.1	20.1
GEN	7.7	8.1	3.3	14.1	5.2	1.8	0	2.4	3.1	1.0
PRO	0	2.7	6.6	3.5	3.4	1.8	2.9	7.6	7.2	5.7
COM	0	21.6	36.1	27.6	27.6	40.0	44.3	40.1	34.0	26.7
ORG	0	0	0	0.6	0	0	0	1.4	1.0	5.7
OTH	0	0	0	0	0	0	0	0	0	1.0
UNK	7.7	29.7	21.3	11.2	15.5	12.7	21.4	4.4	19.6	39.8
N	13	37	61	170	58	55	70	409	194	671

Social Status	First Year of Quinquennium (Last = 1911-13)									1821-1913
	1871	1876	1881	1886	1891	1896	1901	1906	1911	
NBM	27.3	23.4	19.4	18.9	17.6	19.3	16.8	15.0	17.7	21.2
GEN	6.1	9.0	7.9	13.1	10.9	12.3	13.4	9.5	10.4	9.3
PRO	6.4	7.2	10.0	5.4	9.9	11.1	10.9	10.3	13.4	9.6
COM	41.7	44.6	45.8	44.7	47.9	43.9	43.6	38.1	36.1	40.4
ORG	8.0	3.2	4.0	6.8	5.0	2.1	2.4	2.1	2.2	3.5
OTH	0.2	0.4	1.3	1.1	0.9	0.9	3.7	7.0	10.0	3.3
UNK	10.2	12.2	11.5	10.1	7.7	10.4	9.2	18.0	10.1	12.7
N	2,012	531	670	557	777	2,546	1,023	1,836	2,441	14,131

Source: RUSCORP database.

Status Codes: NBM = Noble, Bureaucratic, Military; GEN = Gentry; PRO = Professional; COM = Commercial-Industrial; ORG = Organizations; OTH = Other; UNK = Unknown. Note: Totals diverge from 100 percent because of rounding.

TABLE 3.5 Leading Corporate Founders in Russia, 1851-1913

Rank	Number	Name	Cit.	Eth.	Status	Main HQ	Functions of Corporations
\multicolumn{8}{c}{Cycle 3: 1851-1863}							
1 (tie)	5	Novosel'skii, Nikolai A.	Rus.	Rus.	State Councilor	SPb	Steamship operation, trade
1 (tie)	5	Stieglitz, Aleksandr	Rus.	Ger.	Baron	SPb	Railroads, cotton yarn
3 (tie)	4	Fehleisen, Konstantin	Rus.	Ger.	Gentry	SPb	Sugar, mortgages, lumber
3 (tie)	4	Gonzago-Pavlichinskii, Ivan L.	Rus.	Pol.	Actual S. C'lor	SPb	Mortgages, gold mining, steamship operation
3 (tie)	4	Kaulin, Nikolai I.	Rus.	Rus.	Hered. Hon. Cit.	Moscow	Textiles
3 (tie)	4	Shipov, Dmitrii P.	Rus.	Rus.	Actual S. C'lor	Moscow	Steamship operation
\multicolumn{8}{c}{Cycle 4: 1864-1878}							
1	18	Bekkers, Aleksandr K.	Ger.	Ger.	Hered. Hon. Cit.	Kiev	Beet sugar, banking, iron
2	15	Gubonin, Petr I.	Rus.	Rus.	Actual S. C'lor	Moscow	Machinery, railroads, banking
3	14	Morozov, Timofei S.	Rus.	Rus.	Manuf. C'lor	Moscow	Banking, cotton textiles
4	13	Rau, Wilhelm Ellis	Ger.	Ger.	First-guild Mcht	Podolia	Beet sugar
5 (tie)	12	Iakunchikov, Vasilii I.	Rus.	Rus.	Commercial C'lor	Moscow	Banking, cotton textiles
5 (tie)	12	Soldatenkov, Kuz'ma T.	Rus.	Rus.	Commercial C'lor	Moscow	Textiles, banking
\multicolumn{8}{c}{Cycle 5: 1879-1886}							
1	9	Rau, Wilhelm Ellis	Ger.	Ger.	First-guild Mcht	Warsaw	Beet sugar, iron, machinery
2	5	Rodokonaki, Perikl F.	Rus.	Greek	Hered. Hon. Cit.	Odessa	Flour
3 (tie)	4	Barsukov, Nikolai F.	Rus.	Rus.	Tech. Engineer	Kiev	Beet sugar
3 (tie)	4	Bekkers, Aleksandr K.	Ger.	Ger.	Hered. Hon. Cit.	Moscow	Food products
3 (tie)	4	Rubinskii, Nikolai A.	Rus.	Rus.	Titular C'lor	SPb	Pawnshops (Warsaw, Odessa)
3 (tie)	4	Zawadski, Stanislaw P.	Rus.	Pol.	Gentry	Warsaw	Beet sugar

(Continued next page)

184

Cycle 6: 1887-1905

Rank	Name		Ethnicity	Title	City	Industries
1 (tie)	7	Mscychowski, Kazimierz	Pol.	Transp. Engineer	SPb	Construction materials
1 (tie)	7	Rafalovich, Aleksandr F.	Jew.	Hered. Hon. Cit.	Odessa	Banking, coal, steamships
1 (tie)	7	Wogau, Otto M.	Ger.	Commercial C'lor	Moscow	Food products
4 (tie)	6	Barsukov, Nikolai F.	Rus.	State Councilor	Kiev	Beet sugar, machinery
4 (tie)	6	Golubev, Viktor F.	Rus.	Actual C. C'lor	SPb	Metals, machinery
4 (tie)	6	Kunitzer, Julius	Ger.	Mfg. Councilor	Lodz	Textiles
4 (tie)	6	Kuznetsov, Matvei S.	Rus.	Commercial C'lor	Moscow	Hotels
4 (tie)	6	Mantashev, Aleksandr I.	Arm.	Hered. Hon. Cit.	Baku	Petroleum
4 (tie)	6	Pomerantsev, Andrei A.	Rus.	Colonel	SPb	Electric motors, coal
4 (tie)	6	Rothstein, Adolph Iu.	Ger.	Banker	SPb	International banking

Cycle 7: 1906-1913

Rank		Name	Ethnicity	Title	City	Industries
1	10	Wachter, Konstantin Franz (Loginovich)	Ger.	Privy Councilor	SPb	Construction, coal, concrete
2	9	Sirotkin, Dmitrii V.	Rus.	Commercial C'lor	N.Novg.	Steamships, banking
3 (tie)	8	Fedorov, Mikhail M.	Rus.	Actual S. C'lor	SPb	Railroads, chemicals, banking
3 (tie)	8	Khrulev, Sergei S.	Rus.	Actual S. C'lor	SPb	Railroads, weapons, coal
3 (tie)	8	Lianozov, Stepan G.	Arm.	Court Councilor	SPb	Petroleum, cement, machinery
3 (tie)	8	Putilov, Aleksei I.	Rus.	Actual S. C'lor	SPb	Railroads, petroleum
7	7	Tishchenko, Iurii M.	Ukr.	Gentry	SPb	Petroleum, chemicals

Source: RUSCORP database.

TABLE 3.6 Corporate Entrepreneurship of 102 Largest Landowning Families
(Selected Indicators)

Number of Companies Founded (COS)	Number of Families (FAMS)	Total Land (Desiatinas) (TLAND)	Total Companies (TCOS)	Total Capital (Mil. r.) (TCAP)	Land per Family (Desiatinas) (ALAND)	Capital per Family (Mil. r.) (ACAP)
0	59	10,297,225	0	0	174,529	0
1	20	2,530,994	20	53.670	126,550	2.684
2	11	2,248,403	22	46.810	204,400	4.255
3	5	376,729	15	34.950	75,346	6.990
4	3	411,047	12	97.964	137,016	32.655
5	2	361,158	10	13.650	180,579	6.825
6	2	140,932	12	12.500	70,466	6.250
Totals	102	16,366,488	91	259.544	--	--

Sources: Minarik, Kharakteristika, 13-19; RUSCORP database.

TABLE 3.7 Corporate Entrepreneurship and Landholding of 102 Largest
Landowning Families (Coefficients of Correlation)

	COS	FAMS	TLAND	TCOS	TCAP	ALAND	ACAP
COS	--						
FAMS	-.8034*	--					
TLAND	-.7758*	.9935**	--				
TCOS	.0640	-.5903	-.6119	--			
TCAP	.0200	-.4068	-.4211	.4966	--		
ALAND	-.4057	.3528	.4181	-.0663	-.0169	--	
ACAP	.3910	-.4501	-.4337	.0246	.8016*	-.1108	--

Sources: Minarik, Kharakteristika, 13-19; RUSCORP database.

Codes: Same as in Table 3.6   *$p < .05$ **$p < .0001$

TABLE 3.8 Foreign Corporations Operating in the Russian Empire, 1914

Country	N	Total Capital*	Average Capital*	Largest Corporation	Capital*
Belgium	78	144.775	1.856	Providence Russe à Marioupol	14.622
Britain	69	187.706	2.720	Baku Russian Petroleum Co. (tie)	13.245
				Russian Petroleum Co. (tie)	13.245
France	57	167.411	2.937	Société des selles gemmes et houille	9.000
Germany	33	39.580	1.199	Gewerkschaft "Graf Renard"	8.431
Switzerl.	9	13.388	1.488	Moskauer Textil-Manufaktur AG	4.500
USA	4	78.535	19.634	International Harvester Co. in Russia	77.735
Netherl.	4	1.547	0.387	Société hollandaise pour selles gemmes	0.800
Sweden	3	8.482	2.827	Svensk-Dansk-Ryska telefonactiebolaget	5.656
Austria	2	6.493	3.247	AG Sägemühle vorm. P. und Sch. Goertz	5.993
Italy	2	0.750	0.375	Soc. Itala-Russa per l'Amianto Torino	0.563
Denmark	1	0.521	0.521	Aktieselskabet [United Shoe Machinery]	0.521
Totals	262	649.188	--	--	--

Source: RUSCORP database.

*Millions of rubles.

TABLE 3.9 Entrepreneurial and Managerial Quotients of Major Ethnic Groups, c. 1900

Ethnic Group	A % Total 1897	B % Urban 1897	C % Founders 1896-1900	D % Managers 1905	E % Managers 1914	F C/A	G D/A	H E/A	I C/B	J D/B	K E/B	L Composite Quotient
RUS	44.3	52.5	34.4	35.2	37.4	0.78	0.79	0.84	0.66	0.67	0.71	0.74
UKR	17.8	7.5	1.0	0.9	1.0	0.06	0.05	0.06	0.13	0.12	0.13	0.09
POL	6.3	1.0	10.8	8.2	6.8	1.71	1.30	1.08	10.80	8.20	6.80	4.98
RGER	1.4	2.5	20.3	20.1	19.3	14.50	14.36	13.79	8.12	8.04	7.72	11.09
RJEW	4.0	14.9	11.0	10.6	12.7	2.75	2.65	3.18	0.74	0.71	0.85	1.81
ARM	0.9	1.6	4.0	1.7	1.8	4.44	1.89	2.00	2.50	1.06	1.13	2.17

Sources: Columns A and B: Bauer, Kappeler, and Roth, eds., Nationalitäten, vol. 2, 74; columns C, D, and E: RUSCORP database; columns F, G, H, I, J, and K: by computation; column L: average of F, G, H, I, J, and K.

Ethnic codes: same as in Table 3.1.

TABLE 3.10 Ethnicity of Corporate Managers in Ten Russian Cities, 1905
            (Percentages)

City	Ethnic Category									
	RUS	UKR	POL	RGER	RJEW	ARM	OTH	FOR	UNK	N
St. Petersburg	34.5*	1.3	3.7	22.9	7.8	0.6	0.8	15.2	13.0	1,556
Moscow	62.7*	0.4	0.1	15.4	4.4	1.3	0.3	7.5	7.9	1,160
Warsaw	4.1	0	42.3*	16.1	14.6	0	0	8.9	13.9	459
Kiev	18.0	2.2	7.5	10.1	36.7*	0	0	6.4	19.1	267
Odessa	14.8	1.6	0.8	21.9*	18.0	0	3.9	16.4	22.7	128
Riga	4.8	0	1.1	61.9*	5.3	0	0	16.4	10.6	189
Kharkov	46.1*	0	10.5	10.5	7.9	0	0	9.2	15.8	76
Lodz	2.5	0	4.5	47.1*	25.5	0	0	12.1	8.3	157
Baku	29.7	0	0	4.0	6.9	42.6*	4.0	3.0	9.9	101
Rostov-on-Don	45.5*	10.9	1.8	5.5	10.9	1.8	3.6	1.8	18.2	55
Empire	35.2*	0.9	8.2	20.1	10.6	1.7	0.7	10.5	12.0	5,243

Source: RUSCORP database.

Ethnic codes: Same as in Table 3.1. *Largest percentage. Note: Totals diverge from 100 percent because of rounding.

TABLE 3.11 Ethnicity of Corporate Managers in Ten Russian Cities, 1914
            (Percentages)

City	Ethnic Category									
	RUS	UKR	POL	RGER	RJEW	ARM	OTH	FOR	UNK	N
St. Petersburg	38.0*	1.2	1.3	19.7	10.4	2.2	0.5	9.2	17.4	2,786
Moscow	57.3*	0.3	0.3	17.0	9.1	0.3	0.5	4.5	10.8	1,693
Warsaw	1.6	0	45.5*	21.3	14.5	0	0.1	3.6	13.4	703
Kiev	28.9	2.9	5.8	8.5	36.8*	0	1.2	1.8	14.0	342
Odessa	12.4	1.6	0	20.2	31.8*	0.8	4.7	6.2	22.5	129
Riga	4.6	0	0	74.3*	9.6	0.5	0	4.1	6.9	218
Kharkov	43.8*	1.4	1.4	7.5	28.8	0	0	4.1	13.0	146
Lodz	1.1	0	12.6	44.3*	28.2	0	0	3.4	10.3	174
Baku	27.3	1.6	0.8	5.8	5.0	29.8*	11.6	3.3	14.9	121
Rostov-on-Don	41.4*	1.7	0	6.0	17.2	6.9	6.9	2.6	17.2	116
Empire	37.4*	1.0	6.8	19.3	12.7	1.8	1.0	5.7	14.4	8,090

Source: RUSCORP database.

Ethnic codes: Same as in Table 3.1. *Largest percentage. Note: Totals diverge from 100 percent because of rounding.

TABLE 4.1 Main Provisions of the Corporate Laws of the USSR, the Russian Federation, and Lithuania, 1990-1991

Law and Type of Enterprise	Minimum Capitalization	Procedure of Incorporation
USSR, June 19, 1990		
Corporation, open type	500,000 rubles	Local registration, national register
Corporation, closed type	[Not specified]	same
Limited-liability company	50,000 rubles	same
Russia, December 25, 1990		
Corporation, open type	100,000 rubles	[Not specified]
Corporation, closed type	10,000 rubles	[Not specified]
Lithuania, June 30, 1990		
Corporation, open type	250,000 rubles	Local registration
Corporation, closed type	None	same

Sources: On Soviet law, "Polozhenie ob aktsionernykh obshchestvakh"; on Russian law, Maggs, "Forms," 184; on Lithuanian law, Lithuania, Selected Anthology.

TABLE 6.1 Varieties of Russian Capitalism, 1890 and 1990

Weberian Category	Corporations in 1890		Orientations in 1990		
	Joint-Stock Company	Share Partnership	Reformist	Statist	Reactionary
Rational Accounting	4	3	4	3	2
Open Access to Markets	4	3	5	4	2
Application of Technology and Capital	5	3	5	5	3
Objective Legal Norms	2	2	5	3	2
Free Market in Labor	3	3	5	4	3
Public Sale of Stock	4	2	5	2	2
Totals	22	16	29	21	14

Categories from Weber, Economic History, 276-8. Numerical scores represent author's assessments, expressed in quantitative terms (1 = low, 5 = high).

D

Figures

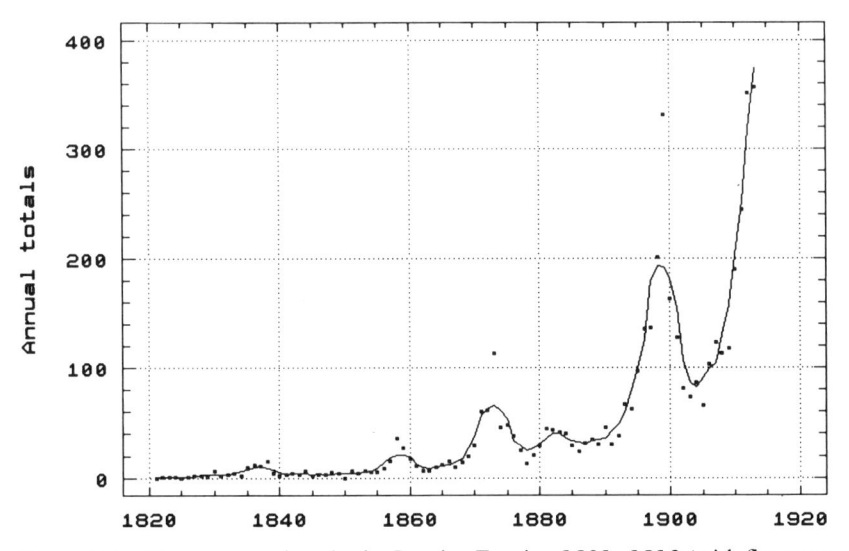

Figure 2.1 New corporations in the Russian Empire, 1821–1913 (with five-year moving average). *Source:* RUSCORP database.

Appendix D   191

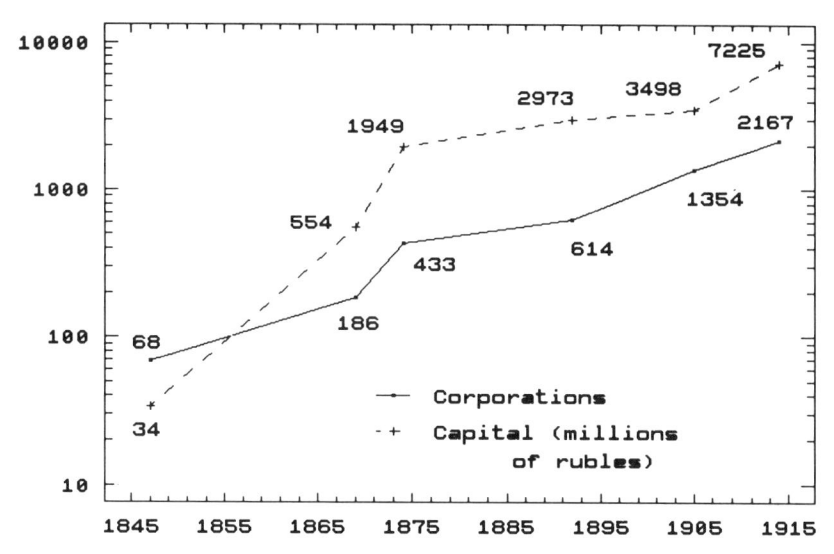

Figure 2.2 Corporations in existence and corporate capital, 1847–1914. *Source:* RUSCORP database.

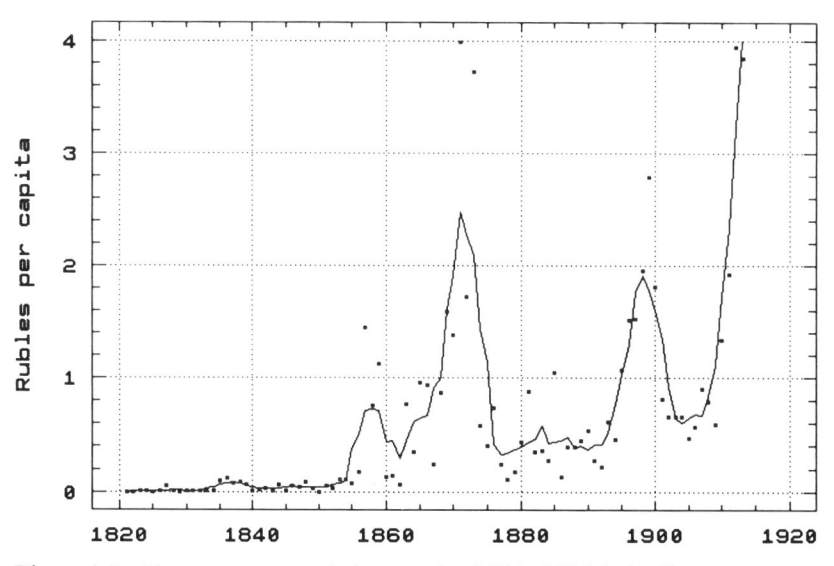

Figure 2.3 New corporate capital per capita, 1821–1913 (with five-year moving average). *Sources:* RUSCORP database; Mitchell, *European Historical Statistics*, 36.

Appendix D

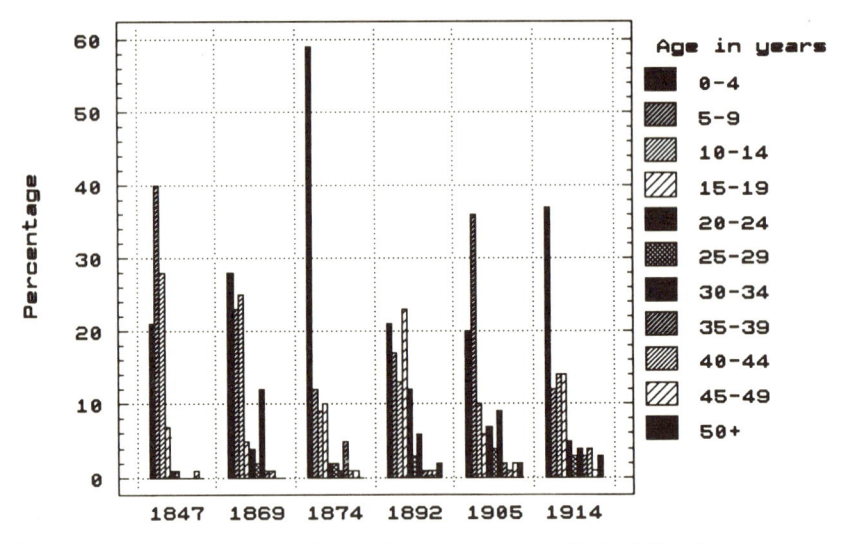

Figure 2.4 Age structure of surviving corporations, 1847–1914 (percentages).
Source: RUSCORP database.

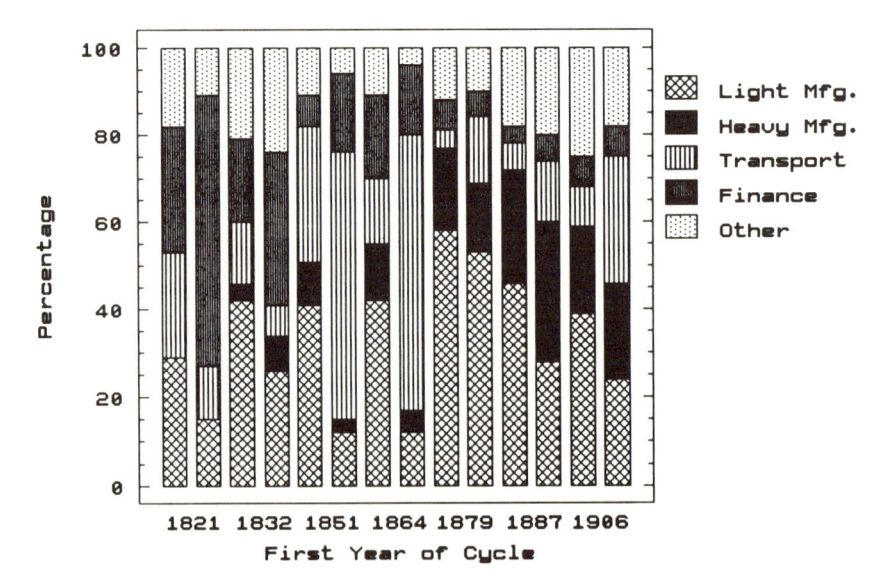

Figure 2.5 New corporations and corporate capital, 1821–1913, by function.
Source: RUSCORP database.

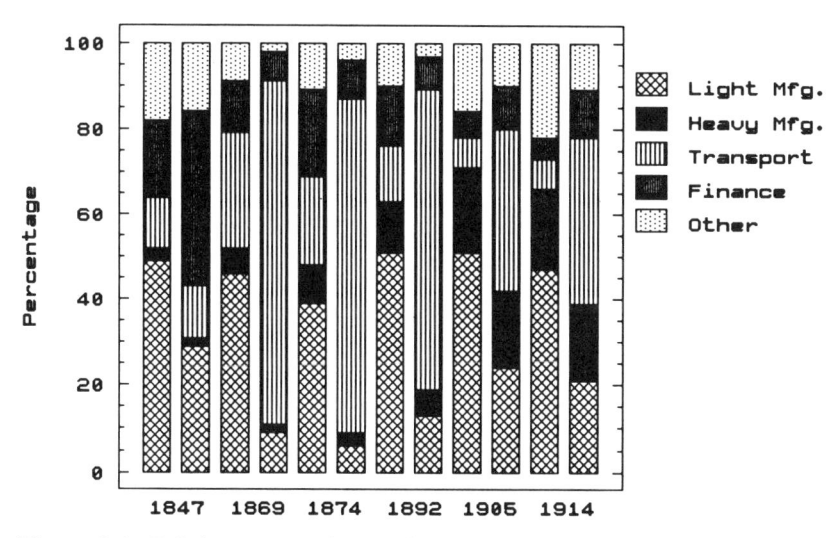

Figure 2.6 Existing corporations and capitalization, 1847–1914, by function. *Source:* RUSCORP database.

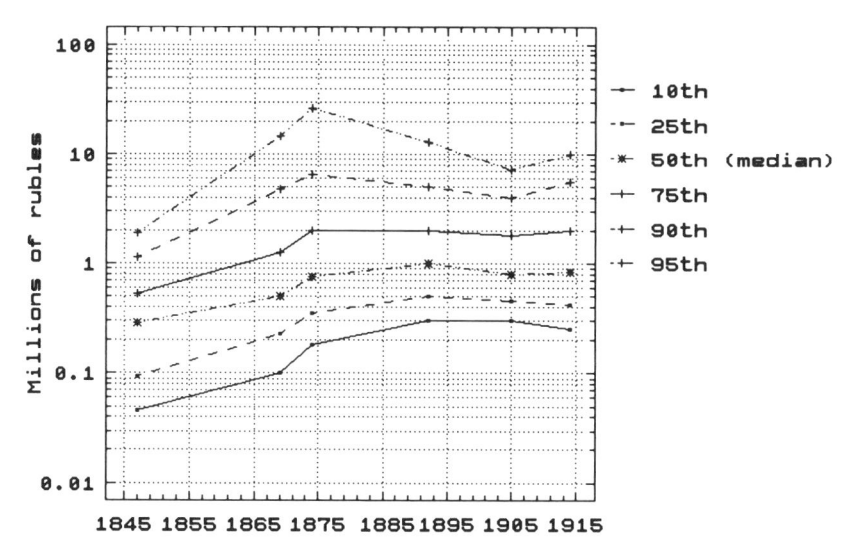

Figure 2.7 Capitalization of surviving corporations, 1847–1914 (selected percentiles). *Source:* RUSCORP database.

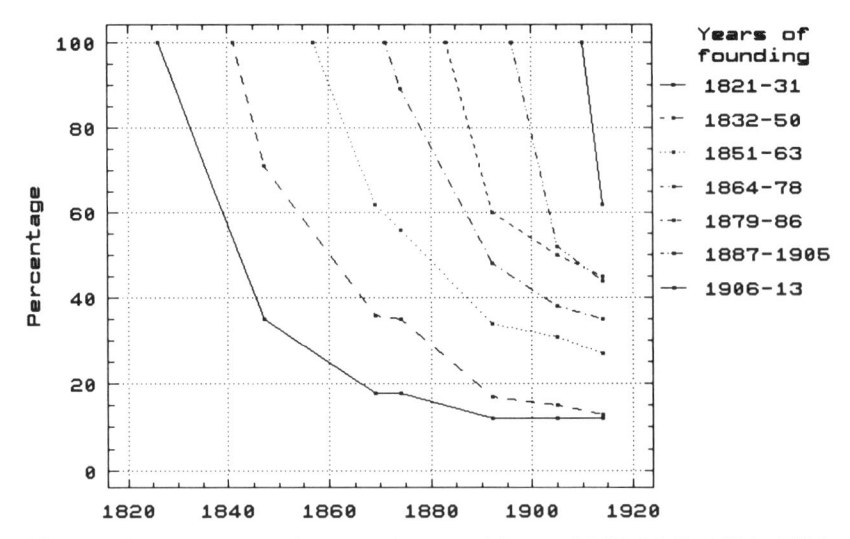

Figure 2.8 Percentages of corporations surviving to 1847, 1869, 1874, 1892, 1905, and 1914. *Source:* RUSCORP database.

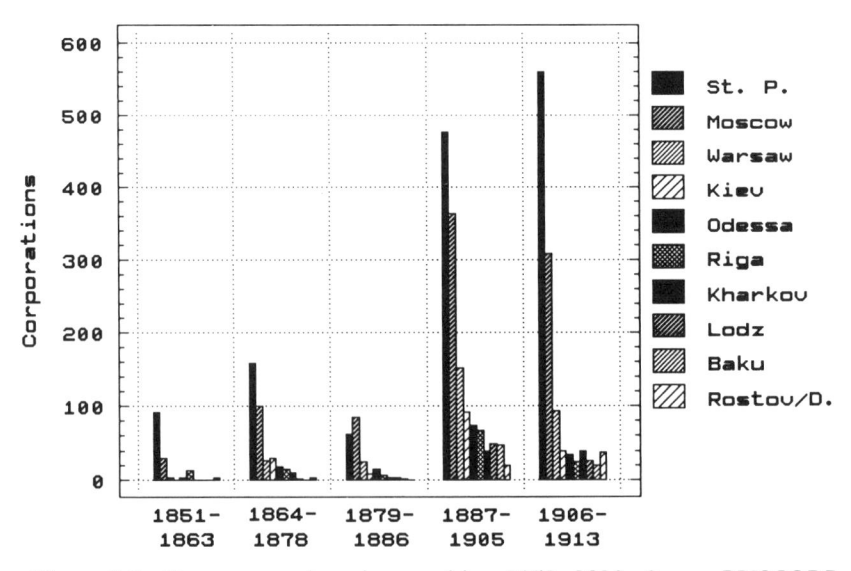

Figure 2.9 New corporations in ten cities, 1851–1913. *Source:* RUSCORP database.

Appendix D   195

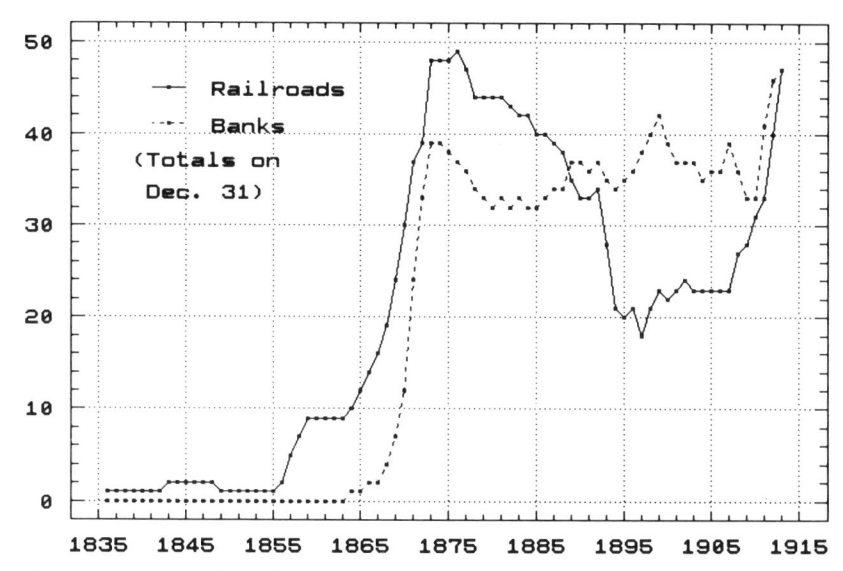

Figure 2.10 Number of corporations engaged in railroad management and banking, 1836–1913. *Source:* RUSCORP database.

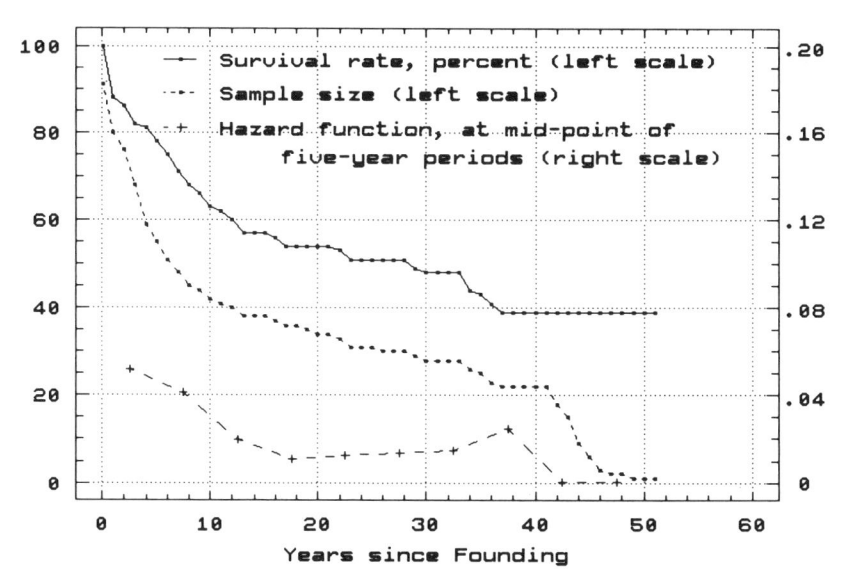

Figure 2.11 Survival rate, sample size, and hazard function of Russian commercial banks. *Source:* RUSCORP database.

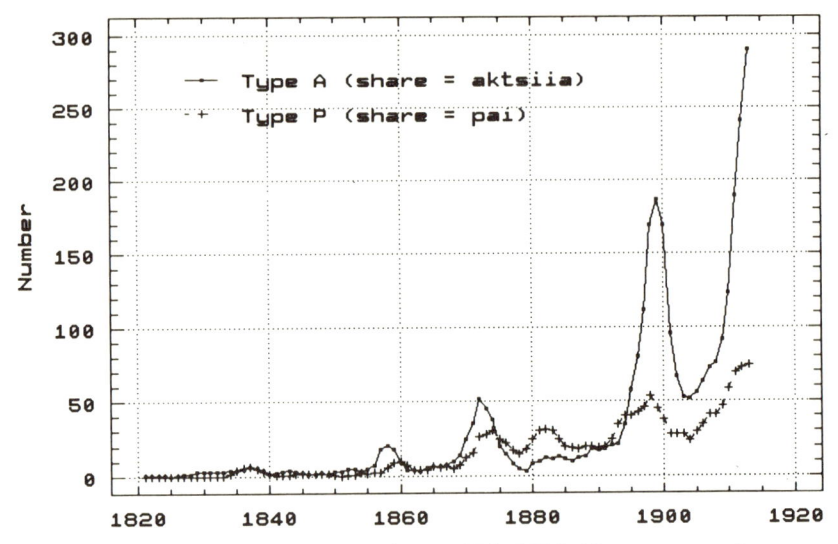

Figure 2.12 Types of new corporations, 1821–1913 (three-year moving averages). *Source:* RUSCORP database.

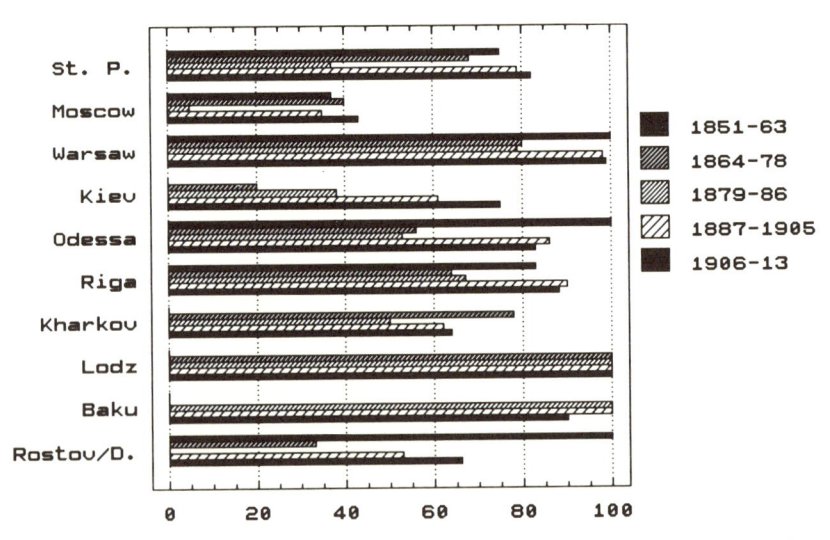

Figure 2.13 Percentage of Type-A corporations founded in ten major cities, 1851–1913. *Source:* RUSCORP database.

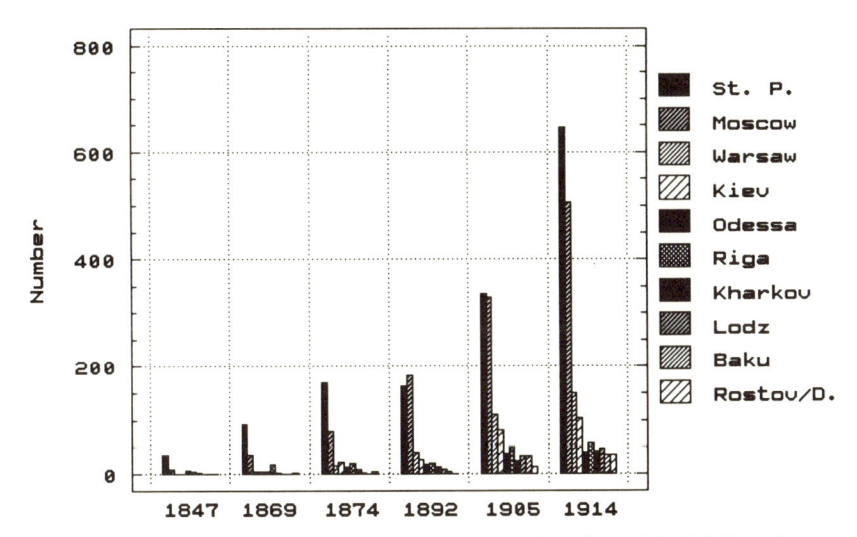

Figure 2.14 Corporations in existence in ten major cities, 1847–1914. *Source:* RUSCORP database.

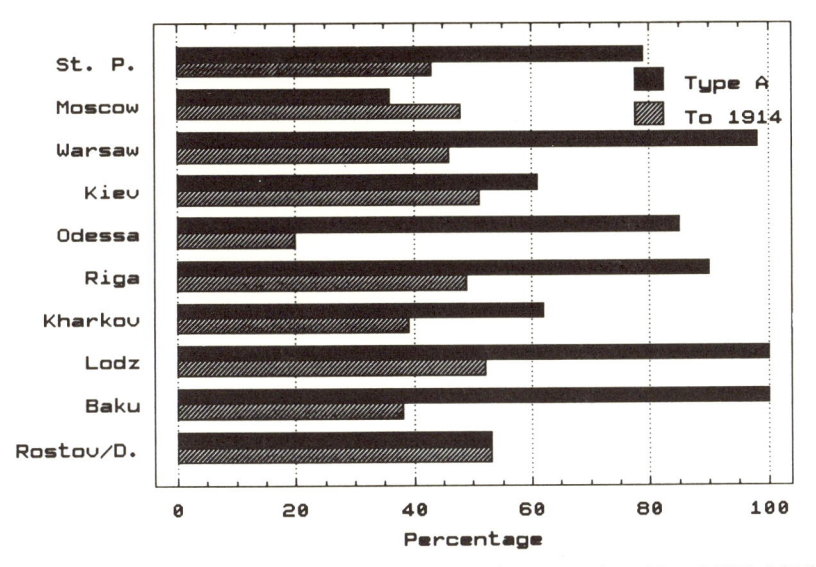

Figure 2.15 New Type-A corporations founded in ten major cities, 1887–1905, and their survival to 1914. *Source:* RUSCORP database.

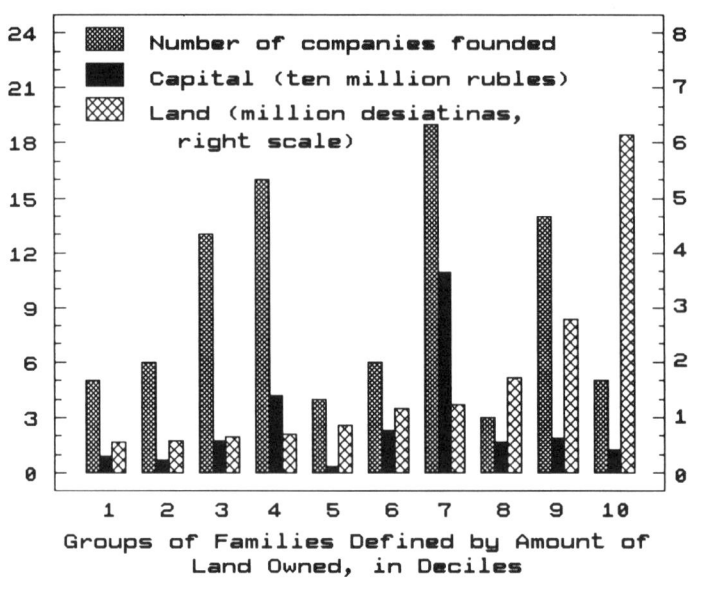

Figure 3.1 Corporate entrepreneurship of 102 largest landholding families. *Sources:* Minarik, *Kharakteristika*, 13–19; RUSCORP database.

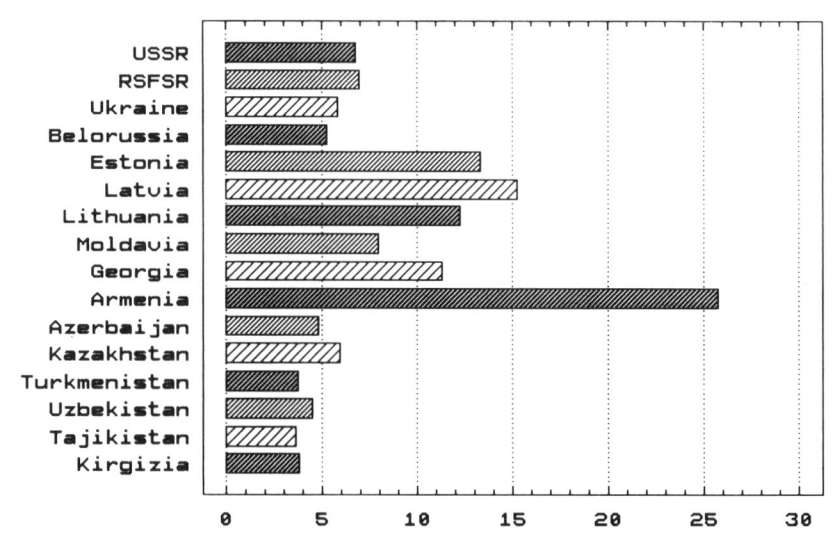

Figure 4.1 Cooperatives in the Soviet Republics per 10,000 inhabitants, January 1990. *Source:* Slider, "Entrepreneurs," 803; data on cooperatives from Jan. 1990; population data from 1989.

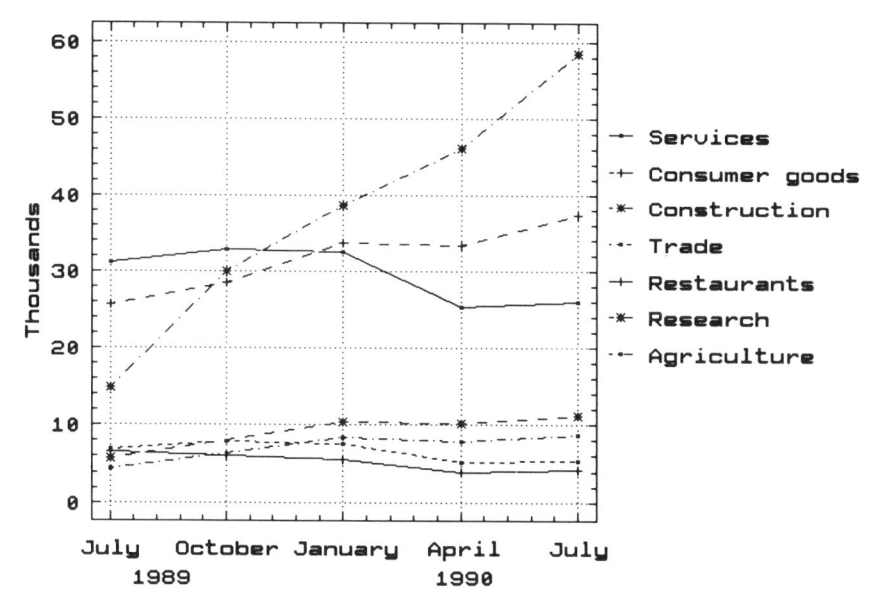

Figure 4.2 Cooperatives in the Soviet Union, by sector, July 1989–July 1990. *Source:* Slider, "Entrepreneurs," 804.

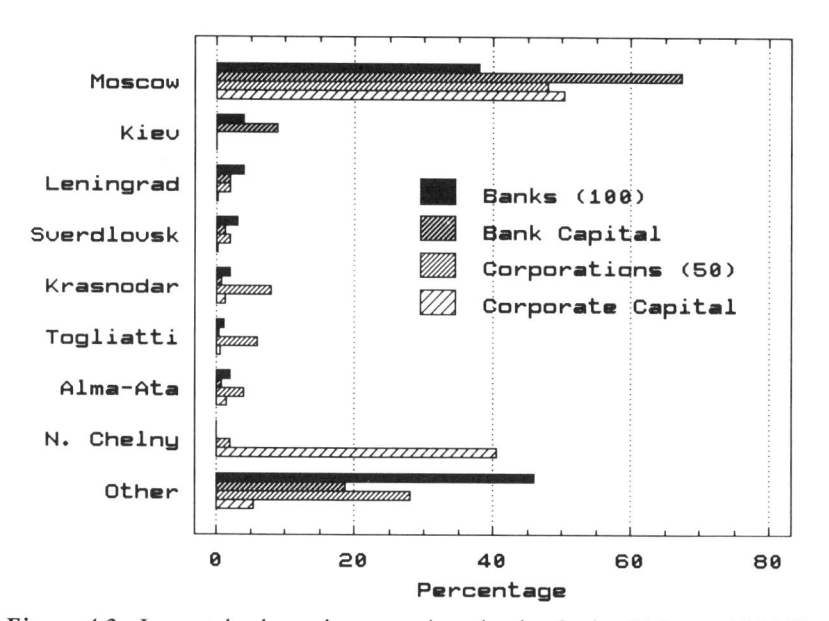

Figure 4.3 Largest banks and corporations in the Soviet Union, mid-1991. *Sources:* On banks, Brady, "In the Red," 231; on corporations, Korobkova, "Societies," 20–1.

Notes

Chapter 1

1. *Herakleitos and Diogenes,* trans. Guy Davenport (Bolinas, Calif.: Grey Fox Press, 1983), 18.

2. Bertram D. Wolfe, comment in *Revolutionary Russia,* ed. Richard Pipes (Cambridge: Harvard University Press, 1968), 330.

3. *General Economic History,* trans. Frank H. Knight (New York: Greenberg, 1927), 276–8.

4. See the classic studies by the late David Granick; and, on illegal entrepreneurship, Konstantin M. Simis, *USSR—The Corrupt Society: The Secret World of Soviet Capitalism,* trans. Jacqueline Edwards and Mitchell Schneider (New York: Simon and Schuster, 1982).

5. See Roger Boyes, *The Hard Road to Market: Gorbachev, the Underworld and the Rebirth of Capitalism* (London: Secker and Warburg, 1990); Gregory Grossman, "The Second Economy: Boon or Bane for the Reform of the First Economy?" in *Berkeley-Duke Occasional Papers on the Second Economy in the USSR,* no. 11 (Dec. 1987), 2.1–2.25; and Arkady Vaksberg, *The Soviet Mafia,* trans. John and Elizabeth Roberts (New York: St. Martin's Press, 1991).

6. For an overview of radical opinion, see Andrzej Walicki, *The Controversy over Capitalism: Studies in the Social Philosophy of the Russian Populists* (Oxford: Clarendon Press, 1969). Mendeleev's efforts to promote Russian industry are examined in Beverly Almgren, "Mendeleev: The Third Service" (doctoral dissertation, Brown University, 1968) and Francis M. Stackenwalt, "The Thought and Work of Dmitrii Ivanovich Mendeleev on the Industrialization of Russia, 1867–1907" (doctoral dissertation, University of Illinois, 1976). On Struve's defense of Russian capitalism at the turn of the century, see Richard Pipes, *Struve: Liberal on the Right, 1905–1944* (Cambridge: Harvard University Press, 1980), esp. ch. 4.

7. The classic study of tsarist economic policy remains Theodore H. Von Laue, *Sergei Witte and the Industrialization of Russia* (New York: Columbia University Press, 1963). On early Russian entrepreneurship, the best studies are those of Samuel H. Baron, "Entrepreneurs and Entrepreneurship in Sixteenth/Seventeenth-Century Russia," in *Entrepreneurship in Imperial Russia and the Soviet Union,* ed. Gregory Guroff and Fred V. Carstensen (Princeton: Princeton University Press, 1983), 27–58, and the many works of Eric Amburger, cited in Chapters 2 and 3. A good overview is M. C. Kaser, "Russian Entrepreneurship," in *The Cambridge Economic History of Europe,* vol. 7, part 2, ed. Peter Mathias and M. M. Postan (Cambridge: Cambridge University Press, 1978), 416–93. The contention of Joseph T. Fuhrmann, *The Origins of Capitalism in Russia* (Chicago: Quadrangle, 1972), that capitalist institutions worthy of the name already existed in Russia in the seventeenth century is unconvincing. On eighteenth-century industrial activities of the Russian landed elite, see Aristide Fenster, *Adel und Ökonomie im vorindustriellen Russland: Die unternehmerische Betätigung der Gutsbesitzer in der grossgewerblichen Wirtschaft im 17. und 18. Jahrhundert* (Wiesbaden: Franz Steiner, 1983). The fates of specific firms and individuals in the nineteenth century are explored in the case studies of Amburger, Friedgut, Kirchner, Lieberman, McKay, Ruud, and Tolf. For a recent assessment of the impact of tsarist economic policy in the late imperial period, see Paul R. Gregory, *Before Command: An Economic History of Russia from Emancipation to the First Five-Year Plan* (Princeton: Princeton University Press, 1994), esp. ch. 4. The social history of merchants is explored in Alfred J. Rieber, *Merchants and Entrepreneurs in Imperial Russia* (Chapel Hill: University of North Carolina Press, 1982), and in studies of regional elites cited in Chapter 3. Some recent monographs on workers' attitudes in the late imperial period are cited in Chapter 5.

8. For a copious list of Soviet works published before 1980, see the bibliography in Heiko Haumann, *Kapitalismus im zaristischen Staat 1906–1917: Organisationsformen, Machtverhältnisse und Leistungsbilanz im Industrialisierungsprozess* (Königstein/Ts.: Hain, 1980). The first post-Soviet analysis of the prerevolutionary economy, Boris V. Anan'ich, *Bankirskie doma v Rossii, 1860–1914 gg.: Ocherki istorii chastnogo predprinimatel'stva* (Leningrad: Nauka, 1991), contained a wealth of new archival material analyzed in a refreshingly straightforward, unpolemical manner. The most thorough analyses of the so-called Russian bourgeoisie were those of Vladimir Ia. Laverychev, *Krupnaia burzhuaziia v poreformennoi Rossii* (Moscow: Mysl', 1974), which paid particular attention to political evolution from the 1860s to 1900, and Aleksandr N. Bokhanov, *Krupnaia burzhuaziia Rossii: konets XIX v.–1914 g.* (Moscow: Nauka, 1992), an account of managers of corporations and unincorporated firms in imperial Russia from the late nineteenth century to 1914, based on an exhaustive analysis of biographical information in corporate directories. Bokhanov's findings are examined critically in Chapter 3.

9. Sergei A. Pervushin, *Khoziaistvennaia kon''iunktura: vvedenie v izuchenie dinamiki russkogo narodnogo khoziaistva za polveka* (Moscow: Ekonomicheskaia zhizn', 1925).

10. Leonid E. Shepelev, "Aktsionernoe uchreditel'stvo v Rossii (istoriko-statisticheskii ocherk)," in *Iz istorii imperializma,* ed. Mikhail P. Viatkin (Leningrad: Nauka, 1959), 134–82; "Aktsionernaia statistika v dorevoliutsionnoi Rossii," in *Monopolii i inostrannyi kapital v Rossii,* ed. Mikhail P. Viatkin (Moscow: Nauka, 1962), 165–207; and *Aktsionernye kompanii v Rossii* (Leningrad: Nauka, 1973).

11. Shepelev, *Aktsionernye kompanii*, 55; *Tsarizm i burzhuaziia v 1904–1914 gg.: problemy torgovo-promyshlennoi politiki* (Leningrad: Nauka, 1987), 244–58.

12. Shepelev, *Aktsionernye kompanii*, 58.

13. Fernand Mallieux, *La Société anonyme d'après le Droit Civil Russe* (Paris: L. Larose, 1902), 26; and Arcadius Kahan, *The Plow, the Hammer, and the Knout: An Economic History of Eighteenth-Century Russia* (Chicago: University of Chicago Press, 1985), 234.

14. On eight companies, Mallieux, *Société;* on ten companies, quotation from William L. Blackwell, *The Beginnings of Russian Industrialization, 1800–1860* (Princeton: Princeton University Press, 1968), 93, citing no reference. Forty charters recorded in RUSCORP database, described in Appendix A. Shepelev, *Aktsionernye kompanii*, and the RUSCORP manual, 39–46, cite the vast but uneven primary and secondary literature on Russian corporations.

15. Andrei G. Golikov, "K voprosu of sostave, soderzhanii i sokhrannosti dokumentov aktsionernykh kompanii," in *Istochnikovedenie otechestvennoi istorii: sbornik statei, 1979,* ed. V. I. Budagov (Moscow: Akademiia nauk, 1980), 134–56.

16. Andrei G. Golikov and G. R. Naumova, "Istochniki po istorii aktsionirovaniia promyshlennosti," in *Massovye istochniki po sotsial'no-ekonomicheskoi istorii Rossii perioda kapitalizma,* ed. Ivan D. Koval'chenko (Moscow: Nauka, 1979), 87–120; and, in the same volume, Valerii I. Bovykin and G. R. Naumova, "Istochniki po istorii monopolii i finansovogo kapitala," 120–60.

17. Inna A. Simonova, "'Muzh sil'nogo dukha i deiatel'nogo sertsa,'" *Literaturnaia Rossiia* 1535 (July 3, 1992): 14–15, on the Slavophile banker and railroad magnate Fedor V. Chizhov (1811–77). In the same issue of this staunchly nationalist newspaper appeared a denunciation of the state-controlled Russian television system by Igor Shafarevich (3) and an interview with Natalia D. Solzhenitsyna, wife of the Nobel laureate (6). *Byloe,* a monthly supplement to the newspaper *Delovoi mir/Business World,* contains brief but copiously illustrated profiles of prerevolutionary Russian industrialists, for example, the history of the Smirnov family, manufacturers of fine vodka, in the July 1993 issue, 8–9.

18. Alfred J. Rieber, "The Sedimentary Society," in *Between Tsar and People: Educated Society and the Quest for Public Identity in Late Imperial Russia,* ed. Edith W. Clowes, Samuel D. Kassow, and James L. West (Princeton: Princeton University Press, 1991), 343. For an examination of one portion of the Russian commercial-industrial elite from this dual point of view, see Thomas C. Owen, *Capitalism and Politics in Russia: A Social History of the Moscow Merchants, 1855–1905* (New York: Cambridge University Press, 1981). The political aspirations of Siberian merchants were discussed in Iia G. Mosina, *Formirovanie burzhuazii v politicheskuiu silu v Sibiri* (Tomsk: Izdatel'stvo Tomskogo universiteta, 1978). A survey of the major business organizations was contained in Rieber, *Merchants.* The best Soviet analyses of policy debates between business organizations and the tsarist bureaucracy were the two volumes by Shepelev, *Tsarizm . . . 1914 g.* and *Tsarizm i burzhuaziia vo vtoroi polovine XIX veka: problemy torgovo-promyshlennoi politiki* (Leningrad: Nauka, 1981). Business organizations in the last decade of the tsarist period were also analyzed briefly in Haumann, *Kapitalismus,* and Johann Hartl, *Die Interessenvertretungen der Industriellen in Russland 1905–1914* (Vienna: Hermann Böhlaus Nachf., 1978).

19. On the most influential national business organization, see Ruth A. Roosa, "The Association of Industry and Trade, 1906–1914: An Examination of the Economic Views of Organized Industrialists in Prerevolutionary Russia" (doc-

toral dissertation, Columbia University, 1967); Roosa, "Russian Industrialists and 'State Socialism', 1906–1917," *Soviet Studies* 23, no. 3 (Jan. 1972): 395–417; and Carl A. Goldberg, "The Association of Industry and Trade, 1906–1917: The Successes and Failures of Russia's Organized Businessmen" (doctoral dissertation, University of Michigan, 1974). Major regional organizations were analyzed in Susan P. McCaffray, "The Association of Southern Coal and Steel Producers and the Problems of Industrial Progress in Tsarist Russia," *Slavic Review* 47, no. 3 (Fall 1988): 464–82; Victoria King, "The Emergence of the St. Petersburg Industrialist Community, 1870–1905: The Origins and Early Years of the Petersburg Society of Manufacturers" (doctoral dissertation, University of California, Berkeley, 1982); and Heather Hogan, *Forging Revolution: Metalworkers, Managers, and the State in St. Petersburg, 1890–1914* (Bloomington: Indiana University Press, 1993).

20. On the poor quality of corporate statistics, the direct result of the lack of a uniform system of corporate bookkeeping in Russia, see Ivan A. Gorbachev, *Tovarishchestva . . . aktsionernye i paevye kompanii: zakon i praktika s senatskimi raz''iasneniiami* (Moscow: I. K. Golubev, 1910), 230. The bankers' complaint appeared in Komitet s''ezdov predstavitelei aktsionernykh kommercheskikh bankov, *Obzor deiatel'nosti s''ezdov predstavitelei aktsionernykh kommercheskikh bankov i ikh organov, 1 iuliia 1916 g.–1 ianvaria 1918 g.* (Petrograd: Svoboda, 1918), 128–9. For a study of Austrian corporations using data on basic capitalization, cash flow, and profits, see Alois Mosser, *Die Industrieaktiengesellschaft in Österreich 1880–1913: Versuch einer historischen Bilanz- und Betriebsanalyse* (Vienna: Akademie, 1980).

21. See Gerschenkron's classic article, "Economic Backwardness in Historical Perspective," first published in 1952, in *Economic Backwardness in Historical Perspective* (Cambridge: Harvard University Press, 1966), 5–30. Gerschenkron's scheme and others advanced in the following decades are reviewed critically in Gregory, *Before Command.*

22. "Perestroika and the October Revolution in Soviet Historiography," *Russian Review* 51, no. 4 (Oct. 1992): 566–76; quotations from 573, 575.

23. Shepelev, *Aktsionernye kompanii;* Thomas C. Owen, *The Corporation under Russian Law, 1800–1917: A Study in Tsarist Economic Policy* (New York: Cambridge University Press, 1991); Harold J. Berman, *Law and Revolution: The Formation of the Western Legal Tradition* (Cambridge: Harvard University Press, 1983); and Douglass C. North, *Institutions, Institutional Change, and Economic Performance* (Cambridge: Cambridge University Press, 1990).

24. Alan M. Ball, *Russia's Last Capitalists: The Nepmen, 1921–1929* (Berkeley: University of California Press, 1987).

25. Hedrick Smith, *The New Russians* (New York: Knopf, 1991), 205. For a qualification of this concept, see Chapter 5.

26. Barrington Moore, Jr., *Social Origins of Dictatorship and Democracy: Lord and Peasant in the Making of the Modern World* (Boston: Beacon Press, 1966), 485–6.

27. North, *Institutions,* 59. This trenchant survey of the state of economic development theory examined cases from economic history worldwide, with special attention to Britain, Spain, the United States, and Latin America. In 1993, Professor North shared the first Nobel Prize in economics to be awarded in the field of economic history. On the contribution of legal structures to the evolution of corporate capitalism in various countries, see, for example, Bishop Carleton

Hunt, *The Development of the Business Corporation in England, 1800–1867* (Cambridge: Harvard University Press, 1936); Charles E. Freedman, *Joint-Stock Enterprise in France, 1807–1867: From Privileged Company to Modern Corporation* (Chapel Hill: University of North Carolina Press, 1979); Freedman, *The Triumph of Corporate Capitalism in France, 1867–1914* (Rochester: University of Rochester Press, 1993); Kurt Bösselmann, *Die Entwicklung des deutschen Aktienwesens im 19. Jahrhundert: Ein Beitrag zur Frage der Finanzierung gemeinwirtschaftlicher Unternehmungen und zu den Reformen des Aktienrechts* (Berlin: W. de Gruyter & Co., 1939); Paul Fischer, *Die Aktiengesellschaft in der nationalsozialistischen Wirtschaft: Ein Beitrag zur Reform des Gesellschaftsrechts* (Munich: Duncker und Humblot, 1936); Norbert Horn and Jürgen Kocka, eds. *Recht und Entwicklung der Grossunternehmen im 19. und frühen 20. Jahrhundert* (Göttingen: Vandenhoeck und Ruprecht, 1979), containing articles in German and English; and Herbert Hovenkamp, *Enterprise and American Law, 1836–1937* (Cambridge: Harvard University Press, 1991).

28. North, *Institutions,* 100, 99, 111–12.

29. Moore, *Social Origins,* 508.

30. Jeffrey D. Sachs, "Privatization in Russia: Some Lessons from Eastern Europe," *American Economic Review* 82, no. 2 (May 1992): 43–8; and Sachs, "Goodwill Is Not Enough," *Economist,* Dec. 21, 1991, 101–4.

31. Stephen F. Cohen, "American Policy and Russia's Future: Illusions and Realities," *Nation* (Apr. 12, 1993): 478.

32. Tim McDaniel, *Autocracy, Capitalism, and Revolution in Russia* (Berkeley: University of California Press, 1988).

33. Quoted in *From Max Weber: Essays in Sociology,* trans. and ed. H. H. Gerth and C. Wright Mills (New York: Oxford University Press, 1958), 71.

34. David E. Schrader, *The Corporation as Anomaly* (Cambridge: Cambridge University Press, 1993), 134. See also Robert A. Dahl, *A Preface to Economic Democracy* (Berkeley: University of California Press, 1985); and Samuel Bowles and Herbert Gintis, *Democracy and Capitalism: Property, Community, and the Contradictions of Modern Social Thought* (New York: Basic Books, 1986).

35. Quoted without reference in Cohen, "American Policy," 481.

36. This pessimistic theme permeated two journalistic accounts: A. Craig Copetas, *Bear Hunting with the Politburo* (New York: Simon and Schuster, 1991); and Bill Thomas and Charles Sutherland, *Red Tape: Adventure Capitalism in the New Russia* (New York: Dutton, 1992).

37. Jude Wanniski, "The Future of Russian Capitalism," *Foreign Affairs* 71, no. 2 (Spring 1992): 17–25.

Chapter 2

1. Johan Huizinga, "Historical Conceptualization" (1934), trans. Rosalie Colie, in *The Varieties of History: From Voltaire to the Present,* ed. Fritz Stern, rev. ed. (New York: Vintage, 1973), 299–300.

2. Gregory, *Before Command;* quotations from 29, 83.

3. Howard E. Aldrich, *Organizations and Environments* (Englewood Cliffs, N.J.: Prentice-Hall, 1979), 27–28. For an early statement of the theory, see Michael T. Hannan and John Freeman, "The Population Ecology of Organizations," *American Journal of Sociology* 82 (March 1977): 929–64. Achievements of the

method are discussed in Glenn R. Carroll, "Organizational Ecology," *Annual Review of Sociology* 10 (1984): 71–93.

4. See Alfred D. Chandler, Jr., and Herman Daems, eds., *Managerial Hierarchies: Comparative Perspectives on the Rise of the Modern Industrial Enterprise* (Cambridge: Harvard University Press, 1980); and Michael T. Hannan and John Freeman, *Organizational Ecology* (Cambridge: Harvard University Press, 1989).

5. See Jean-Benoît Scherer, *Histoire raisonnée du commerce de la Russie*, 2 vols. (Paris: Cuchet, 1788); Nikolai N. Firsov, *Russkie torgovo-promyshlennye kompanii v pervuiu polovinu XVIII stoletiia* (Kazan: Universitet, 1896); Aleksandr S. Lappo-Danilevskii, "Russkie promyshlennye i torgovye kompanii v pervoi polovine XVIII veka," *Zhurnal ministerstva narodnogo prosveshcheniia* 320, no. 12 (Dec. 1898), part 2: 306–66; and 321, no. 2 (Feb. 1899), part 2: 371–436; and Aleksandr I. Iukht, "Torgovye kompanii v Rossii v seredine XVIII v.," *Istoricheskie zapiski* 111 (1984): 238–95.

6. *PSZ* 1-7906, dated Sept. 21, 1739; and 1-1706, dated Oct. 27, 1699. In 1-8237, dated Sept. 11, 1740, the Governing Senate admitted that no one had responded to the earlier appeal to merchants to set up a China trade company. The renewed invitation of 1740 likewise had no effect.

7. *PSZ* 1-11489, dated Mar. 28, 1762, voided the charters of these three companies; and 1-11630, dated July 31, 1762, definitively abolished them.

8. For recent scholarship which contains references to the older historical literature on this company, see Mary E. Wheeler, "The Russian American Company and the Imperial Government: Early Phase," in *Russia's American Colony*, ed. S. Frederick Starr (Durham: Duke University Press, 1987), 43–62; and other essays in that volume. Still useful are Hans Pilder, *Die Russisch-Amerikanische Handels-Kompanie bis 1825* (Berlin: G. J. Göschen, 1914); S. B. Okun', *Rossiisko-Amerikanskaia kompaniia* (Moscow: Gosudarstvennoe sotsial'no-ekonomicheskoe izdatel'stvo, 1939); A. A. Preobrazhenskii, "O sostave aktsionerov Rossiisko-Amerikanskoi kompanii v nachale XIX v.," *Istoricheskie zapiski* 67 (1960): 286–98; and P. A. Tikhmenev, *A History of the Russian-American Company*, trans. and ed. Richard A. Pierce and Alton S. Donnelly (Seattle: University of Washington Press, 1978). On the granting of limited liability to investors in 1821, see *PSZ* 1-28756. For an incisive analysis of the success of the Hudson's Bay Company, see Ann M. Carlos and Stephen Nicholas, "Agency Problems in Early Chartered Companies: The Case of the Hudson's Bay Company," *Journal of Economic History* 50, no. 4 (Dec. 1990): 853–75.

9. See the insurance company's jubilee history: *V pamiat' 75-ti letnego iubileia Pervogo Rossiiskogo strakhovogo obshchestva, uchrezhdennogo v 1827 godu* (St. Petersburg: Marks, 1903); and Amburger, *Deutsche in Staat, Wirtschaft und Gesellschaft Russlands: Die Familie Amburger in St. Petersburg 1770–1920* (Wiesbaden: Harrassowitz, 1986), which describes the role of several Amburgers in this venerable company.

10. Of the many works on foreign corporations in Russia, among the most important are: Bachschi Ischchanian, *Die ausländischen Elemente in der russischen Volkswirtschaft* (Berlin: F. Siemenroth, 1913); Isaak I. Levin, *Germanskie kapitaly v Rossii*, 2d ed., rev. (Petrograd: I. Shurkht, 1918); John P. McKay, *Pioneers for Profit: Foreign Entrepreneurship and Russian Industrialization, 1885–1913* (Chicago: University of Chicago Press, 1970); Joachim Mai, *Das deutsche Kapital in Russland 1850–1894* (Berlin: Deutscher Verlag der Wissenschaften, 1970); René

Girault, *Emprunts russes et investissements français en Russie, 1887–1914* (Paris: A. Colin, 1973); Fred V. Carstensen, *American Enterprise in Foreign Markets: Studies of Singer and International Harvester in Imperial Russia* (Chapel Hill: University of North Carolina Press, 1984); and Walther Kirchner, *Die deutsche Industrie und die Industrialisierung Russlands 1815–1914* (St. Katharinen: Scripta Mercaturae, 1986).

The precise amount of foreign investment in the Russian economy has yet to be established, the well-known work by Ol' (Ohl) having received trenchant criticism in Fred V. Carstensen, "Foreign Participation in Russian Economic Life: Notes on British Enterprise, 1865–1914," in *Entrepreneurship,* ed. Guroff and Carstensen, 143–7.

11. Suggestions of cyclical patterns were presented by Shepelev, *Aktsionernye kompanii,* 23, 63, 66, 84, 92–3, 135, 225, 234, but some of his tables included both domestic and foreign companies. Valerii I. Bovykin, *Formirovanie finansovogo kapitala v Rossii: konets XIX v.–1908 g.* (Moscow: Nauka, 1984), presented the best charts and graphs in Soviet scholarship on this subject.

12. See Owen, *The Corporation under Russian Law.* On this and other aspects of imperial corporate law, Shepelev, *Aktsionernye kompanii,* provided a wealth of documentation, much of it verbatim, from the ministerial archives.

13. Shepelev, *Aktsionernye kompanii,* 30.

14. Ibid., 28 (on the reduction from a percent to 4 percent in 1830); 67 (on the reduction from 4 percent to 3 percent in mid-1857); 83 (on the cessation of stock exchange speculation by the issuing of 5 percent banknotes in mid-1869); 144 (on reductions from 5 percent and 4.5 percent to 4 percent of the interest rate on government-guaranteed bonds in 1889–94); and 145 (on reductions in land banks from 6 percent to 5 percent in 1891–2 and from 5 percent to 4.5 percent in 1898).

15. William L. Crum, *The Age Structure of the Corporate System* (Berkeley: University of California Press, 1953).

16. A Spearman coefficient of $+1.0$ indicates perfect agreement in the rank order of two lists; 0 denotes the presence of as many similarities as differences; and -1.0 signifies a complete reversal of rank order in the two lists.

17. Aldrich, *Organizations,* 68–9.

18. Carstensen, *American Enterprise,* on large capitalizations, 231 (quoted); on defeat of competitors, 232; on Singer's sales network, 230 (quoted); on International Harvester's marketing, 206; on mistakes of its managers, 174, 204, 205 (quoted).

19. See Mikhail Ia. Gefter, "Iz istorii monopolisticheskogo kapitalizma v Rossii: sakharnyi sindikat," *Istoricheskie zapiski* 38 (1951): 151, on the importance of excise taxes in the state budget; and Vladimir Ia. Laverychev, *Gosudarstvo i monopolii v dorevoliutsionnoi Rossii* (Moscow: Mysl', 1982), 101–17. Roger Munting, "The State and the Beet Sugar Industry in Russia before 1914," in *Crisis and Change in the International Sugar Economy,* ed. Bill Albert and Adrian Graves (Norwich, U.K.: ISC Press, 1984), 21–9, is a good overview in English. The last account to appear in the Soviet period, M. A. Davydov, "Soglasheniia rafinerov (1900–1914 gg.)," in *Monopolisticheskii kapitalizm v Rossii,* ed. Valerii I. Bovykin (Moscow: Akademiia nauk, 1989), 104–23, paid due attention to internal tensions within the cartel and occasional disagreements between it and the tsarist authorities.

20. Bovykin's account, *Formirovanie*, ch. 4, although markedly empirical by Soviet standards, bore a traditionally teleological subtitle: "Consolidation of the Monopolies." The efforts of the tsarist bureaucracy to weaken the coal cartel shortly before World War I were discussed in Shepelev, *Tsarizm . . . 1904–1914 gg.*, 235, and by a mining engineer in the coal industry, Aleksandr I. Fenin, *Coal and Politics in Late Imperial Russia: Memoirs of a Russian Mining Engineer,* trans. Alexandre Fediaevsky, ed. Susan P. McCaffray (DeKalb: Northern Illinois University Press, 1990), 53–4. For a contemporary complaint, see S———m, "Pochemu podpisyvaiut dogovory s kaznoiu," *Gorno-zavodskoe delo* 18, no. 10 (Mar. 12, 1910): 337. Useful material on cartels may be found in Rieber, *Merchants*. The essays in Bovykin, ed., *Monopolisticheskii kapital,* tended to use published financial data uncritically.

21. Aldrich, *Organizations*, 69.

22. Paul R. Gregory, *Russian National Income, 1885–1913* (New York: Cambridge University Press, 1982), 149.

23. Pervushin, *Kon''iunktura*, 184–213; Boris N. Mironov, *Khlebnye tseny v Rossii za dva stoletiia (XVIII–XIX vv.)* (Leningrad: Nauka, 1985), 151–3.

24. Aldrich, *Organizations*, 171.

25. W. T. Easterbrook, "The Climate of Enterprise," in *Explorations in Enterprise,* ed. Hugh G. J. Aitken (Cambridge: Harvard University Press, 1965), 76 (quoted), 78.

26. David H. Kamens and Tormod K. Lunde, "Institutional Theory and the Expansion of the Central State Organizations, 1960–1980," in *Institutional Patterns and Organizations: Culture and Environment,* ed. Lynne G. Zucker (Cambridge, Mass.: Ballinger Publishing Company, 1988), 171.

27. Aldrich, *Organizations*, 169–70, on Peter the Great, citing Reinhard Bendix, *Work and Authority in Industry* (New York: Wiley, 1956). Governmental policies inimical to enterprise under Peter I and Catherine II are stressed in Kahan, *Plow,* 263–4. On the lack of a coherent industrial policy under Nicholas II, see Haumann, *Kapitalismus,* 49. The importance of the Glorious Revolution of 1688 in securing property rights that stimulated the emergence of both public and private capital markets in England is made clear in North, *Institutions,* 138–40.

28. Letter dated Dec. 19, 1803, cited in Alison Blakely, "American Influences on Russian Reformist Thought in the Era of the French Revolution," *Russian Review* 52, no. 4 (Oct. 1993): 460.

29. Quoted from *Slovo* in *Gorno-zavodskii listok,* the newspaper of the Association of Southern Coal and Steel Producers, Apr. 9, 1905, 7699–7700. For numerous other examples of manufacturers' complaints of bureaucratic ineptitude, see Shepelev's two volumes entitled *Tsarizm i burzhuaziia;* and McDaniel, *Autocracy,* esp. 19–24 on the weakness of laws and contracts under the tsarist regime. The restrictions on ethnic minorities are discussed in Shepelev, *Aktsionernye kompanii,* 122–3, and Owen, *Corporation,* 118–32. The protest of the sugar men appeared in "Polozhenie sakharnoi promyshlennosti . . . (zapiski sakharozavodchikov)," *Pravo* (Mar. 27, 1905), col. 918.

30. Roosa, "'State Socialism.'"

31. Gregory, *Before Command,* 82. On the tariff debates in 1850, 1857, 1868, 1877, and 1891, see Owen, *Capitalism,* 20, 37–8, 61–3, 118, 136–7.

32. On tariffs and other aspects of economic policy, see Arcadius Kahan, *Russian Economic History: The Nineteenth Century,* ed. Roger Weiss (Chicago: University of Chicago Press, 1989), ch. 2, a classic article originally published in

1967. Isaak I. Levin, *Aktsionernye kommercheskie banki v Rossii*, vol. 1 [no more published] (Petrograd: I. R. Belopol'skii, 1917), 230–1, gives a richly detailed account of Reutern's handling of the bank crisis of 1875.

33. Generally negative assessments are offered in Owen, *Corporation;* Steven G. Marks, *Road to Power: The Trans-Siberian Railroad and the Colonization of Asian Russia, 1850–1917* (Ithaca: Cornell University Press, 1991); and Jonathan Coopersmith, *The Electrification of Russia, 1880–1926* (Ithaca: Cornell University Press, 1992). For an examination of the effects of corporate tax policies, see Linda Bowman, "Russia's First Income Taxes: The Effects of Modernized Taxes on Commerce and Industry, 1885–1914," *Slavic Review* 52, no. 2 (Summer 1993): 256–82.

34. Robin L. Marris, "An Introduction to Theories of Corporate Growth," in *The Corporate Economy: Growth, Competition, and Innovative Potential*, ed. Robin Marris and Adrian Wood (Cambridge: Harvard University Press, 1971), 4–5.

35. Peter D. McClelland, *Causal Explanation and Model Building in History, Economics, and the New Economic History* (Ithaca: Cornell University Press, 1975), 223.

36. Conversation with author, Harvard Business School, May 19, 1988; Herman Daems, *The Holding Company and Corporate Control* (Boston: Nijhoff, 1978).

37. On the interaction of organizational networks and political power, see Aldrich, *Organizations,* ch. 13.

38. On unincorporated trading and banking firms, respectively, see Bokhanov, *Krupnaia burzhuaziia*, ch. 2.; and Anan'ich, *Bankirskie doma*.

39. Alfred D. Chandler, Jr., *Strategy and Structure: Chapters in the History of the American Industrial Enterprise* (Cambridge: MIT Press, 1962), 23 (quoted), 32–8 (quoted); chaps. 2–5 on the multidivisional giants.

40. Oskar Mertens, "1882–1911: Dreissig Jahre russischer Eisenbahnpolitik," *Archiv für Eisenbahnwesen* 40 (1917): 427. On the financial woes of railroads in the 1880s, see also Pavel I. Georgievskii, *Finansovye otnosheniia gosudarstva i chastnykh zh.-dorozhnykh obshchestv v Rossii i v Zapadno-evropeiskikh gosudarstvakh* (St. Petersburg: Benke, 1887), esp. 101–4, 286–307.

41. Aida M. Solov'eva, *Zheleznodorozhnyi transport Rossii vo vtoroi polovine XIX v.* (Moscow: Nauka, 1975), part 3.

42. Survival data from RUSCORP; mileage figures from John N. Westwood, *A History of Russian Railways* (London: Allen and Unwin, 1964), 142. On railroads generally, see Westwood; I. A. Tikhotskii, *Kratkii ocherk razvitiia nashei zheleznodorozhnoi seti za desiatiletie 1904–1913 g.g.* (St. Petersburg: Ministerstvo finansov, 1914); and "Nasha zheleznodorozhnaia set' i ee istoricheskoe razvitie," *Vestnik finansov, promyshlennosti i torgovli* 16 (Apr. 20, 1914): 131–5, esp. 133 on strategic lines built in 1904–13. Mertens, "1882–1911," 429–30, also stressed the military purpose of short rail lines extending to the western border of the empire.

43. Aida M. Solov'eva, "Iz istorii vykupa chastnykh zheleznykh dorog v Rossii v kontse XIX veka," *Istoricheskie zapiski* 82 (1968): 116. Mertens, "1882–1911," 439, described the growth of the six largest companies from 1892 to 1911.

44. On the allocation of freight cars by the southern coal and steel producers in 1879–89, after which the Ministry of Transportation established its own committee for coal and iron cars (*Komitet po perevozka gorno-zavodskikh gruzov*), see *Nikolai Stepanovich Avdakov* (Kharkov, 1915; appendix to *Gorno-zavodskoe delo* 46–47, 1915), 10–11. On piles of grain, Mertens, "1882–1911," 425.

45. Girault, *Emprunts*, 561–6.

46. On the Bolsheviks' dictatorial control over the crumbling rail network, the logistical key to their victory in the Russian Civil War of 1918–20, see the sophisticated geographical treatment of Robert Argenbright, "Bolsheviks, Baggers and Railroaders: Political Power and Social Space, 1917–1921," *Russian Review* 52, no. 4 (Oct. 1993): 506–27.

47. Shepelev, "Aktsionernoe uchreditel'stvo," appendix on banks and railroads; J. Lewin [Isaak I. Levin], *Der heutige Zustand der Aktienhandelsbanken in Russland (1900–1910)* (Freiburg: Poppen, 1912), 15–19.

48. SAS Institute, *SAS User's Guide: Statistics, Version 5* (Cary, N.C.: SAS Institute, 1985), ch. 22: "The LIFETEST Procedure."

49. Shepelev, "Aktsionernoe uchreditel'stvo," 169–74, traced the establishment and the demise of Russian commercial banks, but his list was not complete before 1900.

50. Peter Gatrell, book review, in *Business History* 34, no. 4 (Oct. 1992): 110.

51. Komitet s''ezdov predstavitelei aktsionernykh kommercheskikh bankov, *O zhelatel'nykh izmeneniiakh v postanovke aktsionernogo bankovogo dela v Rossii* (Petrograd: Al'fa, 1917), 23-8; on "depression" of 1900–8 [*sic*], 25; quotation from 29: *razvitie bankov opredeliaet i razvitie khoziaistvennoi deiatel'nosti*. The pamphlet also contained, 8–19, an informative survey of tsarist legislation on commercial banks from 1864 to 1916.

52. r^2 is the percentage obtained by squaring a coefficient of correlation. It indicates the percentage of variation in the dependent variable attributable to variation in the independent variable or variables. p is another indication of statistical significance in regression analysis, closely related to the coefficient of correlation and r^2. $p = .05$ means that the relationship in question would occur by chance in only one in twenty cases; $p = .01$, in one in a hundred; $p = .005$, in one in two hundred; and $p = .001$, in one in a thousand. Significant statistical relationships are those with high coefficients of correlation (whether positive or negative), high r^2, and low p, conventionally defined as falling between .05 and 0. Whenever the number of cases is reasonably large, r^2 and p vary inversely. That is, a large r^2 and small p combine to indicate a significant statistical relationship between the two variables.

53. Boris V. Anan'ich and Valerii I. Bovykin, "Foreign Banks and Foreign Investment in Russia," in *International Banking, 1870–1914*, ed. Rondo Cameron and Valerii I. Bovykin (Oxford: Oxford University Press, 1991), appendix, 277–90, compiled with the assistance of S. K. Lebedev.

54. For analyses of the banking system and its role in industry, see Levin, *Banki*; Iosif F. Gindin, *Banki i promyshlennost' v Rossii do 1917 g.: k voprosu o finansovom kapitale v Rossii* (Moscow: Promizdat, 1927); Iosif F. Gindin and Leonid E. Shepelev, "Bankovskie monopolii v Rossii nakanune velikoi oktiabr'skoi sotsialisticheskoi revoliutsii," *Istoricheskie zapiski* 66 (1960): 20–95; Olga Crisp, *Studies in the Russian Economy before 1914* (New York: Macmillan, 1976), esp. ch. 5: "Banking in the Industrialization of Tsarist Russia, 1860–1914"; Bovykin, *Formirovanie;* and Anan'ich, *Bankirskie doma*.

55. Crisp, *Studies,* 141–7, provided a succinct overview of the relationship between corporate banks and industry, with useful statistics from 1895, 1900, 1908, and 1914 showing the leading role of the St. Petersburg banks in these and other forms of advanced financial activities.

56. "Enemies of the People," in *The Lenin Anthology,* ed. Robert C. Tucker (New York: Norton, 1975), 306 (emphasis in original).

57. Gindin, *Banki i promyshlennost'*, 42. For a brief review of the extensive Soviet historical literature, see Bovykin, *Formirovanie*, introduction.

58. George W. Edwards, *The Evolution of Finance Capitalism* (New York: Longmans, Green, 1938), 4.

59. On Baku, see John P. McKay, "Entrepreneurship and the Emergence of the Russian Petroleum Industry, 1813–1883," *Research in Economic History* 8 (1983): 47–91; and Robert W. Tolf, *The Russian Rockefellers: The Saga of the Nobel Family and the Russian Oil Industry* (Stanford: Hoover Institution Press, 1976).

60. Iosif F. Gindin, *Gosudarstvennyi bank i ekonomicheskaia politika tsarskogo pravitel'stva (1861–1892 gody)* (Moscow: Gosfinizdat, 1960), 128–53, 322–7; and Gindin, "Pravitel'stvennaia podderzhka ural'skikh magnatov vo vtoroi polovine XIX–nachale XX v," *Istoricheskie zapiski* 82 (1968): 120–62.

61. These distinctions are made clear in Gorbachev, *Tovarishchestva*, a manual published in 1910 for the benefit of merchants and lawyers.

62. Three excellent monographs make this contrast clear: Anders Henriksson, *The Tsar's Loyal Germans: The Riga German Community, Social Change and the Nationality Question, 1855–1905* (Boulder, Colo.: East European Monographs, 1983); Steven J. Zipperstein, *The Jews of Odessa: A Cultural History, 1794–1881* (Stanford: Stanford University Press, 1985); and Patricia Herlihy, *Odessa: A History, 1794–1914* (Cambridge: Harvard Ukranian Research Institute, 1986), on Greeks, Italians, and Jews in the southern grain trade.

63. For a recent survey of the activities of Jewish business leaders in Kiev, see Michael F. Hamm, *Kiev: A Portrait, 1800–1917* (Princeton: Princeton University Press, 1993), ch. 5. Arcadius Kahan, "Notes on Jewish Entrepreneurship in Russia," in *Entrepreneurship*, ed. Guroff and Carstensen, 104–24, is the most sophisticated analysis of the complicated subject of Jewish entrepreneurship, on which a large literature exists in Russian, Polish, and Yiddish.

64. The preference for family-centered share partnerships based on previously existing limited partnerships in this period was noted by Shepelev, *Aktsionernye kompanii*, 245–6, who, however, did not apply any statistical tests to his data. A statistical expression of this dichotomy was first published in Thomas C. Owen, "Entrepreneurship and the Structure of Enterprise in Russia, 1800–1880," in *Entrepreneurship*, ed. Guroff and Carstensen, 71, in a table comparing joint-stock companies and share partnerships founded in the regions of St. Petersburg and Moscow in 1855–80. The table summarized data drawn from the *PSZ* and analyzed in Whitney A. Coulon III, "The Structure of Enterprise in the Russian Empire, 1855–1880" (M.A. thesis, Louisiana State University, 1979). On the Moscow merchants and their entrepreneurial habits, see Owen, *Capitalism*; Rieber, *Merchants*; Jo Ann S. Ruckman, *The Moscow Business Elite: A Social and Cultural Portrait of Two Generations, 1840–1905* (DeKalb: Northern Illinois University Press, 1984); and James L. West, "The Riabushinskii Circle: *Burzhuaziia* and *Obshchestvennost'* in Late Imperial Russia," in *Between Tsar and People*, ed. Clowes, Kassow, and West, 41–56.

65. In the copious secondary literature on Warsaw and Lodz, the most impressive works are Ireneusz Ihnatowicz, *Przemysł łódzki w latach 1860–1900* (Warsaw: Akademia nauk, 1965); Ihnatowicz, *Burżuazja warszawska* (Warsaw: Państwowe Wydawnictwo Naukowe, 1972); Johanna Hensel, *Burżuazja warszawska drugiej połowy XIX w. w świetle akt notarialnych* (Warsaw: Akademia nauk, 1979), a computerized analysis of notarial records in Warsaw; Ryszard Kołodziejczyk and Ryszard Gradowski, *Zarys dziejów kapitalizmu w Polsce* (Wrocław: Państwowe Wydawnictwo Naukowe, 1974); Kołodziejczyk, ed., *Dzieje burżuazji w Polsce: Studia i*

materiały (Wroclaw: Akademia nauk, 1974, 1980, 1983); and Irena Pietrzak-Pawłowska, ed., *Uprzemysłowienie ziem polskich w XIX i XX wieku: Studia i materiały* (Warsaw: Zakład narodowy im. Ossolińskich, 1970), a general survey of industrialization in Poland.

66. See Thomas C. Owen, "The Russian Industrial Society and Tsarist Economic Policy, 1867–1905," *Journal of Economic History* 45, no. 3 (Sept. 1985): 587–606; Owen, "Impediments to a Bourgeois Consciousness in Russia, 1880–1905: The Estate Structure, Ethnic Diversity, and Economic Regionalism," in *Between Tsar and People,* ed. Clowes, Kassow, and West, 75–89; and Muriel Joffe, "Regional Rivalry and Economic Nationalism: The Central Industrial Region Industrialists' Strategy for the Development of the Russian Economy, 1880s–1914," *Russian History* 11 (Winter 1984): 389–421.

67. Nikolai P. Shmelyov [Shmelev] and Vladimir Popov, *The Turning Point: Revitalizing the Soviet Economy,* trans. Michele A. Berdy (New York: Doubleday, 1989), 93–4; Gregory, *Before Command,* ch. 5.

68. Quotation from Marks, *Road,* 124. Józef Kaczkowski, "Towarzystwo akcyjne w państwe rosyjskiem: studium prawno-ekonomiczne," *Ekonomista* 8 (1908), vol. 1, 103–4; Shepelev, *Aktsionernye kompanii,* 115, 196–201; Owen, *Corporation,* chaps. 3, 5.

69. Carstensen, *American Enterprise,* 180, quoting Bary's statement in the International Harvester Archive.

70. Ruth A. Roosa, "Banking and Financial Relations between Russia and the United States," in *International Banking,* ed. Cameron and Bovykin, 291–318.

71. *Government, Industry and Rearmament in Russia, 1900–1914: The Last Argument of Tsarism* (Cambridge: Cambridge University Press, 1994), 256 (quoted), 257, 154; Gregory, *Before Command,* 32 (quoted).

72. [G. P. Nebol'sin], "Aktsionernye obshchestva v Rossii," *Sovremennik,* 1847, no. 5 (Sept.), *smes',* part 4, 14–15; quotations from 14. Shepelev, *Aktsionernye kompanii,* 64, identified the author of this anonymous article. The RUSCORP database contains no information about the Tsna River company. On early Russian shipping enterprises, including corporations, see Richard M. Haywood, "The Development of Steamboats on the Volga River and Its Tributaries, 1817–1856," *Research in Economic History* 6 (1981): 127–92.

73. C. Skalkovsky [Konstantin A. Skal'kovskii], *Les Ministres des finances de la Russie, 1802–1890,* trans. P. de Nevsky (Paris: Guillaumin, 1891), 170.

74. See *Entrepreneurship,* ed. Guroff and Carstensen; Tolf, *Russian Rockefellers;* Manfred Hildermeier, *Bürgertum und Stadt in Russland 1760–1870: Rechtliche Lage und soziale Struktur* (Cologne: Böhlau Verlag, 1986), esp. 370–544; and Amburger, *Deutsche.*

75. Albert J. Beveridge, *The Russian Advance* (New York: Harper and Brothers, 1903), 264–6.

76. Hannan and Freeman, *Organizational Ecology,* 10.

Chapter 3

1. Sir Lewis Namier, "History" (1952), reprinted in Stern, ed., *Varieties of History,* 379.

2. Valentin S. Diakin, ed., *Krizis samoderzhaviia v Rossii, 1895–1917* (Leningrad: Nauka, 1984), which appeared on the eve of perestroika, contained essays by five of the leading Leningrad historians of the reign of Nicholas II. The

chapters on economic policy by Anan'ich on Witte and by Diakin on the period after 1905 summarized the best of Soviet scholarship, but the editor saw fit to cite no sources except the works of Lenin in the concluding chapter.

3. Roosa, "'State Socialism'"; Owen, *Capitalism* and *Corporation;* McDaniel, *Autocracy;* West, "Riabushinskii Circle"; and Gatrell, *Government*.

4. On the sixteenth and seventeenth centuries, see Baron, "Entrepreneurs," 53–8; on the period from Catherine II's reign to the Great Reforms, see Hildermeier, *Bürgertum*.

5. Arno J. Mayer, *The Persistence of the Old Regime: Europe to the Great War* (New York: Pantheon, 1981).

6. *Entsiklopedicheskii slovar' Brokgauz-Efrona*, vol. 91A (1904), 884. No information on Fedorov appeared in the *Russkii biograficheskii slovar'*.

7. Shepelev, *Tsarizm . . . 1904–1914 gg.*, 39; Shepelev, *Aktsionernye kompanii*, 255 (quoted); Valentin S. Diakin, *Samoderzhavie, burzhuaziia i dvorianstvo v 1907–1911 gg.* (Leningrad, Nauka, 1978), 118, 187; Diakin, ed., *Krizis*, 307, 639. Mention of Fedorov's vice-presidency of the Russian National Committee (*Russkii national'nyi komitet*) appears in the protocol of a meeting of this organization, dated June 1922, in item 54466, pp. 136–7, Harold Whitmore Williams papers, Department of Manuscripts, British Library, London.

8. Barry Supple, "The Nature of Enterprise," in *The Cambridge Economic History of Europe*, vol. 5, ed. E. E. Rich and C. H. Wilson (Cambridge: Cambridge University Press, 1977), 452.

9. Moore, *Social Origins*, 442.

10. Liudmila P. Minarik, *Ekonomicheskaia kharakteristika krupneishikh zemel'nykh sobstvennikov Rossii kontsa XIX–nachala XX v.* (Moscow: Sovetskaia Rossiia, 1971), 19, 21; 24–30 on industries; quotation from 30. Professor Terence Emmons kindly drew my attention to this important work.

11. Fenster, *Adel*, lists of individuals, 271–328, and appendix 8, 329–34.

12. R. H. Coase, quoted by T. Dudley Wallace and cited in Stanley Lieberson, *Making It Count: The Improvement of Social Research and Theory* (Berkeley: University of California Press, 1985), 98.

13. Erik Amburger, "Das Haus Wogau & Co. in Moskau und der Wogau-Konzern, 1840–1917," in *Russland und Deutschland: Festschrift für Georg von Rauch*, ed. Uwe Liszkowski, vol. 22 of *Kieler Historische Studien* (Stuttgart: E. Klett, 1974), 186. Bokhanov, *Krupnaia burzhuaziia*, 116, correctly noted that its declared capitalization of 90,000 rubles belied its enormous economic role.

14. For biographical details, see Owen, *Capitalism*. Details of Gubonin's background are given in N. P. Chulkov, "Moskovskoe kupechestvo XVIII i XIX vv.," *Russkii arkhiv*, 1907, vol. 3, 495.

15. BASF advertisement in *Business in the USSR*, no. 3 (July–Aug. 1990): 29: "As long ago as 1874, shortly after the founding of our company 125 years ago, we set up a branch office in Moscow, and three years later a production plant went on stream." According to corporate directories published in 1914, the Moscow agency of BASF received permission to operate under "conditions of activity" (*usloviia deiatel'nosti*) issued in 1887. Data on Siemens and Halske from RUSCORP; on its pivotal role in Russian electrification, see Coopersmith, *Electrification*, 38, who attributed the prominence of German firms in electrical engineering not to their capital investments but to "their aggressive and thorough marketing," the German salesmen's command of the Russian language, and their ability to "arrange long-term credit, a vital consideration." On German capital in the Russian electric power industry, see also Valentin S. Diakin, *Germanskie kapitaly v*

Rossii: elektroindustriia i elektricheskii transport (Leningrad: Nauka, 1971). Kirchner, *Deutsche Industrie,* 104–23, provides a vivid analysis of the activities of Bayer in Moscow. The point about enterprise outweighing capital as a factor in the success of German businesses in Russia was made as early as 1918 by Levin, *Germanskie kapitaly.*

16. Erik Amburger, "Der fremde Unternehmer in Russland bis zur Oktoberrevolution im Jahre 1917," *Tradition: Zeitschrift für Firmengeschichte und Unternehmerbiographie* 2, no. 4 (Oct. 1957): 349.

17. *Entrepreneurship,* ed. Guroff and Carstensen; RUSCORP manual.

18. Pavel A. Buryshkin, *Moskva kupecheskaia* (New York: Chekhov Publishing Company, 1954), 58–9.

19. Nikolai A. Naidenov, *Vospominaniia o vidennom, slyshannom i ispytannom,* 2 vols. (Moscow, 1903–5; reprinted Newtonville, Mass.: Oriental Research Partners, 1976), vol. 2, 34, 117 (quoted), 129–33. Levin, *Banki,* 213–25, provided details on the financial aspects of this crash, which involved illegal dealing on the part of the Berlin banker Strousberg.

20. Octave Marie Joseph Kerim Homberg, *Les Coulisses de l'histoire: souvenirs 1898–1928* (Paris: A. Fayard, 1938), 99, 100 (quoted). For additional evidence of poor corporate management by former military officers and bureaucrats, see Owen, *Corporation,* 49–50, 89–97.

21. Skal'kovskii served as vice-director of the Mining Department for almost thirteen years before becoming director in 1891. He was one of many fascinating characters in Russian economic history deserving of a full-scale biography. For a brief account, see Thomas C. Owen, "Skal'kovskii, Konstantin A.," *Modern Encyclopedia of Russian and Soviet History,* 35: 157–60. Bertenson, whose brother married Skal'kovskii's sister in 1878, wrote the most detailed account of his life but burned all "letters of a personal nature" in Skal'kovskii's apartment in Paris after his death; V. B. Bertenson, *Iz vospominanii o K. A. Skal'kovskom* (St. Petersburg, 1912), 12, 18. The Soviet article is Aleksandr A. Fursenko, "Materialy o korruptsii tsarskoi biurokratii (po bumagam K. A. Skal'kovskogo)," in *Issledovaniia po otechestvennomu istochnikovedeniiu: sbornik statei, posviashchennykh 75-letniiu professora S. N. Valka,* edited by N. E. Nosov (Leningrad: Nauka, 1964), 149–56. The anecdote appeared in Aleksandr Kliagin, *Strana vosmozhnostei neobychainykh* (Paris: n.p., n.d. [1947]), 73, a reference kindly provided by Dimitri Arensburger, a distant relative of Skal'kovskii.

22. Maurice Verstraete, "Sur les routes de mon passé," unpublished autobiography, 1949, Hoover Institution Archives, Stanford University; vol. 1, 238–43 on corruption; quotations from 238.

23. On Sushchov, see Fenin, *Coal,* 68–9; Owen, *Corporation,* 49–50; and the sources cited there. Quotation from Sergei Iu. Witte, *The Memoires of Count Witte,* trans. and ed. Sidney Harcave (Armonk, N.Y.: M. E. Sharpe, 1990), 320.

24. Bokhanov, *Krupnaia burzhuaziia,* 133–5, 139–43, and 200–13, identified all managers of five or more corporations in existence in 1896, 1902, and 1914, who numbered 44, 59, and 123, respectively; percentages for 1914, from 214 and 216. (He did not use the corporate directory of 1905, utilized in RUSCORP.) Bokhanov also listed, 182–5, the fifty-three men who held corporate positions and seats in the State Duma and State Council in 1914, in an effort to show how leading legislators belonged to the corporate elite and therefore were positively disposed toward it.

25. Catherine L. Johnstone, *The British Colony in Russia* (London: Roxburghe Press, 1897), a brief survey of the period from 1553 to the 1890s.

26. Stephen Charles Ellis, "Management in the Industrialization of Russia, 1861–1917" (doctoral dissertation, Duke University, 1980), 175, 185–98.

27. Anders Henriksson, "Nationalism, Assimilation and Identity in Late Imperial Russia: The St. Petersburg Germans, 1906–1914," *Russian Review* 52, no. 3 (July 1993): 341–53; quotations from 353, 342; the phrase "the German colony" appeared on 346.

28. Henriksson, *Germans,* presented an excellent portrait of German life in Riga, including a list of corporations. Other important sources are Wilhelm Lenz, *Die Entwicklung Rigas zur Grosstadt* (Kitzingen/Main: Holzner-Verlag, 1954); and Wilhelm Lenz, ed., *Deutschbaltisches biographisches Lexikon 1710–1960* (Cologne: Böhlau Verlag, 1970), a reference tool for the study of Germans in the Baltic region of which there is no counterpart in the scholarship on other regions of the Russian Empire.

29. McKay, *Pioneers,* 199–200. Biographies of these "old Russian hands," as McKay called them, remain to be written. Verstraete's memoir, "Sur la route," contains much useful autobiographical detail. For brief tributes to Pierre Darcy, who founded the Prodameta metallurgical cartel, represented the Banque de l'Union Parisienne in Russia, and died in Moscow in December 1918 after a brutal incarceration by the Cheka, see Paul Darcy, "Au service de la France en Russie," *Revue de Paris,* Sept. 15, 1927, 364–78, and Oct. 1, 631–53; and Homberg, *Coulisses,* 100–1.

30. Ernst Jenny, *Die Deutschen im Wirtschaftsleben Russlands* (Berlin: Carl Heymanns Verlag, 1920); quotations from 4, 8, 9.

31. Jenny, *Deutschen,* 28–9, 30 (quoted), 31 (quoted twice).

32. Ibid., 28.

33. Quoted in Kirchner, *Industrie,* 126.

34. Amburger, *Deutsche;* conversation with author in Heuchelheim, West Germany, July 8, 1987.

35. Franz Karlovich San-Galli, *Curriculum vitae zavodchika i fabrikanta Frantsa Karlovicha San-Galli* (St. Petersburg: P. O. Iabolonskii, 1903).

36. Herbert Swann, *Home on the Neva: A Life of a British Family in Tsarist St. Petersburg—And after the Revolution* (London: Gollanz, 1968), 30–1.

37. James Whishaw, *Memoirs of James Whishaw,* ed. Maxwell S. Leigh (London: Methuen and Co., 1935), 66–7, 88, 91; quotations from 121.

38. Georg Spies, *Erinnerungen eines Ausland-Deutschen,* Beilageband 2 of *Spiess'sche Familien-Zeitung* (Marburg: Moritz Spiess, 1926–8), 23–4, 27–9 on Robert Spies; 126–9 on the "colony"; quotation from 129.

39. Ibid., 28, 29 (quoted).

40. Ibid., 19 on Stjernvall; 78 (quoted); section 38 on the Clason family.

41. Richard Falck, *Familienbuch Rau: Geschichte einer kurmainzischen Schiffersippe aus Höchst, Eltville und Mainz* (Düsseldorf: Walter Rau Verlag, 1956), 114–16; quotation from 114. Rau ranked fourth in Cycle four and first in Cycle five among corporate founders. The historical obscurity of Rau, who stood in the front rank of corporate founders for several decades, showed the abysmal state of business history in Russia and Poland.

42. Ibid., 117–18.

43. Harvey Pitcher, *The Smiths of Moscow: A Story of Britons Abroad* (Cromer, Norfolk: Swallow House Books, 1984), 34.

44. Sir Robert H. Bruce Lockhart, *British Agent* (Garden City, N. Y.: Garden City Publishing Co., 1933), 66–7.

45. Spies, *Erinnerungen,* 130.

46. Jenny, *Deutschen*, 31, 9, 31, 33, 27.

47. For a fascinating commentary on other foreign stereotypes, positive and negative, including those of businessmen, in both the tsarist and Soviet periods, see Valentin Kiparsky, *English and American Characters in Russian Fiction* (Berlin: Steinkopf & Sohn, 1964).

48. For a concise review of the shortcomings of previous work on entrepreneurship, see Sidney M. Greenfield and others, "Studies in Entrepreneurial Behavior: A Review and an Introduction," in *Entrepreneurs in Cultural Context,* ed. Sidney Greenfield, Arnold Strickon, and Robert T. Aubey (Albuquerque: University of New Mexico Press, 1979), 4–10.

49. Burton Benedict, "Family Firms and Firm Families: A Comparison of Indian, Chinese, and Creole Firms in Seychelles," in *Entrepreneurs,* ed. Greenfield, Strickon, and Aubey, 305–26.

50. Greenfield and Strickon, conclusion to *Entrepreneurs,* ed. Greenfield, Strickon, and Aubey, 348–9.

51. Janet T. Landa, "Culture and Entrepreneurship in Less-Developed Countries: Ethnic Trading Networks as Economic Organizations," in *The Culture of Entrepreneurship,* ed. Brigitte Berger (San Francisco: ICS Press, 1992), 56–9; quotation from 59.

52. Landa, "Culture," 60, 65 (quoted); emphasis in original.

53. Arnold Strickon, "Ethnicity and Entrepreneurship in Rural Wisconsin," in *Entrepreneurs,* ed. Greenfield, Strickon, and Aubey, 188 (quoted), 186 (quoted); Harry W. Strachan, "Nicaragua's Grupos Económicos: Scope and Operations," in *Entrepreneurs,* ed. Greenfield, Strickon, and Aubey, 243–4 (quoted).

54. On Kokorev, the only extensive analysis is Paul Lieberman, "V. A. Kokorev: An Industrial Entrepreneur in Nineteenth-Century Russia" (doctoral dissertation, Yale University, 1982), but his idiosyncratic enterprises were also discussed in Gindin, *Gosudarstvennyi bank;* Owen, *Capitalism;* Rieber, *Merchants;* and David Christian, *"Living Water": Vodka and Russian Society on the Eve of Emancipation* (Oxford: Oxford University Press, 1990).

55. Greenfield and others, "Studies," 16.

56. Ludwig Knoop, letter to his brother, Julius, dated May 30 (N.S.), 1877, describing the celebration on May 3/16. The letter was published verbatim in Adele Wolde, *Ludwig Knoop: Erinnerungsbilder aus seinem leben* (Bremen: C. Schünemann, 1928), 43–4. Quotation from biographical sketch by Friedrich Prüser in Wolde, *Knoop,* separate pagination, 249–50.

57. Karl Khagelin [Hagelin], *Moi trudovoi put'* (New York: Grenich Printing Corp., 1945), 235, 236 (quoted) on Nobels; 228 on Azeris. The only comprehensive account of the Nobel Brothers Petroleum Company is Tolf, *Russian Rockefellers.*

58. Coopersmith, *Electrification,* 16–21.

Chapter 4

1. Mikhail S. Gorbachev, "Main Guidelines for the Stabilization of the Economy and Transition to the Market," *Reprints from the Soviet Press* 52, no. 1 (Jan. 15, 1991): 5–6.

2. "On Cooperation," in *The Lenin Anthology,* ed. Tucker, 707–13; quotation from 710.

3. Stephen F. Cohen, *Bukharin and the Bolshevik Revolution: A Political Biography, 1888–1938* (New York: Vintage, 1975), ch. 6.

4. This account is based on the detailed analysis of the decree of February 1987 and the law of May 1988 in John E. Tedstrom, "The Reemergence of Soviet Cooperatives," in *Socialism, Perestroika, and the Dilemmas of Soviet Economic Reform*, ed. John E. Tedstrom (Boulder, Colo.: Westview Press, 1990), esp. 114–21.

5. Law on cooperatives issued in late May 1988, discussed in Smith, *New Russians*, 264; Brigitte Quinton, "Des petits entrepreneurs en URSS: les patrons des cooperatives," *Le Courrier des pays de l'Est* 360 (May–June 1991), 29, on the minimum of three founders.

6. Darrell Slider, "Embattled Entrepreneurs: Soviet Cooperatives in an Unreformed Economy," *Soviet Studies* 43, no. 5 (1991): 799.

7. A. Shaposhnikov, "What Are Cooperatives and How Should They Be Dealt With?" *Problems of Economics* 34, no. 5 (Sept. 1991): 66–7; quotation from 67. For data from January 1989 on cooperatives, their functions, work force, and output, see Tedstrom, "Reemergence," tables 2–4.

8. On the conventions of removing outliers in regression analysis and reporting results with and without outliers, see George W. Bohrnstedt and David Knoke, *Statistics for Social Data Analysis* (Itasca, Ill.: F. E. Peacock Publishers, 1982), 265–7.

9. Smith, *New Russians*, 268, citing Simis, *USSR*, on crime patterns; quotation from 268.

10. Slider, "Entrepreneurs," 806.

11. Leonid Dobrokhotov, quoted by Smith, *New Russians*, 286.

12. Slider, "Entrepreneurs," 808–9.

13. Esther B. Fein, "Millionaire's Bad Fortune: Why Is K.G.B. Calling?" *New York Times*, Mar. 5, 1991, sec. A., p. 4.

14. Steve Coll and Michael Dobbs, "Rampant Corruption Fuels Capital Flight from Russia," *Washington Post*, Jan. 31, 1993, sect. A, p. 4.

15. Slider, "Entrepreneurs," 809; Marshall I. Goldman, *What Went Wrong with Perestroika*, rev. ed. (New York: Norton, 1992), 113–14.

16. Anatoly Sobchak, *For a New Russia: The Mayor of St. Petersburg's Own Story of the Struggle for Justice and Democracy* (New York: Free Press, 1992), 39–41 (quoted).

17. John M. Litwack, "Legality and Market Reform in Soviet-Type Economies," *Journal of Economic Perspectives* 5, no. 4 (Fall 1991): 87.

18. Sergei Glaziev, "Transformation of the Soviet Economy: Economic Reforms and Structural Crisis," *National Institute Economic Review* 138 (Nov. 1991): 99–100.

19. Slider, "Entrepreneurs," 805.

20. On bodyguards, Quinton, "Des petits entrepreneurs," 39; quotation from Quinton's interview with a manager, 38.

21. William A. Clark, "Crime and Punishment in Soviet Officialdom, 1965–90," *Europe-Asia Studies* 45, no. 2 (1993): 272 (quoted), 276, 277 (quoted). Clark cited the copious literature on the second economy and the black market from the mid-1960s to the mid-1980s.

22. Slider, "Entrepreneurs," 807–8.

23. Quotations from Slider, "Entrepreneurs," 810, and Quinton, "Des petits entrepreneurs," 30.

24. For a detailed analysis of this three-cornered struggle, see Paul B. Stephan

III, *Soviet Economic Law: The Paradox of Perestroyka* (Pittsburgh: University of Pittsburgh Center for Russian and East European Studies, 1990). Baruch A. Hazan, *Gorbachev and His Enemies: The Struggle for Perestroika* (Boulder, Colo.: Westview Press, 1990), 222–35, examines the various forms of bureaucratic harassment of individual and cooperative economic activity.

25. Quinton, "Des petits entrepreneurs," 32, citing *Sotsialisticheskaia industriia,* Feb. 1989.

26. Ibid., 34.

27. Smith, *New Russians,* 284.

28. Shmelyov and Popov, *Turning Point,* 267.

29. Slider, "Entrepreneurs," 813–17. On 815, Slider provided a table of maximum rates adopted by thirteen republics (excluding Ukraine and Uzbekistan) for seven kinds of cooperatives by mid-1989; on 816–17, he listed the revised rates for 1989–91.

30. Slider, "Entrepreneurs," 808, 816, 812.

31. *Turning Point,* 251–2; quotations from 252.

32. Goldman, *What Went Wrong,* 229; Grigorii Khanin, "The Soviet Economy—From Crisis to Catastrophe," in *The Post-Soviet Economy: Soviet and Western Perspectives,* ed. Anders Aslund (New York: St. Martin's Press, 1992), 9–24.

33. Paul R. Gregory and Robert C. Stuart, *Soviet and Post-Soviet Economic Structure and Performance,* 5th ed. (New York: HarperCollins, 1994), 202–3, cited some of this literature.

34. David K. Shipler, *Russia: Broken Idols, Solemn Dreams,* rev. ed. (New York: Penguin, 1989), 226. The text of this book, which appeared in 1983, remained unchanged in the revised edition, except for the addition of an epilogue.

35. John Newhouse, "Chronicling the Chaos," *New Yorker,* Dec. 31, 1990, 64 (quoted), 72.

36. Quoted from *Novyi mir,* Sept. 1988, in Smith, *New Russians,* 205; Zaslavskaia quoted in Smith, *New Russians,* 194; on resentment of family contract teams, Tatyana Zaslavskaya, *The Second Socialist Revolution: An Alternative Soviet Strategy,* trans. Susan M. Davies with Jenny Warren (Bloomington: Indiana University Press, 1990), 56 (quoted).

37. Quinton, "Des petits entrepreneurs," 40.

38. Smith, *New Russians,* 199–200; Sobchak quoted on 204. Sobchak, *Russia,* 138, gave a slightly different rendition of the parable and attributed this mentality to "Communist ideology."

39. Edward L. Keenan, "Muscovite Political Folkways," *Russian Review* 45, no. 2 (Apr. 1986); 123–8; quotations from 125, 126.

40. Esther Kingston-Mann, "Peasant Communes and Economic Innovation: A Preliminary Inquiry," in *Peasant Economy, Culture, and Politics of European Russia, 1800–1921,* ed. Esther Kingston-Mann and Timothy Mixter (Princeton: Princeton University Press, 1991); quotations from 50, 39.

41. Leonid Dobrokhotov, quoted in Smith, *New Russians,* 286.

42. Keenan, "Folkways," 169; conversation with author, Cambridge, Mass., May 27, 1993.

43. Otto Latsis, article in *Rabochaia tribuna,* Mar. 27, 1990, quoted in Smith, *New Russians,* 192.

44. Quotation from an undated article in *Voprosy filosofii,* cited in Anthony

Jones and William Moskoff, *Ko-ops: The Rebirth of Entrepreneurship in the Soviet Union* (Bloomington: Indiana University Press, 1991), 96.

45. Hazan, *Gorbachev,* 231; quotations from *Moscow News,* July 24, 1988. For a report on harassment of Belorussian farmers by envious neighbors, see N. Matikovskii, "Zavist' i len'," *Izvestiia,* Aug. 8, 1988. Matikovskii's title referred to the "envy and laziness" traditionally attributed to the Russian peasantry.

46. Slider, "Entrepreneurs," 805.

47. Quotation from Slider, "Entrepreneurs," 817. For details of extortion of a Russian-language training cooperative by three police officers in Moscow in 1991, see Igor Svinarenko, "Crooked Cops Hooked by Co-op President," *Commersant,* Aug. 5, 1991, 14.

48. John Lloyd, "Russian Reforms Hit Private Sector," *Financial Times,* July 16, 1992, 3.

49. Jones and Moskoff, *Ko-ops,* 129.

50. Donald A. Filtzer, "The Contradictions of the Marketless Market: Self-financing in the Soviet Industrial Enterprise, 1986–1990," *Soviet Studies* 43, no. 6 (1991); quotations from 991, 999.

51. B. P. Kurashvili, "Restructuring and the Enterprise," in *Perestroika and the Economy: New Thinking in Soviet Economics,* ed. Anthony Jones and William Moskoff (Armonk, N.Y.: M. E. Sharpe, 1989), 28 (quoted). For brief assessments of the Law on State Enterprises, see Gregory and Stuart, *Structure,* 328–30; and Goldman, *What Went Wrong,* 118–20, 139–42. Goldman cited the figures of 70 percent (139) and 85 percent (119).

52. Filtzer, "Contradictions," 990 (quoted), 993, 991 (quoted).

53. "Zakon Soiuza Sovetskikh Sotsialisticheskikh Respublik o predpriiatiiakh v SSSR," *Vedomosti s''ezda narodnykh deputatov SSSR i Verkhovnogo soveta SSSR,* 1990, no. 25 (June 20, 1990), law no. 460, dated June 4, 1990: 639–55; English translation in International Chamber of Commerce, *Foreign Investment in the USSR: Key 1990 Legislation* (Paris: ICC Publishing Corp., 1991), 23–42. Parenthetical references are to specific articles and sections.

54. The English translation of this sentence in International Chamber of Commerce, *Foreign Investment,* 26, erroneously read: "Refusal of the registration of a State enterprise. . . ."

55. On the scientific-production associations, inaugurated in 1967, and production associations developed on the basis of the law of March 27, 1974, see Stanislaw Pomorski, "Administration of Socialist Property in the USSR: New Trends and Institutions," in *Soviet Law after Stalin,* part III: *Soviet Institutions and Administration of Law,* ed. by F. J. M. Feldbrugge, in series *Law in Eastern Europe* 20 (1979), 124–6. On the decline in productivity, see Gregory and Stuart, *Structure,* part 3; and the brilliant schematic presentation in Padma Desai, *Perestroika in Perspective: The Design and Dilemmas of Soviet Reform* (Princeton: Princeton University Press, 1989), 195–9.

56. "Polozhenie ob aktsionernykh obshchestvakh i obshchestvakh s ogranichennoi otvetstvennost'iu," *Sobranie postanovlenii pravitel'stva Soiuza Sovetskikh Sotsialisticheskikh Respublik,* part 1, 1990, no. 15, decree no. 82, dated June 19, 1990, 331–56; English translation in International Chamber of Commerce, *Foreign Investment,* 46–60. Parenthetical references are to specific articles and sections.

57. Peter B. Maggs, "Legal Forms of Doing Business in Russia," *North Caro-*

lina *Journal of International Law and Commercial Regulation*, 18, no. 1 (Fall, 1992): 185.

58. Lithuania, *Selected Anthology of Institutional, Economic, and Financial Legislation*, trans. Olimpija Armalyte et al. (Vilnius: State Publishing Center, 1991), cited articles. The sources of the Lithuanian law—the legal traditions of independent Lithuania between the world wars, German legislation, another body of law, or a combination—remain unclear.

59. Larisa Korobkova, "Joint-Stock Societies, Soviet Style," *Business in the USSR* 15 (Sept. 1991): 20–1. Data on KamAZ from Filtzer, "Contradictions," 993.

60. Simon Brady, "In the Red," *Euromoney,* July 1991, 19.

61. Ibid., 20 (quoted), 22.

62. Glaziev, "Transformation," 100.

63. Igor Filatotchev, Trevor Buck, and Mike Wright, "Privatisation and Buy-Outs in the USSR," *Soviet Studies* 44, no. 2 (1992): 277.

64. Roman Frydman, Andrzej Rapaczynski, and John S. Earle, *The Privatization Process in Russia, Ukraine, and the Baltic States* (New York: Central European University Press, 1993), 25, 26.

65. "Stock Market in Moscow," *New York Times,* Nov. 14, 1990, Sec. D, p. 16, a bulletin from the Associated Press.

66. Korobkova, "Societies," 18.

67. Litwack, "Legality," 87–8. In describing institutional contrasts between the USSR and Western Europe, where economic legality grew over the centuries, Litwack drew on the historical studies of Douglass C. North, especially *Institutions*.

68. Nikolai P. Shmelyov [Shmelev], "The Rebirth of Common Sense," in *Voices of Glasnost: Interviews with Gorbachev's Reformers,* ed. Stephen F. Cohen and Katrina vanden Heuvel (New York: W. W. Norton, 1989), 152–3.

69. "Market Relations—with the People's Consent," *Reprints from the Soviet Press* 51, no. 2 (July 31, 1990): 20–1; quotations from both pages. The resolution appeared in Russian in the trade-union newspaper *Trud,* Apr. 24, 1990.

70. Press release of Goskomstat SSSR, dated Feb. 8, 1991, presented in Filatotchev, Buck, and Wright, "Privatization," 272, table 4.

71. Filtzer, "Contradictions," 1003 (quoted), and n. 96 (quoted).

Chapter 5

1. Anton Chekhov, "The Duel," in *Seven Short Novels,* trans. Barbara Makanowitzky, introd. Gleb Struve (New York: Norton, 1971), 31–2.

2. Ruckman, *Elite,* 71, quoting an essay by Ianzhul published in 1904.

3. Gerkhart fon Shul'tse-Gevernits [Gerhart von Schulze-Gävernitz], *Ocherki obshchestvennogo khoziaistva i ekonomiki Rossii,* trans. B. V. Avilov and P. P. Rumiantsev, intro. Petr B. Struve (St. Petersburg: Knizhnoe delo, 1900), 116.

4. Mark D. Steinberg, *Moral Communities: The Culture of Class Relations in the Russian Printing Industry, 1867–1907* (Berkeley: University of California Press, 1992), quotations from 231, 232, 234.

5. Reginald E. Zelnik, trans. and ed., *A Radical Worker in Tsarist Russia: The Autobiography of Semen Ivanovich Kanatchikov* (Stanford: Stanford University Press, 1986).

6. Theodore H. Friedgut, *Iuzovka and Revolution: Society and Politics in the Donbass, 1869–1924* (Princeton: Princeton University Press, 1989), 197.

7. Victoria E. Bonnell, ed., *The Russian Worker: Life and Labor under the Tsarist Regime* (Berkeley: University of California Press, 1983), 120–1, citing a Soviet collection of documents and the memoirs of a worker, F. P. Pavlov (Moscow, 1901). Protests against sexual molestation of female workers by male supervisors, Russian and foreign, are documented in Rose L. Glickman, *Russian Factory Women: Workplace and Society, 1880–1914* (Berkeley: University of California Press, 1984), 142–4, 166, 205. She also chronicled a huge strike of male and female workers protesting poisoning by hazardous chemicals at the Russian-American Triangle rubber factory in St. Petersburg in March 1914 but did not stress the fact of foreign ownership of the company.

8. Paraphrase in Friedgut, *Iuzovka*, 311, n. 186.

9. Charters Wynn, *Workers, Strikes, and Pogroms: The Donbass-Dnepr Bend in Late Imperial Russia, 1870–1905* (Princeton: Princeton University Press, 1992), esp. ch. 7 and 261–2; quotation from 219.

10. McKay, *Pioneers,* 193 (quotation from French archive), 196 (quoted).

11. Quoted in Hogan, *Forging Revolution,* 223. She specified, 222, that the plant was founded in 1898 and transformed into a joint-stock company in 1912. Corporate details from RUSCORP database.

12. Daniel R. Brower, "Labor Violence in Russia in the Late Nineteenth Century," *Slavic Review* 41, no. 3 (Fall 1982): 417–31; Wynn, *Workers,* ch. 4.

13. Quoted in *Torgovo-promyshlennyi iug,* no. 4 (Feb. 1, 1912), col. 86.

14. Alexander Herzen, *My Past and Thoughts: The Memoirs of Alexander Herzen,* trans. Constance Garnett, ed. Dwight Macdonald (Berkeley: University of California Press, 1982), 655–76; quotations from 672, 674, 675. On affinities between Herzen and the Slavophiles, see Andrzej Walicki, *The Slavophile Controversy: History of a Conservative Utopia in Nineteenth-Century Russian Thought,* trans. Hilda Andrews-Rusiecka (Oxford: Clarendon Press, 1975), ch. 16: "Slavophilism and Populism: Alexander Herzen's 'Russian Socialism.'"

15. Martin Malia, *Alexander Herzen and the Birth of Russian Socialism* (New York: Grosset and Dunlap, 1965), 402–3. Malia's study remains the best analysis of Herzen's ideological evolution.

16. *Controversy over Capitalism,* 98. See also Deborah Hardy, *Petr Tkachev, the Critic as Jacobin* (Seattle: University of Washington Press, 1977), 252–3, 309.

17. Quoted without reference in Pavel A. Berlin, *Russkaia burzhuaziia v staroe i novoe vremia,* 2d ed. (Moscow: Kniga, 1925), 326.

18. "Everything the Other Is Not: Islam and the West," *Economist,* Aug. 1, 1992, 34 (quoted twice). Janet G. Vaillant, *Black, French, and African: A Life of Léopold Sédar Senghor* (Cambridge: Harvard University Press, 1990), 261, drew an explicit parallel between Russian Slavophilism of the 1840s and the twentieth-century *négritude* movement, which included the distinguished Senegalese poet and political leader Léopold Senghor.

19. Liah Greenfeld, *Nationalism: Five Roads to Modernity* (Cambridge: Harvard University Press, 1992); quotations from 254, 258. Likewise, the general German resentment of English and French commercial power underlay Friedrich List's program of German economic nationalism, described in Greenfeld, 377–8. List's influence on Russian economic thought has been demonstrated by Von Laue and others. See, for example, Roman Szporluk, *Communism and Nationalism: Karl*

Marx versus Friedrich List (New York: Oxford University Press, 1988), ch. 13: "List and Marx in Russia."

20. *Controversy over Capitalism*, 107–31, quoted a variety of xenophobic statements by Russian populists. Schulze-Gävernitz, *Ocherki*, ch. 3, also gave an insightful critique of the opposition of the agrarian socialists to Russian capitalism.

21. "Po povodu gosudarstvennoi rospisi," in *Sochineniia*, 4th ed., vol. 5 (Leningrad: Gosudarstvennoe izdatel'stvo politicheskoi literatury, 1946), 306–7; emphasis in original. Lenin resorted to xenophobic rhetoric on other occasions, as noted by Iurii B. Solov'ev, "Protivorechiia v praviashchem lagere Rossii po voprosu ob inostrannykh kapitalakh v gody pervogo promyshlennogo pod''ema," in *Iz istorii imperializma v Rossii*, ed. Mikhail P. Viatkin, (Leningrad: Nauka, 1959), 372, nn. 5 and 6.

22. *Nationalism*, 385–6; 388–95; quotation from 393. On Russophobic prejudice in Europe generally, and among socialists in particular, see Bruno Naarden, *Socialist Europe and Revolutionary Russia: Perception and Prejudice, 1848–1923* (New York: Cambridge University Press, 1992).

23. Louise McReynolds, "V. M. Doroshevich: The Newspaper Journalist and the Development of Public Opinion in Civil Society," in *Between Tsar and People*, ed. Clowes, Kassow, and West, 243 (quotation from Doroshevich), 245, 242–3.

24. Walter Laqueur, *Black Hundred: The Rise of the Extreme Right in Russia* (New York: HarperPerennial, 1994), 165, wrote that Viazemskii invented the term. Quotation from Petr A. Valuev, diary entry of April 10, 1866, *Dnevnik P. A. Valueva, ministra vnutrennikh del*, 2 vols., ed. P. A. Zaionchkovskii (Moscow: Akademiia nauk SSSR, 1961), vol. 2, 118.

25. Quotations from Friedrich Diestelmeier, *Soziale Angst: Konservative Reaktionen auf liberale Reformpolitik in Russland unter Alexander II. (1855–1866)* (Frankfurt/Main: Peter Lang, 1985), 167–71; Zipperstein, *The Jews of Odessa*, 125; and Abbott T. Gleason, "The Terms of Russian Social History," in *Between Tsar and People*, ed. Clowes, Kassow, and West, 18.

26. *A Writer's Diary*, trans. Kenneth Lantz, 2 vols. (Evanston, Ill.: Northwestern University Press, 1993–4), vol. 2; 914–15, on the Christian idea; 1340, on railroads. Emphasis in original.

27. Ibid., vol. 2, 1135, on cohesion; 1320, on workers.

28. Nikolai Strakhov, *Bor'ba s zapadom v nashei literature: istoricheskie i kriticheskie ocherki*, 3 vols., 3d ed. (Kiev: Chokolov, 1897–8; reprinted, The Hague: Mouton, 1969), vol. 1, on Herzen, 1–137; quotation from Aksakov obituary, 385; on Renan and Taine, 320–46.

29. Iurii B. Solov'ev, "Ob''edinennoe dvorianstvo i proekt sozdaniia ekonomicheskogo soiuza," in *Monopolii i ekonomicheskaia politika tsarizma v kontse XIX–nachale XX v.*, ed. S. I. Potolov (Leningrad: Nauka, 1987), 219, citing *Vestnik Vserossiiskoi sel'sko-khoziaistvennoi palaty*, 1914, nos. 5–6 and 7–8. Quotation on "conquest of power" by Pavlov at VIII Congress of United Gentry, March 1912, cited in Solov'ev, 217.

30. Solov'ev, "Ob''edinennoe dvorianstvo," 219. On the failure to adopt political action, Geoffrey A. Hosking and Roberta T. Manning, "What Was the United Nobility?" in *The Politics of Rural Russia, 1905–1914*, ed. Leopold H. Haimson (Bloomington: Indiana University Press, 1979), 170–2; on private property rights, 156. Wallace, *Russia: On the Eve of War and Revolution*, ed. Cyril E. Black (New York: Vintage, 1961), 506–9; quotation from 507.

31. Komitet s''ezdov, *O zhelatel'nykh izmeneniiakh,* 4.
32. Shatsillo, conversation with the author at the Institute of Russian History, Moscow, May 29, 1992.
33. For examples of outbursts, see McKay, *Pioneers,* 192; Baron Nikolai E. Vrangel', *Vospominaniia (ot krepostnogo prava do bol'shevikov)* (Berlin: Slovo, 1924), 158; and Witte, *Memoirs,* 319 (quoted). On restrictive legislation against foreigners, Jews, and Poles in the western borderlands of the empire, see Owen, *Corporation,* ch. 5.
34. John Hubback, *Russian Realities* (New York: John Lane, 1915), ch. 21: "The German in Russia," 246–56; quotation from 254.
35. Autobiography, Ziablov Papers, Bakhmeteff Archive of Russian Culture and Civilization, Columbia University, New York; 22, on resentment; 24, on humiliations; 30, on promotion to the board of directors; 34–5, on shortage of injectors; 22, on "German domination" of the Kolomna company. On medal, personnel record dated Jan. 18, 1916, Ziablov Papers.
36. Thomas Riha, *A Russian European: Paul Miliukov in Russian Politics* (Notre Dame: University of Notre Dame Press, 1969), 93, 149 (quoted), 94 (quoted); on Crane, 39, 49.
37. R. J. Barrett, *Russia's New Era* (London: The Financier and Bullionist, 1908), 223, 260; on Nicholas II, 14; on increasing social tranquillity, 288.
38. See Owen, *Capitalism,* ch. 2; Rieber, *Merchants,* ch. 4; and Schulze-Gävernitz, *Ocherki,* ch. 3.
39. Buryshkin, *Moskva* (1954 ed.), 60, on treatment of workers; 100, on attitudes toward wealth.
40. For a brief review of the rise of the labor question in the Central Industrial Region from the 1880s onward, see Owen, *Capitalism,* 120–36.
41. On the labor struggles of 1905, see Owen, *Capitalism,* 199–200. The best analysis of such an organization, Hogan, *Forging Revolution,* captures the drama of the struggle in St. Petersburg. McCaffray, "Association," and Steinberg, *Moral Communities,* also address the issue of manufacturers' paternalism toward workers. The lack of solid historical research on the dozens of business organizations in the Russian Empire, including employers' associations, prevents the drawing of comparisons among regions.
42. Chizhov, lead editorial in *Aktsioner* [The Stockholder], no. 1 (Jan. 5, 1863): 1. On the "merchant-Slavophile alliance," see Owen, *Capitalism,* ch. 2; Stuart R. Grover, "Savva Mamontov and the Mamontov Circle, 1870–1905: Art Patronage and the Rise of Nationalism in Russian Art" (doctoral dissertation, University of Wisconsin, Madison, 1971); and Rieber, *Merchants,* ch. 4.
43. Naidenov, *Vospominaniia,* vol. 2, 76.
44. Kahan, *Plow,* 134 (quoted), 137. Kahan identified this official as Kurt Alexander Schönberg; he was named von Shemburg in the charter of the Lapland and Verkhoture Mining Company (PSZ 1-07767, dated March 3, 1739).
45. M. S. Anderson, *Britain's Discovery of Russia, 1553–1815* (New York: St. Martin's Press, 1958), 12–13.
46. Richard Hellie, ed. and trans., *Readings for Introduction to Russian Civilization: Muscovite Society,* 2d ed. (Chicago: University of Chicago Press, 1970), ch. 6; 73–4 on the charter to Garrand; quotations from 63 (Hellie's commentary), 70, 88. Professor Hellie kindly brought this selection of documents to my attention.
47. Iurii Krizhanich, *Russian Statecraft: The Politika of Iurii Krizhanich,* ed.

and trans. John M. Letiche and Basil Dmytryshyn (New York: Basil Blackwell, 1985), 18, 29. The sections on "xenomania" (128–9) and "xenophobia" (228–33) are also relevant. On the Russian merchants' success in 1667, Baron, "Entrepreneurs," 49 (quoted).

48. Wallace, *Russia,* 206; P. S. Smirnov, *Istoriia russkogo raskola staroobriadchestva,* 2d ed. (St. Petersburg: Glavnoe upravlenie udelov, 1895; reprinted Westmead, England: Gregg, 1971), 4. In *Merchants,* section on "Cultural Foundations: Old Believers and Slavophiles," 139–48, Rieber did not raise the issue of influences. In *Capitalism,* ch. 2, I attributed the leading ideological role to the Slavophiles. For a recent review of the Old Belief from the standpoint of social history, see Manfred Hildermeier, "Alter Glaube und neue Welt: Zur Sozialgeschichte des Raskol im 18. und 19. Jahrhundert," *Jahrbücher für Geschichte Osteuropas* 38, no. 3 (Sept. 1990): 372–98, and no. 4 (Dec. 1990): 504–25.

49. *Kontora Knop i ee znachenie* (St. Petersburg: Golike, 1895), quoting from *Russkie vedomosti* (Mar. 3, 1895), 5, on "bondage"; 4–5, on finances; 6, on "lesson" and "measures."

50. Ibid., 8, on colony; 15, on outmoded English machines; 13 on contempt; 16–23, 40–3, on English foremen. On Knoop's contributions to Russian industry, see Schulze-Gävernitz, *Ocherki,* 82; and Spies, *Erinnerungen,* 121.

51. On the Sergeev trial, *Ocherki,* 84–5; quotations from 83; On the Lapino factory, Spies, *Erinnerungen,* 160.

52. Quotations from Spies, *Erinnerungen,* 112–113.

53. Sergei F. Sharapov, "Rech' o promyshlennoi konkurentsii Lodzi i Sosnovits s Moskvoiu" (1885), in *Sochineniia,* 3 vols. in 2 (St. Petersburg: Izdatel'stvo Russko-slavianskogo knizhnogo sklada, 1892–9), vol. 1, 70–94; quotation from 93–4. Löwe, *Antisemitismus und reaktionäre Utopie: Russischer Konservatismus im Kampf gegen den Wandel von Staat und Gesellschaft, 1890–1917* (Hamburg: Hoffmann und Campe, 1978), 26 (quoted). On his career, see Owen, *Capitalism,* 129, 143; and Rieber, *Merchants,* 182–3. His critique of Witte is analyzed in Von Laue, *Witte.* The only detailed account is Thomas Trice, "Sergei A. Sharapov, A Reactionary Russian Journalist, 1855–1911" (M.A. thesis, Louisiana State University, 1987). Data on Sharapov's company from RUSCORP database.

54. *V pamiat' 50-ti letnego iubileia Rossiiskogo strakhovogo ot ognia obshchestva, uchrezhdennogo v 1827 g.* (St. Petersburg: V. Velling, 1877), xiii.

55. A. P. Panov, "O neobkhodimosti reformy birzhevogo ustava 1832 goda," appendix to M. Slavianinov, *Birzha i gil'dii* (St. Petersburg, 1894), 48, on the number of foreigners on the committee; 51, on the large proportion of foreigners among first-guild merchants; 56, on the need to allow second-guild merchants to vote; and 57, on presidents.

56. I. V. D'iakonov, *V khrame Vaala: etiudy po voprosam promyshlennosti i torgovli* (Moscow: E. I. Pichugina, 1889), esp. 19–20, on German-speaking foreigners, Tatars, Turks, Persians, Armenians, and Jews; 35, on railroad men; 52, on Lodz; ii, on his article.

57. "Rech' S. T. Morozova," *Moskovskie vedomosti,* Aug. 16, 1893, 1. Buryshkin, *Moskva* (1954 ed.), 74, noted that this speech irritated tsarist bureaucrats and Suvorin, the editor of *Novoe vremia* in St. Petersburg. On 73, Buryshkin quoted part of Morozov's speech but gave no citation. The merchant Krestovnikov's gross biological metaphor occurred in an interview in *Novoe vremia,* 1893, cited without reference in Buryshkin, *Moskva* (1954 ed.), 180–1. The editors of

the 1991 edition of this book did not supply the reference. English translations of other sections of these speeches appear in Owen, *Capitalism,* 136–7.

58. West, "Riabushinskii Circle," 49 (quoted), 54. Long quotation from Mikhail P. Riabushinskii's strategic plan of 1916, in Iosif F. Gindin, ed., "K istorii kontserna br. Riabushinskikh," in *Dokumenty po istorii monopolisticheskogo kapitalizma v Rossii,* ed. A. L. Sidorov and others, vol. 6 of *Dokumenty po istorii SSSR* (Moscow: Akademiia nauk SSSR, 1959), 632. The analysis of the Riabushinskii family's banking business in Anan'ich, *Bankirskie doma,* ch. 5, surpasses all previous scholarship on this subject.

59. On the Black Hundreds, see Hans Rogger, "Was There a Russian Fascism?" *Journal of Modern History* 36, no. 4 (Dec. 1964): 398–415; and Laqueur, *Black Hundred,* ch. 2.

60. *Moskva* (1954 ed.), quotations from 10, 322.

61. I. O., "Bankovoe delo v sovremennom khoziaistve," in *Banki Rossii (Finansovye i torgovo-promyshlennye svedeniia),* 2d ed. (Moscow: SVOP, 1911), 10 (quoted), on speculation; 6 (quoted), on stage theory; 13 (quoted), on credit societies; 14 (quoted), on renaissance. The most likely author of this article appeared to be the Moscow economist Ivan Kh. Ozerov.

62. Buryshkin, *Moskva* (1954 ed.), 94–5.

63. Owen, "Impediments," 81–9.

64. Ivan Time, "Inostrannye kapitaly," *Gorno-zavodskii listok* 12, no. 3 (Feb. 1, 1899): 3663.

65. Nikolai S. Avdakov, "Germanskie zhelaniia," *Gorno-zavodskii listok,* 1892, no. 22 (Nov. 15): 1376–7. This article also appeared in *Moskovskie vedomosti* and as a twelve-page pamphlet: *Germanskie zhelaniia: pis'mo k izdateliu "Moskovskikh vedomostei" gornogo inzhenera N. S. Avdakova* (Kharkov, 1892). On the campaign to require fluency in Russian, Friedgut, *Iuzovka,* 22.

66. Quotations from Yanni Kotsonis, "Arkhangel'sk, 1918: Regionalism and Populism in the Russian Civil War," *Russian Review* 51, no. 4 (Oct. 1992): 529, 530; and Witte, *Memoirs,* 320.

67. Ischchanian, *Die ausländischen Elemente.*

68. On this complex subject, Ruth Roosa's pioneering research on the Association of Industry and Trade was especially illuminating. For example, in "Russian Industrialists during World War I: The Interaction of Economics and Politics," in *Entrepreneurship,* ed. Guroff and Carstensen, 183, she concluded that by 1916 "the divisions separating the various entrepreneurial elements from one another had become deeper and more apparent than ever."

69. Lockhart, *British Agent,* 92.

70. Ibid., 110.

71. Riha, *Russian European,* 266, n. 71 (quoted), 266–8.

72. On this controversy, see Robert Service, *Lenin: A Political Life,* vol. 2, *Worlds in Collision* (Bloomington: Indiana University Press, 1991), 247–51; Chaikovskii quoted in Kotsonis, "Arkhangel'sk," 535.

73. John Reed, *Ten Days That Shook the World,* ed. Bertram D. Wolfe (New York: Vintage, 1960), 60, quoting Tereshchenko (emphasis in original); 7–8, quoting Lianozov; 9, on pro-German merchants.

74. "The Communist Manifesto" (1848), part 2, in Robert C. Tucker, ed., *The Marx-Engels Reader* (New York: Norton, 1972), 350.

75. Mikhail Agursky, *The Third Rome: National Bolshevism in the USSR* (Boulder, Colo.: Westview Press, 1987).

76. Lenin in *Pravda,* May 4, 1917, quoted in John Shelton Curtiss, *The Russian Revolutions of 1917* (New York: Van Nostrand, 1957), 126.

77. Quotation from "The Foreign Policy of the Russian Revolution," in *The Lenin Anthology,* ed. Tucker, 539.

78. Quotation from Service, *Worlds,* 246–7.

79. Quotations from the résumé of Miliukov's speech to the Council of the Republic, October 31, 1917 (N. S.), in Reed, *Ten Days,* 64, 67. Reed misspelled Kireevskii "Keroyevsky."

80. Agursky, *Third Rome,* ch. 3, referred to the Russian Revolution as "the culmination of the Russian-German contest." See also his discussion of "red patriotism" in the early Soviet period, 203–12.

81. For an early analysis of the relationship of Tkachev's ideas to those of Lenin, see Michael Karpovich, "Forerunner of Lenin: P. N. Tkachev," *Review of Politics,* 6, no. 3 (July 1944): 336–50. Hardy, *Tkachev,* 312–14, surveyed the historiography of this interesting question, including Soviet articles of the 1920s that stressed temperamental affinities between the two revolutionaries. Richard Pipes, "The Origins of Bolshevism: The Intellectual Evolution of Young Lenin," in *Revolutionary Russia,* ed. Richard Pipes (Cambridge: Harvard University Press, 1968), 61–2 (quoted); Bertram D. Wolfe, *Three Who Made a Revolution,* rev. ed. (New York: Dell, 1964), 156.

82. Wolfe, *Three,* 567 (quoted); John O. Norman, "Pavel Tretiakov and Merchant Art Patronage, 1850–1900," in *Between Tsar and People,* ed. Clowes, Kassow, and West, 93–107.

83. Agursky, *Third Rome,* 206–7, citing V. Peletin in *Molodaia gvardiia,* 1969, no. 12, 272, and Lunacharskii's *Sobranie sochinenii* (1963–8), vol. 1, 189, and vol. 7, 306–7.

84. Volobuev, "Perestroika," 573.

85. Diane Koenker, *Moscow Workers and the 1917 Revolution* (Princeton: Princeton University Press, 1981), 239.

86. "New Perspectives on the Civil War," in *Party, State, and Society in the Russian Civil War,* ed. Diane P. Koenker, William G. Rosenberg, and Ronald Grigor Suny (Bloomington: Indiana University Press, 1989), 13, 15. She made these cogent points in passing, without documentation, and did not discuss xenophobia in *The Russian Revolution, 1917–1932* (New York: Oxford University Press, 1984).

87. Stephen White, *The Bolshevik Poster* (New Haven: Yale University Press, 1988), illustrations 3.29, 3.30, 1.10, and 3.9.

88. "The Chief Task of Our Day," (March 1918), in *The Lenin Anthology,* ed. Tucker, 436; Mark R. Beissinger, *Scientific Management, Socialist Discipline, and Soviet Power* (Cambridge: Harvard University Press, 1988), 28.

89. Daniel Orlovsky, "The Lower Middle Strata in Revolutionary Russia," in *Between Tsar and People,* edited by Clowes, Kassow, and West; 252, 268 (quoted), 249 (quoted).

90. Kotsonis, "Arkhangel'sk," 543, on dependence; 541, quoting demonstrators.

91. B. M. Dvorniak, ed., *Istoriia dal'nevostochnogo parokhodstva: ocherki* (Moscow: Morskoi transport, 1962), 70, 73.

92. Dvorniak, ed., *Istoriia,* 64, quoting the *Vestnik* of the Maritime Region Provisional Government, March 3, 1920; ellipses in Dvorniak.

93. Martin Malia made a strong case for this scenario in his incisive analysis

of the Russian Revolution: *Comprendre la révolution russe* (Paris: Seuil, 1980), 87–90; quotation from 89.

94. Comments of Thompson and Seton-Watson in *Revolutionary Russia*, ed. Pipes, 160, 300.

95. *The Icon and the Axe: An Interpretive History of Russian Culture* (New York: Vintage, 1970), 532–49; quotations from 549, 529. Jeffrey Brooks, "Official Xenophobia and Popular Cosmopolitanism in Early Soviet Russia," *American Historical Review* 97, no. 5 (Feb. 1992): 1431–48.

96. John B. Dunlop, *The New Russian Nationalism* (New York: Praeger, 1985), 29–32, 77–80; quotations from *Mnogaia leta*, ed. Gennadii M. Shimanov, 1980 ed., cited in Dunlop, *Nationalism*, 66, 72–73, and 1981 ed., 148, cited in Dunlop, 77.

97. Description of *Slovo i delo* in catalog of Russian House, New York City. Dunlop, *Nationalism*, 76 ff., noted the popularity of Pikul' as a novelist on nationalistic themes.

98. On Ligachev's call for economic revitalization without market reforms and his stress on competition with the West, Aslund, *Gorbachev's Struggle*, 48–52; quotation from 49. For a condemnation of economic ties with the West by Kriuchkov, head of the KGB, see the *New York Times*, Dec. 23, 1990, sec. 1, 1. On Pavlov's accusation of economic destabilization by Canadian and U.S. bankers, *New York Times*, Feb. 13, 1991, sec. A, p. 3, and Feb. 15, 1991, sec. A, p. 6, and editorial, sec. A, p. 34. Quotation from Polozkov's speech in Jones and Moskoff, *Ko-ops*, 68.

99. Goldman, *What Went Wrong*, 161–9; quotation from 163. Goldman completed this analysis in April 1991, well before the dissolution of the USSR. On the financial mechanisms employed by foreign corporations in the Soviet Union under Gorbachev, see Hertzfeld, "Joint Ventures." On the views of various Russian nationalists under perestroika, with some attention to economic grievances, see Smith, *New Russians*, ch. 17: "Backlash in Mother Russia"; and John B. Dunlop, *The Rise of Russia and the Fall of the Soviet Empire* (Princeton: Princeton University Press, 1993), ch. 4: "The Statists."

100. David Remnick, "Russian Nationalists Jeer Gorbachev, Zionists," *Washington Post*, Jan. 24, 1990, sec. A, p. 24; Nina Andreeva, "Letter to the Editorial Office from a VUZ Lecturer: I Cannot Abandon My Principles," *Sovetskaia Rossiia*, March 13, 1988, 3; English translation of Andreeva's letter in Hazan, *Gorbachev*, 302–11; quotation from 306.

101. Interview with *Sovetskaia Rossiia* (Soviet Russia), reported in the *New York Times*, Nov. 22, 1990, sec. A, p. 3; on the inherent flaws of Stalin's planning system, Holland Hunter and Janusz M. Szyrmer, *Faulty Foundations: Soviet Economic Policies, 1928–1940* (Princeton: Princeton University Press, 1992).

102. Hazan, *Gorbachev*, 237.

103. Dmitrii Vasil'ev, "Az buki vede glagol' dobro," *Pamiat'*, no. 2 (Jan. 1991), 5. The second quoted sentence appeared in capital letters in the original.

104. Mark Deich and Leonid Zhuravlev, *"Pamiat'" kak ona est'* (Moscow: Tsunami, 1991), 29, on capitalism and cooperatives; 30–1 (quoted), on reparations; 75, on reforms; 100, on World War II. In a published interview, 62–70, he made similarly preposterous assertions.

105. Quotations from Katherine Verdery, "Nationalism and National Sentiment in Post-socialist Romania," *Slavic Review* 52, no. 2 (Summer 1993): 186–7, 196, 197; on stereotypes of Gypsies and Jews, 197–9.

106. Quoted in Bill Keller, "Russian Nationalists: Yearning for an Iron Hand," *New York Times Magazine,* Jan. 28, 1990, 18–21, 46, 48, 50; quotations from 19, on spiritual culture; 48, on economic policy; 50, on workers' resentments.

107. Interview with the *Washington Post* and *Newsweek,* May 1988, quoted in Shipler, *Russia,* 419.

Chapter 6

1. North, *Institutions,* 100.
2. Ralf Dahrendorf, *Reflections on the Revolution in Europe* (New York: Times Books, 1990), 66.
3. Daniel Yergin and Thane Gustafson, *Russia 2010—and What It Means for the World,* rev. ed. (New York: Vintage, 1994).
4. Barrington Moore, Jr., *Terror and Progress—USSR: Some Sources of Change and Stability in the Soviet Dictatorship* (Cambridge: Harvard University Press, 1954), esp. the final chapter, on "images of the future."
5. Quotation from "Russia: Ungovernable?" *Economist,* Jan. 15, 1994, 50. On the illegality of bribery, Armin A. Brott, "How to Avoid Bear Traps," *Nation's Business,* Sept. 1993, 50. On the growth of organized crime, "Crime in Russia: The High Price of Freeing Markets," *Economist,* Feb. 19, 1994, 57.
6. North, *Institutions,* 103, 117, 67.
7. Lynn D. Nelson and Irina Y. Kuzes, *Property to the People: The Struggle for Radical Economic Reform in Russia* (Armonk, N.Y.: M. E. Sharpe, 1994), 157.
8. Kathryn Hendley, "Legal Development and Privatization in Russia: A Case Study," *Soviet Economy* 8, no. 2 (1992): 130–57, based on the experience of the Saratov Aviation Plant in 1992.
9. Jenny, *Deutschen,* 43.
10. Carstensen, *American Enterprise,* 144; on the location of the Liubertsy plant, 167.
11. Quoted in Nelson and Kuzes, *Property,* 167; emphasis in original.
12. McKay, *Pioneers,* 199–200.
13. Nelson and Kuzes, *Property,* 220–1, table B-8.5.
14. Sobchak, *Russia,* 144.
15. North, *Institutions,* 138.
16. Quoted in Alma Guillermoprieto, *The Heart That Bleeds: Latin America Now* (New York: Knopf, 1994), 252.
17. Nelson and Kuzes, *Property,* tables B-A.3, B-A.5, B-A.7.
18. "Talking to Gaidar," *Economist,* Apr. 25, 1992, 17–20; quotation from 18. On Ivan V. Vernadskii, the foremost Russian proponent of free trade and private property in the era of the Great Reforms, see Owen, *Capitalism,* 59–64; Kingston-Mann, "Peasant Communes," 23–5; and the sources cited therein.
19. John Lloyd, "New Times, New Comrades, New May Day in Moscow," *Financial Times,* May 2, 1992, 2.
20. Kahan, *Russian Economic History,* 99–100.
21. Metropolitan Ioann, "Puti russkogo vozrozhdeniia (national'no-pravoslavnyi vzgliad)," supplement to *Russkii vestnik,* 1993; quotations from 7, 6, 10, back cover; on disputes among monarchists, "Zaiavlenie," a statement of members of the Union of Descendants of the Russian Gentry, *Russkii vestnik,* no. 36 (119), Sept. 1993, 6; Dahrendorf, *Reflections,* 111–16; quotation from 115.

22. Parenthetical references in this paragraph are to *Pravda Zhirinovskogo,* the party's campaign newspaper (issue / page). Issues of this periodical bore no date except the year, 1993, but at least twenty-two issues appeared. Issue 1 announced the party congress scheduled for Apr. 24–5, and issue 22 contained radio and television schedules for Dec. 1–10.

23. Vladimir Zhirinovskii, "Russkie idut!" *Sokol Zhirinovskogo,* 1993, no. 7 (Nov. 5, 1993): 5–6; quotation from 6.

24. For a treatise on the alleged evils of the corporation by a Nazi legal expert, see Fischer, *Aktiengesellschaft.* Jeffrey Herf, *Reactionary Modernism: Technology, Culture, and Politics in Weimar and the Third Reich* (New York: Cambridge University Press, 1984) analyzed the intertwining of tradition and modernity in twentieth-century German culture.

25. Laqueur, *Black Hundred,* 262–4.

26. Nelson and Kuzes, *Property,* 83–5.

27. Keenan, "Folkways," 165.

28. Brenda Meehan-Waters, *Autocracy and Aristocracy: The Russian Service Elite of 1730* (New Brunswick, N.J.: Rutgers University Press, 1982), 161–6.

29. Quotations from "Arkadii Vol'skii: tsentrizm bez zolotoi seredinoi," *Voina i mir,* special edition, December 1993, 1; and electoral program of Civic Union, same issue, 4. On state enterprises and wage and price controls, Nelson and Kuzes, *Property,* 83.

30. "The World's Worst Central Banker," *Economist,* Oct. 16, 1993, 90. On his dismissal, *Economist,* Oct. 22, 1994, 91.

31. Carstensen, *Enterprise,* 175. On questionnaire results in 1992, Nelson and Kuzes, *Property,* 172.

32. On the flight of capital from Russia in the late imperial period, see Roosa, "Association," ch. 3. On the same phenomenon after the collapse of perestroika, see the three-part series by Steve Coll and Michael Dobbs, "The Profits of Chaos," *Washington Post,* Jan. 31, Feb. 1, and Feb. 2, 1993, all sec. A, p. 1; and Marshall Goldman, "Do Business in Russia? For Now, No," *New York Times,* Aug. 7, 1994, sec. 3, p. 9.

33. "High Stakes on the High Steppes," *Economist,* Oct. 16, 1993, 89–93; quotations from 89, 93.

34. Pekka Sutela, "The Role of the External Sector during the Transition," in *Economy,* ed. Aslund, 100, n. 4.

35. Dahrendorf, *Reflections,* 100. For a discussion of the many forms of interplay between cultural tradition and modern capitalist behavior in modern Europe and the United States, see Thomas L. Haskell and Richard F. Teichgraeber III, eds., *The Culture of the Market: Historical Essays* (New York: Cambridge University Press, 1993). Professor Samuel C. Ramer kindly drew my attention to this volume.

36. Aleksandr I. Solzhenitsyn, *Letter to the Soviet Leaders,* trans. Hilary Sternberg (New York: Harper and Row, 1974), 36–7 (quoted); on modes of transport, 49. See also Valentin Rasputin, *Siberia on Fire: Stories and Essays,* trans. Gerald Mikkelson and Margaret Winchell (DeKalb: Northern Illinois University Press, 1989).

37. Aleksandr I. Solzhenitsyn, *Rebuilding Russia: Reflections and Tentative Proposals,* trans. Alexis Klimoff (New York: Farrar, Straus, and Giroux, 1991), quotations 38, 33, 36–7.

38. Douglas R. Weiner, paraphrased in Gregory D. Crowe, "Science and

Technology with a Human Face: Russian-American Perspectives," *Slavic Review* 52, no. 2 (Summer 1993): 319–32; quotations from 325.

39. On addiction, declaration of an advisory panel of the U.S. Food and Drug Administration, reported in Philip J. Hilts, "Addictive Substances: Nicotine Is Compared to Cocaine and Heroin," *New York Times,* Aug. 7, 1994, sec. 4, p. 2. On East Germany and Kazakhstan, "The Search for El Dorado," *Economist,* May 16, 1992, 22; on Petersburg, "The Cradle of Capitalism," *Economist,* Nov. 6, 1993, 94.

40. Michael Janofsky, "Moscow Takes a Stand on Cigarette and Liquor Ads," *New York Times,* July 20, 1993, sec. D, p. 1.

Works Cited

This list includes archival documents, primary sources, articles, theses, dissertations, and books. Newspaper articles are cited only in the notes.

Agursky, Mikhail. *The Third Rome: National Bolshevism in the USSR*. Boulder, Colo.: Westview Press, 1987.

Aitken, Hugh G. J., ed. *Explorations in Enterprise*. Cambridge: Harvard University Press, 1965.

Aldrich, Howard E. *Organizations and Environments*. Englewood Cliffs, N.J.: Prentice-Hall, 1979.

Almgren, Beverly S. "Mendeleev: The Third Service." Unpublished doctoral dissertation, Brown University, 1968.

Amburger, Erik. "Der fremde Unternehmer in Russland bis zur Oktoberrevolution im Jahre 1917." *Tradition: Zeitschrift für Firmengeschichte und Unternehmerbiographie* 2, no. 4 (Oct. 1957): 337–55. Reprinted in Amburger, *Fremde und Einheimische*.

―――. "Das Haus Wogau & Co. in Moskau und der Wogau-Konzern, 1840–1917." In *Russland und Deutschland: Festschrift für Georg von Rauch*, edited by Uwe Liszkowski, vol. 22 of *Kieler Historische Studien*, 171–92. Stuttgart: E. Klett, 1974. Reprinted in *Fremde und Einheimische*.

―――. *Fremde und Einheimische im Wirtschafts- und Kulturleben des neuzeitlichen Russland: Ausgewählte Aufsätze*. Ed. Klaus Zernack. Wiesbaden: Franz Steiner, 1982.

―――. *Deutsche in Staat, Wirtschaft und Gesellschaft Russlands: Die Familie Amburger in St. Petersburg, 1770–1920*. Wiesbaden: Harrassowitz, 1986.

Anan'ich, Boris V. *Bankirskie doma v Rossii, 1860–1914 gg.: Ocherki istorii chastnogo predprinimatel'stva*. Leningrad: Nauka, 1991.

Anan'ich, Boris V., and Valerii I. Bovykin. "Foreign Banks and Foreign Investment in Russia." In *International Banking, 1870–1914,* edited by Rondo Cameron and Valerii Bovykin, 253–90. Oxford: Oxford University Press, 1991.
Anderson, M. S. *Britain's Discovery of Russia, 1553–1815.* New York: St. Martin's Press, 1958.
Anfimov, A. M. "On the History of the Russian Peasantry at the Beginning of the Twentieth Century." Translated by Greta Bucher. *The Russian Review* 51, no. 3 (July 1992): 396–407.
Argenbright, Robert. "Bolsheviks, Baggers and Railroaders: Political Power and Social Space, 1917–1921." *The Russian Review* 52, no. 4 (Oct. 1993): 506–27.
Aslund, Anders. *Gorbachev's Struggle for Economic Reform.* Ithaca: Cornell University Press, 1989.
———, ed. *The Post-Soviet Economy: Soviet and Western Perspectives.* New York: St. Martin's Press, 1992.
Ball, Alan M. *Russia's Last Capitalists: The Nepmen, 1921–1929.* Berkeley: University of California Press, 1987.
Baron, Samuel H. "Entrepreneurs and Entrepreneurship in Sixteenth/Seventeenth-Century Russia." In *Entrepreneurship in Imperial Russia and the Soviet Union,* edited by Gregory Guroff and Fred V. Carstensen, 27–58. Princeton: Princeton University Press, 1983.
Barrett, R. J. *Russia's New Era.* London: The Financier and Bullionist, 1908.
Bauer, Henning, Andreas Kappeler, and Brigitte Roth, eds. *Die Nationalitäten des Russischen Reiches in der Volkszählung von 1897.* 2 vols. Stuttgart: Franz Steiner, 1991.
Beissinger, Mark R. *Scientific Management, Socialist Discipline, and Soviet Power.* Cambridge: Harvard University Press, 1988.
Bendix, Reinhard. *Work and Authority in Industry.* New York: Wiley, 1956.
Benedict, Burton. "Family Firms and Firm Families: A Comparison of Indian, Chinese, and Creole Firms in Seychelles." In *Entrepreneurs in Cultural Context,* edited by Sidney M. Greenfield, Arnold Strickon, and Robert T. Aubey, 305–26. Albuquerque: University of New Mexico Press, 1979.
Berger, Brigitte, ed. *The Culture of Entrepreneurship.* San Francisco: ICS Press, 1992.
Berlin, Pavel A. *Russkaia burzhuaziia v staroe i novoe vremia.* 2d ed. Moscow: Kniga, 1925.
Berman, Harold J. *Law and Revolution: The Formation of the Western Legal Tradition.* Cambridge: Harvard University Press, 1983.
Bertenson, V. B. *Iz vospominanii o K. A. Skal'kovskom.* St. Petersburg, 1912.
Beveridge, Albert J. *The Russian Advance.* New York: Harper and Brothers, 1903.
Billington, James H. *The Icon and the Axe: An Interpretive History of Russian Culture.* New York: Vintage, 1970.
Blackwell, William L. *The Beginnings of Russian Industrialization, 1800–1860.* Princeton: Princeton University Press, 1968.
Blakely, Alison. "American Influences on Russian Reformist Thought in the Era of the French Revolution." *The Russian Review* 52, no. 4 (Oct. 1993): 451–71.
Bohrnstedt, George W., and David Knoke. *Statistics for Social Data Analysis.* Itasca, Ill.: F. E. Peacock Publishers, 1982.

Bokhanov, Aleksandr N. *Krupnaia burzhuaziia Rossii: konets XIX v.–1914 g.* Moscow: Nauka, 1992.

Bonnell, Victoria E., ed. *The Russian Worker: Life and Labor under the Tsarist Regime.* Berkeley: University of California Press, 1983.

Bösselmann, Kurt. *Die Entwicklung des deutschen Aktienwesens im 19. Jahrhundert: Ein Beitrag zur Frage der Finanzierung gemeinwirtschaftlicher Unternehmungen und zu den Reformen des Aktienrechts.* Berlin: W. de Gruyter & Co., 1939.

Bovykin, Valerii I. *Formirovanie finansovogo kapitala v Rossii: konets XIX v.–1908 g.* Moscow: Nauka, 1984.

———, ed. *Monopolisticheskii kapitalizm v Rossii.* Moscow: Akademiia nauk, 1989.

Bovykin, Valerii I., and G. R. Naumova. "Istochniki po istorii monopolii i finansovogo kapitala." In *Massovye istochniki po sotsial'no-ekonomicheskoi istorii Rossii perioda kapitalizma,* edited by Ivan D. Koval'chenko, 120–60. Moscow: Nauka, 1979.

Bowles, Samuel, and Herbert Gintis. *Democracy and Capitalism: Property, Community, and the Contradictions of Modern Social Thought.* New York: Basic Books, 1986.

Bowman, Linda. "Russia's First Income Taxes: The Effects of Modernized Taxes on Commerce and Industry, 1885–1914." *Slavic Review* 52, no. 2 (Summer 1993): 256–82.

Boyes, Roger. *The Hard Road to Market: Gorbachev, the Underworld and the Rebirth of Capitalism.* London: Secker and Warburg, 1990.

Brady, Simon. "In the Red." *Euromoney,* July 1991: 19–23.

Brooks, Jeffrey. "Official Xenophobia and Popular Cosmopolitanism in Early Soviet Russia." *American Historical Review* 97, no. 5 (Feb. 1992): 1431–48.

Brott, Armin A. "How to Avoid Bear Traps." *Nation's Business* (Sept. 1993): 49–50.

Brower, Daniel R. "Labor Violence in Russia in the Late Nineteenth Century." *Slavic Review* 41, no. 3 (Fall 1982): 417–31.

Buryshkin, Pavel A. *Moskva kupecheskaia.* New York: Chekhov Publishing Company, 1954. Reprinted, with intro. and commentary by G. N. Ul'ianova and Mikhail K. Shatsillo, Moscow: Vysshaia shkola, 1991.

Cameron, Rondo, and Valerii I. Bovykin, eds. *International Banking, 1870–1914.* Oxford: Oxford University Press, 1991.

Carlos, Ann M., and Stephen Nicholas. "Agency Problems in Early Chartered Companies: The Case of the Hudson's Bay Company." *Journal of Economic History* 50, no. 4 (Dec. 1990): 853–75.

Carroll, Glenn R. "Organizational Ecology." *Annual Review of Sociology* 10 (1984): 71–93.

Carstensen, Fred V. "Foreign Participation in Russian Economic Life: Notes on British Enterprise, 1865–1914." In *Entrepreneurship in Imperial Russia and the Soviet Union,* edited by Gregory Guroff and Fred V. Carstensen, 140–58. Princeton: Princeton University Press, 1983.

———. *American Enterprise in Foreign Markets: Studies of Singer and International Harvester in Imperial Russia.* Chapel Hill: University of North Carolina Press, 1984.

Chandler, Alfred D., Jr., *Strategy and Structure: Chapters in the History of the American Industrial Enterprise.* Cambridge: MIT Press, 1962.

Chandler, Alfred D., Jr., and Herman Daems, eds. *Managerial Hierarchies: Com-*

parative Perspectives on the Rise of the Modern Industrial Enterprise. Cambridge: Harvard University Press, 1980.

Chekhov, Anton P. *Seven Short Novels.* Translated by Barbara Makanowitzky. Introd. by Gleb Struve. New York: Norton, 1971.

Christian, David. *"Living Water": Vodka and Russian Society on the Eve of Emancipation.* New York: Oxford University Press, 1990.

Chulkov, N. P. "Moskovskoe kupechestvo XVIII i XIX vv." *Russkii arkhiv,* 1907, vol. 3: 489–502.

Clark, William A. "Crime and Punishment in Soviet Officialdom, 1965–90." *Europe-Asia Studies* 45, no. 2 (1993): 259–79.

Clowes, Edith W., Samuel D. Kassow, and James L. West, eds. *Between Tsar and People: Educated Society and the Quest for Public Identity in Late Imperial Russia.* Princeton: Princeton University Press, 1991.

Cohen, Stephen F. *Bukharin and the Bolshevik Revolution: A Political Biography, 1888–1938.* New York: Vintage, 1975.

———. "American Policy and Russia's Future: Illusions and Realities." *The Nation* (Apr. 12, 1993): 476–85.

Connor, Walter D. "Entrepreneurship in the Soviet Economy, 1986–1989." In *The Culture of Entrepreneurship,* edited by Brigitte Berger, 189–209. San Francisco: ICS Press, 1992.

Coopersmith, Jonathan. *The Electrification of Russia, 1880–1926.* Ithaca: Cornell University Press, 1992.

Copetas, A. Craig. *Bear Hunting with the Politburo.* New York: Simon and Schuster, 1991.

Coulon, Whitney A., III. "The Structure of Enterprise in the Russian Empire, 1855–1880." Unpublished M. A. thesis, Louisiana State University, 1979.

Crisp, Olga. *Studies in the Russian Economy before 1914.* New York: Macmillan, 1976.

Crowe, Gregory D. "Science and Technology with a Human Face: Russian-American Perspectives." *Slavic Review* 52, no. 2 (Summer 1993): 319–32.

Crum, William L. *The Age Structure of the Corporate System.* Berkeley: University of California Press, 1953.

Curtiss, John Shelton. *The Russian Revolutions of 1917.* New York: Van Nostrand, 1957.

Daems, Herman. *The Holding Company and Corporate Control.* Boston: Nijhoff, 1978.

Dahl, Robert A. *A Preface to Economic Democracy.* Berkeley: University of California Press, 1985.

Dahrendorf, Ralf. *Reflections on the Revolution in Europe.* New York: Times Books, 1990.

Darcy, Paul. "Au service de la France en Russie." *Revue de Paris,* Sept. 15, 1927, 364–78; Oct. 1, 631–53.

Davies, R. W., ed. *From Tsarism to the New Economic Policy: Continuity and Change in the Economy of the USSR.* Ithaca: Cornell University Press, 1991.

Davydov, M. A. "Soglasheniia rafinerov (1900–1914 gg.)." In *Monopolisticheskii kapitalizm v Rossii,* edited by Valerii I. Bovykin, 104–23. Moscow: Akademiia nauk, 1989.

Deich, Mark, and Leonid Zhuravlev. *"Pamiat' " kak ona est'.* Moscow: Tsunami, 1991.

Desai, Padma. *Perestroika in Perspective: The Design and Dilemmas of Soviet Reform.* Princeton: Princeton University Press, 1989.
Diakin, Valentin S. *Germanskie kapitaly v Rossii: elektroindustriia i elektricheskii transport.* Leningrad: Nauka, 1971.
———. *Samoderzhavie, burzhuaziia i dvorianstvo v 1907–1911 gg.* Leningrad, Nauka, 1978.
———, ed. *Krizis samoderzhaviia v Rossii, 1895–1917.* Leningrad: Nauka, 1984.
D'iakonov, I. V. *V khrame Vaala: etiudy po voprosam promyshlennosti i torgovli.* Moscow: E. I. Pichugina, 1889.
Diestelmeier, Friedrich. *Soziale Angst: Konservative Reaktionen auf liberale Reformpolitik in Russland unter Alexander II. (1855–1866).* Frankfurt/Main: Peter Lang, 1985.
Dostoevsky, Fyodor [Dostoevskii, Fedor M.] *A Writer's Diary.* Translated by Kenneth Lantz. 2 vols. Evanston, Ill.: Northwestern University Press, 1993–4.
Dunlop, John B. *The New Russian Nationalism.* New York: Praeger, 1985.
———. *The Rise of Russia and the Fall of the Soviet Empire.* Princeton: Princeton University Press, 1993.
Dvorniak, B. M., ed. *Istoriia dal' nevostochnogo parokhodstva: ocherki.* Moscow: Morskoi transport, 1962.
Easterbrook, W. T. "The Climate of Enterprise." In *Explorations in Enterprise,* edited by Hugh G. J. Aitken, 65–79. Cambridge: Harvard University Press. Reprinted from *The American Economic Review,* 1949.
Edwards, George W. *The Evolution of Finance Capitalism.* New York: Longmans, Green, & Co., 1938.
Ellis, Stephen Charles. "Management in the Industrialization of Russia, 1861–1917." Unpublished doctoral dissertation, Duke University, 1980.
Entsiklopedicheskii slovar' Brokgauza-Efrona. 41 vols. in 82. St. Petersburg: Brokgauz i Efron, 1890–1904. Supplement: 2 vols. in 4. 1905–7.
Falck, Richard. *Familienbuch Rau: Geschichte einer kurmainzischen Schiffersippe aus Höchst, Eltville und Mainz.* Düsseldorf: Walter Rau Verlag, 1956.
Fenin, Aleksandr I. *Coal and Politics in Late Imperial Russia: Memoirs of a Russian Mining Engineer.* Translated by Alexandre Fediaevsky. Edited by Susan P. McCaffray. DeKalb: Northern Illinois University Press, 1990.
Fenster, Aristide. *Adel und Ökonomie im vorindustriellen Russland: Die unternehmerische Betätigung der Gutsbesitzer in der grossgewerblichen Wirtschaft im 17. und 18. Jahrhundert.* Wiesbaden: Franz Steiner, 1983.
Filatotchev, Igor, Trevor Buck, and Mike Wright. "Privatisation and Buy-Outs in the USSR." *Soviet Studies* 44, no. 2 (1992): 265–82.
Filtzer, Donald A. "The Contradictions of the Marketless Market: Self-financing in the Soviet Industrial Enterprise, 1986–1990." *Soviet Studies* 43, no. 6 (1991): 989–1009.
Firsov, Nikolai N. *Russkie torgovo-promyshlennye kompanii v pervuiu polovinu XVIII stoletiia.* Kazan: Universitet, 1896.
Fischer, Paul. *Die Aktiengesellschaft in der nationalsozialistischen Wirtschaft: Ein Beitrag zur Reform des Gesellschaftsrechts.* Munich: Duncker und Humblot, 1936.
Fitzpatrick, Sheila. "New Perspectives on the Civil War." In *Party, State, and Society in the Russian Civil War,* edited by Diane P. Koenker, William G.

Rosenberg, and Ronald Grigor Suny, 3–24. Bloomington: Indiana University Press, 1989.

———. *The Russian Revolution, 1917–1932.* New York: Oxford University Press, 1984.

Freedeman, Charles E. *Joint-Stock Enterprise in France, 1807–1867: From Privileged Company to Modern Corporation.* Chapel Hill: University of North Carolina Press, 1979.

———. *The Triumph of Corporate Capitalism in France, 1867–1914.* Rochester: University of Rochester Press, 1993.

Friedgut, Theodore H. *Iuzovka and Revolution.* 2 vols. Princeton: Princeton University Press, 1989–94.

Frydman, Roman, Andrzej Rapaczynski, and John S. Earle. *The Privatization Process in Russia, Ukraine, and the Baltic States.* New York: Central European University Press, 1993.

Fuhrmann, Joseph T. *The Origins of Capitalism in Russia.* Chicago: Quadrangle, 1972.

Fursenko, Aleksandr A. "Materialy o korruptsii tsarskoi biurokratii (po bumagam K. A. Skal'kovskogo)." In *Issledovaniia po otechestvennomu istochnikovedeniiu: sbornik statei, posviashchennykh 75-letiiu professora S. N. Valka,* edited by N. E. Nosov, 149–56. Leningrad: Nauka, 1964.

Gatrell, Peter W. *The Tsarist Economy, 1850–1917.* New York: St. Martin's Press, 1986.

———. *Government, Industry, and Rearmament in Russia, 1900–1914.* Cambridge: Cambridge University Press, 1994.

Gefter, Mikhail Ia. "Iz istorii monopolisticheskogo kapitalizma v Rossii: sakharnyi sindikat." *Istoricheskie zapiski* 38 (1951): 104–53.

Georgievskii, Pavel I. *Finansovye otnosheniia gosudarstva i chastnykh zh.-dorozhnykh obshchestv v Rossii i v Zapadno-evropeiskikh gosudarstvakh.* St. Petersburg: Benke, 1887.

Gerschenkron, Alexander. *Economic Backwardness in Historical Perspective.* Cambridge: Belknap Press of Harvard University Press, 1966.

———. *Continuity in History, and Other Essays.* Cambridge: Belknap Press of Harvard University Press, 1968.

Gindin, Iosif F. *Banki i promyshlennost' v Rossii do 1917 g.: k voprosu o finansovom kapitale v Rossii.* Moscow: Promizdat, 1927.

———. *Russkie kommercheskie banki.* Moscow: Gosfinizdat, 1948.

———. "Moskovskie banki v period imperializma (1900–1917)." *Istoricheskie zapiski* 58 (1956): 38–106.

———. *Gosudarstvennyi bank i ekonomicheskaia politika tsarskogo pravitel'stva (1861–1892 gody).* Moscow: Gosfinizdat, 1960.

———. "Pravitel'stvennaia podderzhka ural'skikh magnatov vo vtoroi polovine XIX-nachale XX v." *Istoricheskie zapiski* 82 (1968): 120–62.

———, ed. "K istorii kontserna br. Riabushinskikh." In *Dokumenty po istorii monopolisticheskogo kapitalizma v Rossii,* edited by A. L. Sidorov and others, vol. 6 of *Materialy po istorii SSSR,* 603–40. Moscow: Akademiia nauk SSSR, 1959.

Gindin, Iosif F., and Leonid E. Shepelev. "Bankovskie monopolii v Rossii nakanune velikoi oktiabr'skoi sotsialisticheskoi revoliutsii." *Istoricheskie zapiski* 66 (1960): 20–95.

Girault, René. *Emprunts russes et investissements français en Russie, 1887–1914.* Paris: A. Colin, 1973.

Glaziev, Sergei. "Transformation of the Soviet Economy: Economic Reforms and Structural Crisis." *National Institute Economic Review* 138 (Nov. 1991): 97–108.

Gleason, Abbott T. "The Terms of Russian Social History." In *Between Tsar and People: Educated Society and the Quest for Public Identity in Late Imperial Russia,* edited by Edith W. Clowes, Samuel D. Kassow, and James L. West, 15–27. Princeton: Princeton University Press, 1991.

Glickman, Rose L. *Russian Factory Women: Workplace and Society, 1880–1914.* Berkeley: University of California Press, 1984.

Goldberg, Carl A. "The Association of Industry and Trade, 1906–1917: The Successes and Failures of Russia's Organized Businessmen." Unpublished doctoral dissertation, University of Michigan, 1974.

Goldman, Marshall I. *What Went Wrong with Perestroika.* Rev. ed. New York: Norton, 1992.

Golikov, Andrei G. "K voprosu o sostave, soderzhanii i sokhrannosti dokumentov aktsionernykh kompanii." In *Istochnikovedenie otechestvennoi istorii: sbornik statei, 1979,* edited by V. I. Budagov, 134–56. Moscow: Akademiia nauk, 1980.

Golikov, Andrei G., and G. R. Naumova. "Istochniki po istorii aktsionirovaniia promyshlennosti." In *Massovye istochniki po sotsial'no-ekonomicheskoi istorii Rossii perioda kapitalizma,* edited by Ivan D. Koval'chenko, 87–120. Moscow: Nauka, 1979.

Gorbachev, Ivan A. *Tovarishchestva . . . aktsionernye i paevye kompanii: zakon i praktika s senatskimi raz''iasneniiami.* Moscow: I. K. Golubev, 1910.

Gorbachev, Mikhail S. "Main Guidelines for the Stabilization of the Economy and Transition to the Market." *Reprints from the Soviet Press* 52, no. 1 (Jan. 15, 1991): 5–46. Full translation, from *Pravda,* Oct. 18, 1990.

Greenfeld, Liah. *Nationalism: Five Roads to Modernity.* Cambridge: Harvard University Press, 1992.

Greenfield, Sidney M., and others. "Studies in Entrepreneurial Behavior: A Review and an Introduction." In *Entrepreneurs in Cultural Context,* edited by Sidney M. Greenfield, Arnold Strickon, and Robert T. Aubey, 3–18. Albuquerque: University of New Mexico Press, 1979.

Greenfield, Sidney M., Arnold Strickon, and Robert T. Aubey, eds. *Entrepreneurs in Cultural Context.* Albuquerque: University of New Mexico Press, 1979.

Gregory, Paul R. *Russian National Income, 1885–1913.* New York: Cambridge University Press, 1982.

———. *Before Command: An Economic History of Russia from Emancipation to the First Five-Year Plan.* Princeton: Princeton University Press, 1994.

Gregory, Paul R., and Robert C. Stuart. *Soviet and Post-Soviet Economic Structure and Performance.* 5th ed. New York: HarperCollins, 1994.

Grossman, Gregory. "The Second Economy: Boon or Bane for the Reform of the First Economy?" In *Berkeley-Duke Occasional Papers on the Second Economy in the USSR,* no. 11 (December 1987), 2.1–2.25.

Grover, Stuart R. "Savva Mamontov and the Mamontov Circle, 1870–1905: Art Patronage and the Rise of Nationalism in Russian Art." Unpublished doctoral dissertation, University of Wisconsin, Madison, 1971.

Guillermoprieto, Alma. *The Heart That Bleeds: Latin America Now.* New York: Knopf, 1994.

Guroff, Gregory, and Fred V. Carstensen, eds. *Entrepreneurship in Imperial Russia and the Soviet Union*. Princeton: Princeton University Press, 1983.

Hamm, Michael F. *Kiev: A Portrait, 1800–1917*. Princeton: Princeton University Press, 1993.

Hannan, Michael T., and John Freeman. "The Population Ecology of Organizations." *American Journal of Sociology* 82 (March 1977): 929–64.

———. *Organizational Ecology*. Cambridge: Harvard University Press, 1989.

Hardy, Deborah. *Petr Tkachev, the Critic as Jacobin*. Seattle: University of Washington Press, 1977.

Hartl, Johann. *Die Interessenvertretungen der Industriellen in Russland 1905–1914*. Vienna: Hermann Böhlaus Nachf., 1978.

Haskell, Thomas L., and Richard F. Teichgraeber III, eds. *The Culture of the Market: Historical Essays*. New York: Cambridge University Press, 1993.

Haumann, Heiko. *Kapitalismus im zaristischen Staat 1906–1917: Organisationsformen, Machtverhältnisse und Leistungsbilanz im Industrialisierungsprozess*. Königstein/Ts.: Hain, 1980.

Haywood, Richard M. "The Development of Steamboats on the Volga River and Its Tributaries, 1817–1856." *Research in Economic History* 6 (1981): 127–92.

Hazan, Baruch A. *Gorbachev and His Enemies: The Struggle for Perestroika*. Boulder, Colo.: Westview Press, 1990.

Hellie, Richard, ed. and trans. *Readings for Introduction to Russian Civilization: Muscovite Society*. 2d. ed. Chicago: University of Chicago Press, 1970.

Hendley, Kathryn. "Legal Development and Privatization in Russia: A Case Study." *Soviet Economy* 8, no. 2 (1992): 130–57.

Henriksson, Anders. *The Tsar's Loyal Germans: The Riga German Community, Social Change and the Nationality Question, 1855–1905*. Boulder, Colo.: East European Monographs, 1983.

———. "Nationalism, Assimilation and Identity in Late Imperial Russia: The St. Petersburg Germans, 1906–1914." *The Russian Review* 52, no. 3 (July 1993): 341–53.

Hensel, Joanna. *Burżuazja warszawska drugiej połowy XIX w. w świetle akt notarialnych*. Warsaw: Akademia nauk, 1979.

Herakleitos and Diogenes. Translated by Guy Davenport. Bolinas, Calif.: Grey Fox Press, 1983.

Herf, Jeffrey. *Reactionary Modernism: Technology, Culture, and Politics in Weimar and the Third Reich*. New York: Cambridge University Press, 1984.

Herlihy, Patricia. *Odessa: A History, 1794–1914*. Cambridge: Harvard Ukrainian Research Institute, 1986.

Hertzfeld, Jeffrey M. "Joint Ventures: Saving the Soviets from Perestroika." *Harvard Business Review* (Jan.–Feb. 1991): 80–91.

Herzen, Alexander. *My Past and Thoughts: The Memoirs of Alexander Herzen*. Translated by Constance Garnett. Edited by Dwight Macdonald. Berkeley: University of California Press, 1982.

Hildermeier, Manfred. *Bürgertum und Stadt in Russland 1760–1870: Rechtliche Lage und soziale Struktur*. Cologne: Böhlau Verlag, 1986.

———. "Alter Glaube und neue Welt: Zur Sozialgeschichte des Raskol im 18. und 19. Jahrhundert." *Jahrbücher für Geschichte Osteuropas* 38, no. 3 (Sept. 1990): 372–98, and no. 4 (Dec. 1990): 504–25.

Hogan, Heather. *Forging Revolution: Metalworkers, Managers, and the State in St. Petersburg, 1890–1914*. Bloomington: Indiana University Press, 1993.

Homberg, Octave Marie Joseph Kerim. *Les Coulisses de l'histoire: souvenirs 1898–1928*. Paris: A. Fayard, 1938.
Horn, Norbert, and Jürgen Kocka, eds. *Recht und Entwicklung der Grossunternehmen im 19. und frühen 20. Jahrhundert*. Göttingen: Vandenhoeck und Ruprecht, 1979.
Hosking, Geoffrey A., and Roberta T. Manning. "What Was the United Nobility?" In *The Politics of Rural Russia, 1905–1914,* edited by Leopold H. Haimson, 142–83. Bloomington: Indiana University Press, 1979.
Hovenkamp, Herbert. *Enterprise and American Law, 1836–1937*. Cambridge: Harvard University Press, 1991.
Hubback, John. *Russian Realities*. New York: John Lane, 1915.
Huizinga, Johan. "Historical Conceptualization" (1934). Translated by Rosalie Colie. Reprinted in *The Varieties of History: From Voltaire to the Present,* edited by Fritz Stern, rev. ed., 290–303. New York: Vintage, 1973.
Hunt, Bishop Carleton. *The Development of the Business Corporation in England, 1800–1867*. Cambridge: Harvard University Press, 1936.
Hunter, Holland, and Janusz M. Szyrmer. *Faulty Foundations: Soviet Economic Policies, 1928–1940*. Princeton: Princeton University Press, 1992.
I. O. "Bankovoe delo v sovremennom khoziaistve." In *Banki Rossii (Finansovye i torgovo-promyshlennye svedeniia),* 5–14. 2d ed. Moscow: SVOP, 1911.
Ihnatowicz, Ireneusz. *Przemysł łódzki w latach 1860–1900*. Warsaw: Akademia nauk, 1965.
———. *Burżuazja warszawska*. Warsaw: Państwowe Wydawnictwo Naukowe, 1972.
International Chamber of Commerce. *Foreign Investment in the USSR: Key 1990 Legislation*. Paris: ICC Publishing Corp., 1991.
Ischchanian, Bachschi. *Die ausländischen Elemente in der russischen Volkswirtschaft*. Berlin: F. Siemenroth, 1913.
Iukht, Aleksandr I. "Torgovye kompanii v Rossii v seredine XVIII v." *Istoricheskie zapiski* 111 (1984): 238–95.
Jenny, Ernest. *Die Deutschen im Wirtschaftsleben Russlands*. Berlin: Carl Heymanns Verlag, 1920.
Joffe, Muriel. "Regional Rivalry and Economic Nationalism: The Central Industrial Region Industrialists' Strategy for the Development of the Russian Economy, 1880s–1914." *Russian History* 11 (Winter 1984): 389–421.
Johnstone, Catherine L. *The British Colony in Russia*. London: Roxburghe Press, 1897.
Jones, Anthony, and William Moskoff. *Ko-ops: The Rebirth of Entrepreneurship in the Soviet Union*. Bloomington: Indiana University Press, 1991.
———, eds. *Perestroika and the Economy: New Thinking in Soviet Economics*. Armonk, N.Y.: M. E. Sharpe, 1989.
Kaczkowski, Józef. "Towarzystwo akcyjne w państwe rosyjskiem: studium prawno-ekonomiczne." *Ekonomista* 8 (1908), vol. 1: 81–128.
Kahan, Arcadius. "Capital Formation during the Period of Early Industrialization in Russia, 1890–1913." In *The Cambridge Economic History of Europe,* vol. 7, part 2, 265–307. Cambridge: Cambridge University Press, 1978.
———. "Notes on Jewish Entrepreneurship in Russia." In *Entrepreneurship in Imperial Russia and the Soviet Union,* edited by Gregory Guroff and Fred V. Carstensen, 104–24. Princeton: Princeton University Press, 1983.
———. *The Plow, the Hammer, and the Knout: An Economic History of Eighteenth-Century Russia*. Chicago: University of Chicago Press, 1985.

———. *Russian Economic History: The Nineteenth Century.* Edited by Roger Weiss. Chicago: University of Chicago Press, 1989.
Kamens, David H., and Tormod K. Lunde. "Institutional Theory and the Expansion of the Central State Organizations, 1960–1980." In *Institutional Patterns and Organizations: Culture and Environment,* edited by Lynne G. Zucker, 169–95. Cambridge, Mass.: Ballinger Publishing Company, 1988.
Karpovich, Michael. "Forerunner of Lenin: P. N. Tkachev." *Review of Politics* 6, no. 3 (July 1944): 336–50.
Kaser, M. C. "Russian Entrepreneurship." In *The Cambridge Economic History of Europe,* vol. 7, part 2, edited by Peter Mathias and M. M. Postan, 416–93. Cambridge: Cambridge University Press, 1978.
Keenan, Edward L. "Muscovite Political Folkways." *The Russian Review* 45, no. 2 (Apr. 1986): 115–81.
Khagelin [Hagelin], Karl. *Moi trudovoi put'.* New York: Grenich Printing Corp., 1945.
Khanin, Grigorii. "The Soviet Economy—From Crisis to Catastrophe." In *The Post-Soviet Economy: Soviet and Western Perspectives,* edited by Anders Aslund, 9–24. New York: St. Martin's Press, 1992.
King, Victoria. "The Emergence of the St. Petersburg Industrialist Community, 1870–1905: The Origins and Early Years of the Petersburg Society of Manufacturers." Unpublished doctoral dissertation, University of California, Berkeley, 1982.
Kingston-Mann, Esther. "Peasant Communes and Economic Innovation: A Preliminary Inquiry." In *Peasant Economy, Culture, and Politics of European Russia, 1800–1921,* edited by Esther Kingston-Mann and Timothy Mixter, 23–51. Princeton: Princeton University Press, 1991.
Kiparsky, Valentin. *English and American Characters in Russian Fiction.* Berlin: Steinkopf & Sohn, 1964.
Kirchner, Walther. *Die deutsche Industrie und die Industrialisierung Russlands 1815–1914.* St. Katharinen: Scripta Mercaturae, 1986.
Kliagin, Aleksandr. *Strana vosmozhnostei neobychainykh.* Paris: n.p., n.d. [1947].
Koenker, Diane. *Moscow Workers and the 1917 Revolution.* Princeton: Princeton University Press, 1981.
Koenker, Diane P., William G. Rosenberg, and Ronald Grigor Suny, eds. *Party, State, and Society in the Russian Civil War.* Bloomington: Indiana University Press, 1989.
Kołodziejczyk, Ryszard, ed. *Dzieje burżuazji w Polsce: Studia i materiały.* Wrocław: Akademia nauk, 1974, 1980, 1983.
Kołodziejczyk, Ryszard, and Ryszard Gradowski. *Zarys dziejów kapitalizmu w Polsce.* Wrocław: Państwowe Wydawnictwo Naukowe, 1974.
Komitet s''ezdov predstavitelei aktsionernykh kommercheskikh bankov. *O zhelatel'nykh izmeneniiakh v postanovke aktsionernogo bankovogo dela v Rossii.* Petrograd: Al'fa, 1917.
———. *Obzor deiatel'nosti s''ezdov predstavitelei aktsionernykh kommercheskikh bankov i ikh organov, 1 iuliia 1916 g.–1 ianvaria 1918 g.* Petrograd: Svoboda, 1918.
Kontora Knop i ee znachenie. St. Petersburg: Golike, 1895.
Korobkova, Larisa. "Joint-Stock Societies, Soviet Style." *Business in the USSR* 15 (Sept. 1991): 16–21.
Kotsonis, Yanni. "Arkhangel'sk, 1918: Regionalism and Populism in the Russian Civil War." *The Russian Review* 51, no. 4 (Oct. 1992): 526–44.

Krizhanich, Iurii. *Russian Statecraft: The* Politika *of Iurii Krizhanich*. Edited and translated by John M. Letiche and Basil Dymtryshyn. New York: Basil Blackwell, 1985.

Kurashvili, B. P. "Restructuring and the Enterprise." In *Perestroika and the Economy: New Thinking in Soviet Economics,* edited by Anthony Jones and William Moskoff, 21–44. Armonk, N.Y.: M. E. Sharpe, 1989.

Landa, Janet T. "Culture and Entrepreneurship in Less-Developed Countries: Ethnic Trading Networks as Economic Organizations." In *The Culture of Entrepreneurship,* edited by Brigitte Berger, 53–72. San Francisco: ICS Press, 1992.

Lappo-Danilevskii, Aleksandr S. "Russkie promyshlennye i torgovye kompanii v pervoi polovine XVIII veka." *Zhurnal ministerstva narodnogo prosveshcheniia* 320, no. 12 (Dec. 1898), part 2: 306–66; and 321, no. 2 (Feb. 1899), part 2: 371–436.

Laqueur, Walter. *Black Hundred: The Rise of the Extreme Right in Russia*. New York: HarperPerennial, 1994.

Laverychev, Vladimir Ia. *Krupnaia burzhuaziia v poreformennoi Rossii: 1861–1900*. Moscow: Mysl', 1974.

———. *Gosudarstvo i monopolii v dorevoliutsionnoi Rossii*. Moscow: Mysl', 1982.

Lenin, Vladimir I. "Po povodu gosudarstvennoi rospisi." *Sochineniia,* 4th ed., vol. 5, 304–9. Leningrad: Gosudarstvennoe izdatel'stvo politicheskoi literatury, 1946. Reprinted from *Iskra,* no. 15 (Jan. 15, 1902).

———. "Enemies of the People" (June 1917). In *The Lenin Anthology,* edited by Robert C. Tucker, 305–6. New York: Norton, 1975.

———. "The Foreign Policy of the Russian Revolution" (June 1917). In *The Lenin Anthology,* edited by Robert C. Tucker, 537–9. New York: Norton, 1975.

———. "The Chief Task of Our Day" (March 1918). In *The Lenin Anthology,* edited by Robert C. Tucker, 433–7. New York: Norton, 1975.

———. "On Cooperation" (January 1923). In *The Lenin Anthology,* edited by Robert C. Tucker, 707–13. New York: Norton, 1975.

Lenz, Wilhelm. *Die Entwicklung Rigas zur Grosstadt*. Kitzingen/Main: Holzner-Verlag, 1954.

———, ed. *Deutschbaltisches biographisches Lexikon 1710–1960*. Cologne: Böhlau Verlag, 1970.

Levin, Isaak I. *Aktsionernye kommercheskie banki v Rossii*. Vol. 1 [no more published]. Petrograd: I. R. Belopol'skii, 1917.

———. *Germanskie kapitaly v Rossii*. 2d. ed., rev. Petrograd: I. Shurkht, 1918.

Lewin, J. [Levin, Isaak I.] *Der heutige Zustand der Aktienhandelsbanken in Russland (1900–1910)*. Freiburg: Poppen, 1912.

Lieberman, Paula. "V. A. Kokorev: An Industrial Entrepreneur in Nineteenth-Century Russia." Unpublished doctoral dissertation, Yale University, 1982.

Lieberson, Stanley. *Making It Count: The Improvement of Social Research and Theory*. Berkeley: University of California Press, 1985.

Lithuania. *Selected Anthology of Institutional, Economic, and Financial Legislation*. Translated by Olimpija Armalyte et al. Vilnius: State Publishing Center, 1991.

Litwack, John M. "Legality and Market Reform in Soviet-Type Economies." *Journal of Economic Perspectives* 5, no. 4 (Fall 1991): 77–89.

Lockhart, Sir Robert H. Bruce. *British Agent*. Garden City, N.Y.: Garden City Publishing Co., 1933.

Löwe, Heinz-Dietrich. *Antisemitismus und reaktionäre Utopie: Russischer Konservatismus im Kampf gegen den Wandel von Staat und Gesellschaft, 1890–1917.* Hamburg: Hoffmann und Campe, 1978.

Maggs, Peter B. "Legal Forms of Doing Business in Russia." *North Carolina Journal of International Law and Commercial Regulation* 18, no. 1 (Fall 1992): 173–92.

Mai, Joachim. *Das deutsche Kapital in Russland 1850–1894.* Berlin: Deutscher Verlag der Wissenschaften, 1970.

Malia, Martin. *Alexander Herzen and the Birth of Russian Socialism.* New York: Grosset and Dunlap, 1965.

———. *Comprendre la révolution russe.* Paris: Seuil, 1980.

Mallieux, Fernand. *La Société anonyme: d'après le Droit Civil Russe.* Paris: L. Larose, 1902.

Marks, Steven G. *Road to Power: The Trans-Siberian Railroad and the Colonization of Asian Russia, 1850–1917.* Ithaca: Cornell University Press, 1991.

Marris, Robin L. "An Introduction to Theories of Corporate Growth." In *The Corporate Economy: Growth, Competition, and Innovative Potential,* edited by Robin Marris and Adrian Wood, 1–36. Cambridge: Harvard University Press, 1971.

Mayer, Arno J. *The Persistence of the Old Regime: Europe to the Great War.* New York: Pantheon, 1981.

McCaffray, Susan P. "The Association of Southern Coal and Steel Producers and the Problems of Industrial Progress in Tsarist Russia." *Slavic Review* 47, no. 3 (Fall 1988): 464–82.

McClelland, Peter D. *Causal Explanation and Model Building in History, Economics, and the New Economic History.* Ithaca: Cornell University Press, 1975.

McDaniel, Tim. *Autocracy, Capitalism, and Revolution in Russia.* Berkeley: University of California Press, 1988.

McKay, John P. *Pioneers for Profit: Foreign Entrepreneurship and Russian Industrialization, 1885–1913.* Chicago: University of Chicago Press, 1970.

———. "Entrepreneurship and the Emergence of the Russian Petroleum Industry, 1813–1883." *Research in Economic History* 8 (1983): 47–91.

McReynolds, Louise, "V. M. Doroshevich: The Newspaper Journalist and the Development of Public Opinion in Civil Society." In *Between Tsar and People: Educated Society and the Quest for Public Identity in Late Imperial Russia,* edited by Edith W. Clowes, Samuel D. Kassow, and James L. West, 233–47. Princeton: Princeton University Press, 1991.

Meehan-Waters, Brenda. *Autocracy and Aristocracy: The Russian Service Elite of 1730.* New Brunswick, N.J.: Rutgers University Press, 1982.

Mertens, Oskar. "1882–1911: Dreissig Jahre russischer Eisenbahnpolitik." *Archiv für Eisenbahnwesen* 40 (1917): 415–59, 699–729; 41 (1918): 442–67, 563–98; 42 (1919): 687–714, 858–907.

Minarik, Liudmila P. *Ekonomicheskaia kharakteristika krupneishikh zemel'nykh sobstvennikov Rossii kontsa XIX–nachala XX v.* Moscow: Sovetskaia Rossiia, 1971.

Mironov, Boris N. *Khlebnye tseny v Rossii za dva stoletiia (XVIII–XIX vv.)* Leningrad: Nauka, 1985.

Mitchell, B. R. *European Historical Statistics, 1750–1975.* 2d rev. ed. New York: Facts on File, 1980.

Moore, Barrington, Jr. *Terror and Progress—USSR: Some Sources of Change and*

Stability in the Soviet Dictatorship. Cambridge: Harvard University Press, 1954.

———. *Social Origins of Dictatorship and Democracy: Lord and Peasant in the Making of the Modern World.* Boston: Beacon Press, 1966.

Mosina, Iia G. *Formirovanie burzhuazii v politicheskuiu silu v Sibiri.* Tomsk: Izdatel'stvo Tomskogo universiteta, 1978.

Mosser, Alois. *Die Industrieaktiengesellschaft in Österreich 1880–1913: Versuch einer historischen Bilanz- und Betriebsanalyse.* Vienna: Akademie der Wissenschaften, 1980.

Munting, Roger. "The State and the Beet Sugar Industry in Russia before 1914." In *Crisis and Change in the International Sugar Economy,* edited by Bill Albert and Adrian Graves, 21–9. Norwich, U.K.: ISC Press, 1984.

Naarden, Bruno. *Socialist Europe and Revolutionary Russia: Perception and Prejudice, 1848–1923.* New York: Cambridge University Press, 1992.

Naidenov, Nikolai A. *Vospominaniia o vidennom, slyshannom i ispytannom.* 2 vols. Moscow, 1903–5; reprinted Newtonville, Mass.: Oriental Research Partners, 1976.

Namier, Sir Lewis. "History" (1952). Reprinted in *The Varieties of History: From Voltaire to the Present,* edited by Fritz Stern, rev. ed., 372–81. New York: Vintage, 1973.

[Nebol'sin, G. P.] "Aktsionernye obshchestva v Rossii." *Sovremennik,* 1847, no. 5 (Sept.), *smes',* part 4: 1–25.

Nelson, Lynn D., and Irina Y. Kuzes. *Property to the People: The Struggle for Radical Economic Reform in Russia.* Armonk, N.Y.: M. E. Sharpe, 1994.

Newhouse, John. "Chronicling the Chaos." *The New Yorker,* Dec. 31, 1990, 38–72.

Nikolai Stepanovich Avdakov. Kharkov, 1915. [Appendix to *Gorno-zavodskoe delo* 46–47 (1915).]

Norman, John O. "Pavel Tretiakov and Merchant Art Patronage, 1850–1900." In *Between Tsar and People: Educated Society and the Quest for Public Identity in Late Imperial Russia,* edited by Edith W. Clowes, Samuel D. Kassow, and James L. West, 93–107. Princeton: Princeton University Press, 1991.

North, Douglass C. *Institutions, Institutional Change, and Economic Performance.* Cambridge: Cambridge University Press, 1990.

Okun', S. B. *Rossiisko-Amerikanskaia kompaniia.* Moscow: Gosudarstvennoe sotsial'no-ekonomicheskoe izdatel'stvo, 1939.

Orlovsky, Daniel. "The Lower Middle Strata in Revolutionary Russia." In *Between Tsar and People: Educated Society and the Quest for Public Identity in Late Imperial Russia,* edited by Edith W. Clowes, Samuel D. Kassow, and James L. West, 248–68. Princeton: Princeton University Press, 1991.

Owen, Thomas C. *Capitalism and Politics in Russia: A Social History of the Moscow Merchants, 1855–1905.* New York: Cambridge University Press, 1981.

———. "Entrepreneurship and the Structure of Enterprise in Russia, 1800–1880." In *Entrepreneurship in Imperial Russia and the Soviet Union,* edited by Gregory Guroff and Fred V. Carstensen, 59–83. Princeton: Princeton University Press, 1983.

———. "Skal'kovskii, Konstantin A." *Modern Encyclopedia of Russian and Soviet History* 35: 157–60.

———. "The Russian Industrial Society and Tsarist Economic Policy, 1867–1905." *Journal of Economic History* 45, no. 3 (Sept. 1985): 587–606.

———. "A Standard Ruble of Account for Russian Business History, 1769–1914: A Note." *Journal of Economic History* 49, no. 3 (Sept. 1989): 699–706.

———. *The Corporation under Russian Law, 1800–1917: A Study in Tsarist Economic Policy.* New York: Cambridge University Press, 1991.

———. "Impediments to a Bourgeois Consciousness in Russia, 1880–1905: The Estate Structure, Ethnic Diversity, and Economic Regionalism." In *Between Tsar and People: Educated Society and the Quest for Public Identity in Late Imperial Russia,* edited by Edith W. Clowes, Samuel D. Kassow, and James L. West, 75–89. Princeton: Princeton University Press, 1991.

———. "RUSCORP: A Database of Corporations in the Russian Empire, 1700–1914." Machine-readable data file no. 9142, distributed by the Inter-University Consortium for Political and Social Research, Ann Arbor, Michigan. Rev. ed., 1992.

Panov, A. P. "O neobkhodimosti reformy birzhevogo ustava 1832 goda." Memorandum published as appendix to M. Slavianinov, *Birzha i gil'dii,* 35–57. St. Petersburg, 1894. Originally published in *Birzhevye vedomosti,* Apr. 10, 1888.

Pervushin, Sergei A. *Khoziaistvennaia kon''iunktura: vvedenie v izuchenie dinamiki russkogo narodnogo khoziaistva za polveka.* Moscow: Ekonomicheskaia zhizn', 1925.

Pietrzak-Pawłowska, Irena, ed. *Uprzemysłowienie ziem polskich w XIX i XX wieku: Studia i materiały.* Warsaw: Zakład Narodowy im. Ossolińskich, 1970.

Pilder, Hans. *Die Russisch-Amerikanische Handels-Kompanie bis 1825.* Berlin: G. J. Göschen, 1914.

Pipes, Richard. "The Origins of Bolshevism: The Intellectual Evolution of Young Lenin." In *Revolutionary Russia,* edited by Richard Pipes, 26–52. Cambridge: Harvard University Press, 1968.

———. *Struve: Liberal on the Right, 1905–1944.* Cambridge: Harvard University Press, 1980.

Pitcher, Harvey. *The Smiths of Moscow: A Story of Britons Abroad.* Cromer, Norfolk: Swallow House Books, 1984.

"Polozhenie ob aktsionernykh obshchestvakh i obshchestvakh s ogranichennoi otvetstvennost'iu." *Sobranie postanovlenii pravitel'stva Souiza Sovetskikh Sotsialisticheskikh Respublik,* part 1, 1990, no. 15, decree no. 82, dated June 19, 1990, 331–56. [English translation: International Chamber of Commerce, *Foreign Investment in the USSR: Key 1990 Legislation,* 46–60. Paris: ICC Publishing Corp., 1991.]

Pomorski, Stanisław. "Administration of Socialist Property in the USSR: New Trends and Institutions." *Soviet Law after Stalin,* part 3: *Soviet Institutions and Administration of Law,* edited by F. J. M. Feldbrugge. *Law in Eastern Europe* 20 (1979): 123–38.

Preobrazhenskii, A. A. "O sostave aktsionerov Rossiisko-Amerikanskoi kompanii v nachale XIX v." *Istoricheskie zapiski* 67 (1960): 286–98.

Quinton, Brigitte. "Des petits entrepreneurs en URSS: les patrons des cooperatives." *Le Courrier des pays de l'Est* 360 (May–June 1991): 25–44.

Rasputin, Valentin. *Siberia on Fire: Stories and Essays.* Translated by Gerald Mikkelson and Margaret Winchell. DeKalb: Northern Illinois University Press, 1989.

Reed, John. *Ten Days That Shook the World.* Edited by Bertram D. Wolfe. New York: Vintage, 1960.

Rieber, Alfred J. *Merchants and Entrepreneurs in Imperial Russia*. Chapel Hill: University of North Carolina Press, 1982.

———. "The Sedimentary Society." In *Between Tsar and People: Educated Society and the Quest for Public Identity in Late Imperial Russia*, edited by Edith W. Clowes, Samuel D. Kassow, and James L. West, 343–66. Princeton: Princeton University Press, 1991.

Riha, Thomas. *A Russian European: Paul Miliukov in Russian Politics*. Notre Dame: University of Notre Dame Press, 1969.

Rogger, Hans. "Was There a Russian Fascism?" *Journal of Modern History* 36, no. 4 (Dec. 1964): 398–415.

Roosa, Ruth A. "The Association of Industry and Trade, 1906–1914: An Examination of the Economic Views of Organized Industrialists in Prerevolutionary Russia." Unpublished doctoral dissertation, Columbia University, 1967.

———. "Russian Industrialists and 'State Socialism', 1906–1917." *Soviet Studies* 23, no. 3 (Jan. 1972): 395–417.

———. "Russian Industrialists during World War I: The Interaction of Economics and Politics." In *Entrepreneurship in Imperial Russia and the Soviet Union*, edited by Gregory Guroff and Fred V. Carstensen, 159–87. Princeton: Princeton University Press, 1983.

———. "Banking and Financial Relations between Russia and the United States." In *International Banking, 1870–1914*, edited by Rondo Cameron and Valerii I. Bovykin, 291–318. Oxford: Oxford University Press, 1991.

Ruckman, Jo Ann S. *The Moscow Business Elite: A Social and Cultural Portrait of Two Generations, 1840–1905*. DeKalb: Northern Illinois University Press, 1984.

Ruud, Charles A. *Russian Entrepreneur: Publisher Ivan Sytin of Moscow, 1851–1934*. Montreal: McGill–Queen's University Press, 1990.

SAS Institute. *SAS User's Guide: Statistics, Version 5*. Cary, N.C.: SAS Institute, 1985.

Sachs, Jeffrey D. "Privatization in Russia: Some Lessons from Eastern Europe." *American Economic Review* 82, no. 2 (May 1992): 43–8.

San-Galli, Franz Karlovich. *Curriculum vitae zavodchika i fabrikanta Frantsa Karlovicha San-Galli*. St. Petersburg: P. O. Iabolonskii, 1903.

Scherer, Jean-Benoît. *Histoire raisonnée du commerce de la Russie*. 2 vols. Paris: Cuchet, 1788.

Schrader, David E. *The Corporation as Anomaly*. Cambridge: Cambridge University Press, 1993.

Service, Robert. *Lenin: A Political Life*. Vol. 2, *Worlds in Collision*. Bloomington: Indiana University Press, 1991.

Shaposhnikov, A. "What Are Cooperatives and How Should They Be Dealt With?" *Problems of Economics* 34, no. 5 (Sept. 1991): 64–78.

Sharapov, Sergei F. "Rech' o promyshlennoi konkurentsii Lodzi i Sosnovits s Moskvoiu" (1885), vol. 1, 70–94. In *Sochineniia*. 3 vols. in 2. St. Petersburg: Izdatel'stvo Russko-slavianskogo knizhnogo sklada, 1892–9.

Shepelev, Leonid E. "Chastnokapitalisticheskie torgovo-promyshlennye predpriiatiia Rossii v kontse XIX–nachala XX vv. i ikh arkhivnye fondy." Glavnoe arkhivnoe upravlenie, *Informatsionnyi biulleten'* 10 (1958): 76–107.

———. "Aktsionernoe uchreditel'stvo v Rossii (istoriko-statisticheskii ocherk)." In *Iz istorii imperializma v Rossii*, edited by Mikhail P. Viatkin, 134–82. Leningrad: Nauka, 1959.

———. "Aktsionernaia statistika v dorevoliutsionnoi Rossii." In *Monopolii i inostrannyi kapital v Rossii,* ed. Mikhail P. Viatkin, 165–207. Moscow: Nauka, 1962.
———. *Aktsionernye kompanii v Rossii.* Leningrad: Nauka, 1973.
———. *Tsarizm i burzhuaziia vo vtoroi polovine XIX veka: problemy torgovo-promyshlennoi politiki.* Leningrad: Nauka, 1981.
———. *Tsarizm i burzhuaziia v 1904–1914 gg.: problemy torgovo-promyshlennoi politiki.* Leningrad: Nauka, 1987.
Shipler, David K. *Russia: Broken Idols, Solemn Dreams.* Rev. ed. New York: Penguin, 1989.
Shmelyov [Shmelev], Nikolai P. "The Rebirth of Common Sense." In *Voices of Glasnost: Interviews with Gorbachev's Reformers,* edited by Stephen F. Cohen and Katrina vanden Heuvel, 140–56. New York: W. W. Norton, 1989.
Shmelyov [Shmelev], Nikolai P., and Vladimir Popov. *The Turning Point: Revitalizing the Soviet Economy.* Translated by Michele A. Berdy. New York: Doubleday, 1989.
Shul'tse-Gevernits, Gerkhart fon [Schulze-Gävernitz, Gerhart von]. *Ocherki obshchestvennogo khoziaistva i ekonomiki Rossii.* Translated by B. V. Avilov and P. P. Rumiantsev. Introduction by Petr B. Struve. St. Petersburg: Knizhnoe delo, 1900.
Simis, Konstantin M. *USSR—The Corrupt Society: The Secret World of Soviet Capitalism.* Translated by Jacqueline Edwards and Mitchell Schneider. New York: Simon and Schuster, 1982.
Simonova, Inna A. "'Muzh sil'nogo dukha i deiatel'nogo sertsa.'" *Literaturnaia Rossiia* 1535 (July 3, 1992): 14–15.
Skalkovsky, C. [Skal'kovskii, Konstantin A.] *Les Ministres des finances de la Russie, 1802–1890.* Translated by P. de Nevsky. Paris: Guillaumin, 1891.
Slider, Darrell. "Embattled Entrepreneurs: Soviet Cooperatives in an Unreformed Economy." *Soviet Studies* 43, no. 5 (1991): 797–821.
Smirnov, P. S. *Istoriia russkogo raskola staroobriadchestva.* 2d ed. St. Petersburg: Glavnoe upravlenie udelov, 1895. Reprinted, Westmead, England: Gregg, 1971.
Smith, Hedrick. *The New Russians.* New York: Knopf, 1991.
Sobchak, Anatoly. *For a New Russia: The Mayor of St. Petersburg's Own Story of the Struggle for Justice and Democracy.* New York: The Free Press, 1992.
"Società." *Enciclopedia Italiana di Scienze, Lettere ed Arti,* 38 vols. Rome: Istituto della Enciclopedia Italiana, 1929–49.
Solov'ev, Iu. B. "Protivorechiia v praviashchem lagere Rossii po voprosu ob inostrannykh kapitalakh v gody pervogo promyshlennogo pod''ema." In *Iz istorii imperializma v Rossii,* edited by Mikhail P. Viatkin, 371–88. Leningrad: Nauka, 1959.
———. "Ob''edinennoe dvorianstvo i proekt sozdaniia ekonomicheskogo soiuza." In *Monopolii i ekonomicheskaia politika tsarizma v kontse XIX–nachale XX v.,* edited by S. I. Potolov, 200–22. Leningrad: Nauka, 1987.
Solov'eva, Aida M. "K voprosu o roli finansovogo kapitala v zheleznodorozhnom stroitel'sve Rossii nakanune pervoi mirovoi voiny." *Istoricheskie zapiski* 55 (1956): 173–209.
———. "Iz istorii vykupa chastnykh zheleznykh dorog v Rossii v kontse XIX veka." *Istoricheskie zapiski* 82 (1968): 89–119.
———. *Zheleznodorozhnyi transport Rossii vo vtoroi polovine XIX v.* Moscow: Nauka, 1975.

Solzhenitsyn, Aleksandr I. *Letter to the Soviet Leaders.* Translated by Hilary Sternberg. New York: Harper and Row, 1974.

———. *Rebuilding Russia: Reflections and Tentative Proposals.* Translated by Alexis Klimoff. New York: Farrar, Straus, and Giroux, 1991.

Spies, Georg. *Erinnerungen eines Ausland-Deutschen.* Beilageband 2 of *Spiess'sche Familien-Zeitung.* Marburg: Moritz Spiess, 1926–8.

Stackenwalt, Francis M. "The Thought and Work of Dmitrii Ivanovich Mendeleev on the Industrialization of Russia, 1867–1907." Unpublished doctoral dissertation, University of Illinois, 1976.

Steinberg, Mark D. *Moral Communities: The Culture of Class Relations in the Russian Printing Industry, 1867–1907.* Berkeley: University of California Press, 1992.

Stephan, Paul B. III. *Soviet Economic Law: The Paradox of Perestroyka.* Carl Beck Papers, no. 805. Pittsburgh: University of Pittsburgh Center for Russian and East European Studies, 1990.

Stern, Fritz, ed. *The Varieties of History: From Voltaire to the Present.* Rev. ed. New York: Vintage, 1973.

Strachan, Harry W. "Nicaragua's Grupos Económicos: Scope and Operations." In *Entrepreneurs in Cultural Context,* edited by Sidney M. Greenfield, Arnold Strickon, and Robert T. Aubey, 243–76. Albuquerque: University of New Mexico Press, 1979.

Strakhov, Nikolai. *Bor'ba s zapadom v nashei literature: istoricheskie i kriticheskie ocherki.* 3 vols. 3d ed. Kiev: Chokolov, 1897–98; reprinted The Hague: Mouton, 1969.

Strickon, Arnold. "Ethnicity and Entrepreneurship in Rural Wisconsin." In *Entrepreneurs in Cultural Context,* edited by Sidney M. Greenfield, Arnold Strickon, and Robert T. Aubey, 159–89. Albuquerque: University of New Mexico Press, 1979.

Supple, Barry. "The Nature of Enterprise." In *The Cambridge Economic History of Europe,* vol. 5, edited by E. E. Rich and C. H. Wilson, 394–461. Cambridge: Cambridge University Press, 1977.

Sutela, Pekka. "The Role of the External Sector during the Transition." In *The Post-Soviet Economy: Soviet and Western Perspectives,* edited by Anders Aslund, 85–101. New York: St. Martin's Press, 1992.

Swann, Herbert. *Home on the Neva: A Life of a British Family in Tsarist St. Petersburg—And after the Revolution.* London: Gollanz, 1968.

Szporluk, Roman. *Communism and Nationalism: Karl Marx versus Friedrich List.* New York: Oxford University Press, 1988.

Tedstrom, John E. "The Reemergence of Soviet Cooperatives." In *Socialism, Perestroika, and the Dilemmas of Soviet Economic Reform,* edited by John E. Tedstrom, 104–34. Boulder, Colo.: Westview Press, 1990.

Thomas, Bill, and Charles Sutherland. *Red Tape: Adventure Capitalism in the New Russia.* New York: Dutton, 1992.

Tikhmenev, P. A. *A History of the Russian-American Company.* Translated and edited by Richard A. Pierce and Alton S. Donnelly. Seattle: University of Washington Press, 1978.

Tikhotskii, I. A. *Kratkii ocherk razvitiia nashei zheleznodorozhnoi seti za desiatiletie 1904–1913 g.g.* St. Petersburg: Ministerstvo finansov, 1914.

Tolf, Robert W. *The Russian Rockefellers: The Saga of the Nobel Family and the Russian Oil Industry.* Stanford: Hoover Institution Press, 1976.

Trice, Thomas. "Sergei A. Sharapov, A Reactionary Russian Journalist, 1855–1911." Unpublished M.A. thesis, Louisiana State University, 1987.
Tucker, Robert C., ed. *The Marx-Engels Reader*. New York: Norton, 1972.
———, ed. *The Lenin Anthology*. New York: Norton, 1975.
V pamiat' 50-ti letnego iubileia Rossiiskogo strakhovogo ot ognia obshchestva, uchrezhdennogo v 1827 g. St. Petersburg: V. Velling, 1877.
V pamiat' 75-ti letnego iubileia Pervogo Rossiiskogo strakhovogo obshchestva, uchrezhdennogo v 1827 godu. St. Petersburg: Marks, 1903.
Vaillant, Janet G. *Black, French, and African: A Life of Léopold Sédar Senghor*. Cambridge: Harvard University Press, 1990.
Vaksberg, Arkady. *The Soviet Mafia*. Translated by John and Elizabeth Roberts. New York: St. Martin's Press, 1991.
Valuev, Petr A. *Dnevnik P. A. Valueva, ministra vnutrennikh del*. 2 vols. Edited by P. A. Zaionchkovskii. Moscow: Akademiia nauk SSSR, 1961.
Verdery, Katherine. "Nationalism and National Sentiment in Post-socialist Romania." *Slavic Review* 52, no. 2 (Summer 1993): 179–203.
Verstraete, Maurice. "Sur les routes de mon passé." Unpublished autobiography, 1949. Hoover Institution Archives, Stanford University.
Viatkin, Mikhail P., ed. *Iz istorii imperializma v Rossii*. Leningrad: Nauka, 1959.
Volobuev, P. V. "Perestroika and the October Revolution in Soviet Historiography." *The Russian Review* 51, no. 4 (Oct. 1992): 566–76.
Von Laue, Theodore H. *Sergei Witte and the Industrialization of Russia*. New York: Columbia University Press, 1963.
Vrangel', Baron Nikolai E. *Vospominaniia (ot krepostnogo prava do bol'shevikov)*. Berlin: Slovo, 1924.
Walicki, Andrzej. *The Controversy over Capitalism: Studies in the Social Philosophy of the Russian Populists*. Oxford: Clarendon Press, 1969.
———. *The Slavophile Controversy: History of a Conservative Utopia in Nineteenth-Century Russian Thought*. Translated by Hilda Andrews-Rusiecka. Oxford: Clarendon Press, 1975.
Wallace, Donald Mackenzie. *Russia: On the Eve of War and Revolution*. Edited by Cyril E. Black. New York: Vintage, 1961.
Wanniski, Jude. "The Future of Russian Capitalism." *Foreign Affairs* 71, no. 2 (Spring 1992): 17–25.
Weber, Max. *General Economic History*. Translated by Frank H. Knight. New York: Greenberg, 1927.
———. *From Max Weber: Essays in Sociology*. Translated and edited by H. H. Gerth and C. Wright Mills. New York: Oxford University Press, 1958.
West, James L. "The Riabushinskii Circle: *Burzhuaziia* and *Obshchestvennost'* in Late Imperial Russia." In *Between Tsar and People: Educated Society and the Quest for Public Identity in Late Imperial Russia*, edited by Edith W. Clowes, Samuel D. Kassow, and James L. West, 41–56. Princeton: Princeton University Press, 1991.
Westwood, John N. *A History of Russian Railways*. London: Allen and Unwin, 1964.
Wheeler, Mary E. "The Russian American Company and the Imperial Government: Early Phase." In *Russia's American Colony*, edited by S. Frederick Starr, 43–62. Durham: Duke University Press, 1987.
Whishaw, James. *Memoirs of James Whishaw*. Edited by Maxwell S. Leigh. London: Methuen and Co., 1935.

White, Stephen. *The Bolshevik Poster.* New Haven: Yale University Press, 1988.
Wilken, Paul H. *Entrepreneurship: A Comparative and Historical Study.* Norwood, N.J.: Ablex Publishing Company, 1979.
Williams, Harold Whitmore. Papers. Department of Manuscripts. British Library, London.
Witte, Sergei Iu. *The Memoirs of Count Witte.* Translated and edited by Sidney Harcave. Armonk, N.Y.: M. E. Sharpe, 1990.
Wolde, Adele. *Ludwig Knoop: Erinnerungsbilder aus seinem Leben.* Bremen: C. Schünemann, 1928.
Wolfe, Bertram D. *Three Who Made a Revolution.* 4th rev. ed. New York: Dell, 1964.
Wynn, Charters. *Workers, Strikes, and Pogroms: The Donbass-Dnepr Bend in Late Imperial Russia, 1870–1905.* Princeton: Princeton University Press, 1992.
Yergin, Daniel, and Thane Gustafson. *Russia 2010—and What It Means for the World.* Rev. ed. New York: Vintage, 1994.
"Zakon Soiuza Sovetskikh Sotsialisticheskikh Respublik o predpriiatiiakh v SSSR." *Vedomosti s''ezda narodnykh deputatov SSSR i Verkhovnogo soveta SSSR,* 1990, no. 25 (June 20, 1990), law no. 460, dated June 4, 1990: 639–55. [English translation: International Chamber of Commerce, *Foreign Investment in the USSR: Key 1990 Legislation,* 23–42. Paris: ICC Publishing Corp., 1991.]
Zaslavskaya, Tatyana. *The Second Socialist Revolution: An Alternative Soviet Strategy.* Translated by Susan M. Davies with Jenny Warren. Bloomington: Indiana University Press, 1990.
Zelnik, Reginald E., trans. and ed. *A Radical Worker in Tsarist Russia: The Autobiography of Semen Ivanovich Kanatchikov.* Stanford: Stanford University Press, 1986.
Ziablov, Aleksei A. Papers. Bakhmeteff Archive of Russian Culture and Civilization, Columbia University, New York.
Zipperstein, Steven J. *The Jews of Odessa: A Cultural History, 1794–1881.* Stanford: Stanford University Press, 1985.

Index

Aeroflot, 110
Agursky, Mikhail, 140–41
Aitken, Hugh G. J., 78
Aivaz, Iakov M., 118
Aksakov, Ivan S., 123, 126, 132
Alaska, 18
Aldrich, Howard E., 27
Aleksii, Patriarch of the Russian Orthodox Church, 162
Alexander I, Emperor, 28
Alexander II, Emperor, 121
Alexander III, Emperor, 133
Alksnis, Lt. Col. Viktor, 148
All-Russian Chamber of Agriculture, 123
Alma-Ata (now Almaty), 109–10
Amburger, Erik, 75
Amburger family, 73, 75
Andreeva, Nina, 148, 150
Andropov, Iurii, 166
Anna Ivanovna, Empress, 18, 148, 150
Anti-Semitism, 121; of Black Hundreds, 135; in environmentalism, 170; of Marx, 120; in Odessa, 122; of Pamiat, 148–49; of populists, 119; of reactionaries, 123; in Russian Revolution, 144
Antonov, Mikhail F., 149
"April Theses" of V. I. Lenin (1917), 139–40

Archangel, 129; rebellion against Bolshevik power in, 139, 145; trade in, 18; xenophobia of merchants in, 137
Armenians, 53, 68–69, 87–88, 99
Aschenbach family, 75
Aslund, Anders, 147
Association of Industry and Trade (AIT), 28, 57, 118, 137–38
Astrakhan Shipping Company (1752), 18
Austria, 65
"Autocratic capitalism," 13
Avdakov, Nikolai S., 118, 137
Avtomatika-Nauka-Tekhnika (ANT) cooperative, 89–90
Avtovazbank, 110
Azerbaijan, 87
Azeris, 82
Azov, 38

Babeuf, François-Noël, 119
Baku, 39, 82, 126; black market in, 88
Bakunin, Mikhail A., 120
Baltic republics, 87, 88
Banks, 33–37, Figures 2.10, 2.11, 4.3; in Moscow, 66–67; in St. Petersburg, criticized in Moscow, 136–37
Bansa family, 75–76
Baranov Commission, 31
Barnaul, 109

Barrett, R. J., 126
Bary, Alexander, 47
BASF, 64, 74
Bayer Chemical Company, 64
Bednyi, Dem'ian, 144
Beet-sugar refining, 38
Bekkers, Alexander K., 64
Belgium, 65
Belorussia, 161
Belov, Vasilii, 147
Berdiansk, 167
Berdichev, 34
Bering machine plant, 117–18
Beveridge, Albert J., 48 (quoted)
Billington, James H., 146
Black Hundreds, 135
Black market, 88
Bleichröder, Gerson von, 120, 140
Bokhanov, Aleksandr N., 71, 83
Bolderaa, 38
Borovoi, Konstantin, 165
Bourgeoisie, Russian, 6, 8–9, 71, 121, 138
Boxer Rebellion, 119
Brady, Simon, 110–11 (quoted)
Briansk, 109
Britain, 65; entrepreneurship in, 79
Brooks, Jeffrey, 146
Bukharin, Nikolai I., 85–86, 99
Bureaucrats, as founders of corporations, 55–58; as managers of corporations, 70–71
Burlakov, M. P., 163
Buryshkin, Pavel A., 127, 135
Business History Review, 78
Business organizations, 7

Camin, Aguilar, 159
Canada, 16, 19
Capitalism, defined, 4; reactionary, 155, 160–66; reformist, 155–60; Russian, before Revolution, 8–10; statist, 155, 166–68; tsarist and Soviet, compared, Table 6.1
Carey, Henry C., 160
Carstensen, Fred V., 25, 178
Cartels, 26
Caspian Sea, 18
Catherine the Great, Empress, 9, 18, 27
Catoire, André, 75
Central Asia, 87, 99, 110
Central Council of Trade Unions, 113
Chaikovskii, Nikolai V., 139
Chancellor, Richard, 129
Chandler, Alfred D., 30

Chasprom Watch Company, 110
Chekhov, Anton P., 98
Chernobyl disaster, 170
Chernomyrdin, Viktor, 155
China, 140
China Caravan Company, 18
Chinese, as entrepreneurs, 79
Chizhov, Fedor V., 121, 126, 128
Chubais, Anatolii, 155, 165
Chukchi Peninsula, 70
Cigarette industry, 170–71
Civic Union, 155
Clark, William A., 91–92 (quoted)
Clason, Henriette, 76
Coase, R. H., 62 (quoted)
Coca-Cola, 157, 171
Cochran, Thomas C., 78–79
Cockerill family, 77
Cohen, Stephen F., 13 (quoted)
Collective farms, 86
Commodity exchanges, Soviet, 111
Communist Party of the Soviet Union, 85–86; criminals in, 91–92
Confederate States of America, 120
Congress of Civic and Patriotic Organizations (Feb. 1992), 164
Constantinople Trade Company (1757), 18
Constitutional Democratic (Kadet) Party, 125–26
Cooperatives, attached to state enterprises, 86–87; decrees on, February 1987 and May 1988, 85; geographical concentration of, 87–88, Figure 4.1; in 1920s, 85–86; numbers of, in late 1980s, 87, Figure 4.2; as objects of envy, 95–99; restrictions on, 92–93; taxation of, 93–94
Corporations, age structure of, 21–22, Figure 2.4; development of, 17–22, Tables 2.1, 2.2, Figures 2.1, 2.3, 2.5, 2.6; foreign, 64, 72, Table 3.8; geographical concentration of, 22–24, 37–45; Tables 2.3, 2.4, Figures 2.9, 2.14; size of, 22–23, Figure 2.7; survival of, 23–24, Figures 2.2, 2.6, 2.8; in Soviet Union, 109–14, Figure 4.3
Crane, Charles R., 126
Crimean War, 19
Council of Ministers, Soviet, 93, 109, 113

Dabrowo, 38
Daems, Herman, 29–30
Dahrendorf, Ralf, 153, 161, 168

Darwinian biology, 79
Deni, Viktor N., 144
Denikin, Gen. Anton I., 145
Dergunov, S. F., 163
Derwies, Pavel G., 134
D'iakonov, I. V., 134
Dickens, Charles, 127
Donets basin, 32, 117
Doroshevich, Vlas M., 121
Dostoevskii, Fedor M., 122, 132, 134, 143
du Pont de Nemours, E. I., and Company, 30

Easterbrook, W. T., 27
Economic Freedom Party, 165
Edwards, George W., 37 (quoted)
England. *See* Britain
Entrepreneurship, 51–58, 78–83; of Russian landed elite, 58–62
Environmental protection, 168–70
Estonia, 87, 162
Exchange committees, 7

Far Eastern Republic, 145
Fascism, post-Soviet, 161
Fedorov, Boris, 155, 167
Fedorov, Mikhail M., 56–57
Fehleisen, Konstantin, 64
Fenster, Aristide, 61
Finance capital, 5, 63
First Russian Fire Insurance Company (from 1896: First Russian Insurance Company), 19, 21; closed to foreign investors, 123
Fitzpatrick, Sheila, 143–44
Foreigners, 35, 52–52; colonies of, 71–77; concessions to, in 1920s, 169; as founders of corporations, 64, 68
Founders of corporations, Table 3.5; ethnicity of, 51–54, Tables 3.1, 3.2, 3.3, 3.9; foreigners as, 64, 68; social status of, 54–64, Tables 3.4, 3.6, 3.7, Figure 3.1
France, 65, 89; entrepreneurship in, 63, 79; lower middle class in, 145
Franco-Russian agreement (Dec. 1913), 32
Freeman, John, 23, 48–49
Friedgut, Theodore H., 117 (quoted)
Fronstein, merchant in Rostov-on-Don, 128
Full cost accounting, 101, 102, 106

Gaidar, Egor, 13, 155, 159, 171
Garrand, William, 129

Gatrell, Peter, 34–35 (quoted), 47
General Motors Corporation, 30
Georgia, Soviet, 87–88
Georgians, 99
Gerashchenko, Viktor, 167
Germans, 53, 68–69; colonies of, 72–77; environmental technology of, 170
Germany, 58, 65; banks in, 37; GmbH in (1892), 106; lower middle class in, 145; nationalism in, 119
Gerschenkron, Alexander, 8, 16–17, 47
Giliarov-Platonov, Nikita P., 134
Gindin, Iosif F., on banks, 37; on "irregular loans," 40
Gintsburg, Goratsii I., 64
Glaser, Carl, 74
Glasnost' (Public Discussion), 150
Glaziev, Sergei, 90–91 (quoted), 111 (quoted)
Glazunov, Il'ia, 147
Goldenberg, merchant in Odessa, 128
Goldman, Marshall I., 94, 148
Gorbachev, Mikhail S., corporate laws of, 102–8; lack of economic legality under, 112; and New Economic Policy, 99, 106; reforms of, 3, 84–86, 89; relaxed censorship under, 94; on Sergei Grigor'iants, 150
Goujon, Jules, 73
Grand Duchy of Finland, 51
Gras, N. S. B., 78
Great Reforms, 23, 51; shortcomings of, 31, 46, 78, 82
Greaves, George, 167
Greenfeld, Liah, 120
Greenfield, Sidney M., 79 (quoted), 81
Gregory, Paul R., 16–17, 26; on government spending, 28, 47
Grigor'iants, Sergei, 150
Gubonin, Petr I., 64, 80
Gustafson, Thane, 153

Haffenberg, merchant in Riga, 128
Hagelin, Karl W., 82
Hagen, Everett, 79, 81
Haniel family, 76
Hannon, Michael T., 23, 48–49
Hazan, Baruch, 148–49 (quoted)
Henriksson, Anders, 72–73
Herzen, Aleksandr I., 118–19, 120, 122–23
Hilferding, Rudolf, 37
Hitler, Adolf, 145
Homberg, Octave, 66–67
Hubback, John, 125 (quoted)
Hudson's Bay Company, 19

Ianzhul, Ivan I., 116
Iasin, Evgenii, 99
Iavlinskii, Grigorii, 155
India, 79
Indians, as entrepreneurs, 79
International Harvester Company, 30; in Russia, 25, 65, 157
International Paper Company, 30
Ioann, Metropolitan of St. Petersburg, 161, 164
Irkutsk, 109
Isergin, Afinogen S., 132
Islam, 119–20, 162
Istok (Source) cooperative, 89
Ivan IV, Tsar, 129

Japan, 16; entrepreneurship in, 58, 79, 83
Jaurès, Jean, 140
Jenny, Dr. Ernst, 74, 77, 78, 157, 169
Jews, 35, 52–53, 68–69; Dostoevskii's attack on, 122; in Europe, 63, 79; in grain and flour trade, 123; under Nazis, 164; as objects of labor violence, 117; pogrom against, in Odessa (1871), 122
Joffre, Gen. Joseph Jacques Césaire, 32
Johnstone, Catherine L., 71 (quoted)
Joint-stock company, defined, 40; on size and location, 43, 46
Jones, Anthony, 99

Kadet (Constitutional Democratic) Party, 125–26
Kahan, Arcadius, 36, 129 (quoted)
KamAZ automobile plant, 109, 114
Kamenets-Podolsk, 34
Kanatchikov, Sergei I., 117
Karakozov, Dmitrii V., 121
Karelin, Feliks, 147
Kazakhstan, 87; cigarette factory in, 170
Keenan, Edward L., 96–97, 165
Keller, Bill, 150 (quoted)
Kennedy, B. A., 47
Kerch, 34
Kerenskii, Aleksandr F., 141
Kharkov, 39–40
Kherson, 34
Khomiakov, Aleksei S., 124
Kiev, 39
Kingdom of Poland, 39
Kingston-Mann, Esther, 97
Kireevskii, Ivan V., 141
Kirov automobile factory, 114
Klopov family, 130
Knoop, Ludwig, 82, 130–32; house burned, 138

Knoop family, 75, 167
Knoop trading firm, 130–32
Kochergin, Nikolai, 144
Kokorev, Vasilii A., 80–81
Kokovtsov, Vladimir N., 32, 67; criticized by Bary, 47
Kolomna Machinery Company, 125
Korobkova, Larisa, 112 (quoted)
Korotich, Vitalii, 95
Kotsonis, Yanni, 135 (quoted), 145 (quoted)
Kozlov, 34
Krasnodar, 109–10
Krasnoiarsk, 109
Kriuchkov, Vladimir A., 147
Krivoi Rog, 32
Krizhanich, Iurii, 129
Kronstadt, 34
Krupskaia, Nadezhda, 142
Kulaks, 10
Kunitzer, Julius, 64
Kursk, 34
"Kvas patriotism," 121, 128, 146
Kyshtym Mining Company, 62

Labor collectives (STK), 113–14
Labor unions, Soviet, 88
La Harpe, Frédéric-César de, 28
Land and Freedom movement, 119
Landa, Janet T., 79–80, 81
Landlords, 58–62, Tables 3.6, 3.7, Figure 3.1
Lapino Manufacturing Company, 130–31
Laski, Aleksander Karol Bernard von, 76
Latin America, 154; entrepeneurship in, 79–80
Latsis, Otto, 98 (quoted)
Law, commercial, 9
Law, corporate, 9, 27, Table 4.1; in Lithuania (June 1990), 108–9; in Russia (December 1990), 108; in Soviet Union (June 1990), 102–8
Law on banking deregulation (Dec. 11, 1990), 111
Law on cooperatives (May 26, 1988), 92
Law on the State Enterprise (1987), 100–101
Lebanese, as entrepreneurs, 79
Left Socialist Revolutionary Party, 139
Lena Goldfields massacre (April 1912), 118
Lenin, Vladimir I., on cooperatives, 85–86; on finance capital, 36–37; influence of populists on, 141–42; on learning from Germans, 144; on liberals, 140–41; on spontaneity and

consciousness, 142; on World War I, 143; xenophobia of, 120, 139–40
Leningrad, black market in, 88; cooperatives in, 110
Lianozov, Stepan G., 64, 139
Lianozov's Sons, S. G., Petroleum Company, 42
Libau, 34
Liberal Democratic Party, 161–64
LIFETEST, 34
Ligachev, Egor K., 147
Limited-liability company, Soviet, 106–8
Linda Steamship Company, 51–52
List, Friedrich, 160
List, Gustav, Machinery Company, 117
Lithuania, 100, 108–9
Litwack, John M., 90 (quoted)
Liubertsy, 157
Lockhart, Sir Robert H. Bruce, 138 (quoted)
Lodz, 38–39; attacked by D'iakonov and Sharapov, 133–34; target of Slavophile capitalism, 137
Löwe, Heinz-Dietrich, 133
Lunacharskii, Anatolii V., 142–43

Machine Tractor Stations, 86
Mafia. *See* Organized crime
Maggs, Peter B., 108 (quoted)
Malia, Martin, 119, 146 (quoted)
Mamontov, Savva I., 134
Managers of corporations, ethnicity of, 67–70, Tables 3.9, 3.10, 3.11; foreigners as, 71–78; social status of, 65–67, 70–71
Mantashev, Aleksandr I., 64
Marc family, 75
Marks, Steven G., 46–47 (quoted)
Marx, Karl, anti-Semitism of, 120; rejected by Herzen, 119
Marxism, post-Soviet, 160
Marxists, German, 141; Russian, 120
Maxwell cotton-textile factory, 117
Mayer, Arno J., 56
McClelland, David, 79
McClelland, Peter D., 29
McDaniel, Timothy, 13
McDonald's, 171
McKay, John P., 73–74 (quoted), 117–18, 158 (quoted)
McReynolds, Louise, 121
Meck, Karl F., 134
Mediterranean Trade Company (1763), 18
Mel'gunov, Sergei P., 138–39
Meller-Zakomel'skii, Vladimir V., 62
Mendeleev, Dmitrii I., 5

Merchants, 64–66; negative stereotype of, 98
Meshcherskii, Prince Vladimir P., 67
Mezhkniga, 109–10
Middle class, 55
Middle East, 162
Miliukov, Pavel N., 57, 126, 138–39; on Lenin's xenophobia, 141
Mill, John Stuart, 123
Minarik, Liudmila P., 58–62, 71, 83
Ministry of Aviation, Soviet, 110
Ministry of Finance, Soviet, 93
Monopolies, 5, 166; under Catherine II, 18
Moor, Dmitrii S., 144
Moore, Barrington, Jr., 10–11, 12–13, 154
Morozov, Savva T., 134
Morozov, Timofei S., 64, 80
Morozov's Son, Savva, Manufacturing Company, 66
Moscow, 39–40; banks in, 33; black market in, 88; as center of Soviet coorporate activity, 109–11; strikes in (1903–5), 116–17
Moscow Bank of Trade, 66
Moscow Commercial Loan Bank, 66
Moscow Exchange Society, 66
Moscow Federation of Trade Unions, 160
Moscow Stock Exchange, 112
Moscow Union Bank, 66
Moskoff, William, 99
Mscychowski, Kazimierz, 64
Musin-Pushkin, Aleksei I., 62

Naberezhnye Chelny, 109
Naidenov, Nikolai A., 66, 128 (quoted)
Nakhichevan-on-Don, 38
National Biscuit Company, 30
Nazis, 148; economic policies of, 164
Nebol'sin, G. E., 47–48 (quoted)
Négritude movement, 119
Neo-Slavophile capitalism, 160, 165
Nepman, 10
New Aivaz Company, 118, 137
New Economic Policy (NEP), 85–86, 113
New Trade Charter (1667), 129
New York Air Brake Company, 157
Nicaragua, 80
Nicholas I, Emperor, 19, 22
Nicholas II, Emperor, 8, 28; murder of, 161; on preparations for World War I, 32
Nikon, Patriarch, 130
Nizhnii Novgorod, 57, 165; fair at, 131
Nizhnii Novgorod Grain Company (1767), 18

Nobel, Emmanuel, 73
Nobel Brothers Petroleum Company, 31, 82
Nomenklatura (Soviet elite), 111
North, Douglass C., 11–12; on corruption, 166; on effects of economic processes, 159; on governments in North and South America, 154–55; on path dependence, 153
Norwegians in Wisconsin, 80
Novgorod, medieval, 157, 169; under Peter the Great, 28
Novosibirsk, 109
Novyi Uzen, Kazakhstan, 99

Oblomov, 78, 130
Odessa, 39; black market in, 88; pogrom in (1871), 122; trade and insurance companies in, 19
Old Believers, 64–65, 80–81, 129–30
On-call accounts, 36
Orekhovo-Zuevo, 127
Organized crime, Soviet, 91–92, 154
Orlovsky, Daniel T., 145–46
Ostrovskii, Aleksandr N., 98
Ostrowiec Iron Company, 77
Ottoman Empire, 26

Pamiat (Memory) organization, 148–49, 165
"Partisans of Renaissance," 147
Partnerships, full, 40; limited, 40. *See also* Share partnership
Party of Peaceful Renewal, 57
Pastor, George, 76
Pastor family, 76
Path dependence, 12, 153
Pavlov, N. A., 123
Pavlov, Valentin S., 147
Pennsylvania Railroad, 30
Pepsi-Cola, 157
Perestroika, 84, 94; xenophobia in era of, 147–48
Perm, 109
Persia, 26, 140
Persian Trade Company (1758), 18
Pervushin, Ivan A., 26
Peter the Great, Emperor, 8–9, 18, 135, 165; autocratic economic policies of, 27, 124
Philip Morris, 170
Pikul', V., 147
Pipes, Richard, 141–42
Pitcher, Harvey, 77 (quoted)

Plemkonesoiuz Cattle-Breeding Company, 110
Poklewski-Koziełł, Vikentii A., 62
Poklewski-Koziełł, Władysław V., 62
Poles, 35, 52–53, 68–69
Poliakov, S. L., 57
Polozkov, Ivan K., 89, 148
Popov, Vladimir, 93, 94
Population ecology of organizations, 17; elements of: capacity, 17–22; concentration, 24; defense, 24–26; homogeneity, 22–23; stability, 23–24; turbulence, 26–28
Presidium of the USSR Supreme Soviet, 93
Produgol', 26
Prokhanov, Aleksandr, 170
Provisional Government (1917), 139–41
Prowe family, 75
Prüser, Friedrich, 82 (quoted)
Pskov, 129

Quinton, Brigitte, 92, 93, 96 (quoted)
Quotients of entrepreneurial and managerial activity, 68–69, Table 3.9

R. J. Petro, 171
Rabeneck, Franz, Company, 131
Rabeneck family, 76
Rafalovich, Aleksandr F., 64
Railroads, 30–33, Figure 2.10. *See also specific railroads*
Ransome, Sims, and Jefferies, 74
Rasputin, Valentin, 147, 168
Rat'kov-Rozhnov, A. N., 57
Rau, Heinrich, 76
Rau, Johann Wilhelm Ellis, 76–77
Rau, Karl Jacob, 76
Rau, Wilhelm, 76
Rau family, 76–77
"Red-Brown alliance," 166
Renan, Ernest, 123
Reutern, Mikhail Kh., 29, 34, 46
Reval (now Tallinn), 52
Revolution of 1905, 26; xenophobic outbursts in, 117
Riabushinskii, Mikhail P., 134–35
Riabushinskii, Pavel P., 57, 134, 136
Rieber, Alfred J., 7
Riga, 38–39; bank in (1991), 109; black market in, 88; seized by Germans in World War I, 139, 141
RJR, 171
Romania, 149
Roscher, Wilhelm, 160

Rostov-on-Don, 38
Rothmans, 170
Rothschild, Baron Alphonse, 120, 140
Rothstein, Adolph, 64
RUSCORP database, 17, 173–74
Russia Company, 129
Russian-American Company (1799), 6, 18–19
Russian-American Triangle Rubber Company, 132
Russian Banking Association, 7, 35, 124
Russian Civil War, 142–46
Russian Industrial Society, 132
Russian Livestock Insurance Company, 19
Russian National Committee, 57
Russian Orthodox Church, 11
Russian People's Assembly, 164–65
Russian Railroad Company, 23
Russian Union of Industrialists and Entrepreneurs, 99
Russians, as founders of corporations, 68; as managers of corporations, 69–70
Russkie vedomosti (Russian News), 130, 132
Russkii vestnik (The Russian Herald), 161
Rybinsk, 34
Ryzhkov, Nikolai, 89–90

Sachert, Wilhelm, 128
Sachs, Jeffrey D., 13, 167
St. Petersburg, 24, 38–39; banks in, 33, 36, 127, 136; as both bureaucratic and capitalist center, 56; cigarette industry in, 170–71; employers' unions in, 128; strikes in (1903–5), 116–17; as target of Slavophile capitalism, 136–37; xenophobia in, 133–34
St. Petersburg Exchange Committee, 134
St. Petersburg-Moscow Railroad, 48
St. Petersburg Telegraph Agency, 56
Samara, 109
Saratov, 109
Scandinavia, medieval, 157
Schlock, 38
Schulze-Gävernitz, Gerhart von, 116 (quoted), 127, 131
Schumpeter, Joseph A., 65
Sears, Roebuck and Company, 30
Sergeev, Nikita F., 121
Service, Robert, 141
Seton-Watson, Hugh, 146
Seychelles islands, 79
Shafarevich, Igor, 147
Shamsi, 82
Sharapov, Sergei F., 132–33

Share, defined, 40–41
Share partnership, defined, 40–41; location and organization of, 45; size of, 43
Shatsillo, Kornelii F., 124
Shemburg, Kurt Aleksandr von, 233 n. 44
Shepelev, Leonid E., 5–6
Shipler, David K., 95 (quoted)
Shmelev, Nikolai P., 93, 94, 113
Shumakher, Danilo D., 66
Siberia, 169
Siemens and Halske, 64, 117
Singer Company, 25
Sirotkin, Dmitrii V., 57
Skal'kovskii, Konstantin A., 48 (quoted), 67
Slavophile capitalism, 160–65; defense of industrial development in, 135–38; economic xenophobia in, 128–35; myth of benevolent employer in, 127–28
Slavophiles, agrarianism of, 127; and Aleksandr I. Herzen, 119; analyzed by Pavel N. Miliukov, 141; contributions of Aleksei S. Khomiakov to, 124; and Fedor M. Dostoevskii, 122; and gentry, 135; and Moscow merchants, 128–32; and Old Believers, 120; on peasants, 96; and Sergei F. Sharapov, 132
Slider, Darrell, 91, 92, 99 (quoted)
Smith, Hedrick, 10; on "culture of envy," 95–96
Snickers candy bars, 157
Sobchak, Anatolii, on ANT cooperative, 89–90; on envy, 96; on state ownership of corporations, 159
Society of Russian Sugar Producers, 25–26
Soldatenkov, Kuz'ma T., 64, 80
Solzhenitsyn, Aleksandr I., 147; on Russian North, 168–69
Southeast Asia, 79
Sovremennye izvestiia (Contemporary News), 134
Spanish Trade Company (1724), 18
Spies, Georg, 75–76, 77, 131–32
Spies, Robert, 75
Stalin, Iosif V., 4, 9, 11; collectivization under, 86; Five-Year Plans of, 98; purges of, 152; xenophobia of, 146, 170
Stalinists, 89
Standard Oil of New Jersey, 30
State Arbitration Agency (Gosarbitrazh), 89

State Bank, Russian, 167; tsarist, 36, 40
State based on the rule of law, 57
State Committee for Supply (Gossnab), 88, 110
State Duma, 166
State Insurance Agency (Gosstrakh), 110
Steinberg, Mark D., 116–17 (quoted)
Stieglitz, Baron Aleksandr, 64
Stieglitz, Baron Ludwig, 133
Stjernvall, Knut von, 76
STK (labor collectives), 113–14
Stock exchanges, 111–12; as financial supporter of the Russian People's Assembly, 165
Strachan, Harry W., 80 (quoted)
Strakhov, Nikolai, 123
Strauss, David, 123
Strickon, Arnold, 79–80 (quoted)
Struve, Petr B., 5
Stucken family, 75
Stürmer, Boris V., 138
Suermondt, Robert, 76
Suermondt family, 76
Sukhomlinov, Gen. Vladimir A., 32
Supple, Barry, 58
Supreme Soviet, 93, 94
Surgutneftegazbank, 110
Sushchov, Nikolai N., 70
Sutela, Pekka, 168 (quoted)
Sverdlovsk, 109–10
Swann, Alfred, 75
Sweden, 65
Syndicates, 26

Taine, Hippolyte, 123
Tarasov, Artem, 88–89
Tariff protection, 29, 160; in political platform of Vladimir V. Zhirinovskii, 162
Tashkent, 88
Tatishchev, Prince V. S., 66–67
Taylor, Frederick W., 118, 137, 144
Tbilisi, 88
Tekhnika (Technique) cooperative, 88–89
Tereshchenko, Mikhail I., 139
Thompson, John M., 146
Tishchenko, Iurii M., 57
Third International (Comintern), 141
Third World, 11
Tkachev, Petr N., 119, 141–42
Togliatti, 113
Tokobank, 110
Tolstoi, Lev N., 121
Trading firms, 30, 40; as founders of corporations, 54

Tret'iakov, Pavel M., 77, 142
Tret'iakov, Sergei M., 77, 142
Tsarskoe selo Railroad (1836), 48
Turgenev, Ivan S., 118
Turkey, 140
Turkmenistan, 99
Type-A corporations, 41–42, Figures 2.12, 2.13; survival of, 44–45, Figure 2.15
Type-P corporations, 41–43, Figure 2.12

Ufa, 109
Ukraine, 38–39, 87, 161
Ukrainians, 68–69
Union (Soiuz) faction, 148
Union of Councils of Labor Collectives and Workers' Committees, 114
Union of Entrepreneurs, 154
Union of Sailors (Vladivostok), 145–46
United Nations, 170
United Nobility, 123
United States, 16, 65; constitution of, 154; corporations in, 30; environmental technology of, 170; food industry of, 157; and law against bribery in foreign countries, 154; Lunacharskii's attack on, 143; and purchase of Alaska, 18; Riabushinskii's attack on, 134–35; Zhirinovskii's attack on, 162
United States Steel Corporation, 30
Ural mountains, 28
Usher, A. P., 78

Valuev, Petr A., 121, 126
Varangians, 169
Vasil'ev, Dmitrii D., 148–49
Veinshtein, Grigorii E., 57
Verdery, Katherine, 149 (quoted)
Verstraete, Maurice, 67 (quoted)
Veselovskii, A. K., 56
Viazemskii, Prince Petr A., 121
Vilnius, 88
Vishniakov, Aleksei S., 137
Volga Automobile Plant (VAZ), 113–14
Volga-Don Railroad, 48
Volga-Kama Bank, 62
Volgograd, 98, 109
Volobuev, P. V., 8, 143 (quoted)
Vol'skii, Arkadii, 155, 166, 171
Volunteer Fleet, 145
Von Laue, Theodore H., 16
Vonliarliarskii, Vladimir M., 70
Voronezh Grain Company (1772), 18
Vorontsov Trade Company (1760), 18
Voucher system of privatization, 165

Wachter, Konstantin Franz, 64
Walicki, Andrzej, 120
Wallace, Sir Donald M., 124, 130
Warsaw, 39
Weber, Max, 4, 13–14, 156, 171
Weiner, Douglas R., 170
Wertheim, Juliusz, 128
"What Is To Be Done?" (1902), 142
Whishaw, James, 57, 75
White Army, in Russian Civil War, 144–45
Williamson, Oliver E., 79
Witte, Sergei Iu., on banks, 34–35; honesty under, 67; industrial drive under, 23; Lenin's attack on, 120, 140; and Russian xenophobia, 124; Sharapov's attack on, 133; statist views of, 46–47; on Vonliarliarskii, 70
Wogau, Hugo von, 76
Wogau and Company trading firm, 30, 64
Wogau family, 73, 75
Wolfe, Bertram, 142
Workers' control, 105
Wrangel, Petr N., 145
Wynn, Charters, 117 (quoted)

Xenophobia, 10, 158, 169–70; in Archangel, 137; in Bolshevik ideology, 139–46; economic, 166; in perestroika, 147–50; in post-Stalin era, 147; in Russian Civil War, 145–46; among Russian radicals, 118–21; among Russian reactionaries, 121–24; among Russian workers, 116–18; in Slavophile capitalism, 128–35; in Stalinist ideology, 146

Yeltsin, Boris N., 13, 14, 165–66
Yergin, Daniel, 153

Zaslavskaia, Tat'iana, 95–96
Zawadski, Stanisław P., 64
Zemstvos, 54
Zenker family, 75
Zgierz, 38
Zhirinovskii, Vladimir V., 161–64, 170, 171
Ziablov, Aleksei A., 125
ZIL automobile plant, 114
Zimmerwald Left, 141